Indian Politics and Society since Independence

This book focuses on politics and society in India. It explores new areas enmeshed in the complex social, economic and political processes in the country. Linking structural characteristics with broader sociological context, the book emphasizes the strong influence of sociological issues on politics, such as the shaping of the social milieu and the articulation of the political in day-to-day events. Political events are connected with the ever-changing social, economic and political processes in order to provide an analytical framework to explain 'peculiarities' of Indian politics. The main argument of the book is that three major ideological influences have provided the foundational values of Indian politics: colonialism, nationalism and democracy. The colonial, nationalist and democratic articulation of the political have shaped Indian politics in a complex way. Structured thematically, with a multitude of pedagogical features, this work is a useful text for students of political science, sociology and South Asian Studies.

Bidyut Chakrabarty is Professor of the Department of Political Science at the University of Delhi. His main research areas are public administration and modern Indian political thought. He has published extensively on the subjects, and is the author of *The Partition of Bengal and Assam, 1932–47* (Routledge, 2004), *Social and Political Thought of Mahatma Gandhi, 1933–1943* (Routledge, 2006), *Forging Power: Coalition Politics in India* (Oxford University Press, 2006), *Reinventing Public Administration: The Indian Experience* (Orient Longman, 2007) and *Mahatma Gandhi: A Historical Biography* (Roli Books, 2007).

Indian Politics and Society since Independence

Events, processes and ideology

Bidyut Chakrabarty

Routledge
Taylor & Francis Group

LONDON AND NEW YORK

First published 2008
by Routledge
2 Park Square, Milton Park, Abingdon, Oxon OX14 4RN

Simultaneously published in the USA and Canada
by Routledge
270 Madison Ave, New York, NY 10016

*Routledge is an imprint of the Taylor & Francis Group, an informa
business*

© 2008 Didyut Chakrabarty

Typeset in Times New Roman by Prepress Projects Ltd, Perth, UK
Printed and bound in Great Britain by MPG Books Ltd, Bodmin, Cornwall

British Library Cataloguing in Publication Data
A catalogue record for this book is available from the British Library

Library of Congress Cataloging in Publication Data
A catalog record for this book has been requested

ISBN10: 0-415-40867-9 (hbk)
ISBN10: 0-415-40868-7 (pbk)

ISBN13: 978-0-415-40867-7 (hbk)
ISBN13: 978-0-415-40868-4 (pbk)

Dedicated to Tutun, Barbie, Pablo and my friend-philosopher-guide, Dipakda.

Contents

Tables

Preface

This book is an outcome of my sustained interaction, over the years, with colleagues, analysts and friends who are equally keen to unravel the dynamics of Indian politics. The idea of writing a book on Indian politics dawned in our regular evening meetings at the Beavers' Retreat of the London School of Economics. I fondly remember Professor W. H. Morris Jones, Professor Tom Nossiter, Professor Meghnad Desai and Dr David Taylor for having kindled and also sustained my interest in the subject. I am thankful to the anonymous reviewers for their comments and suggestions, which are very useful for revising the manuscript in the form of the present book. As this book is intended for general readers I have tried, as far as possible, to leave nothing unexplained.

Portions of this book were presented in various seminars and workshops around the globe. I am thankful to the participants who made perceptive comments that helped to sharpen some of the major arguments in the book. The book has developed over the course of several years and some of my earlier essays foreshadowed some of the points that I pursued in it. I owe a great deal to Mr Dipak Bhattacharya, who always remained a constant source of inspiration. It would not have been possible for me to concentrate on my academic pursuits without the support that Mr Bhattacharya extended whenever I asked for it. I also put on record my heartfelt gratitude to Professor Mohit Bhattacharya, who helped me understand the intricate processes that are at work in Indian politics. By being very supportive in a very chilly winter in Hamburg, Professor Tatiana Oranskaia, Dr Ramprasad Bhatt and Dr Barbara Schuler never allowed me to feel homesick. My colleagues in the Asien–Afrika Institut of the University of Hamburg provided all facilities, including a well-equipped office that was a very useful aid to my academic pursuits. I am thankful to Mr Sunil Sharma for his critical inputs in comprehending the changing nature of 'grassroots politics' in the context of the rise of the socio-economically peripheral sections of Indian society. I appreciate Mr Gopinath of Routledge India for his help. I shall be failing in my duties if I do not mention the contribution of the editors of Routledge London in publishing my three books in a row. I am indebted to my graduate students for their critical role in making this work seem worthwhile.

Without the support of my family, my wife and two most inquisitive children,

Pablo and Barbie, it would not have been possible to write on such a complex theme as Indian politics. By dedicating this book to them, I have just put on record my endorsement of their contribution, which, I know, can never be gauged. Despite her severe illness, my mother always encouraged me to venture out into the 'unknown', which both inspired and gave me confidence to undertake projects on a variety of themes. Tinku and Mini sustain my zeal for creativity by being supportive and their daughters, Mitul and Rimpi, always make my visits to Calcutta worthwhile. I also fondly remember my students around the globe who contributed to my academic sharpness by being perhaps the staunchest critics of whatever I had presented before them. Without their inputs, the book would not have been the same.

Bidyut Chakrabarty
Hamburg, Germany
January 2008

Abbreviations

ABVP	Akhil Bharatiya Vidyarthi Parishad
AGP	Assom Gana Parishad
AIADMK	All India Anna Dravida Munnetra Kazagham
AICC	All India Congress Committee
ARC	Administrative Reforms Commission
BJP	Bharatiya Janata Party
BJS	Bharatiya Jana Sangh
BLD	Bharatiya Lok Dal
BSP	Bahujan Samaj Party
CAD	*Constituent Assembly Debates*
CPI	Communist Party of India
CPI(M)	Communist Party of India (Marxist)
CPI(ML)	Communist Party of India (Marxist and Leninist)
CWC	Congress Working Committee
DMK	Dravida Munnetra Kazagham
FDI	foreign direct investment
FERA	Foreign Exchange Regulation Act
FICCI	Federation of Indian Chambers of Commerce and Industries
FPTP	first past the post
GATT	General Agreement on Tariffs and Trade
GDP	gross domestic product
IAS	Indian Administrative Service
ICS	Indian civil service
INC	Indian National Congress
IPR	Industrial Policy Resolution
IPS	Indian Police Service
JD(U)	Janata Dal (United)
JP	Jayaprakash Narayan
KHAM	acronym for a combination involving Kshatriyas, Harijans, Adivasis and Muslims
LF	Left Front
MDMK	Marumalarchi Dravida Munnetra Kazagham

MISA	Maintenance of Internal Security Act
MLA	Member of Legislative Assembly
MNC	Multinational corporations
MP	Member of Parliament
MRTP Act	Monopoly and Restrictive Trade Practices Act
NDA	National Democratic Alliance
NDC	National Development Council
NF	National Front
NRI	non-resident Indian
OBC	other backward classes/other backward castes
OECD	Organization for Economic Cooperation and Development
PMK	Pattali Makkal Katchi
PMO	Prime Minister's Office
POTA	Prevention of Terrorist Act
POTO	Prevention of Terrorism Ordinance
PR	proportional representation
PSUs	public sector units
RJD	Rashtriya Janata Dal
RLD	Rashtriya Lok Dal
RSS	Rashtriya Swayamsevak Sangh
SAD	Shiromani Akali Dal
SC	scheduled castes
SJM	Swadeshi Jagaran Manch
SJP	Samajwadi Janata Party
SP	Samajwadi Party
ST	scheduled tribe
TADA	Terrorist and Disruptive Activities (Prevention) Act
TDP	Telegu Desam Party
TMC	Tamil Manila Congress
TMC	Trinamul Congress
TNC	Tamil National Congress
UF	United Front
UPA	United Progressive Alliance
VHP	Vishwa Hindu Parishad
WBIDC	West Bengal Industrial Development Corporation
WEBEL	West Bengal Electronic Corporation
WTO	World Trade Organization

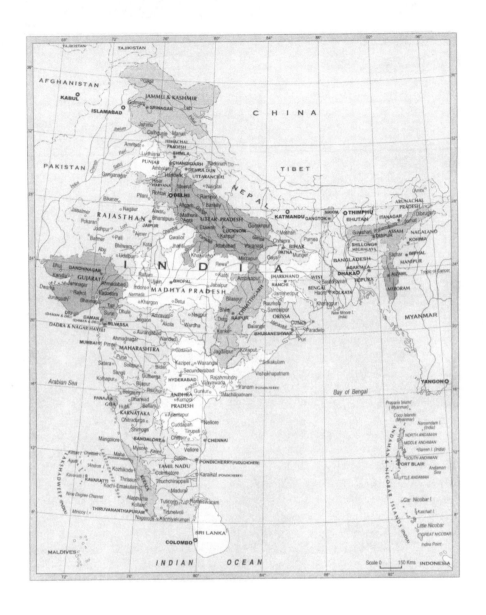

Introduction

I

India's freedom struggle culminated in the transfer of power in 1947. The Indian Independence Act of 1947 ratified the change. A new era dawned and Jawaharlal Nehru captured that historic moment in his famous 'tryst with destiny' speech which runs as follows:

> Long years ago, we made a tryst with destiny, and now the time comes when we shall redeem our pledge, not wholly or in full measure, but very substantially. At the stroke of the midnight hour, when the world sleeps, India will awake to life and freedom. A moment comes, which comes out rarely in history, when we step out from the old to the new, when an age ends, and when the soul of a nation, long suppressed, finds utterance.
>
> The future [of India] is not one of ease or resting but of incessant striving so that we might fulfil the pledges we have so often taken and the one we shall take today. The service of India means the service of the millions who suffer. It means the ending of poverty and ignorance and disease and inequality of opportunity. The ambition of the greatest man of our generation [Mahatma Gandhi] has been to wipe every tear from every eye. That may be beyond us but as long as there are tears and suffering, our work will not be over.[1]

India became a free nation in 1947 through what is known as 'the transfer of power'. Yet a great deal of what we see in independent India can be attributed to 'legacies' of one kind or another. Was independent India a break with the past or in continuity? Did India, as Nehru claimed, 'step out of the old to the new'? These are the questions that baffle historians given the clear continuities in terms of not only institutions of governance, but also the values that inform these institutions. Was the change that India saw following decolonization merely cosmetic then? There is also the argument that the influences of almost 200 years of colonialism seem to have been entrenched in India's society, economy and polity simply because of its long duration. Hence it was almost impossible for those who presided over India's destiny at the early phases of her nationhood to completely do away with the prevalent system of governance, so critical for the British Raj. Besides the system of governance, political liberalism of the British variety remained a significant ideological force even after the withdrawal of colonial administration on 15 August 1947. Although 'a new age', as Nehru enthusiastically characterized it, had arrived when 'the soul of a nation . . . finds utterance', the language had hardly changed simply because of its articulation in the classical liberal mould. Those who remained outside the Congress fold did not approve of continuing the colonial system of governance, but Nehru and his colleagues had perhaps no alternative but to accept the colonial administration, which successfully dealt with the communal violence that broke out in Bengal and Punjab following the declaration of independence by the British. It was perhaps the only option available to the nationalists, at a critical juncture of India's history when the administration that the British left was useful for the new ruling authority in India. So it was an ideological choice that the nationalists exercised perhaps on account of the exigencies of the circumstances, which more or less ruled out the search for alternatives. The year of 1947 cannot therefore be seen as 'marking a total disjuncture between the colonial and post-colonial'. What governed the nationalist choice for instruments of colonial administration were perhaps the unique circumstances of communal riots in which these instruments of power became useful to Indian rulers who had hardly any experience of managing the state.[2] Given the well-entrenched administrative legacy of the British Raj, the post-colonial state in India is hardly a break with its immediate past.

Three major ideological influences seem to have been critical in Indian politics: colonialism, nationalism and democracy. The colonial, nationalist and democratic articulation of 'the political' remains therefore crucial in comprehending Indian politics even after decolonization. Two points need to be kept in mind. First, although colonialism and nationalism are surely antagonistic to each other there is no doubt that the former provoked circumstances in which nationalism emerged as a powerful ideology to articulate the voices of the colonized. Second, colonialism also led to a slow process of democratization by gradually involving people who were favourably disposed towards the alien administration. The colonial state had permitted some measures of representation to carefully selected Indian interests. But it had also ensured that 'the state had always operated at a level removed from the society which it governed'. Appropriating 'the executive privilege' for itself, the colonial state appeared to 'stand outside the realm of and therefore free to be arbiter over, social conflict and political competition [and its relationship with the subject] continued to be conducted in the language of supplication and concession, grants and demands, charters and petition, grievances and repression'.[3] The British were admittedly influenced by their own 'theories of liberalism and self-government'. Through a mixture of motives that included 'self interests and ideological commitments', the colonial government introduced principles of representation, appropriate for its rule, into the colonial legislature.[4] The British imperial attitudes in India seem to be 'highly ambiguous' resulting from their efforts to negotiate their liberal regard for self rule as the best form of government and their vested interests in being imperial masters.[5]

Modelled on the British North America Act, 1867, which established the Canadian federation, the 1935 Government of India Act is certainly a powerful constitutional intervention that the colonial rulers seriously made to accommodate the nationalist zeal within, of course, the colonial administrative format. This is also illustrative of efforts at legitimizing the growing democratic aspirations of the ruled in India through a constitutional intervention. Interestingly, the 1935 Act remained the strongest influence during the making of the 1950 Constitution for free India. Some 250 clauses of the present Constitution were, in fact, lifted from the Government of India Act. Although the political system of independent India draws its sustenance from universal adult franchise and political sovereignty, the governing rules are undoubtedly derived from its colonial past. The most striking provisions that the Constitution of India derived from its 1935 counterpart are the 'emergency provisions' that enable the President to suspend democratically elected governments and fundamental rights of the citizens. Furthermore, colonial provisions for 'preventive detention' of the so-called 'politically subversive individuals' remain in forces in independent India in different forms. The infamous 1972 Maintenance of Internal Security Act (MISA), Terrorist and Disruptive Activities (Prevention) Act (TADA) of the early 1980s and Prevention of Terrorist Act (POTA) in recent times are some of the examples that draw on the colonial and authoritarian legislation of the colonial past. Nonetheless, the 1935 Government of India Act is undoubtedly a very significant concession that the colonial government was forced to make to the rising tide of nationalism and democratization.

There is no doubt that the post-colonial state in India inherited its habits of governance from colonial practices. And its *weltanschauung* (world view) is based on 'the mixed legacies of colonial rule' that also upheld rule of law, bureaucracy, citizenship, parasitic landlords, modern political institutions and 'two-track tradition' of protest and participation.[6] What accounts for relative stability for colonialism in India was certainly its ability to adapt to the changed socio-political circumstances and also gradual but steady 'internalization' of domination by the subjects of colonial rule, which led Ashis Nandy to characterize colonialism as 'an intimate enemy' because the dominated saw 'the virtues of being dominated' for their own betterment.[7] Colonialism was not seen as an absolute evil. For the subjects, as Nandy argues,

> it was a product of one's own emasculation and defeat in legitimate power politics. For the rulers, colonial exploitation was an incidental and regrettable by-product of a philosophy of life that was in harmony with superior forms of political and economic organization. This was the consensus that rulers of India sought, consciously or unconsciously . . . [while] the subjects collaborated on a long-term basis [because] they seemed to have accepted the ideology of the system, either as players or as counter-players. This is the only way they could preserve a minimum of self-esteem in a situation of unavoidable injustice.[8]

Colonialism drew on such a cultural consensus, which was further strengthened by evolving mechanisms to defuse threats and also nationalist ire as and when it required. For instance, when the British model of unitary governance proved relatively ineffective for a diverse country like India, the colonial rulers began introducing by degrees doses of 'decentralization' and 'federalism', from the 1920s, in which the 1935 Government of India Act was the most significant institutional step.[9] Although the colonial state was hardly federal in its classical sense, the federal arrangement that the Act stipulated seemed to have provided critical inputs to the founding fathers when they deliberated on federalism in the Constituent Assembly.

These selective examples are illustrative of the argument underlining the critical importance of the three ideological forces of colonialism, nationalism and democratization in charting out a distinctive path for India. The argument that this book seeks to make draws on the dialectical interaction between colonialism, nationalism and democratization over a historical time leading to India's independence and its aftermath. Hence, it is intended neither to suggest that political freedom from colonial rule wrought no changes to Indian polity nor to argue that post-colonial India is just a continuation of her colonial past. Major political institutions, despite their clear colonial roots, have undergone dramatic metamorphoses in independent India. A careful look at the evolution of institutions in India clearly shows that they evolved creatively to adjust to the changing circumstances. The Westminster model of parliamentary democracy that India adopted was not a clone, for instance, but was responsive to the situation-specific ethos and the existent socio-cultural milieu. Similarly, there is no more persuasive example of 'deepening of democracy' than the 1977 and 2004 national polls, which were announced by the incumbent ruling authority, allegedly not favourably disposed towards 'democratic values and procedures'. In other words, the holding of the 1977 elections – called by Indira Gandhi, who had proven dictatorial tendencies – and of the 2004 elections – called by the BJP, who did not exactly appreciate democratic procedures – were both testimony to 'the deep roots that democracy had struck in the soil of India'.[10] Furthermore, the changing socio-economic profile of the legislative assemblies and national parliament is also indicative of a trend toward a genuinely inclusive democracy. Given the growing politicization of the peripheral sections of society, the elite-centric governance is fading away with the consolidation of people-centric governance. The change of political authority at regular intervals through elections is an eloquent testimony to the depth of the democratic processes, which are not merely articulated in periodic elections.[11] The introduction of adult suffrage transformed India's politics beyond recognition. Democracy is, therefore, no longer confined to electoral participation of the voters; it is also articulated in the 'everyday struggle' in which people are involved while exercising their rights as citizens.

There is however a note of caution. Colonialism contributed to nationalism, but not to a nation-state in India, for a variety of reasons connected with India's socio-cultural diversity. Post-colonial India was therefore hardly a nation-state, but rather a state-nation, simply because the institutions of governance, very much part of

British legacy, were already in place when the 1947 transfer of power took place. The nationalist leaders, except M. A. Jinnah, deliberately avoided the nationalist language that could be devastating in view of the absence of cultural and moral unity in India that characterized the rise of nations in the west. The nation, as a conscious political articulation, hardly figured in the political discourse of the day. Indian nationalism was not based on a shared language, religion or ethnic identity. Perhaps the presence of a common enemy, namely, British colonialism, 'united men and women from different parts of the subcontinent in a common and shared endeavour'.[12] A nation was consolidated, but followed a completely different path that was not at all derivative of the European sources. The nation that India is does not privilege a single language or a religious faith. Although the majority of its citizens are Hindus, India is not a 'Hindu Pakistan'. Its constitution does not discriminate between people on the basis of faith, nor did the nationalist movement that resulted in decolonization. Although the joy of freedom was marred by partition on the basis of religious chasm between Hindus and Muslims, the failure to avoid the division made Gandhi's political successors determined to construct independent India as a secular republic.

India can thus never be a nation in its catholic sense, though the 1992 Babri Masjid demolition is illustrative of attempts to unite Hindus on the basis of a nationalist criterion, namely religion. The fact that the political forces that spearheaded the campaign for Hindu consolidation remain peripheral in contemporary India is also suggestive of the weaknesses of a clear nationalist ideology. The relative decline of the nationalist ideology is perhaps matched by the rise of the 'regionalists', who seemed to have gained enormously with the growing involvement of the people in the political processes. Bringing people from India's periphery in terms of religion, elite caste status, or geographic distance from the centre, the regionalists have, in the context of coalition politics, redefined not only the contour of Indian politics, but also its vocabulary. In consequence, the terms of political discourse in contemporary India no longer resonate the values of the erstwhile Congress era, but are the outcome of the processes of 'deepening' of democracy. Articulating the voice of the regions, the regionalists seem to have erected a platform for an effective dialogue between the centre and periphery. It is thanks to these regionalists that the emerging multi-party democracy of India 'is not merely an anomic battle for power and short-term gain, but releasing a pent-up creativity and visions that provide a fertile and a cohesive backdrop to the realignment of social forces'.[13] The history of independent India is thus testimony to a creative articulation of democracy that is neither ethno-centric nor exactly imitative of the western experiences, but *sui generis*.

II

The making of free India's constitution by the Constituent Assembly over a period of little more than three years is reflective of the efforts that the founding fathers undertook to translate the nationalist and democratic aspirations of an independent polity following decolonization. Furthermore, although the Constitution is a continuity at least in structural and procedural terms, it was also a clear break with the past, since the 1950 Constitution drew on an ideology that sought to establish a liberal democratic polity following the withdrawal of colonialism. There can be no greater evidence of the commitment to constitutionalism and rule of law on the part of the founding fathers than the Constitution that they framed despite serious difficulties due to partition. The commitment to liberal democratic values, as the Constituent Assembly proceedings suggest, remained paramount in the making of the Constitution. For instance, though the constitution-makers valorized the idea of popular sovereignty, they redefined it and adopted the liberal representative principle to create 'a Nehruvian statist political order'. Popular sovereignty was thus defined in the Habermasian proceduralized sense, in which 'popular opinion and will formation in informal and voluntary public spheres could seek to influence the channels of legitimate law-making'.[14]

Set up as a result of negotiations between the nationalist leaders and the members of the Cabinet Mission over the possible constitutional arrangement in post-war India, the Constituent Assembly began its deliberations on 9 December 1946 and concluded with the passage of the Constitution on 24 January 1950. This period, slightly over three years, was one in which the joy of freedom was severely marred by national trauma, associated with the partition and violence, that resulted in the killing of Mahatma, besides the butchering of innocent people in the wake of the transfer of population in the immediate aftermath of the declaration of freedom. The Indian Constitution was born, argues Paul Brass, 'more in fear and trepidation than in hope and inspiration'.[15] There is hardly a strong argument to dispute this proposition because of the context in which the Constituent Assembly began and concluded its proceedings. The Constitution was thus a pragmatic response to the reality that the Assembly confronted while drawing the roadmap for free India. The founding fathers practised, as has been appropriately suggested, 'the art of the possible and never allowed [their ideological cause] to blind them to reality'.[16]

Although they appreciated India's pluralistic social texture, there was a near unanimity among the Assembly members for a strong state.[17] Even those who were critical of the emergency provisions also defended a centralized state to contain tendencies threatening the integrity of the country. Emergency provisions in the Constitution were justified because 'disorder' or 'mis-governance' endangers India's existence as 'a territorial state'. Such concerns could only have reflected, argues Paul Brass, 'another kind of continuity' between the new governing elite and the former British rulers, namely 'an attitude of distrust' of the ordinary politicians of the country and 'a lack of faith' in the ability of the newly enfranchised population to check 'the misdeeds' of their elected rulers.[18] Nonetheless, the fear of 'disorder' was probably the most critical factor in favour of the arguments for a centralized state despite its clear incompatibility with the cherished ideal of the nationalist leaders for a federal state. B. R. Ambedkar's contradictory stances on federalism, for instance, thus may appear whimsical independent of the circumstances. In 1939, Ambedkar was clearly in favour of a federal form of government for its political viability in socio-culturally diverse India.[19] By 1946, he provided a radically different view by saying that 'I like a strong united Centre, much stronger than the Centre we had created under the Government of India Act of 1935'.[20] While presenting the final report of the Union Powers Committee, Jawaharlal Nehru also argued in favour of a strong state by stating that:

> [w]e are unanimously of the view that it would be injurious to the interest of the country to provide for a weak central authority which would be incapable of ensuring peace, of coordinating vital matters of common concern and of speaking effectively for the whole country in the international sphere.[21]

As is evident, federalism did not appear to be an appropriate structural form of governance in the light of the perceived threats to the existence of the young Indian nation. Hence the constitution-makers recommended a strong centre because the constitutional design of a country is meant to serve 'the normative-functional requirements of governance'. The constitution was to reflect 'an ideology of governance' regardless of whether it articulated the highly cherished ideals of the freedom struggle that a majority of the Assembly members had nurtured while participating in the struggle. As G. L. Mehta believed, 'we have to build up the system on the conditions of our country [and] not on any abstract theories'.[22] Along the same lines, Alladi Krishnaswamy Ayyar argued that 'our constitutional design is relative to the peculiar conditions obtaining here, according to the peculiar exigencies of our country [and] not according to a prior or theoretical considerations'.[23] In the making of the constitution for governance, they were guided more by their views on statecraft, which would surely have been different without the traumatic experience preceding the inauguration of the Constitution in 1950. Hence one can safely suggest that 'hard-headed pragmatism and not abstract governmental theories' was what guided 'the architects of our Constitution'.[24]

Yet it was not the entire Assembly that wrote the document. It was clearly the hard work 'of the government wing of the Congress, and not the mass party' and the brunt of the task fell upon 'the Canning Lane Group', so named because 'they lived while attending Assembly sessions on Canning Lane'.[25] There is another dimension of the functioning of the Assembly that is also instructive. According to Granville Austin, Indian's constitutional structure is perhaps 'a good example' of decision-making by consensus and accommodation, which he defends by examining the debates on various provisions of the Constitution.[26] Scholars, however, differ because, given the Congress hegemony in the Assembly, views held by the non-Congress members were usually bulldozed. As S. K. Chaube argued, at least on two major issues – political minorities and language – both these principles were conveniently sacrificed. As regards political minority, there was no consensus and the solution to the language problem was, as Austin himself admits, 'a half-hearted compromise'.[27] By dubbing the Assembly 'a packed house', the diminished Muslim League expressed the feeling of being alienated from the house. Even Ambedkar underlined the reduced importance of the Assembly since on a number of occasions, as he admitted, 'they had to go to another place to obtain a decision and come to the Assembly'.[28]

Decision by consensus may not be an apt description of the processes of deliberation. But, as the proceedings show, there was near unanimity on most occasions and divisions of opinion among the Congress Party members, who constituted a majority, were sorted out politically. As Ambedkar admits, '[t]he possibility of chaos was reduced to nil by the existence of the Congress Party inside the Assembly which brought into its proceedings a sense of order and discipline. . . . The Party is therefore entitled to all the credit for the smooth sailing of the Draft Constitution in the Assembly'.[29] As Shiva Rao informs us, on a number of controversial issues, efforts were made to eliminate or at least to minimize differences through informal meetings of the Congress Party's representatives in the Constituent Assembly.[30] If the informal discussion failed to resolve the differences, 'the Assembly leadership . . . exercised its authority formally by the Party Whip'.[31] It is evident that in the Constituent Assembly no attempt was made to force a decision, the accent being on unanimity presumably because 'the leaders were alive to the fact that the constitution adopted on the principle of majority vote would not last long'.[32] It was not therefore surprising that Rajendra Prasad, the president of the Constituent Assembly, preferred to postpone debate and allow them to work out agreed solutions rather than take a vote that might, as he apprehended, result 'in something not wanted by anybody'.[33]

Two important points emerge out of the preceding discussions. First, the making of the Indian Constitution was a difficult exercise not only because of the historical context but also on account of the peculiar social texture of the Indian reality that had to be translated in the Constitution. The collective mind in the Assembly was defensive as a consequence of the rising tide of violence taking innocent lives immediately after partition. Second, the founding fathers seem to have been obsessed with their own notion of integrated national life. The aim of the Constitution was to provide 'an appropriate ordering framework' for India. As Rajendra Prasad equivocally declared on the floor of the Assembly, '[p]ersonally I do not attach any importance to the label which may be attached to it – whether you call it a Federal Constitution or a Unitary Constitution or by any other name. It makes no difference so long as the Constitution serves our purpose.'[34] On the whole, a unitary mind produced 'an essentially unitary constitution doused with a sprinkling of permissive power for a highly supervised level of constituent units'.[35]

III

The national polls in 1999 and 2004 are a watershed in India's recent political history for at least two reasons. First, these elections have ushered in an era of coalition in India that can hardly be reversed because of radical socio-economic changes at the grassroots due to 'deepening' of democracy. There is hardly a stable vote bank for any party involved in elections. Parties win or lose not because of the ideology they represent but because of their electoral strategy to muster support at the time of elections. Second, the 2004 election was also a new era for a voter's calculations of his/her pay-off by deciding strategically at a time when mobilization based on caste or ethnic identities did not seem to be as critical as it was before. The three Ms of the 1990s – Mandal, Mandir and Market – hardly remained effective in garnering votes. Hindutva, for or against, had lost its appeal and the incumbent ruling party, BJP, had to draw on the 'India shining' campaign, which failed to sway the voters. Political parties thus tell 'a story of gradual withdrawal from linkages of one's performance and capabilities'.[36] Local issues – be it electricity, roads or water – became critical in deciding the poll outcomes in a large number of constituencies. This also suggests that 'the issue of governance' – primarily performance – is what mattered most in voter's calculations.

The 2004 national election seems to be a continuation of the pattern that the 1999 election confirmed, namely coalitions of parties as the only option for government formation on account of the fractured poll verdict. Nonetheless, it would be wrong to suggest that the coalition era had begun in 1999 because the experiment, though ephemeral in duration, was conducted earlier in India. Although in 1967 coalition governments were formed in as many as nine Indian states – Punjab, Haryana, Uttar Pradesh, Bihar, Madhya Pradesh, West Bengal, Orissa, Tamil Nadu and Kerala – the first national experiment of coalition government was articulated in 1977 when the Janata Party captured power at the Union level. The Janata experiment of 1977–79 is a class by itself for at least two fundamental reasons. First, this was the first attempt at forming a coalition government at the national level.[37] The non-Congress catch-all coalition governments that came into being in 1967 were merely state-level experiments with no obvious impact on the union government. In a way, regionalization of Indian politics was inevitable when the politically pervasive Congress system appeared to have lost its all-India appeal. Second, although at a different level, the Janata government was a continuation in the sense that not only did it drew upon anti-Congress sentiments, but it also brought within its fold parties with diverse ideological beliefs on the basis of certain common socio-economic and political goals. The importance of the 1975–77 Emergency cannot be glossed over in uniting parties and political forces against the Indira Gandhi-led Congress (I) immediately in the aftermath of the 1977 election. With the Janata coalition at the centre, the state-level parties rub shoulders with national issues as members of the union government and national-level parties get the feel of the polity of the state and still lower levels.

The Emergency was an assault not only on the Constitution but also on the liberal democratic practices that had evolved with the Constitution since independence. Seeking to gag the democratic processes, the authoritarian state created an opportunity for the opposition parties to unite irrespective of ideology against the party in power. The 1975–77 Emergency was thus a watershed in India's post-colonial history not only because it led to circumstances for the emergence and consolidation of coalition politics but also because it strengthened the processes of democratization by provoking spontaneous movements challenging the authoritarian rule. It was easier for various political groups to mobilize massive support for their cause because of the participation of the people, mainly in urban centres, in movements against the suspension of fundamental rights and privileges to which a citizen in a democratic polity had access.

Two dimensions of this coming together of opposition parties seem important: on the one hand, those opposed to Indira Gandhi drew primarily on anti-Congressism, defined vaguely as a political stance against the Congress Party. The other dimension underlined an all-round effort by Jayaprakash Narayan (hereafter JP) to bring together ideologically diverse political parties on the basis of this underlying thread of opposition to the Congress Party. JP's success in cementing the bond suggested a possibility of a political unity among diverse social groups despite serious differences in socio-economic terms. This was how the socialists agreed to downplay the ideological schism with other constituents after the 1975–77 Emergency. Furthermore, the class character of the Bharatiya Lok Dal (BLD) never stood in the way of forming a coalition in which a completely opposite BJS was a significant partner.[38] Even the RSS endorsed the participation of the Jana Sangha in the Janata experiment, as its leader Bala Sahab Deoras realized that, 'to remain in the mainstream of national politics, the RSS should opt for a politics of accommodation' by redefining its exclusivist ideological identity.[39] In fact, the changed RSS attitude was crucial in the formation of the Janata alliance. As soon as the 1977 elections were announced, four opposition parties – Congress (O), the Jana Sangha, the Bharatiya Lok Dal and the Socialist Party – merged to form the Janata Party, which decided to have a common candidate and common symbol in this poll. It was a remarkable success for the party to have prepared a common list of candidates with other parties such as the CPI(M) and Akali Dal, and the result was evident in as many as 425 of 539 seats, where there was virtually a straight contest between Congress and the opposition.

Congress lost and the opposition parties won a majority presumably because of the mass discontent over excesses of the Emergency and the relative success of the movement that JP launched against 'the authoritarian rule'. In a Lok Sabha of 539 seats, the Janata Party won 270, its allies, the Jagjivan Ram-led Congress for Democracy, won 28 seats, the Akali Dal 8 and the CPI(M) 28. Not only did Congress collapse in north India, Indira Gandhi was also defeated in Rae Bareli in UP. History was created. It was a history of non-Congress coalition in India. What was articulated at the state level in the 1967 elections was translated to the national level in the 1977 election. Now, the idea of coalition governments, however nebulous it was, became an important feature of the national political map that was to be redrawn in the light of the declining importance of a single party majority in the central legislature.

As evident, the Janata Party that held power between March 1977 and July 1979 was 'a hastily assembled coalition of quite different opposition parties and groups united mainly by their opposition to Indira Gandhi and the Emergency'.[40] In other words, the unity among the opposition groups was politically expedient and the natural divisions among them began to emerge once the common enemy was defeated. The Janata Party was a coalition, largely dominated by the conservative, but secularist, faction of the Congress Party. Alongside, it also had the Jana Sangha, a party of the 'Hindu Right', representing mainly the high-caste middle-class people in the urban areas in north and central India. As a constituent, the BLD sought to articulate the interest of 'prosperous small peasant proprietors' primarily in the Hindi belt. Its primary ideological goal was to reallocate resources away from the urban, industrial sector towards agriculture. The fourth constituent was the Socialist Party, with a well-entrenched support base among the workers in urban areas and also the rural poor in some areas of north India. Finally the Congress for Democracy was a splinter group from Congress with support among the poor and particularly Dalits in rural India.[41]

The euphoria over the victory of the Janata Party coalition was short-lived. Once the government was formed, holding the party together was a major preoccupation of the leaders. The government received frequent jolts from the constant bickering and infighting in the party both at the centre and in the states. The Janata Party remained 'a coalition of different parties and groups' and was 'a victim of factionalism, manipulation and personal ambitions of its leaders'.[42] Bound by anti-Indira Gandhi sentiments, the coalition was too disparate historically, ideologically and even programmatically to jell together. Jana Sangha, which had ninety MPs, was distinct in its ideology, with clear communal characteristics in view of its organic link with the RSS;[43] Congress (O) was secular but conservative, following more or less the Congress ideology; BLD, though secular, was following a rich-peasant strategy and thus failed to strike roots among the rural masses; the future of the socialists was circumscribed largely by its inability to go beyond Bihar, where it had a base and strong organizational roots. The lack of ideological congruity stood in the way of consolidating a relatively stable coalition.

Although ephemeral in its existence, the Janata coalition is a remarkable experiment in governance by ideologically different but programmatically less incompatible parties. Since the major issue of the 1977 elections was how to reverse the authoritarian usurpation of democratic power, the mandate of the restoration of the constitutional regime 'served as the strongest foundation of support for the Janata coalition'.[44] What is striking is the effort of the Janata Party government to comply with the election pledges as far as possible.[45] In pursuance of this, a rapid reversal of the Emergency regime, the re-establishment of the rule of law and the swift dismantling of the structures of authoritarian control established by Indira Gandhi were probably the most significant achievements of the Janata regime.

The experiment was repeated in 1989 when the Janata Dal government held power in Delhi, though it lasted only for two years until the constituents fell apart on various ideological issues. In view of the failure of a single party to obtain a majority, coalition governments were formed in 1996 and 1998, both of which shared the same fate, and an election was announced in 1999, after which the BJP-led National Democratic Alliance (NDA) secured a majority in the Lok Sabha, the lower house of India's parliament. The 2004 election seems to have confirmed a pattern in Indian political arithmetic, namely that coalition is perhaps the only political mechanism to provide stable governance in India. By bringing together parties opposed to the BJP, the Congress-led United Progressive Alliance (UPA) captured power in New Delhi with the support of the left parties in the lower house. What is most significant is the emergence of regional parties as both major stakeholders in the government and also numerically essential for the continuance of the coalition in case of proving a majority on the floor of the house. With the rising importance of regional political parties in the coalition era, the state-centric issues have gained remarkable salience presumably because of the compulsion of coalition politics. So the emergence of regional parties as serious stakeholders of the system has translated into political pluralism in its true spirit. In this sense, the increasing salience of the parties with roots and support in a particular region contributes to a process of what I call 'regionalization of national politics' and 'nationalization of regional politics'.

Regional parties are now crucial in the continuation of the ruling party in power at the centre. The prominent role that many regional parties played in the formation of the NDA and in jockeying for power in the aftermath of the elections 'created an impression of regionalization of the national political arenas'.[46] For decades, small and regional parties were decried by all parties, especially the Congress, as 'parochial'. They were accused of 'deepening social and regional divisions'. In the political culture of single party dominance, they were dubbed as 'destabilizing forces'. The national politics that pitted the 'nation' against the 'regions' has accorded a legitimate space to the regional and indigenous elite and they cannot be ignored in the new dispensation of political power in India. In other words, with voters' preference for local issues, the political system is forced to structure the process of governance around a coalition of small and regional parties, which, incidentally, happens to be a coalition mostly composed of middle and lower castes in the social hierarchy. This of necessity forced the acceptance of a more federal system of governance (in regional and social terms) than was ever achieved by the proponents of states' rights earlier.[47] The occasional hiccups in the ruling coalition following the reported threat of the AIADMK in 2001 demonstrate the extent to which the constituents of the coalition are significant. The erstwhile NDA coalition led by the Bharatiya Janata Party (BJP) has survived despite a fluid and highly volatile political scenario.[48] The net result of the last national poll in 2004 is, however, that the Indian variety of coalition provides a rather 'moderate' form of government in which large national parties have been forced to accept the need for alliances and accommodations with a variety of new and old parties, including the regional parties. Brushing aside the so-called 'ideological purity', what brings the partners together and largely sustains the coalition is 'the exigency of the situation'. Despite the short duration of the two earlier successive coalition governments at the centre,[49] the continuity of the NDA government for a full term is indicative of a significant change in India's political texture by making coalition inevitable. The presence of the region on the national scene is illustrative of a process of empowerment of various communities, hitherto peripheral. One of the reasons for the growing importance of regional parties is certainly their success in articulating the interests of the assertive backward castes and Dalits. These parties remain 'regional' in terms of geographic location, but are national in terms of raising issues relevant to the country as a whole.[50] The growing importance of regional parties in the national coalition is also indicative of a more competitive and polarized party system. Democracy is indeed moving closer to the people.

The NDA and its successor UPA are therefore powerful experiments in federalism and coalition politics in India. What it suggests is not merely the decline of one party and rise of the regional and smaller parties, but a crisis of majoritarian political culture, based on the dominance of a single party led by a charismatic leader.

The purpose of this brief chronological exposition of India's recent political history is to provide an analytical account of the evolution of coalition politics with reference to the fractured electoral mandate in the last two elections. Two important points emerge. First, appeal to 'nation' does not seem to be effective in garnering a majority in parliament, as the Hindutva brigade attempted by seeking to mobilize Hindus against 'the hated other', namely the Muslims. The espoused Nehruvian goal of 'unity in diversity' as the cultural basis of a tolerant pluralism in India seems to have considerably lost its acceptance particularly in the light of the 1992 Babri Masjid demolition. The single party majority is no longer feasible. The coalition of parties is perhaps the only institutional mechanism to accommodate conflicting pulls of regional and sub-national identities. Grounded on India's well-entrenched pluralism, the coalition may lead to 'banalization' of the concept of nationalism altogether[51] by upholding multicultural nationalism as integral to India's political processes. Secondly, reflective of definite social coalitions, the NDA and later UPA represent a new trend in Indian politics that cannot be reversed. Both these national coalition governments are the result of the coming together of various political parties on the basis of 'programmatic compatibility' notwithstanding serious ideological differences among them. The Bahujan Samaj Party (BSP), which won a majority in the state assembly in 2007, is a coalition of two socially antagonistic socio-political groups, namely Brahmins and Dalits. Drawn on the pro-Dalit views of Ambedkar, the BSP also gained the Brahmins' support by expressing its strong opposition to the Mandal reservation scheme for other backward castes. The outcome of the UP election is indicative of a clear breakdown of social barriers in political mobilization. Brahmins and Dalits may have different, if not antagonistic, social locations. Yet, on the basis of common socio-economic agenda, they can come together to constitute a winning coalition, as the UP election results have demonstrated.

A careful study of the electoral trends in India reveals that the nation in India is highly fractured and an appeal to the nation can never be a meaningful ideological agenda. Furthermore, it has also shown that moderation of shrill ideological overtones is perhaps the most effective way of political mobilization in India's highly competitive politics. Two processes seem to have worked simultaneously: on the one hand, the nation no longer remains a valid electoral plank for mobilizing votes because sub-national issues and identities appear to be critical in deciding the fate of political parties jostling for votes. This clearly suggests, on the other hand, the impact of the processes of democratization that began with the introduction of adult suffrage in independent India. Indian politics is thus not merely a laboratory for different kinds of experiments involving diverse social groups; it is also an arena of diverse social, economic and political activities that are hardly comprehensible if conceptualized in ethnocentric theoretical paradigms.

IV

Indian politics needs to be grasped sociologically. There is no doubt that the political system that India inherited after decolonization was largely based on the Westminster model. Yet it underwent significant changes that hardly had any resemblance to the British system of governance. Herein lies the importance of the socio-economic processes that shaped the political evolution to be clearly distinct in terms of both manifestation and articulation. It was not therefore surprising that 'three different languages of politics, namely, modern, traditional and saintly'[52] seem relevant in Indian politics. The principal argument that this book thus makes revolves around the shifting complexities of the political, which is enmeshed in equally complex socio-economic and cultural circumstances. Indian politics is the study of historically evolved contexts. What is unique about this book is its focus on the dialectical interconnection between society and politics over a historical period. Unlike the conventional studies, the present exercise also dwells on those socio-political and economic variables that have impacted on the evolution of 'the political' in its most complex articulation simply because the Indian context is both reflexive and reflective. The fundamental point that the book seeks to draw out is also concerned with the emergence and consolidation of a democratic polity out of colonialism, nationalism and democratization. These three forces seem to have provided 'the foundational values' on which the political is grounded. There is no doubt that colonialism distorted the evolution of India, which followed neither 'the pure' capitalist path of development nor any routes that do not draw on capitalism. Yet, colonialism, *inter alia*, contributes to 'a critical space' for forces that are opposed to colonialism and inspired by nationalism and democratization. Similarly, nationalism of the Indian variety hardly corresponds to its European counterpart despite being 'derivative' at least in the initial stages. As anti-colonialism gained momentum, nationalism unfolded as an ideology that was interpreted differently by different groups involved in its articulation. Whereas Gandhi was drawn to nationalism for politically bringing together 'the imagined community', Jinnah, persuaded by its classical form, defended 'two nation theory' on the basis of 'homogenizing' nationalist ideology underplaying the inherent divisions even among the Muslims due to a peculiar evolution of Islam in the subcontinent. Nonetheless, nationalism not only unleashed democratic forces but also consolidated them in the course of struggles for freedom. Post-colonial India is therefore not exactly a break with the past because of the institutional and ideational legacies: whereas the former is articulated in the continuity of the structures of governance, the latter was also reflective of the nationalist vision, inspired by values of social and economic justice, political equality and a respect for diversity, especially for the marginalized sections of society. Given the peculiar social context and its equally peculiar evolution in the aftermath of decolonization, India is undoubtedly a unique model that is theoretically innovative owing to the obvious empirical context in which it has evolved. My purpose is to draw on the processes that are critical in 'imagining' and also 're-imagining' India since independence in 1947. Formed in 1946, the Constituent Assembly provided a roadmap for the new nation that was hardly adequate as it gradually became far more complex. The book seeks to provide an interpretative account of shifting politics of India and also of the factors that remained critical in the entire process. There is however a note of caution. The reinvention that is taking place in contemporary India is different from the one which took place in the Constituent Assembly. It is not a considered process, as in the Constituent Assembly, but one of 'contestation and negotiation'. It is, therefore, difficult to comprehend 'the wonder that is India' in one volume. Hence the book seeks to provide 'a contextual interpretation' of Indian politics by drawing on the processes in which ideology seems to be critical as well.

V

With seven chapters, the book is thematically structured and empirically elaborated. Chapter 1 dwells on the evolution of independent India in the wake of the decolonization of the subcontinent. Partition was a watershed. Yet the colonial legacy was so strong that both the institutions of governance and the ideas that informed them after independence drew on values that had been preeminent in colonial governance. Arguments for a strong state were marshalled by those who presided over India's destiny immediately after independence to avoid 'disorder'; this idea seemed to have gained force following the partition riots involving major communities. Chapter 2 concentrates on the multifaceted 'communal' identities in India, revolving around multiple social, economic and cultural axes. In the articulation of the political, the language of identity has gained enormous salience in India's 'patronage democracy' presumably because of the growing importance of ascriptive identities, not only as a social marker, but also as a ladder for political ascendancy. It is also argued that India has a borrowed system of governance. This is partly correct if one considers the institutional legacy of colonial rule. As the book shows, the similarity is perhaps more in the 'nomenclature' of India's governance and less in its substance. The emergence and consolidation of democracy in India seems to be a wonder in liberal political theory since 'free institutions are', as J. S. Mill suggested in his *Representative Government*, 'next to impossible in a country made of different nationalities'.[53] India defied the well-established theory that democracy could strike roots only where there was a *demos* with a common culture. How it is possible that democracy is not only well-rooted in India but also growing stronger day-by-day is the question that Chapter 3 seeks to address. India provides a parliamentary federal form of governance, which is a hybrid system of political decision-making underlining a peculiar mixture of the Westminster model of parliamentary supremacy and the American federal system. Chapter 4 is devoted to this phenomenon, which combines the institutional legacy of colonialism and the nationalist enthusiasm for accommodating India's socio-political diversity.

India is a unique political reality that generally defies some of the well-established theoretical propositions, drawn on liberal democratic experiments elsewhere. Chapters 5, 6 and 7 thus focus on the changing texture of Indian politics since the 1960s. With the failure of the Congress Party to comprehend the changing social texture of Indian politics, several splinter groups that later became political parties came together striving to provide a viable alternative which was undoubtedly symptomatic of a new trend that fully flourished in 1999 with the formation of the NDA-led stable coalition government. Whereas Chapter 5 unravels the dynamics of the embryonic coalition politics in various constituent states of federal India, Chapter 6 is confined to conceptualizing the transformed Marxist-led Left Front in the light of the 2006 state assembly election in West Bengal. Unlike Kerala, the West Bengal Marxists seem to have redefined their ideology in the changed environment of an apparent ascendance of global capital. The new design that the Left Front experiment shows is one of 'corporatized Marxism'. Underlining the growing importance of political alignment regardless of ideology, the final chapter concludes the story by critically evaluating the evolution and consolidation of coalition culture in India as perhaps most inevitable in a highly fragmented polity where the incentives to appeal to a larger constituency seem to have evaporated.

1 Setting the scene
Partition and after

The 1947 partition set the perspective in which India rose as a free nation. The Constitution that was adopted in 1950 was the product of two conflicting cultures: one representing the national leaders' normative concern for India's multicultural personality, shaped by her unique history and geography; and the other underlining their concern for unity, security and administrative efficiency. The former led to the articulation of secularism and federalism in the 1950 Constitution and the latter resulted in the retention of the very state machinery that had consolidated the colonial rule in India. The net result was the emergence of a semi-hegemonic state that drew largely upon the 1935 Government of India Act. If the new Indian political elites received a legacy of government from their predecessors, they assuredly carried over also, argued W. H. Morris-Jones, 'a legacy from their own immediate past, from the experience of the nationalist movement'.[1] Independent India's politics, at least in the initial years, drew on these two legacies. The nationalist ideology, which was hardly derivative, remained the driving force in charting out India's future. Hence political institutions, despite their imperial roots, acted in a manner that was reminiscent of an independent state, imbued with enthusiasm for a new beginning. Yet the importance of the prevalent social order, the divided social structure and the inevitable social conflicts in shaping the political process cannot be overlooked. There were also rich civilizational traditions that preceded the British rule and remained a binding force, despite the triumph of divisive politics with the emergence of Pakistan in 1947 as a precondition for independence from the British rule. There is thus no doubt that Indian politics cannot be grasped without understanding the historical processes that remained most critical even after independence, for reasons connected with the peculiar circumstances in which India emerged in the comity of free nations. It would thus be wrong to suggest that Indian politics even after decolonization remained as it was in the past simply because the historical context underwent massive changes. It would also not be entirely correct to argue that Indian politics was absolutely innovative in its post-colonial phase because the colonial past, though much derided, has, in fact, left behind a substantial political imprint.

The aim of this chapter is thus twofold: first, to briefly discuss the nature of partition and its outcome and, second, by dealing with the ideological basis of the post-colonial political leadership in India that had roots in the nationalist struggle, to draw out the political significance of those principles and values that laid the institutional foundation of a decolonized India.

Partition of the subcontinent

Partition is 'the moment of the constitutional establishment of two dominions with accompanying bloodbath'.[2] Pressing for a separate Muslim state, the 1940 Lahore resolution was the first official pronouncement of the Pakistan or partition by the Muslim League. Though the term 'Pakistan' was nowhere mentioned, by demanding an independent state or states for the Muslims the resolution translated the goal of a sovereign Muslim state into concrete terms.[3] Seeking to organise Indian Muslims around the Pakistan demand, the resolution was thus historically significant for at least two important reasons: first, that the resolution was proposed by Fazlul Haq, the most popular Muslim leader in Bengal, suggests the growing dominance of the League in the Muslim-majority provinces; and second, for the first time an unequivocal demand was formally articulated insisting that the areas in India in which Muslims constituted a majority should be made into an independent state containing autonomous and sovereign units.[4] Furthermore, it argued that Indian Muslims constituted a majority nation in the north-west and the east of India and ought to be treated on a par with the Hindu majority in all future constitutional negotiations.

Despite doubts of Pakistan's viability, the colonial power became increasingly sensitive to the claims advanced by the Muslim League. By 1945, not only did the League insist on 'the division of India as the only solution of the complex constitutional problem of India',[5] its election campaign was also based on the issue of Pakistan. If the Muslims voted in favour of the League in the 1946 elections, 'the League will be entitled to ask for Pakistan without any further investigation or plebiscite'.[6] During the election campaign, Jinnah also identified the areas constituting Pakistan. According to him, those provinces with a clear Muslim majority naturally belonged to Pakistan. Hence, Sind, Baluchistan, the North West Frontier Province and Punjab in the north-west, and Bengal and Assam in the north-east of India were earmarked for Pakistan. The forthcoming elections, he declared, 'will decide the matter once for all and when they are over, Pakistan will become an immediate reality'.[7] In Punjab, Jinnah and his League colleagues were reported to have drawn on the religious sentiments of the Muslim voters by underlining that 'the question a voter is called on to answer is – are you a true believer or an infidel and a traitor'.[8] As the poll outcome revealed, the 1946 election was a referendum for the League.[9] Although in the first provincial poll in 1937 the League failed to make an impact even in the Muslim-majority provinces, within nine years, in 1946, it became the only representative of the Muslims by polling in most, if not all, cases close to its maximum natural strength. This was a remarkable achievement in terms of both leadership and organisation. An unambiguous verdict in favour of the Muslim League in the Muslim-majority provinces in the 1946 elections radically altered India's political landscape in which the League emerged as a stronger party in its negotiations with the British in the last phase of the transfer of power.

The contradictory nature of the reality of 15 August 1947 continues to intrigue the historian even after more than half a century since India was partitioned. Freedom was won but was accompanied by the trauma of partition and mayhem that followed immediately before the transfer of power was formally articulated. So India's independence represents a great paradox of history. The nationalist movement led to freedom, but failed to avoid partition. The success of the nationalist movement was therefore also its failure. Why did it happen? The answer lies in another paradox, namely the success and failure of the anti-imperialist movement, led by Gandhi and his Congress colleagues. In its struggle against the colonial power, the Congress had a twofold task: moulding different classes, communities and groups into a nation and winning freedom for this emerging nation. The Congress had succeeded in mobilizing the nation against the British that accounted for the final withdrawal of the British rule in India; it was however virtually unsuccessful 'in welding the diversity into a nation and particularly failed to integrate the Muslims into this nation'.[10] Underlying this conundrum – the success and failure of the nationalist movement – lies the roots of the paradox of independence that came along with the Great Divide of the subcontinent of India. Independence and partition were, as a commentator argues, 'but the reflection of the success and failure of the strategy of the [Congress-led] nationalist movement'.[11] The 1947 partition was therefore not merely a physical division of the subcontinent; it also radically altered its complexion by seeking to define its members in conformity with the constructed political boundary in the aftermath of the transfer of power. For the Muslims, 1947 was not merely about partition; it was also about freedom from both the British and the Hindu ruling authority. For the Hindus in Bengal, for instance, it created a sense of home[12] – where they were safe and protected.[13] Although it was undoubtedly a watershed in many respects,[14] not everything in India changed irrevocably as a result of these two linked events – independence and partition. Independent India remained, at least in the initial decades of her independence, a hostage of her colonial past.

Political economy of India as a nation-state

India's post-colonial political economy is neither purely capitalist nor feudal but a peculiar admixture of the two. Hence, just like India's evolution as a nation in the aftermath of decolonization in 1947, the path of development that India adopted can never be conceptualized in a straightforward manner. The Preamble to the Constitution of India laid the foundation of the socialistic pattern of society in which the state remained the most critical player. Accordingly, the Directive Principles of State Policy (Part IV of the Constitution) emphasize that the goal of the Indian polity is not unbridled *laissez faire* but a welfare state where the state has a positive duty to ensure to its citizens social and economic justice with dignity of the individual consistent with the unity and integrity of the nation. By making them fundamental in governance, and making the laws of the country and duty of the state to apply these principles, the founding fathers made it the responsibility of future governments to find a middle way between individual liberty and the public good, between preserving the property and privilege of the few and bestowing benefits on the many in order to liberate the powers of individuals equally for contributions to the common good.[15] This new institutional matrix consisted of 'a regulatory regime' comprising (a) public sector expansion, (b) discretionary controls over markets and private economic activities and (c) stringent foreign exchange and import controls. The first two had their roots in the ideology of socialism while the last one had its roots in economic nationalism. Taken together, they articulated 'activism of the newly established nation state'.[16]

In this model of state-directed development, the most significant instrument was the Planning Commission that came into being in January 1950 despite serious opposition of the Gandhians within the Congress Working Committee. However, the cabinet resolution that finally led to the creation of the Commission underlined three major principles as special terms of reference in the preparation of the plans, which largely defused opposition. These principles were: (a) that the citizens, men and women equally, have the right to an adequate means of livelihood; (b) that the ownership and control of the material resources of the country are so distributed as best to subserve the common good; and (c) that the operation of the economic system does not result in the concentration of wealth and means of production to the common detriment.[17] Underlining the ideological commitment of the nation, the 1948 Industrial Policy Resolution therefore begins by stating that

> [t]he nation has now set itself to establish a social order where justice and equality of opportunity shall be secured to all the people. For this purpose, careful planning and integrated efforts over the whole field of national activity are necessary; and the Government of India proposes to establish a National Planning Commission to formulate programmes of development and to secure its execution.
>
> (para. 1)

Accordingly, the 1948 Industrial Policy Resolution insisted that the state should play a progressively active role in the development of critical industries, such as (a) industries manufacturing arms and ammunition, production and control of atomic energy and the ownership and management of railway transport and (b) basic industries, namely iron, coal, steel, aircraft manufacture, shipbuilding and oil. This resolution was reiterated in the 1955 Avadi session of the Congress by underlining that, in view of the declared objective being a socialist pattern of society, the state shall play a vital role in planning and development. The next landmark event confirming the intention of an activist state was the industrial policy resolution of 1956, which was adopted after parliament had accepted in December 1954 a socialist pattern of society as the objective of social and economic policy and the Second Five-Year Plan (also known as the Mahalanobis Plan) articulated this ideological goal in formal terms. P. C. Mahalanobis, the architect of the plan, argued for state-controlled economic development for accelerating the tempo of growth under 'the autarkic industrialization strategy'.[18] Hence he insisted that the basic and heavy industries should remain in the public sector for two reasons: (a) the private sector may not be able to raise adequate resources for these very capital-intensive industries and even if it managed it would command a monopolistic control that was deemed detrimental to social welfare; and (b) by controlling allocation of output of basic and heavy industries according to social priorities, it was certain that the government would be able to channel private sector growth to fulfil its ideological goal. In seeking to fulfil the objective of a socialist pattern of society, the Nehru-led government envisaged an expanded role of public sector and the importance of planning in all-round development of the country.

Planning for development: a panacea or failure?

Planning seems a formidable operational tool to structure the role of the state in accordance with its ideological underpinning. Therefore not only is planning as an instrument tuned to economic regeneration, it is inextricably tied to the regime's political preferences as well. This is, however, not to conceptualize the relationship between planning and the ideological slant of the regime in a deterministic way, but to underline the complex interdependence, which entails, at the same time, an interplay of various pulls and pressures in a rapidly changing social fabric. Planning is thus 'an exercise of instrumental rationality . . . institutionalized . . . outside the normal processes of representative politics [and executed] through a developmental administration'.[19] Notwithstanding the critical significance of planning, the developmental project in India, argues Aseema Sinha, 'was and continues to be constrained by the pattern of mediation between the centre and regions'.[20] Furthermore, a centralized planning also led to the expansion for regionalism in India presumably because of 'haphazard and unequal' development of constituent provinces. Regional differences and politico-economic conflicts arising out of a centrally engineered scheme remain critical in post-independent India's political economy, besides the exogenous influences in the wake of globalization.

Historically, the Congress was persuaded by the arguments supporting planning for development. Contrary to Gandhi's explicit opposition to 'planned development', the Congress Party showed ample interest in socialistic means, including planning and heavy industrialization, as 'essential to make revolutionary changes in the present economic and social structure of society and to remove gross inequalities' since 1929. Within two years, the 1931 Karachi Congress adopted a resolution insisting on state ownership of 'key industries and services, mineral resources, railways, waterways, shipping and other means of public transport'. However in 1934, the Congress Working Committee passed a resolution at Banaras stressing that 'large and organized industries are in no need of the services of Congress organizations or of any Congress effort on their behalf'. Critical of the above, Jawaharlal Nehru rallied support to reformulate the resolution with a view to soliciting Congress backing for industrialization and planning, which, he believed, was the only available means to attain substantial economic development in India.[21] A compromise formula was reached in Bombay at the Congress Working Committee meeting in September 1934. Accordingly, the top priority was accorded to small-scale cottage industries. Encouraged by the partial support of the party, although neither funding nor organizational support was available from the Congress, Nehru in his 1936 Faizpur presidential address argued strongly in favour of heavy industrialization and coordination of human resources through planning.

Planning seems to have provided the Congress stalwarts with a platform to articulate different ideological positions. Drawing on their respective ideological leanings, Nehru hailed industrialism whereas Gandhi opposed it since he felt that, instead of contributing to the general welfare, machine civilization would not only expose Indians to a worse kind of exploitation but also lead to a general degradation of human life. Although Nehru and Gandhi were poles apart on occasions, the former, unlike his militant colleague Subhas Bose, never pursued his differences with the latter to the extent of causing a split within the Congress. Despite the adverse ideological implication of aligning with Gandhi, Nehru as a pragmatist participated wholeheartedly in the Gandhi-led freedom struggle, for he knew that the attainment of independence was prior to ideology. So the controversy involving Gandhi and Nehru vis-à-vis planning and industrialization was just a signpost indicating the likely tension in view of the Congress effort to create an anti-British platform incorporating even contradictory ideologies. By making a case for planning and industrialization there is no doubt that Nehru ushered in a new era in the Indian independence struggle.[22]

The above detailed description of the evolution of planning is illustrative of Nehru's uncritical faith in planning though he acknowledged that planning was to be guided by what he characterized as 'integrated planning'. Hence he observed, '[The] Planning Commission has performed an essential tasks; without which it could not have progressed . . . We are a federal structure and it has served to bring the various states together and have integrated planning. If it had not been there, the central government could not have done its job because immediately difficulties would have arisen that the central government was encroaching the rights of the States.'[23] It was natural that planning was to become an important instrument for development once he took over as India's Prime Minister. This is where Meghnad Desai intervenes with his powerful argument endorsing that planning was detrimental to capitalist development in India. Planning was merely an ideological tool of the state to intrude, rather mechanically, into the economic processes, which may not always follow what is planned in advance. According to him, 'the Green Revolution, and the context of owner-cultivation in which it made its impact, brought capitalism irreversibly to the country side'.[24] This is a significant structural change in Indian economy that 'came independently of planning'. What it had shown was the gradual but steady decline of planning as an instrument of rapid economic development in India, where capitalism had a skewed growth for a variety of historical reasons. Desai thus concludes that 'planning has lost the driving seat it once had [because] . . . the driving force will come from the capitalist social relations in the Indian economy'. Instead of altogether rejecting planning, what it suggests is the changing role of the Planning Commission based on appreciating the capitalist path of development. In the words of Desai:

> Planning [requires to be] interactive and predictive in an econometric way. It will be strategic rather than pervasive. It will start with a given growth rate. The growth rate that will emerge from the interactive predictive quinquennial exercise will set a feasible bound. It will require further iterative and counterfactual work with the available models to explore whether a higher growth path is achievable, and if so, what constraints need to be removed.[25]

This is the quintessence of the argument which Desai puts forward to reorient the instruments for economic development, including planning for a well-defined scheme drawn on the basic principles of capitalist growth, as explained by classical Marxism. Hence 'planning designed for an insulated national economy . . . is not appropriate'.[26] Instead, it has to take into account the new material conditions involving the growing importance of the global economy, especially the non-state actors, such as the IMF, World Bank and other transnational donor agencies. One cannot simply ignore this changed milieu and hence the national economies need to come to terms with them as best as they can. So the most meaningful step for steady economic growth is 'a rapid integration of the Indian economy into capitalism'.[27] The formula works in a spectacular way in the case of China, Taiwan and Korea, where capitalism is not discriminatory but pro-people as well. Socialism in India failed in its basic objective. Those at the bottom continued to suffer. The mixed-economy strategy, seeking also to pursue state-led capitalist development, thus largely failed because the Indian economy 'had grown too slowly to qualify as a capitalist economy . . . [and] by its failure to reduce inequalities had forfeited any claims to being socialist'.[28] Such an argument led Desai to believe that 'India's problem is not so much capitalism but that it is stuck with a backward version of capitalism'.[29] So economic growth is, as Desai argues, rooted in a complete overhauling of the economy, supported by a strong political will endorsing, for instance, various anti-poverty programmes and cutting the subsidies to the rich. Under these changed circumstances, it is also possible for the state to play a dynamic role in pursuing an economic agenda in favour of those at the bottom, who always suffered in the name of the much euphoric socialistic planning.

It is true, as Desai argues, that there is no alternative to economic reforms. It is also true that, without a proper political backing, economic reforms are just mere devices without much substance. In India, the same political leadership that had been the guardian of the old order emerged as the champion of the new. Is this 'a genuine change or [mere] electoral window dressing', Desai asks.[30] Given the present dispensation of power in India, the future of economic reform does not appear to be as bright as in South-East Asian countries or China. One of the primary conditions for a sustained reform package is a government that is ideologically compatible with an adequate numerical strength in the legislature. As of now, the political system does not appear to be stable because elections are too frequent, and it is thus not equipped to pursue economic reforms in a sustained manner. 'An unreformed political system is', Desai laments, 'an obstacle to fundamental and irreversible economic reform'.[31] There is no magical way. What is required is a change of attitude because 'it is quite clear that India must liberalize' for sustained economic growth. Indian resistance to liberalization, as Desai argues, comes from the elite interests and not from the poor. At the forefront are the organized sector industrialists who benefited from the policy of protection and are now scared of competition. The state has a crucial role to play in the changed circumstances. What must be junked is 'state ownership [of unprofitable businesses that are otherwise not viable] as it has proven to be wasteful and growth-retarding'.[32] Still, 'reform is a contentious issue [and] India [as of now] is not an enthusiastic reformer'. Yet there is no doubt that reform is a sure contribution to economic growth, as the examples from South-East Asia demonstrate. For India, clinging to liberalization is 'a resumption of history [because] India as a trading and manufacturing nation [was] able to compete on a world scale [in] cotton textile in the days before independence'.[33]

Changing economic horizon

With the onset of macroeconomic reforms in the 1990s, the state-led developmental plans seem to have lost their significance in a situation where the non-state actors became critical in redefining the state agenda. India has adopted reforms in perhaps a very guarded manner. One probably cannot simply wish away the theoretical justification of state intervention in a transitional economy. Reasons are plenty. Socialist principles may have been forgotten, but the importance of the state in social sector cannot be minimized unless a meaningful alternative is mooted.

Economic liberalization in India ushered in reforms 'by stealth'[34] as it was more or less accepted as a *fait accompli* to avoid the massive balance of payment crisis in 1991. Apart from the domestic compulsion, internationally two major events undermined 'the basic premises of the earlier social consensus regarding the development strategy'.[35] The first was the collapse of the former Soviet Union and its east European satellite states, which moved towards 'a market-oriented economic system' eschewing altogether the model of planned economic development. Second, the spectacular success of 'the socialist market economy' of China with the opening of the economy since 1978 and its concomitant favourable economic outcome cast serious doubts on India's development strategy, based on economic nationalism.

Nonetheless, the importance of the prevalent 'politico-institutional context' cannot be underestimated when conceptualizing the impact of economic reform in India. In a significant way, the institutional legacy of 'a well-entrenched state' affected the post-reform possibilities in India. As a commentator argues, 'India's bureaucratized regime – the license-quota-permit raj – has had major, unintended consequences on post-transition patterns: all [state] governments and central regimes continue to rely on state-led strategies of reform; there is no "Washington Consensus" or "neo-liberal" route to reforms in India'.[36] There is no doubt that economic reforms brought about radical changes in India's political economy. Yet the old regulatory regime of the bygone era remained critical in the path and processes of liberalization in a very decisive way. What thus proliferates across India is 'state-guided routes to liberalization rather than market fundamentalism'.[37] This is reflected in the obvious distortions in India's economy. The author of an empirical study of Andhra Pradesh argues on the basis of her study and other supporting data that 'two economies – one affluent and the other predominantly agricultural economy – are emerging . . . and this division can be seen across the social and regional landscape of India'.[38] The technology-based export-oriented city-centred economy is flourishing in the new economic environment while the agricultural economy remains backward and those associated with this 'have little expectation of a better future [and] remain preoccupied with the daily struggle to secure a livelihood'.[39]

Seeking to articulate the typical Indian response to liberalization, the 1991 Industrial Policy Resolution suggested several steps to 'unshackle the Indian industrial economy from the cobwebs of unnecessary bureaucratic control', though within the overall control of the state. Four specific steps were recommended. First, the government decided to abolish 'industrial licensing policy' except for a short list of industries related to security and strategic concerns, social concerns, hazardous chemicals and overriding environmental considerations. Second, the government also endorsed 'direct foreign investment up to fifty-one percent foreign equity in high priority industries'. To avoid bottlenecks, an amendment to the 1973 Foreign Exchange Regulation Act was suggested. Third, it was also decided to withdraw protection of 'the sick public sector units' and there would be 'a greater thrust on performance improvement' to ensure accountability of those involved in these state-sponsored enterprises. Finally, the 1991 Policy sought to remove 'the threshold limits of assets in respect of those companies functioning under the MRTP (Monopolies and Restrictive Trade Practices) Act'. By seeking to amend this act, the 1991 Policy suggested elimination of 'the requirement of prior approval of the Union Government for establishment of new undertakings, expansion of undertakings, merger, amalgamation and take over and appointments of Directors under certain circumstances'. The Indian response to economic liberalization is most creative, if judged contextually. The Nehruvian socialist pattern of society cannot be so easily dispensed with for historical reasons, and globalization may not be an appropriate strategy for economic development in a poor country such as India because in its present form, argues Joseph Stiglitz, it seems like 'a pact with the devil'. A few people may have become wealthier but, for most of the people, closer integration into the global economy 'has brought greater volatility and insecurity, and more inequality'.[40] Economic liberalization is thus a double-edged device that, while improving the lives of some Indians, has also left millions more untouched. Hence it has been rightly pointed out that the essence of economic liberalization in India can be captured by a Buddhist proverb suggesting that 'the key to the gate of heaven is also the key that could open the gate to hell'. Indeed, the danger and opportunity are so intricately intermingled in economic reforms that 'the journey to the promised land of [economic prosperity] could easily turn into a hellish nightmare of poverty and widening inequality for the majority'.[41]

Public administration in India

Bearing the obvious imprint of British colonial administration, bureaucracy in India – its structure, role, behaviour and interrelationships – has evolved over a long period in history since the designing of the system about the middle of the nineteenth century.[42] The Macaulay Committee Report, 1854, is a watershed in the growth of bureaucracy in India. By recommending a civil service based on the merit system, the Committee sought to replace the age-old patronage system of the East India Company.[43] Defending the idea of a generalist administrator – 'all rounder' – the Committee 'portrayed the ideal administrator as a gifted layman who, moving from job to job irrespective of its subject matter, on the basis of his knowledge and experience in the government'.[44] The efficiency of the members of the Indian civil service (ICS) as administrators may have been exemplary, but it is likely that they were motivated primarily by imperial interests and hence 'the interests of the country were too often postponed to the interests of the [Crown]'.[45] Furthermore, there was a Weberian aspect to the ICS. Drawn from the well-off sections of society, the civil servants came from some of the best universities and were chosen on the basis of a competitive examination. Those within the ICS were therefore secluded from the rest given their exclusive class, caste and educational backgrounds. In other words, they had the special status within the society that Weber felt was essential to a true bureaucracy. Given their peculiar characteristics, the British officials in India formed a most unusual kind of society with no organic links with the society they were to serve.[46] Nonetheless, the Indian civil service held a pivotal position in the system of administration that flourished during the colonial rule. Recognizing its immense importance in sustaining the empire, Lloyd George declared in the House of Commons in 1922 that '[t]hey are the steel frame of the whole structure. I do not care what you build it of – if you take the steel frame out, the fabric will collapse'.[47]

In independent India, the Indian Administrative Service (IAS) succeeded the ICS.[48] Despite its imperial roots, the Indian political leaders chose to retain the structure of the ICS presumably because of its efficient role in conducting Indian administration in accordance with prescribed rules and regulations supporting a particular regime. Thus the pre-1947 experience favourably disposed them towards its continuation, though during the discussion in the Constituent Assembly the house was not unanimous on this issue. The argument opposing its continuation was based on its role as an ally of imperialism. 'The Civil Service as the Steel Frame . . . enslaved us [and] they have been guilty of stabbing Nation during our freedom struggle. [W]e should not, therefore,' as the argument goes, 'perpetuate what we have criticized so far.'[49] Vallabhbhai Patel was probably most vocal in defending the ICS and its steel frame. He knew that without the ICS Pax Britannica would simply have been inconceivable. And he also realized that independent India needed a committed bureaucracy even more simply because of the multifarious responsibilities that the state had to shoulder. Since they were 'patriotic, loyal, sincere [and] able', Patel was persuaded to defend the continuity of the British bureaucracy especially when the country was reeling under chaos towards the close of the colonial rule. As early as 1946, he convened the provincial Premier's Conference to evolve a consensus on the future of what was then All India Services (AIS). In view of their long association with public admin-istration, officers belonging to the AIS 'are most well-equipped to deal with new and complex tasks'. Not only 'are they useful instruments, they will also serve as a liaison between the Provinces and the Government of India and introduce a certain amount of brashness and vigour in the administration both of the Centre and the Provinces'.[50] Later, while speaking in the Constituent Assembly, he cat-egorically stated that '[y]ou will not have a united India if you do not have a good all India service' that had the independence to speak out its mind and enjoyed a sense of security. He also attributed the success of the Constitution to the exist-ence of an all India service by saying, 'if you do not adopt this course, then do not follow this Constitution . . . . This Constitution is meant to be worked by a ring of service which will keep the country intact. . . . If you remove them', Patel thus apprehended, 'I see nothing but a picture of chaos all over the country.'[51] Hence Patel concluded that 'I need hardly emphasize that an efficient, disciplined and contented service, assured of its prospects as a result of diligent and honest work, is a *sine qua non* of sound administration under a democratic regime even more than under an authoritarian rule.'[52]

Even Jawaharlal Nehru, who was very critical of the ICS for its role in sustain-ing the imperial rule in India,[53] seemed persuaded and supported its continuation for 'the security and stability of India, . . . including coping with the slaughter and its aftermath in Punjab, crushing opposition in Hyderabad, and containing it in Kashmir'.[54] Patel's views were translated into Article 311 of the Constitution of India, which states that no civil servant shall be dismissed or removed or reduced in rank except after an enquiry in which he has been informed of the charges and given a reasonable opportunity of being heard in respect of those charges.[55] So an instrument that consolidated the imperial rule in India 'with so slight use of force'[56] survived in completely different political circumstances primarily because there was continuing support for it first from the British Government and then from the Congress Government. Furthermore, its continuance did not pose any threat to the dominant classes that reigned supreme following the 1947 transfer of power in India. The new civil service for all practical purposes was, as a former bureaucrat comments, therefore 'the continuation of the old one with the differ-ence that it was to function in a parliamentary system of government, accepting the undoubted primacy of the political executive which in turn was responsible to the people through their elected representatives in the legislature'.[57] Besides its structure, which is more or less an expansion of the steel frame, the continuity is at a deeper level. Whereas the colonial civil servants had a paternalistic attitude towards the people, and ruled largely by negative discretionary powers, '[t]heir successors, noting the vast unmet development needs of the people, substituted positive discretionary powers of patronage and subsidies, reinforcing the colonial syndrome of dependency on the *mai-baap* state'.[58]

Apart from its functional utility, the fact that the steel frame was retained more or less *intact* was because, as B. P. R. Vithal, himself an IAS officer, argued, 'the Congress leaders who took office . . . shared the social background of the senior civil servants whom they inherited from the colonial state'.[59] Thus, for example, Nehru felt at ease while working with senior civil servants. Similarly, Rajagopala-chari felt more at home with the ICS officers who were placed with him when he was the Prime Minister of Madras (1937–39) than with certain elements in the Congress Party. The political processes subsequent to independence gave rise to changes in the class composition of the political executive that were more far-reaching and rapid than changes in the social composition of the civil service. While the political executives, trained in vernacular education, came largely from rural and semi-urban areas, those in the steel frame were generally urban-based and English-educated. The growing disparity between the class backgrounds of the political executive and the civil servants led to frequent frictions between the administrators and politicians in the Westminster parliamentary system of govern-ance when the politicians had assumed a leading role in building a new nation.

Following independence, government functions have also expanded in scope and content. With the introduction of the parliamentary form of government and the setting up of people's institutions right down to the village level, there has been an inevitable rise in the level of expectations and the gap between expectations and performance has widened. People's institutions were set up with the objective of creating self-governing institutions at the village level. The objective remains distant for ever. Similarly, independence and Five Year Plans were perceived by people as synonymous with economic and social equity and well-being, and free-dom from want and oppression. In the early days of the planning era people did not complain much about the shortage that they confronted with fortitude because the future held hope and promise for them. With the passage of time, they felt their hopes were belied and they were nowhere near the promised land of honesty, plenty and happiness. The ethos of self-governance, decentralization and commu-nity development was greeted with considerable élan and fanfare. For example, the three-tier Panchayati Raj system and the urban local bodies were conceived of as a properly meshed network of institutions to accelerate the development process.[60] The recent Seventy-Third and Seventy-Fourth Amendments (1992) to the Constitution seek to advance the concept of 'self-governance' by providing for (a) regular elections, (b) minimal suppression of Panchayati Raj bodies by administrative fiat and (c) regular finances through statutory distribution by state finance commissions. The aim, argues Kuldeep Mathur, 'is to reduce the margin of political and administrative discretion and to allow the decentralised institutions to gather strength on the basis of people's involvement'.[61] But, for various rea-sons, the political process became what may be termed as 'reversed', and highly centralized and personalized systems of government developed both at the central and state levels. There has been a massive erosion of institutions, whether they are the Parliament and parliamentary institutions, or the party system and democratic procedures in the running of parties, or the judiciary, or indeed the press. Describ-ing the crisis and erosion of institutions as 'the natural and expected consequences of a political process that has undermined both the role and authority of basic institutions',[62] Rajni Kothari has sought to grapple with a peculiar reality in which public administration appears to be largely de-linked from the basic institutions of the democratic system that has flourished in India following independence.[63]

Indian historical experience, both during the British period and immediately afterwards, has led to the emergence of a public administration that was ill-suited to needs and aspiration of the people. The reasons are not difficult to seek as studies have shown that the bureaucrats who have been brought up and trained in the colonial administrative culture are wedded to the Weberian characteristics of hierarchy, status and rigidity of rules and regulations and concerned mainly with the enforcement of order and collection of revenues. This structure was most appropriate for the colonial regime, whereas it is completely unfit to discharge the functions in the changed environment of an administration, geared to the task of development. As the government becomes the main institution for development in the democratic setup that India adopted following independence, the role of the officials has undergone changes. Their sole objective is to 'emphasize results, rather than procedures, teamwork rather than hierarchy and status, [and] flexibility and decentralization rather than control and authority'.[64] Seen as 'the development administrator', the bureaucrat is therefore characterized by 'tact, pragmatism, dynamism, flexibility, adaptability to any situation and willingness to take rapid, ad-hoc decisions without worrying too much about procedures and protocol'.[65]

The concept of governance has led to the recognition of the role of multiple agencies in organizing and undertaking public business. In addition to formal government, the role of non-governmental organizations and community-based organizations has been acknowledged as supplementary to public agencies. Another significant development is decentralization and empowerment of localities for local resources and knowledge-based authentic grassroots governance. The Seventy-Third and Seventy-Fourth Constitutional Amendments (1992) signalled momentous changes in terms of grassroots people's empowerment, whose full potentialities are yet to be realized. Given the clear legal sanction for decentralization, there is no doubt that decentralization through panchayats could bring about an enormous change in the way our democracy functions. This is not only a change in local governance but could provide a way for deepening political democracy by making it more direct, though it will have all the limitations of 'agency-induced instrumental decentralization' so long as the ideological format in which panchayati raj institutions are articulated remains unaltered. Local governments largely execute the plans and programmes, devised elsewhere. And, in view of the interests of global capital in grassroots governance, there is a possibility that these governmental institutions at the localities will end being agents of global capital in India.

The new instrumentalities such as the Lokpal/Lokayaukta for dealing with people's grievances against top functionaries in government still remain a distant dream. Corruption in many forms continues to plague the Indian public system, but its ability to successfully deal with corruption at different levels has fallen short of the requirement. The other instrumentality is the human rights institutions at the national and state levels, which are quite recent in Indian public administration. There are both international and domestic pressures to uphold human rights and ensure effective 'rights regimes' at all levels in the interests of steady democratization of the public sphere.

Governance and the Fifth Pay Commission, 1997

Underlining the new dispensation in public administration, the appointment of the Fifth Pay Commission in 1994 by the government of India was a major intervention in redefining the role of politics in public administration for two important reasons: (a) the Commission undertook the exercise when globalization seemed to have influenced, if not shaped, human life to a significant extent; and (b) there is no doubt that the governance paradigm (which is clearly an antithesis to the state-directed development model) provides a critical reference point for civil service reform in most of the developing countries seeking loans from international agencies. The primary goal of civil service is, as the Commission identifies it, to 'understand customer needs'. Based on this basic concern, the mission statement[66] of the Commission runs as follows:-

a   clarify the goals of the organization in the mind of the management;
b   clarify for staff the purpose of their jobs in meeting the organizational goals,
c   make clear the policy of the Government to ensure that it is interpreted accurately by staff,
d   engender pride in belonging to the organization,
e   provide targets to aim for, against which results can be assessed.

The aim of this section is twofold: first, to identify the sociological roots of the Fifth Pay Commission, which came into existence following the adoption of the 1991 New Economic Policy in India, and second, to evaluate whether the recommendations are merely contextual, independent of the neo-liberal directions of the global forces, or are clearly dictated by the so-called international actors and largely, if not entirely, devoid of national roots.

It is obvious that, even before the onset of liberalization, several measures were adopted to revitalize the administration, which owes its origin to completely different socio-economic concerns when reforms were largely internally generated whereas post-liberalization efforts are mostly externally driven. There has been a clear shift towards a reduced role for the government in all countries. In the words of the Fifth Pay Commission, 'Thatcherism in UK and Reaganomics in USA tried to pull out the State from the morass of over-involvement. The decline of Communism in Eastern Europe has furthered the trend towards economic liberalization and disinvestment in public sector enterprises.'[67] So, the impetus for reducing the role of the government came from outside, as the Commission admits by mentioning that 'India could not have remained unaffected by these global trends'.[68] What was however most critical in the entire process was 'the deep economic crisis of 1991 which pushed [India] on to a new path of development, [which meant that] Government should confine itself primarily to the core functions that cannot be performed by the market. Everything else must be left to the private initiative.'[69] As evident, the Fifth Pay Commission clearly articulates 'a new path of development' underlining the reduced role of the government. Critical of 'the over-involvement' of government, the Commission demarcates certain 'core functions' for the government keeping aside a wide range of functions for the private enterprises. Conceptualizing government within the governance paradigm, the Commission also seeks to negotiate with the neo-liberal thrust in public administration and accordingly suggests 'reform packages' to adapt civil services in India to the changed milieu. The government retreats giving space to private operators discharging functions which it performed traditionally for 'public well being'. By redefining the role of government, the Commission seems to have equipped the state to keep pace with the changes in an interdependent world.

In view of the above well-directed designs for civil service reform, the recommendations of the Fifth Pay Commission are another milestone in this direction. True to the spirit expressed in the 1996 Chief Secretaries conference, the Fifth Pay Commission has recommended: (a) downsizing the government through corporatization of activities that involve 'manufacturing of goods or the provision of commercial services'; (b) transparency, openness and economy in government operation through 'privatization of activities where government does not need to play a direct role' and also 'contracting out of services which can be conveniently outsourced to the private sector';[70] and (c) contractual appointment in selected areas of operations 'for the purpose of maintaining a certain flexibility in staffing both for lateral entry of experts, moderating the numbers deployed depending on the exigencies of work and ensuring availability of most competent and committed personnel for certain sensitive/specialized jobs.'[71]

The central government has been advised to go for a 30 per cent reduction in the strength of the civil service, as the Pay Commission felt that it would be unwise to let the government sector continue as 'an island of inefficiency' and 'inertia'. The normal procedure of voluntary retirement after completing twenty years should be continued. Alongside this, the Commission recommended a special scheme of voluntary retirement in the departments where surplus manpower has been identified. In such cases, there should be a provision for selective retirement of persons, the initiative always resting with the government and for 'a golden handshake'.

The other significant recommendation of the Commission is concerned with 'openness' in administration. Defending the repeal of 'the Official Secrets Act of the old colonial days', the Commission insists on openness, which 'means giving everyone the right to have access to information about the various decisions taken by the Government and the reasoning behind them'.[72] Although what is detrimental to the interests of the nation, the security of the state or its commercial, economic and other strategic interests may not be made public, 'nothing should be held back just to subserve the interests of individual bureaucrats and politicians'.[73] Every important government decision involving 'a shift in policy' should invariably be accompanied by a White Paper 'in the nature of an explanatory memorandum'. As an integral part of civil service reform, the Commission insisted on the formation of 'an efficient grievance redressal machinery [that] has to be effective, speedy, objective, readily accessible and easy to operate'.[74] Drawing upon the examples of Canada, the UK and Malaysia, where effective grievance redressal cells have been functioning efficiently, the idea of a Citizen's Charter – defining the rights of the customers of government schemes and services – was mooted by the Commission. The recognition by the Commission of the citizen's right to information and the procedures suggested in this connection are of seminal importance from the point of debureaucratizing government and making it citizen-friendly. The issues raised by the Pay Commission figured prominently in the 1997 Conference of Chief Ministers, where an action plan was adopted to (a) make the administration accountable and citizen-friendly, (b) ensure transparency and right to information and (c) adopt measures to cleanse and motivate civil services.[75]

Public administration in a network society

The Fifth Pay Commission is a watershed in the evolution of India's public administration for a variety of reasons. This is not a pay commission in the ordinary sense of the term since it has also sought to reshape the bureaucracy in the light of the emerging global trends especially after the collapse of the Soviet system. By suggesting significant changes in the administrative hierarchy, the Commission translates into reality the drive towards 'debureaucratization'. There are two immediate consequences. (a) It draws our attention away from the 'steel frame' to other agencies that are equally crucial in 'public service' but have not been recognized so far formally. In this sense, the Commission provides a powerful critique of Weberian bureaucracy that is strictly hierarchical and largely 'status-quoist'. (b) By recognizing the importance of civil society organizations in public administration, the Commission provides a formal recognition to a space of cooperation between the governmental bureaucracy and these organizations. Such cooperation was discouraged presumably because of the 'sanctity' of the governmental domain in which the state bureaucracy appears to be the only legitimate agency in discharging responsibilities on behalf of the state. Underlining the importance of agencies that are not exactly linked with the government and its peripheral organizations, the Fifth Pay Commission has not only redefined Indian bureaucracy but also expanded its sphere of influence by seeking to involve various non-governmental agencies, the role of which was never recognized under traditional theories of public administration.

The Fifth Pay Commission is also a significant comment on the nature of Indian administration that has a clear colonial hangover. Critical of hierarchical Weberian administration, the Commission is clearly favourably disposed towards 'decentralized' administration that provides room for organizations that are not exactly within the government. In structural terms, decentralized administration underlines the importance of various layers of the decision-making process. What cripples public administration in post-colonial India is, as a World Bank document underlines, 'overregulation', which is both 'a cause and an effect of bloated public employment and the surest route to corruption'.[76] Apart from 'contracting out of the state', the World Bank suggests several specific measures to 'motivate' civil servants 'through a combination of mechanisms to encourage internal competition'.[77] That the Pay Commission recommendations have not been accepted *in toto* by the government of India clearly suggests that the Indian response to the governance-initiated civil service reforms is a guarded one. In India's planned economy, the role that the civil service has discharged is that of a 'regulator' and not a 'facilitator'. And yet, the civil service was not severely challenged presumably because of its structural requirement in governance. The mood does not appear to have changed radically in the context of the interconnected global order. This can perhaps be linked with India's response to globalization, which is equally tempered by her peculiar socio-economic and political circumstances. Hence two contrasting scenes are visible: on the one hand, there are evidences of a growing free market in India though the Indian state is, on the other hand, still very interventionist and the Indian economy is still relatively closed to external goods, finance and investors. The policy trend is thus 'better interpreted as a rightward drift in which the embrace of the state and business continues to grow warmer, leaving many others out in the cold'.[78]

Irrespective of whether the recommendations of the Fifth Pay Commission consititute a rightward drift or not, the fact remains that it has drawn on the neo-liberal theoretical thrust towards globalization. Accepting that bureaucrats in developing countries are also 'rent-seekers', the Commission has raised issues that are pertinent in redefining its role in the changed environment of governance. What is sadly missing is the context in which the recommendations are to be implemented. India is perhaps a unique example, showing the peculiar combination of roles in public bureaucracy that has a distinct colonial flavour due to its obvious historical roots. Structured in the Weberian mould, Indian bureaucracy however reinvented its role and character following the adoption of the state-directed planned economy. Now, governance offers new challenges and the Fifth Pay Commission, by seeking to reorient the Indian civil service, is responding to these challenges. Given the historical nature of Indian bureaucracy, most of the recommendations of the Commission may be inappropriate and thus not worth-while. Nonetheless, there is no doubt that the Commission has played a historical role in the sense that it has drawn our attention to the weaknesses of a well-entrenched bureaucracy and also the advantages of critically assessing its utility in the globalization-inspired social, economic and political circumstances. In some sense, the Fifth Pay Commission brings back the Wilsonian dichotomy between politics and administration, in which administration is defined as an unalloyed technical exercise. Whether or not there is a conclusive resolution of this debate, which had its root in an 1887 article by Woodrow Wilson,[79] one can confidently argue that administration without politics (denoting values or ideologies) is like a fish without water. Administration is a guided action. Hence values seem to be critical in its articulation and manifestation. The Fifth Pay Commission does not seem to have paid adequate attention to this dimension of civil service reform. Instead, it has generally endorsed the ideal of governance in its recommendations. There is no doubt that the recommendations of the Pay Commission are historical in the sense that they approximate to the neo-liberal values; they are ahistori-cal as well because they are non-contextual responses to an environment where globalization continues to remain, for valid socio-economic and political reasons, an anathema.

Concluding observations

Despite more or less the same colonial legacy, independent states in South Asia have adopted completely different forms of governance. India, for instance, has been continuing with democracy, while neither Pakistan nor Bangladesh has succeeded, except temporarily, in this regard. What is puzzling to an analyst is the relative strength of democracy in India and its failure to strike roots either in Bangladesh or Pakistan or elsewhere in the region. The question is therefore why democracy is so strong in India and not elsewhere in South Asia despite almost the same values inherited by them from British colonialism. Elections have been held in both Pakistan and Bangladesh of late, but the ritual of voting cannot be confused with the achievement of substantive democracy resting on social and economic rights of citizenship. Political processes in Bangladesh and Pakistan remain hostage to highly inequitable state structures. Continuing imbalances within the state structures and also between them and civil society foreclose the possibility of a significant reapportioning of political power and economic resources in the near future.

The reasons are not difficult to seek. Historically, India was better-placed than her neighbours at least in two major ways: (a) India's transition to democracy owed a great deal to the Congress Party and its leadership, which respected the nationalist legacy, and (b) religious divisions were cross-cut by numerous regional, language and caste cleavages and also the obvious decline of Muslims as a critical factor in political decisions. There is no doubt that the depth of the Congress organization and its electoral success after independence gave the party's leadership an exceptional political resource. Its elite enjoyed great influence in the process of drawing up the constitution of independent India, and its parliamentary majority gave it 'the freedom to make "hard decisions" in the immediate aftermath of decolonization'.[80]

Like all ideal types, this schematic picture of consensual politics under the Congress system appeared to be divorced from a much more complex reality, which was, *inter alia,* characterized by very low levels of political awareness among the lower castes and poor classes. With the continuity of the major political institutions that held the colonial power even after independence, it is, in fact, plausible to argue that politics in the Nehru era as a whole is basically 'a continuum with the Raj'. Whatever social configurations the Congress party confronted at the various provinces, 'its leader, like the British before them, did not attempt to change the social order but to adapt to it'.[81] Furthermore, it is probably justified to argue that Indian politics in the first two decades after decolonization was built on a kind of consensus based primarily on elite accommodation. The system passed uncontested 'because of its nearness to the mobilization of the national movement, and the relation of implicit trust between its leadership and the masses'. It was a consensus of 'discourse rather than ideological positions'.[82] Soon after Nehru's demise, the system started breaking down – a process that became evident especially from 1969 onwards when Nehru's successor, Indira Gandhi, faced with increasing opposition strength 'rejected the principle of consensus in favour of the majoritarian principle'.[83] Since she carried the masses with her, she ignored the party, which had lost its democratic mainspring. Centralization, which was once considered as 'an instrument of purposive interventions by cohesive and disciplined elite', soon turned out to be 'suicidal to the prevalent party system and the federal structure and wider affiliations that were built through them'.[84]

The adoption of the 1991 New Economic Policy and the growing consolidation of coalition politics are symptomatic of dramatic changes in India's political texture in recent years. Whereas the former seems to have permanently sealed the future of the Nehruvian socialistic pattern of society the latter is surely an outcome of the growing democratization of the politically marginalized and economically backward sections of Indian masses. By accepting the market-oriented economic reforms, the pan-Indian parties, including Congress, have not only redefined their ideological agenda but also set a new course for India's economic development. Regional parties that provide the critical support to two major all-India parties, namely the Congress and BJP, in government formation at the national level seem to have accepted the neo-liberal economic policy more or less as a *fait accompli.* It is thus fair to argue that economic reforms and coalition politics seem to be complementary to each other and cannot be reversed for reasons connected with the failure of the state-led development paradigm in India and elsewhere or the rise of new social constituencies seeking to reinvent the role of hitherto peripheral sections of society in political decision-making and governance. In this changed environment, the political cannot be understood with reference to its manifestation only, simply because of the obvious complexities involved in its articulation. What is thus critical is to understand Indian politics as complex processes with roots in the prevalent socio-economic and political circumstances, which are historically textured and governed. The present exercise is a serious intervention in debates seeking to explore the complexities of Indian politics that cannot be grasped merely by 'received wisdom' or 'derivative discourses' drawn on ethnocentric theoretical paradigms.

2   Shaping Indian politics
The language of identity

The political is constantly reconstituted, translating its characteristics in accordance with the milieu in which it is located. It is both institutional and non-institutional. Therefore what is articulated in the well-entrenched political institutions has its roots invariably in the wider socio-economic processes, very much outside the governmental institutions. This chapter deals with the processes that to a large extent shape, if not determine, the political. Two dimensions are very critical in conceptualizing the political in a socio-politically volatile state: first, the political may be located not only in structured human acts, but also in the historical circumstances fashioning them in a specific way; and second, the process that is crucial in the evolution of the political in a particular way can never be comprehended without taking into account the dialectical interplay of human values and attitudes within a specific historical context. Hence, in any critical study of human behaviour, institutions other than the political remain significant in conceptualizing and also articulating the political. Within this parameter, this chapter responds to three important questions that are relevant in grasping contemporary Indian politics, which provides a unique model that may be meaningful in socio-economic circumstances similar to those of India. First, what is an Indian identity and how is this articulated? Second, is it possible to conceptualize India as a nation given its inherent and historically justified diversity? Third, if India is a conglomeration of nations, what is the thread that links such a vast country, as diverse as Europe? This chapter is also an attempt to comprehend the texture of 'the Indian identity' in terms of both its sociological ingredients and its political attributes, which may not always go hand-in-hand with its acceptable definition in a typical liberal democratic design. The 2006 controversy on the national song, *Vandemataram*, is illustrative here. There is no doubt that this song was appreciated by the freedom fighters for its powerful potential for mobilization, as its stirring words and imagery impelled thousands of Indians to participate in the nationalist struggle despite adverse consequences. But it also provoked controversies even during the nationalist phase because of the predominant religious imagery and 'anthropomorphic depiction' of the Indian nation, which left many uneasy with its adoption as a national song. Yet, in contemporary India, Muslims who were identified as 'the hated other' in the song are divided: although there was a strong opposition when it was decided to sing the song on the day of its centenary year (2006) in schools, including madrassas, equally powerful was the voice in support of the decision because it reflected national sentiments and thus fulfilled a historic purpose during the struggle for freedom.

Conceptualizing identity[1]

Since the modern era brings a multiplicity of identities that hinges on nation, region, class, gender, language, citizenship – identity is always negotiated within a flow of multiple influences. Our identity has therefore two dimensions, 'ontological' and 'epistemological' – the former refers to we are and the latter to who we think we are. The two necessarily shape each other and 'our identity is a constant and dialectical interplay between them'.[2] The modern subject is thus defined 'by its insertion into a series of separate value spheres – each one of which tends to exclude or attempts to assert its priority over the rest'.[3] So, individual identity can never be permanently fixed, but is in constant flux for socio-cultural and political reasons. One of the instances of a radical shift in identity was certainly the outcome of the divisive politics articulated in the 1947 partition of the subcontinent of India. People's identity as Indians, as Asians or as members of the human race, writes Amartya Sen,

> seemed to give way – quite suddenly – to sectarian identification with Hindu, Muslim or Sikh communities. The broadly Indian of January was rapidly and unquestioningly transformed into the narrowly Hindu or finely Muslim of March. The carnage that followed had much to do with unreasoned herd behaviour by which people, as it were, 'discovered' their new divisive and belligerent identities and failed to subject the process to critical examination. The same people were suddenly different.[4]

The contemporary debate on communal identity revolves around concerns in two complementary directions, First, as a community, Indians 'lack' or have lost identity, or it has become diluted, eroded, corrupted or confused. As a corollary to the first, the obvious concern is therefore how to retain, preserve or strengthen the sense of identity. What is thus emphasized is a 'belief' that identity consists in being different from others and is invariably diluted by intercultural borrowing, that an identity is historically fixed, that it is the sole source of political legitimacy, that the state's primary task is to maintain it and that national identity defines the limits of permissible diversity.

The above argument does not appear to hold good since communal identity is not a substance but a cluster of tendencies and values that are neither fixed nor alterable at will, and it needs to be periodically redefined in the light of historically inherited characteristics, present needs and future aspirations. Identity is not something that 'we have', rather it is 'what we are'; it is not a 'property' but 'a mode of being'. So, to talk of preserving, maintaining, safeguarding or losing one's identity is to use misleading metaphors. By its very nature, a community's identity needs to be constantly reconstituted in response to broader historical dynamics and it thus can never be an abstract, sterile and essentialized category.[5] For instance, the contact with the west was a crucial factor in the transformation of modern Indian sensibilities. The contact 'was a catalyst: it triggered off responses and reactions which acquired a life of their own'. The results, manifest in new ways of thinking, feeling and action, 'were very different from their counterparts in the Indian past or the contemporary western experience'.[6] It would therefore be self-defeating to view the Indian sensibilities in stereotypical way. In the Indian context, both the appeal to shared experiences and the drawing of boundaries have, for instance, led to often fatal contradictions probably because the appeal to shared experiences, though often meant as a device for inclusion, usually invoked the experience of one particular group – upper castes, Hindus, the political elite – which was then made an authoritative marker of identity.[7] And the obsession with boundaries has created divisions and often led to exclusions of significant communities and individuals that are as much a part of the cultural and historical fabric of India as anyone else.

Although, at present, the term 'communal' usually refers to division on the basis of religion, particularly to the division between Hindus and Muslims, it had different shades of meaning in north and south India in the pre-1947 period. For instance, in the south, the same term, in such phrases as 'Communal Award' or 'Communal G(overnment) O(rder)', referred to divisions between castes or groups of castes, particularly the one between Brahmins and non-Brahmins. The caste quotas were codified in the 1927 Communal G. O., which laid down a scheme of reservation that lasted till 1947 when it was revised (see Table 2.1).[8] The Constituent Assembly sought to establish a polity in which individual and nation would prevail over caste and community though it concerned itself only with ascriptive social identities. Hence, caste, religion and language were the only three distinct categories of communities that figured prominently in its deliberations.[9] Religion, caste and language continue to remain probably the most effective factors in political mobilization in India even after decades of the successful experiment of electoral democracy.

Table 2.1 The reservation scheme provided in the Communal Government Order of 1927

Community	No. of posts	Percentage
Non-Brahmin Hindus	5 of 12	42
Brahmins	2 of 12	17
Muslims	2 of 12	17
Anglo-Indians	2 of 12	17
Depressed classes	1 of 12	8

Source: *The Report of the Backward Classes Commission* (second part), Vols III to IV, New Delhi: Government of India, 1980, p. 147.

The perspective

Identities are constantly in flux and hence are subject to processes of invention and reinvention making some of them more politically salient than others at particular juncture of history. Hence, first of all the construction of Indian identity needs to be contextualized in the larger social processes in the nineteenth and twentieth century. The two most obvious ones are nationalism and democratization. In the context of the first, the question that deserves careful attention is: why do communities seek to redefine themselves as nations? What mark of distinctiveness does being a nation carry and as a corollary what is denied to a community and its members if they do not claim their status as a nation? After all, the obsessive desire of communities to claim the status of nations or to define India as a nation is historically conditioned and textured. Simply put, after the late nineteenth century the claim to any form of self government was shelved so long as it was not articulated as the claim of a nation. Colonial sovereignty in part rested upon denying that India was a nation. The nationalist project was not simply something that elites dreamt up to define others in their image; it also sought to identify and highlight the distinctive features of a population to justify its claim for nationhood.[10]

The belief in Indian nationhood as a historical fact was based on western models. But it 'was also an emotionally charged reply to the rulers' allegation that India never was and never could be a nation'.[11] The construction of even a vaguely defined Indian nationhood was a daunting task simply because India lacked the basic ingredients of the conventionally conceptualized notion of nation. There was therefore a selective appeal to history to recover those elements transcending the internal schism among those who were marginalized under colonialism. Hence, an attempt was always made in a concerted manner to underline 'the unifying elements of the Indian religious traditions, medieval syncretism and the strand of tolerance and impartiality in the policies of Muslim rulers'.[12] So the colonial milieu was an important dimension of the processes that led to a particular way of imagining a nation in a multi-ethnic context such as India, which is very different from perceptions based on western experience. The political sensibilities of Indian nationalism 'were deeply involved in this highly atypical act of imagining'.[13]

Apart from colonialism, the major factor that contributed to the formation of a political entity that was India was the freedom movement. It is therefore no exaggeration to suggest that the Indian consciousness, as we understand it today, 'crystallized during the national liberation movement'. So national 'is a political and not a cultural referent in India'.[14] This perhaps led the nationalist leaders to recognize that it would be difficult to forge the multi-layered Indian society into a unified nation-state in the European sense.[15] Accepting the basic premise about the essentially 'invented' nature of national identities and the importance of such factors as 'print capitalism' in their spread and consolidation, Partha Chatterjee challenges the very idea of 'modular forms', as articulated by Benedict Anderson,[16] since it ignores the point that, if modular forms are made available, nothing is left to be imagined.[17] It is true that the non-western leaders involved in the struggle for liberation were deeply influenced by European nationalist ideas. They were also aware of the limitations of these ideas in the non-European socio-economic context due to their alien origin. So, while mobilizing the imagined community for an essentially political cause, by the beginning of the twentieth century they began to speak in a 'native' vocabulary. Although they drew upon the ideas of European nationalism they indigenized them substantially by discovering or inventing indigenous equivalents and investing these with additional meanings and nuances. This is probably the reason why Gandhi and his colleagues in the anti-British campaign in India preferred *swadeshi*[18] to nationalism. Gandhi avoided the language of nationalism primarily because he was aware that the Congress flirtation with nationalist ideas in the first quarter of the twentieth century frightened away not only the Muslims and other minorities but also some of the Hindu lower castes. This seems the most pragmatic idea one could possibly conceive of in a country such as India that was not united in terms of religion, race, culture and common historical memories of oppression and struggle. Underlying this is the reason why Gandhi and his Congress colleagues preferred 'the relaxed and chaotic plurality of the traditional Indian life to the order and homogeneity of the European nation state [because they realized] that the open, plural and relatively heterogeneous traditional Indian civilization would best unite Indians'.[19] Drawing on values meaningful to the Indian masses, the Indian freedom struggle developed its own modular form, which is characteristically different from that of the west. Although the 1947 Great Divide of the subcontinent of India was articulated in terms of religion,[20] the nationalist language drawing upon the exclusivity of Islam appeared inadequate in sustaining Pakistan following the creation of Bangladesh in 1971.

The second broader context that appears to have decisively shaped the search for identity is democratization. What sort of 'unity' does democracy require? After all, it was a staple of liberal discourse (J. S. Mill, for instance) that democracy could not flourish in multi-ethnic societies. The important thing about Jinnah and Savarkar is that they were deploying precisely the liberal argument about why a unitary nationhood is necessary for a modern polity. And then they provided their own interpretations of how this was to be attained. Second, democracy complicates the problem of 'representation'. What is being represented and on what terms? After all, the divisions between the Congress and Muslim League turned on issues of representation. This is, however, not to suggest that the state created two monolithic communities and these communities came into being through 'the politics of representation', since the relationship between identity and democracy is far deeper and complex than it is generally construed in contemporary discourses on South Asia. Identity politics is about expressing one's agency and creating new forms of collective agency. In this sense, it becomes part of the democratic ferment – in which people want to fashion identities for themselves. This process will happen at all levels with a complicated relationship between the levels.

Furthermore, democratization is both inclusive and exclusive as well. Inclusive because it unleashes a process to include people, at least theoretically, regardless of class, clan and creed; it is essentially a participatory project seeking to link different layers of socio-political and economic life. As a movement, democracy thus, writes Charles Taylor, 'obliges us to show much more solidarity and commitment to one another in our joint political project than was demanded by the hierarchical and authoritarian societies of yesteryear'.[21] This is also the reason why democratization tends towards exclusion, which itself is a by-product of the need of a high degree of cohesion. Excluded are those who are different in many ways. We are introduced to a situation in which a communal identity can be formed or malformed in contact with significant 'others', generally projected with 'an inferior or demeaning image'.[22] For Charles Taylor, the politics of exclusion is an absolutely modern phenomenon since in the past

> social recognition was built in to the socially derived identity from the very fact that it was based on social categories everyone took for granted. The thing about inwardly derived, personal, original identity is that it doesn't enjoy this recognition a priori. It has to win it through exchange. What has come about with the modern age is not the need for recognition but the conditions in which this can fail. And that is why the need is now *acknowledged* for the first time. In pre-modern times, people didn't speak of "identity" and "recognition" not because people didn't have (what we call) identities or because these didn't depend on recognition, but rather because these were too unproblematic to be thematized as such.[23]

The 1919–21 Non-Cooperation–Khilafat Movement is illustrative here. By a single stroke, both Hindus and Muslims were brought under a single political platform submerging, at one level, their distinct separate identities. At another level, this movement is a watershed in the sense that these two communities remained separate since they collaborated as separate communities for an essentially political project.[24] So, the politics of inclusion also led towards exclusion for the communities, which identified different political agendas to mobilize people.

In the imagination of communal identity, both these forces of nationalism and democratization appeared to have played decisive roles. Nationalism as a concerted effort was not merely unifying, it was also expansive in the sense that it brought together apparently disparate socio-political groups in opposition to an imperial power.[25] The character of the anti-British political campaign gradually underwent radical changes by involving people of various strata, region and linguistic groups. The definition of nation also changed. No longer was the nation confined to the cities and small towns, it consisted in innumerable villages that so far remained peripheral to the political activities generated by the freedom struggle. Whatever the manifestations, the basic point relates to the increasing awareness of those involved in nation-building both during the anti-imperial struggle and afterwards.

The construction of communal identity has thus to be viewed in the context of a search for nationhood and/or a distinct place within the nation by those who apparently felt threatened under the prevalent socio-economic configurations. For instance, one of the first serious attempts to establish the Indian Muslims as a separate community was made by Rahmat Ali and others in 1933 by saying that,

> our religion, culture, history, tradition, economic system, laws of inheritance, succession and marriage are basically and fundamentally different from those of the people living in the rest of India. The differences are not confined to the broad basic principles – far from it. They extend to the minutest details of our lives. We do not inter-dine; we do not inter-marry. Our national customs and calendars, even our diet and dress are different. [Since] we possess a separate and distinct nationality from the rest of India where the Hindu nation lives and has every right to live . . . [w]e, therefore, deserve and must demand the recognition of a separate national status by the grant of a separate Federal Constitution from the rest of India.[26]

Although Rahmat Ali clearly articulated the demand for 'a separate national status' for the Muslims,[27] the 1916 Lucknow Pact appears to be the first well-defined attempt in this direction. In his earlier incarnation as the member of the Congress, Jinnah, underlining the distinctiveness of the Muslims as a community, defended separate electorates for them as 'the only mechanism' to defuse inter-community tension. In an address to the Bombay Provincial Conference at Ahmedabad in October, 1916, he thus warned his fellow-Congressmen:

> rightly or wrongly, the Muslim community is absolutely determined for the present to insist upon separate electorates. . . . I would, therefore, appeal to my Hindu brethren that in the present state of [the] position they should try to win confidence and the trust of Muslims. . . . If they are determined to have separate electorates, no resistance should be shown to their demands.[28]

Such Muslim leaders were clearly in favour of separate electorates for the Muslims for protection of their distinct identity as compared with the Hindus. It was therefore easier for the British to pursue a policy that culminated in the 1932 Communal Award. Underlining the distinct characteristics separating the two communities, the British premier Ramsay Macdonald, the architect of the Award, argued:

> the contrast between these intermingled population[s] extends far beyond a difference in religious faith: differences of race and of history, a different system of law, widely opposed social observances and absence of intermarriage, set up barriers which have no analogy in the distinctions that may exist between religious denominations in any other existing state. It is not therefore altogether surprising that . . . separate representation, namely the grouping of a particular category of voters in territorial constituencies by themselves, so as to assure to them an adequate number of members of their faith and race has been favoured.[29]

Not merely was the Communal Award an institutional device to split the Indian communities on grounds of religion, it was also an obvious choice for the British given the fact that 'Indian society . . . is essentially a congeries of widely separated . . . communities with divergencies of interests and hereditary sentiments which for ages have precluded common action or local unanimity'.[30] The 1932 scheme was the culmination of a series of efforts undertaken by the Muslim leadership to ascertain both the distinctiveness of the community and thus the extent to which it was separate from the Hindus. In the context of the new political arrangement following the adoption of the 1935 Government of India Act, the communal equations appeared to have significantly influenced the course of India's freedom struggle. A. K. Ghuznavi, a prominent Bengali Muslim leader, in his memorandum to the Simon Commission, 1927, emphasized that, as the Muslim community was educationally, economically and politically behind the Hindus of the province, 'further extensions of parliamentary institutions without proper and definite safeguards would place the Muslims permanently in a position subservient to the Hindus'.[31] Jinnah's Fourteen Points Programme was the formulation of the above in concrete terms. These points demanded, *inter alia*, that 'all legislatures in the country and other elected bodies should be reconstituted on the definite [principle] of adequate and effective representation of minorities in every province without reducing the majority of any province to a minority . . . the representation of communal groups shall continue to be by means of separate electorate'.[32] So, what was articulated in the 1932 Communal Award was nothing but a well-prepared design to strengthen the argument that since Muslims were a separate community with a distinct identity their claim for a separate status within British India appeared most logical.

Communal identity and the historical context

Communal identity is multi-layered and diversely textured. However, if one looks at the British perception on communal identity, as codified in the communal award, one is struck by its simplistic nature since it was defined exclusively in terms of religion. Hindus, Muslims and other religious groups were thus placed in neat compartments. The colonial rulers, by according equal status to all religions, placed these identities in competition with each other.[33] Recognizing that Hindus and Muslims had completely different identities, the dominant political group, the Congress, devised a strategy of absorbing dissent in the form of the 1923 Bengal Pact,[34] which sought to accommodate the educated Muslims in the Hindu-dominated white-collar world. What added a new dimension to the debate was the Poona Pact of 1932, which, for the first time, placed the backward classes (later classified as the scheduled castes in the 1935 Government of India Act) on the centre stage of Indian politics with a separate identity.[35] From now on, the scheduled castes invariably figured in any discussion on national identity. Although in Ambedkar the scheduled castes found a powerful leader, they continued to remain a politically significant 'minority' with narrow social, economic and political goals. As a dissenter bent on dismantling an oppressive caste system, Ambedkar therefore 'fulfilled the historical role of dissent not only to question hateful religious dogma but also unbuckle the consolidating ambitions of the secular state within which former religious orthodoxies are subsumed'.[36] What is striking is that, despite having opposed Hindu orthodoxy, manifested in the caste rigidity of which he was a victim, he 'attempted to steer a steady course between a separatist, sectarian stance and unconditional citizenship function in which identity of untouchables would be subsumed within Hinduism'.[37]

The 1932 Poona Pact is the first well-articulated arrangement in which the scheduled castes were identified as a separate group within Hinduism; their emergence with a distinct political identity significantly influenced the provincial elections that followed the 1935 Government of India Act. Apart from the Muslims, who had already asserted their existence as a significant community, the ascendancy of the scheduled castes clearly indicated the complexity of the future course of Indian history, which so far had glossed over the well-entrenched fragmentation of identities among both the Hindus and Muslims. In fact, the Pakistan demand that drew upon Jinnah's 'two nation theory' hinges on the exclusive identities of both the principal communities, Hindus and Muslims, despite their sharing the same socio-economic and politico-cultural milieu. For the nationalists, the idea of separate Hindu and Muslim identity had no natural basis and also the two communities were politically separated through the manoeuvres of communal forces and imperial *divide et impera*.[38] For Jinnah and the Muslim League, the demand for a sovereign and independent Muslim state was logical since Muslims constituted a separate nation with a different religious philosophy, social customs and literature. Hindus and Muslims belonged to two completely different civilizations which drew on conflicting ideas and conceptions.[39] The Hindu counterpart of this logic was articulated by V. D. Savarkar, who argued strongly for a separate Hindu identity because of distinctive features separating Hindus from Muslims, though its root can be traced back to the eighteenth century when the English writing on India clearly provided the Hindus with a distinct identity 'in racial, religious and linguistic terms'.[40] One of the earliest attempts to organize the Hindus as a community was the Hindu Sabha that flourished in Punjab 'to protect the interests of the Hindus by stimulating in them the feelings of self respect, self help and mutual cooperation so that by a combined effort there would be some chance of promoting the moral, social and material welfare of the individuals of which the nation is composed'.[41]

Drawing upon the cultural differences from the Hindus, Jinnah defended his argument for a separate identity for the Muslims. Savarkar too sought to construct the Hindu identity by underlining the well-entrenched cultural distinctiveness of the Hindus. Defining a Hindu as a person 'who regards his land of Bharatvarsha from the Indus to the Seas as his fatherland as well as his holyland', Savarkar identified the following four specific features that distinguish them from the Muslims:

(a) all those sects and panths, whether Vedic or non Vedic in their origin who consider 'Aa Sindhu' Hindustan (i. e. the Indian subcontinent from the river Sindhu to the Indian Ocean) as their fatherland and motherland; (b) all Hindus who belong to the same racial stock; (c) they all share a common cultural heritage; (d) those who regard *Bharat* [India] as their *punyabhumi*, the sacredland (or, holyland in the sense Christianity uses the term holy).[42]

So, Savarkar's construction of Hindu identity is territorial (the land between the Indus and the Indian Ocean), genealogical (fatherland) and religious (holyland).[43] The Hindu *Rashtra* was therefore more of a territorial than a religious nationalism because Hindus represented a cultural and civilizational synthesis which is more 'a secular-rationalist than a religio-fundamentalist construction'.[44] Despite its clarity, the formulation has elements that could be used for other purposes given the attempt at cultural homogenization of multifaceted country like India. Furthermore, this particular conceptualization was also the outcome of a specific politico-ideological debate that unfolded with the propagation of the two nation theory by the Muslim League in the wake of the struggle for freedom in India. So, by highlighting the cultural aspect of Hindu Rashtra, Savarkar, the ideologue of Hindu nationalism, strove to provide an alternative to the construction of Hindus and Muslims as two separate nations. This was the beginning of 'the institutionalization of Hindu nationalism' on the basis of the essence of 'Hindu culture'.[45]

In his formulation, Savarkar underlined the importance of a specific territory that he conceptualized through the notion of *pitribhumi* (fatherland) in the construction of a Hindu nation. He then shifted his emphasis towards Hindu 'sentiments' or 'culture' by arguing that only among Hindus could *pitribhumi* and *punyabhumi* be identical. Hindus are defined in a very catholic way. Whoever can identify India as both *pitribhumi* and *punyabhumi* is a Hindu. This formula holds the core to his idea of *rastra-jati-sanskriti* (nation-race-culture), which seeks to provide a sociological basis for a Hindu nation that could also be a homogeneous nation in cultural and racial terms despite its ingrained diversity. Identification with the Hindu race and nation is made possible by the recognition of *pitribhumi* while identification with culture is justified by the acceptance of India as *punyabhumi*. So, the key exclusions are Muslims and Christians, since they locate their holy land and also their cultural roots outside India.

It was M. S. Golwalkar who sought to construct 'a Hindu society' on the basis of this argument highlighting the cultural uniqueness of the Hindus who 'have set up standards . . . prescribed duties and rights [and] shed their blood in defence of the sanctity and integrity of the Motherland'.[46] While articulating the relationship between the Hindus and the non-Hindus in Hindustan, Golwalkar argued against the ideal of composite nationalism by saying that:

the non-Hindu people must either adopt the Hindu culture and language, must learn to respect and revere Hindu religion, must entertain no idea but the glorification of the Hindu nation, i.e. they must not only give up their attitude of intolerance and ingratitude towards this land and age-long traditions, but must also cultivate the positive attitude of love and devotion instead; in one word, they must cease to be foreigners or *may stay in the*

*country wholly subordinated to the Hindu nation claiming nothing, deserving
no privileges, far less any preferential treatment, not even citizen's rights*
(emphasis added).[47]

What is unique in the exercise undertaken by Golwalkar and those espousing
the cause of Hindu nationalism is the consistent effort to position the Hindus as a
community against its binary opposite – the Muslims.[48] Projecting the Muslims as
'traitors', Golwalkar proclaimed:

> they have developed a feeling of identification with the enemies of this land.
> They look to some foreign lands as holy places. They call themselves Sheikhs
> and Syeds . . . They still think they have come here to conquer and establish
> their kingdoms. So we see that it is not merely a case of change of faith, but
> a change in national identity. *What else is it if not treason, to join the camp of
> the enemy leaving the mother nation in the lurch?*[49]

What Golwalkar develops is similar to that of Savarkar. There is a clear continuity in terms of the conceptual framework in which Hindutva is articulated.
Drawn on Savarkar's idea, Golwalkar devised a formula based around what he
recognizes as 'the five unities' of territory, race, religion, culture and language.
Whereas territory and race are related to *pitribhumi*, religion, culture and language
refer to *punyabhumi*. Like his intellectual mentor, this RSS guru also excludes
Muslims and Christians since they can hardly integrate with the nation for reasons
connected with their religious roots and cultural background.

Conceptually Golwalkar's notion of Hindutva is surely an advancement over
where Savarkar left off though the substance remains the same.[50] Both of them
produced approaches that sought to resolve the threat posed by doctrinal diversity
and fragmentation within Hindu identity by reference to a framework that was
plausible in the context of partition and its aftermath. Deen Dayal Upadhyaya's
notion of *integral humanism* seems to capture Hindutva in the changed environment when the spectre of partition did not appear to be so decisive politically.
Integral humanism is informed by a series of key themes: (a) there is a need
to evolve 'a typical Indian answer' to modern problems (through promoting
swadeshi and small-scale industries, for instance); (b) politics is about values that
need to be upheld in accordance with the *chiti* (specific essence) of the Hindu
nation; (c) dharma is the most critical factor in maintaining balance between the
individual and different institutions in society – institutions such as the family,
caste and the state. As is clear, integral humanism is an effort to redefine Hindutva
by incorporating some of the Gandhian ideas into Hindu nationalist politics. It is
surprising because, when Deen Dayal evolved his model, the votaries of Hindu
nationalist politics, especially Bharatiya Jana Sangh, were keen to join hands with
other anti-Congress political forces in the 1970s to dislodge the Congress Party
from power. In other words, integral humanism is an adaptation of Hindutva to
radically different socio-political circumstances when its original form (as devised
by Savarkar and later Golwalkar) seemed to have run out of steam for historical
reasons.[51]

Consolidating an identity

The idea that Hindus and Muslims are completely different, and hence the genesis of the 1947 Great Divide has to be located in the Hindu–Muslim chasm, figured prominently in the debate on partition immediately after the transfer of power.[52] The importance of ascriptive identity was further reiterated in the Constituent Assembly, which concerned itself only with ascriptive communities. Hence, religion, caste and language were the distinct categories of communities that were considered.[53] Within this perspective, the Constitution sought to protect the rights of those groups that are distinct in terms of socio-cultural characteristics.[54] The Indian nation state at independence was therefore said to have been confronted with the task of evolving a 'unified' national and political society out of a formidable diversity of regional, religious, linguistic and caste identities.

It will be perfectly in order if we look at the deliberations in the Constituent Assembly on minority rights. The aim here is to understand the processes that informed the debates which finally led to the abrogation of preferential policies in favour of the recognized minorities. Diversity is inherent in Indian society perhaps on account of cleavages that are socially nurtured and culturally defended. During the colonial period, the British administration acceded to a separate electorate for the Muslims as an ameliorating step, though the nationalists identified this as a part of the *divide et impera* strategy. Yet the Motilal Nehru Committee suggested the separate electorate in its 1928 report, which runs as follows:

(a) There shall be joint electorates throughout India for the House of Representatives and the provincial legislatures. (b) There shall be no reservation of seats for the House of Representatives except for Muslims in provinces where they are in a minority and non-Muslims in the North Western Frontier (NWF) Province. Such reservation will be in strict proportion to the Muslim population in every province where they are in a minority and in proportion to the non-Muslim population in NWF provinces. The Muslims or non-Muslims where reservation is allowed to them shall have the right to contest additional seats. (c) In the provinces (i) there shall be no reservation of seats for any community in the Punjab and Bengal; (ii) in provinces other than the Punjab and Bengal there will be reservation of seats for Muslim minorities on population basis with the right to contest additional seats; (iii) in the NWF Province there shall be similar reservation of seats for non-Muslims with the right to contest other seats. (d) Reservation of seats where allowed shall be for a period of ten years.[55]

When the Constituent Assembly met to draft the Constitution for free India, there was a long tradition of governmental preferential policies and also the Congress endorsement. The choice was not easy to make because the circumstances in which the Constitution was to be drafted underwent radical metamorphosis. The partition of the country was certainly a significant factor that influenced the deliberations on constitutional protection to minorities. Furthermore, the Congress no longer had to negotiate with the powerful British-patronized Muslim League. Most importantly, the political parties pressing for preferential treatment for the minorities were in shambles and therefore 'unable to present a united front in resisting the revocation of safeguards'.[56] There was also a significant political argument that gained ground, namely that, if the detailed safeguards were included in the Constitution for the minorities, 'they would also serve to perpetuate the separate consciousness of the minorities to work against the basic desire of the Congress to strengthen Indian national unity'.[57] Yet a complete neglect of safeguards for the minorities would have left the Congress with the charge of being 'unrestrainedly majoritarian in practice'.[58]

For B. R. Ambedkar, special constitutional protection to the minorities was morally appropriate given 'the age-old torture' meted out by the majority. He thus sarcastically argued that Indian nationalism had developed a doctrine called 'the divine right of the majority to rule the minorities according to the wishes of the majority. Any claim for the sharing of power by the minority is called communalism while the monopolizing of the whole power by the majority is called nationalism.'[59] Reflective of Ambedkar's sentiments, the Minorities Sub Committee proposed separate electorates and also reservation in legislative bodies, ministries and civil, military and judicial services of the government as well as a minority commission. Dissension was sharply articulated during the discussion of this proposal in the subcommittee; and, following the partition, a separate electorate was vehemently opposed as it was held responsible for creating 'two nations' as competing political blocs. It was finally given up since separate electorates 'sharpened communal differences to a dangerous extent and [had] proved one of the stumbling blocks to the development of a healthy national life'.[60] Jawaharlal Nehru also endorsed this decision by unequivocally saying that 'doing away with this reservation is not only a good thing in itself, good for all concerned, more especially for the minorities, but psychologically too it is a good move for the nation and the world. It shows that we are really sincere about this business of having a secular democracy.'[61]

A perusal of the debates on the policies of group preference suggests that the nationalist argument prevailed over other considerations. The Muslim representatives, for instance, defended separate electorates as they would ensure adequate and proper representation of the minorities in the public sphere. Three major arguments were put forward: first, minorities required special protection since they were socio-culturally different from the rest; second, since they were different, they had to be represented separately in the legislature so that their needs received adequate attention when framing policies; and third, representation would not be authentic unless members of the community chose their representatives, otherwise, representation would be a mockery serving no end whatsoever.

These arguments were forcefully made by a fractured Muslim League.[62] The Assembly, however, rejected them since they were not tenable in the changed political milieu. The arguments were dismissed on grounds that separate electorates did not seem to be relevant when India was being conceptualized as a nation. It was argued that separate electorates gained ground when India was articulated as 'a conglomeration of distinct communities' and not a nation. Moreover, this very idea, which also informed Jinnah's two-nation theory, was at the root of India's 1947 partition and hence its continuation would ruin the effort of creating 'a national political community'. Separation of electorates was questioned on the ground that it stood in contradiction with the principle of secularism as they 'involved the introduction of religious consideration into the political sphere'. Representation on the basis of the religion was simply an anathema in a modern nation-state. Given the acceptance of typical liberal values such as democracy, secularism, rights and justice in defining citizenship in independent India, separate electorates became a system with no organic roots in the changed political circumstances of 1947 and its aftermath.[63]

In May 1949, the Advisory Committee on Minorities, presided over by Vallabhbhai Patel, decided to abandon 'the reserved representation for minority religious groups'. This principle was, however, to be diluted 'by temporary retention of reservation to redress the age-old social discrimination suffered by the Scheduled Castes and Tribes'.[64] This decision, as Patel felt, would lay 'the foundation of a true secular democratic state'.[65] It is true that the Constitution that the Assembly produced was reflective of majoritarian religious sentiments. Nonetheless, at the end of the deliberation what came out was a constitution that recognized the rights of religious minorities and did not privilege the majoritarian views in articulating its provisions.

Other considerations for identity

Although religious identity was the primary basis of aggregating people and identifying minorities the demand for demarcating regions on the basis of a shared language significantly influenced the process of identity formation since the 1905–8 Swadeshi Movement in Bengal. The 1928 All Parties Conference laid down the principles for the redistribution of provinces on a linguistic basis.[66] As an idea, the linguistic regrouping of Indian provinces was greatly appreciated,[67] though its application was likely to complicate the scenario by creating a new majority and minority within a province. For instance, in those Oriya towns adjacent to Andhra Pradesh, Oriya and Telugu are both spoken, but Oriya-speaking people constitute about 60 per cent of the population and hence the Telugus are reduced to the status of a minority. There are areas where religious majority and minorities came to be redefined in the context of these regions.[68] Linguistic reorganization thus blurred the distinction between the majority and minority since people accustomed to seeing themselves as a majority could, in a different location, be reduced to a minority. Simultaneously with the movements for linguistic divisions of provinces, there began what is defined as 'the nativist movements' championing the demands of the 'sons of the soil'. Articulated by the Shiv Sena in Maharashtra and Assom Gana Parishad in Assam, these movements were swept to the top on a staggering wave of popular sympathy within a short period.[69] These movements also captured the aspirations for regional identity[70] that drew upon linguistic, religious and ethnic sentiments of the people concerned. In the movement to create greater internal cohesion and to press more effectively ethnic demands against rival groups, ethnic elites, argues Paul Brass, 'increasingly stress the variety of ways in which the members of the group are similar to each other and collectively different from others'.[71] By asserting the distinctive characteristics in relation to 'the other' the search for identity has led to a process of what S. J. Tambiah calls 'the politicization of ethnicity', a contemporary phenomenon, associated mostly with 'politics of elections'. This political equation, Tambiah argues, 'combined with the capabilities of the mass media, radio, television and print capitalism, so effectively deployed in our time, makes present day ethnic riot crowds very different from the crowds of pre-industrial Europe'.[72]

The gradual consolidation of the Sikh identity during the last two decades of the twentieth century underlines the significance of 'ethnicity' as a factor in the formation of a 'community' that transcends national boundaries. Several studies have firmly established that ethnicity is a broader concept since it accommodates within itself the unifying characteristics of both 'religious' and 'linguistic' distinctiveness.[73] The importance of ethnicity as a powerful determinant of identity is undoubtedly refreshing in the sense that it is a break with the past in which the basic thrust of the debate revolved around caste as the only ascriptive denomination of human existence in India. This is not to belittle the significance of caste as an important marker of one's identity, but to expand its viability as an explanatory tool in association with other factors.[74] Although caste continues to be significant in Indian politics, the centre of gravity appears to have shifted from the upper castes to those characterized as the Other Backward Castes (OBC). Drawing upon the ascriptive identity, the 1980 Mandal Commission Report identifies 3743 OBCs in India.[75] Apart from underlining the complexity of the caste system, the report is an eye-opener for having shown the intimate link between social backwardness and poverty, which remained probably the most important issue in Indian politics following the acceptance of the reservation scheme, as enunciated in the Mandal Commission.

As the above discussion has shown, the context appears to be a significant variable in the construction of both individual and communal identity. The formulation brings out the complexity of tribal identity in the subcontinent that clearly defies the stereotyped understanding of the phenomenon. Since tribal identity is integrally linked with various other and yet distant 'external' influences, it is extremely difficult to capture the so-called general characteristics applicable to different tribal groups, scattered all over the subcontinent. Moreover, the changing nature of tribal identity also captures the varied impact of the external world. In other words, the explanation for the different nature of tribal populations in India has to be located in the socio-cultural milieu which they confront in their day-to-day interaction. Here lies a possible answer to why the Jharkhandis prefer to be accommodated in the nation-state while some of their north-eastern counterparts resort to armed struggle for an autonomous existence.[76] So, instead of identifying the so-called 'fundamental' features of tribal identity, the process that is articulated in its shaping has to be contextualized to grasp the obvious impact of the prevalent socio-economic and political forces on identity. Hence it would not be entirely wrong to argue that the emergence of political Hinduism, of regional voices, and of the claims of caste identities – some of these last created by constitutional law, others worn as a defiant badge of historical oppression – has given 'the question of "who is an Indian (?)" sometimes lethal vitality'.[77]

Concluding observations

The political is enmeshed in identity and its articulation is context-driven. Attributing 'oneness' to Indian identity is sociologically wrong and politically comical for at least two fundamental reasons: first, there is a logical fallacy in assuming that Hindus and Indians are identical for reasons connected with diversity crosscutting religion, language and culture. Despite a uniform political identity of the nation-state, its ingredients do not match its well-accepted liberal description. Second, despite attempts at homogenizing identity, there were serious discourses challenging its basic premises. For Jawaharlal Nehru, imposition of a homogenizing western model of the nation-state was likely 'to fuel apprehensions of assimilation' among religious and regional minorities. Imposition of 'a homogenizing form of Indian nationalism [is] therefore', argues Sudipta Kaviraj, 'likely to disrupt a nation-state instead of cementing its cultural basis'.[78]

Indian identity is therefore neither monolithic nor totalizing. Rabindranath Tagore was perhaps the first to emphatically argue against this view that identity in the subcontinent was unidimensional. Challenging the concept of nation as it undermines the multilayered Indian identity, Tagore reminds us of the combined role of the 'little' and 'great' traditions in shaping what he loosely defined as the Indian nation.[79] India's diversity, Tagore felt, was her 'nature [and] you can never coerce nature into your narrow limits of convenience without paying one day very dearly for it'.[80] Not only 'have religious beliefs cut up society into warring sections . . . social antagonisms [between Hindus and Muslims] have set up impassable barriers every few miles – barriers which are guarded night and day by forces wearing the badge of religion'.[81] For Tagore, the gulf between the communities was largely due to 'the cultural forces' released by British colonialism, which 'fractured the personality of every sensitive exposed Indian and set up the West as crucial vector within the Indian self'.[82] As India's social system got distorted, '[l]ife departed', argued Tagore, 'from her social system and in its place she is worshipping with all ceremony the magnificent cage of countless of compartments that she has manufactured'.[83] While Tagore was critical of artificial division among the communities, created and consolidated by forces supporting colonialism, he was equally alarmed by the drive to gloss over India's diversity for the sake of creating a nation-state as in Europe since it would strike at the very foundation of a civilizational society that flourished in India over the centuries.[84]

Manifested in an ideological design, described as *Hindutva*, the recent endeavour to redefine and restructure identity in India in order to construct a new homogeneous monolithic Hindu identity has posed the issue of identity in a manner that bears considerable resemblance to that in Germany and Canada. The political design seeking homogeneity draws on conceptualizing 'differences' as *a priori* dangerous to alliance, unity, communication and true understanding. They are seen as 'a political threat for any political agenda' striving majority support in a diverse society.[85] The construction of such an overarching homogeneous identity not only debunks the historical and civilizational complexities but also reduces the entire diversity of sects and cults within and other distinctive multi-faceted aspects of India's plural social personality into 'straitjacketed monolithic Hinduism'.[86] The failure to recognize that Indians are instinctively multi-cultural is perhaps the most serious weakness of the Hindutva project. Hindutva is a thus a deliberate ideological construction to erase multiple identities within the category of caste, sect, region, gender, class or belief. The idea itself is a contradiction of the pluralisitic personality of a country such as India that has 'millennia of flourishing diversity in the form of nurturing different religions – what is important to emphasize – diverse non-religious beliefs'.[87] In other words, redefinition of Hinduism as a monolithic and uniform religion is conceptually indefensible[88] because of 'the rich tradition of heterodoxy that has been so central to the history of the Hindu culture'.[89] An inclusionary view of Indian identity, argues Amartya Sen, 'is not only not parasitic on, or partial to, a Hindu identity, it can hardly be a federation of the different religious communities in India' presumably because of the critical role of 'the non-religious beliefs' also in shaping what Indians finally become.[90]

Furthermore, given the increasing proliferation of many other revivalist ascriptive identities around language, caste, tribe and region, the drive for the construction of a Hindu identity drawing solely on religion does not seem to be tenable in the contemporary context. Hence there have been attempts to redefine Hindu nationalism as a cultural referent. The valorization of Ram and Sita is indicative of 'a wider point on the idea' of Hindutva because it 'denotes a set of ideas that consciously articulated as cultural, rather than religious' and yet there is constant slippage into what we might perceive as 'more clearly religious territory'. In other words, this is an imagery, formulated clearly in Savarkarian terms of *pitribhumi* and *punyabhumi*, for inclusion on the basis of cultural logic and yet it is also a specific cultural referent for exclusion on the basis of religious identity.[91]

Similarly, the zeal for a grand celebration to commemorate the centenary year of the *Vandemataram* song is also reflective of a design for gaining political mileage out of cultural referent. There is no doubt that *Vandemataram* played a stirring and historic role in the context of the nationalist struggle against colonialism. Probably because of its typical Hindu imagery, Nehru, despite characterizing the song as 'indisputably the premier national song of India', remarked that 'it represents the position and poignancy of that struggle, but perhaps not so much the culmination of it'.[92] What Nehru was referring to was that, if the song had swayed large sections of Hindus by its cultural appeal, it had obviously alienated non-Hindu minorities, who also remained an integral part of the freedom struggle. Hence it cannot be 'an emblem of modern Indian nationhood'.[93]

Hindutva is thus manifested differently to attain its threefold political goals, namely (a) creating a unitary society, (b) redefining social mobility in an individualistic fashion and (c) using the state to further its ideological goal. Although it may appear to be a mere coincidence, the fact that both Hindutva and neo-liberalism draw on more or less identical ideological goals is perhaps indicative of underlying compatibility of political visions and aims. The decade of the 1980s, which is also known as the decade of possibilities, saw critical changes in Indian political discourse for reasons connected, *inter alia*, with the rise of Dalits and lower castes following the adoption of the Mandal recommendations and also the consolidation of the Hindus for Ramjanmabhumi. This was also the decade in which neo-liberal economic thinking made its appearance. The growing salience of Hindu nationalism and neo-liberal values in contemporary India can perhaps be explained by their clear ideological complementarities.[94] Hence one can safely argue that neo-liberalism would not have gained as much as it did independent of the consolidation of the Hindu nationalist forces that, by seeking to create a united Hindu India, have also paved the way for 'a unified market', the lifeline of the IMF–World Bank-sponsored neo-liberal development packages.

As evident, identity is formed out of contestations and it can never be static but is constantly redefined, keeping more or less intact the core values on which it is grounded. Illustrations from India clearly suggest the difficulty in articulating identity in a single axis presumably because of the complex socio-economic realities in which identity is textured. The political undoubtedly plays a critical role in identity formation. What is significant, as our survey has shown, is also the context, which is reflective of an amalgam of tradition, values and the impact of statecraft. Hence it is not surprising that the *Vandemataram* hardly became a rallying cry for even the Hindus in India. The fractured opinion of the Muslims may have had roots in the fear of majoritarian backlash. But the failure to gain majority support from among the Hindus is certainly indicative of how false is the claim of the Hindu nationalists of their ideological strength. Furthermore, it has also shown that extreme political forces, despite their capacity to wreck the social equilibrium on emotive issues, still remain peripheral to India's basic socio-political fabric, firmly grounded on a well-entrenched pluralistic ethos. Neglect of this dimension amounts to a serious distortion of Indian reality, which is resilient enough to sustain the process of seeking to redefine politics in perhaps the most creative manner.

3 Indian democracy

Liberalism in its reinvented form

Democracy is not merely a guarantee of adult franchise; it also creates conditions for participation in the political process. Has India been successful in this regard? It is difficult to arrive at a conclusive answer because of the apparent paradox one confronts when conceptualizing Indian democracy: on the one hand, popular zeal, which reaches the level of hysteria at times during the elections, almost evaporates once the politicians take over political authority and thus hardly functions as the custodian of both the democratic process and its value system. What is probably more alarming, on the other, is the gradual erosion of the institutions that are critical for democracy in its classical liberal sense. The perversion of the electoral system that fails to neutralize the forces challenging its very existence highlights a major lacuna in the political arrangement forced on India drawing on feudal instincts and primordial loyalties. So, democracy, a western concept, has failed to evolve in India, in its true form. Or, it seems possible, given its short history, that democracy in India is passing through a transition and will triumph eventually. Or, since the form of democracy is linked largely to the socio-economic compulsions of the day, India is likely to redefine its nature and contour since its socio-economic environment is entirely dissimilar to that of the west. Nonetheless, India is perhaps the only example showing that it is possible to maintain, sustain and strengthen a functioning democracy in a very poor country despite enormous diversity in terms of language, religion, culture and ethnicity. It is most striking because according to the classical liberal discourse democracy cannot strike roots in multi-ethnic societies. Democracy in India is thus 'a phenomenon' that, argues a commentator, 'by most accounts, should not have existed, flourished or, indeed long endured'.[1] The growing consolidation of democratic processes can be attributed to the emergence of complementary social and political institutions, nurtured and sustained by an alert people despite the rising tide of communalism and other divisive tendencies. The chapter is devoted to understanding the evolving nature of democracy in India, which hardly corresponds to any copybook description. One can thus safely argue that India is a creative democracy for it is being not only constantly reinvented, but also redesigned to capture the new experiments in a non-western socio-political context.

Democracy and its articulation

The Indian democratic experiment is innovative not only in terms of articulation, but also in substance. Political institutions that hold the spirit of democracy are constantly restructured in view of the constantly changing socio-economic milieu, giving it distinctive localized characteristics within the larger universal paradigm of liberal democracy. Democracy is translated into the expansion of political participation though parliamentary elections that were, in the past, centred on a simple message that could appeal to a broad section of the electorate irrespective of caste, class and creed and became, in effect, 'a single issue referendum'.[2] Describing this phenomenon as 'plebiscitary politics', the Rudolphs have attributed its rise to the de-institutionalization of Congress.[3] The Congress victory is attributed to its strategic resort to populist or plebiscitary politics in terms of electoral and mobilizational strategies. The Lok Sabha elections held so far since 1971 have been decided not by a plethora of promises made in election pledges, but by a single slogan that appeared decisive at a particular point in time because of peculiar historical circumstances,[4] as evident in parliamentary elections: in 1971 it was '*garibi hatao*' (remove poverty); in 1977 'Emergency *hatao*' (remove politicians responsible for the 1975–77 Emergency); in 1980 'Janata *hatao*' (replace the Janata Party government for its chronic instability); in 1984 '*Desh bachhao*' (save the country), which acquired a new majoritarian connotation following the assassination of Indira Gandhi in 1984; in 1989 the campaign 'corruption *hatao*' (remove the Congress government for its involvement in the Bofors scandal) tilted the verdict against Congress, which had had a two-thirds majority in the lower house of the Indian parliament in the 1984 election.

One obvious outcome of the plebiscitary strategies deployed by Congress to sustain its political hegemony has been a long-term tendency towards regionalization of 'oppositional' politics. The regional dimensions of oppositional politics were seen in the growing consolidation of ethnic movements for autonomy and the formation of new parties with an absolute regional agenda. Also, Congress was divided into splinter groups in the regions for its inability to accommodate the new interests that gained salience at local level in a particular historical juncture. In consequence, although politics at the 'national' level continues to be dominated by select political parties that are pan-Indian in electoral and organizational terms, the party system is now highly fractured since there is hardly a dominant pattern in the regions that constitute India. The nature of the party system in the Indian provinces is increasingly being governed by the peculiar regional socio-economic characteristics that influence not only the electoral strategy of the parties but also their mobilizational techniques.[5]

What is, however, alarming in India's successful experience of democracy is the rising tide of violence particularly during and after elections, which is probably an offshoot of criminalization of politics – a phenomenon undermining democratic practices and consolidating muscle power in politics. Violence in the form of communal riots is an age-old phenomenon, which shaped India's destiny during the 1947 transfer of power. Gandhi's assassination is a fall-out of the process unleashed with the acceptance of the Great Divide. The 1952 national election went off smoothly because of the mass euphoria following the attainment of independence. Voters exercised their franchise enthusiastically. There was a new awakening among the urban and rural women, there was a new consciousness of equality among the backward and the poor, who asserted their newly acquired right in large numbers.[6] The situation is different now. The perversion of the electoral system is reaching abysmal depths. All political parties want to capture power or secure a place in the legislature by any means, fair or foul. This results in the increasing reduction of the electoral process to mere mockery. Election on occasions thus becomes a slur on democracy.

The process, known as 'criminalization of politics', began in north India in the 1950s. This was perhaps the outcome of contradictions between the newly emerging middle-caste peasantry and the prevalent feudal forces trying desperately to grab post-independence benefits and maintain the status quo. The upper castes, which monopolized power, wealth and status, continued to maintain their hegemony by resorting to these acts. The upper castes seized the new opportunities in politics as well, where their musclemen proved to be of great help. Not only did they resort to physical violence to force the voters to stamp the ballots in favour of their patrons, they captured polling booths as well to ensure adequate number of votes for the individual or the party of their choice. The benefit of keeping the musclemen led the politicians to offer protection to those who, in the eyes of law, were criminals. With the participation of the musclemen, who so far remained peripherally linked to politics, in parliamentary and state assembly elections, the phenomenon of criminalization of politics has become more vivid than ever.

The upper castes held their hegemony in rural India till the rise of the so-called 'backward castes', which experienced economic prosperity after the 'green revolution' and the resultant social benefits. And the government policy of reducing land revenue contributed to further prosperity. The process of ensuring their economic well-being brought closer the prospect of political dominance among the middle castes, who found in Ram Manohar Lohia their ideologue. By arguing for 'preferential treatment', Lohia made the middle castes aware of their importance in Indian politics. In fact, the argument defending preferential treatment for the middle castes on the ground of social justice triggered off the 1978–79 struggles on the issue of reservation for the backward castes during the Janata rule. Not only did these movements challenge the predominance of the upper castes in the white collar world, they brought about the radical changes in the traditional power hierarchy as well. The contradiction between the upper castes and the rest saw a new turn when the economically prosperous castes, so far neglected politically, gave up the old practice of imitating the upper-caste culture (the process of *sanskritization*) and prepared for direct political confrontation for their share in politics. In the face of such a well-articulated resistance, the traditional upper castes (especially in the Hindi 'heartland'), who controlled access to government jobs and economic resources, resorted to 'political devices' that were not exactly constitutional. This was a significant factor behind the consolidation of the process of criminalization of politics that undoubtedly undermined the very basis of India's democratic system.[7]

In the context of increasing violence, the so-called popular verdict, obtained through election, may appear deceptive. What is more shocking is the lack of interest in the entire electoral process because it hardly changes the political landscape of the country in any substantial way. This raises serious doubts about the basis of India's democracy, which, according to some, approximates to a functioning anarchy. With the rising tide of violence, the anarchical component seems to have assumed a frightening magnitude and, as a result, political rivalry is sorted out not by debate but by naked physical force. The process thus begun has contributed over the years to 'the debasement of our legislatures . . . and the prospect of the gun and intimidation replacing the ballot box in a distressing number of constituencies'.[8]

Electoral dynamics

Of the all the national elections held so far, the 1991 Lok Sabha poll is a watershed for a variety of reasons. First, it was perhaps the most protracted election, having been punctuated by the assassination of Rajiv Gandhi. Although this dastardly killing of a Congress leader was most unfortunate, it gave the Congress party an extra political mileage especially in the light of its decline at least in the Hindi heartland. Second, despite the absence of an electoral pact among the opposition parties, the two major issues of Mandal and Mandir placed them at an advantage over Congress. Third, the 1991 election was also unique in the sense that it was held when Indian policy makers more or less reconciled to the structural adjustment programme of the neo-liberal variety.

The election manifestos released by the national political parties on the eve of the 1991 election contain promises that are peripheral to the major issues for the campaign. The obvious issues on view for some time were Mandal, which for a sizeable section of population means the caste card; Mandir, perceived as a fundamentalist twist to a faith and instigating Hindu–Muslim rivalry to the extent of setting one community against another; and stability, which for many of the electorate is merely a euphemism for unbridled power.[9] Despite reference to various other pledges, the political parties in the fray hammered on one particular issue, which appeared effective in gaining votes in the context of divisive tendencies drawing on social cleavages. The Janata Dal accorded priority to the implementation of the Mandal Report striving to cash in on the caste card; the Bharatiya Janata Party (BJP), by intelligently organizing the Rath Yatra, mobilized Hindu support across the country for the construction of a temple of Ram in Ayodhya. Under the stewardship of its slain leader, Rajiv Gandhi, Congress tried to cash on its promise to provide a stable government and therefore all-round economic development. The party also pleaded to tone up the administration with a view to attaining the stipulated goal. The stability card seems to have had an appeal to a broad cross-section of the electorate in the light of the collapse of two successive non-Congress (I) governments, which had assumed power following the failure of the Rajiv Gandhi-led Congress (I) to obtain an absolute majority in the 1989 Lok Sabha elections.

The rise of plebiscitary politics led to the decline of the party system. In order to obtain votes, individual leadership appeal became far more important than the party, which appeared insignificant in elections. Between 1947 and the death of Jawaharlal Nehru in 1964, however, the Congress Party remained a crucial political institution sustaining India's democracy. Nehru, who described the Congress Party as the central fact of India, guarded the party that won freedom against tendencies undermining its democratic structure. So strong and widespread was its organization throughout India that the Congress Party appeared to be the only viable option to run the state. Commentators like W. H. Morris-Jones and Rajni Kothari[10] who were impressed by the continuity of the party as a ruler despite serious challenges attributed the durability of the 'one party dominance' or 'the Congress system' to its historic role in the freedom struggle and its ability to mediate between different conflicting interests that were dominant on the contemporary political scene. The party held India's democracy in safe custody because, as James Manor explains, it was 'a huge, hierarchically structured party, broadly rooted throughout the country side, [that] apparently provided the mechanism whereby a plurality of elites, sub elites and groups could both voice their claims and attempt to realize them'.[11] At the same time, the Congress could adequately mediate and settle these multiple and often conflicting claims. If necessary, it could count on the extreme faith in the constitutional and legal system and also the fact that the ruling party, which had fought for independence, was held in high esteem and therefore what was decided by the Congress Party and its leadership was accepted by the masses at large. Moreover, the party also mirrored grievances of other groups too. 'The principle of consensus' helped the Congress system work so smoothly for the first two decades after independence.

Soon after Nehru's demise in 1964, the Congress system started breaking down – a process that became evident especially from 1969 onwards when Nehru's successor, Indira Gandhi, faced with increasing opposition strength 'rejected the principle of consensus in favour of the majoritarian principle'.[12] The legitimacy of the party and its structure was supplanted by an altogether more unstable and inherently ephemeral legitimacy of individuals. Since she carried the masses with her, she ignored the party, which lost momentum considerably with the passage of time. Centralization, which was once appreciated as 'an instrument of purposive interventions by a cohesive and disciplined elite soon turns out . . . suicidal to the prevalent party system and the federal structure and of wider affiliations that were built through them'.[13]

Moreover, the breakdown of the Congress system led to the rise of various other structures, both political and non-political, which became formidable in the era of mass politics. Despite Nehru's limitation as a statesman, the Congress party under his tutelage both absorbed new demands and strove to provide avenues for their fulfilment. With the collapse of the party as an institution and 'the unwillingness of the system to create new institutional modes of the masses,'[14] the chasm that was created between the party and the people became unbridgeable. The result was 'the politicization of the masses outside the defined and confined structure laid out by the Congress'.[15]

The deinstitutionalization of the Congress party contributed immensely to the erosion of the party's federal structure: not only did the process lead to massive concentration of power in the central leadership, it also deprived the party of seasoned national and state party officials. What was worse was a calculated drive on the part of the coterie, glued to the leadership, of 'substituting loyalists and favourites at the state and constituency levels for party officials and candidates with local knowledge and support'.[16] The growing consolidation of personal politics under Indira Gandhi's stewardship also 'obviated the need for an organization capable of articulating with society, serving and leading the political community and fighting elections'.[17] She could afford to ignore the party as an instrument for creating a constituency of her own because she succeeded in establishing 'a direct and unmediated link with the people who had transported enormous faith in her charisma and her image as a deliverer and secular messiah'.[18]

Indira Gandhi's ascendance was partly due to the adoption of a number of radical programmes and partly due to her ability to sway the Indian masses by her populist rhetoric. What it implies is that despite her shortcoming as a premier she presided over India's destiny confidently for so many years probably because she gained legitimacy[19] for her rule. In the process, instead of restructuring the party and inducing the people 'in its framework and composition', she depended heavily on 'the sinews of the state'. Notwithstanding populist rhetoric, she was interested neither in restructuring the state nor in its policy apparatus 'for actually redistributing power, wealth and opportunities'. As a result, she ended up creating 'a top heavy and an increasingly insensitive structure of the state, so that all that remained was herself'.[20] Not only was the party identified with her, the state, as it were, lost its independent existence, for the slogan 'Indira is India, India is Indira' stated much of what was true of Indira Gandhi's regime.

What probably enabled Indira Gandhi to continue as an otherwise effective ruler was the opposition disunity and successful suppression of the grassroots-level political movements in a context when the country was distressingly divided by its peculiar socio-cultural environment and exogenous influences, alleged to have instigated and nurtured divisive tendencies within it. By her direct contact with the people, Indira Gandhi became, as it were, a representative of the people irrespective of caste, class and creed. Her image as the reconciler of conflicting interests earned her a strong support base which was consolidated gradually independent of the party. Her emergence by the early 1970s as an invincible political leader lies not so much in the failure of the parties opposed to her, but in appropriating the opposition politics based on the economic demands of various exploited classes. By adopting policies for the alleviation of conditions for landless agricultural labourers and the working class and various other poverty-eradication programmes especially for the backwards, scheduled castes and tribes, she expressed her sincerity to attain the well-publicized socialist goal.[21] In the context of plebiscitary democracy, the appeal in terms of the alleviation of the poor seemed most effective because it meant survival to a majority of the population. Whatever the structure of the appeal as a policy decision, the well-devised slogan 'garibi hatao', which paid off Indira Gandhi electorally in 1971, drew heavily on the so-called appropriation of opposition politics.

Rajiv Gandhi's entry into politics: old pattern survived

Indira Gandhi's tragic end catapulted her son, Rajiv Gandhi, a reluctant entrant to politics, into centre stage of Indian politics. With the democracy still plebiscitary, the slogan '*Desh bachhao*', which gained currency in view of the consolidation of fissiparous tendencies, swayed the Indian electorates and the Rajiv Gandhi-led Congress (I) obtained a two-thirds majority in the Lok Sabha with 49 per cent of the votes to its credit – a rare achievement for the Congress Party because neither Jawaharlal Nehru nor Indira Gandhi had ever garnered as much support as Rajiv Gandhi did. With his pronounced zeal for modernization Rajiv Gandhi was hailed as someone who would revitalize the democratic system 'by attacking corruption and patronage, reinstitutionalizing the Congress, halting the erosion of other institutions and promoting healthy two party competition between the Congress (I) and the opposition parties at the centre'.[22] Despite India's remarkable technological advancement during his tenure as the premier, Rajiv Gandhi failed miserably in bringing about changes in the political arena, which continued to appreciate old values, idioms and styles, as is common in a transitional society such as India. What it probably draws out is the fact that, without developing an appropriate political culture, mere adoption of political institutions that are integral to democracy in the advanced western capitalist societies hardly changes the contours of any political system. Rajiv's managerial approach to politics and remote control style of functioning kept himself away from the reality, which, instead of being adapted to 'the computer age', polarized the communities more on primordial considerations such as caste and religion than on class antagonism. The rise of a powerful coterie comprising those dissociated from the ground reality of India around the prime minister, who increasingly depended on them for advice, ruled out the possibility of a different kind of politics altogether. Since the Congress Party drew heavily on the Nehru–Indira Gandhi lineage on account of its structural weakness, there was not a single effective threat to the continuation of Rajiv Gandhi as a leader. Factionalism, which appeared serious on occasions, thus never assumed alarming proportions.

The ninth general election, held in 1989, conforms to the plebiscitary democracy model. The incumbent prime minister, Rajiv Gandhi, went to the polls with the electoral pledge 'power to the people' through the panchayati raj against a united opposition, a conglomeration of parties with conflicting ideologies, which cashed in on the slogan 'corruption hatao' in the context of the Bofors scandal, in which the top Congress (I) leadership was allegedly involved. Neither of the slogans was effective enough to garner majority support for either of the contending parties. Though the Congress (I), routed almost completely in the Hindi heartland but compensated by its gains in south India, emerged as the single largest party in parliament, it did not stake its claim to form the government as it failed to get a clear verdict. This provided the National Front with an opportunity to rule India

with numerical support from the BJP, which readily agreed despite its serious ideological differences with the Front constituents because it was politically expedient
for the party. For the BJP, the decision to back the National Front government on
the floor of parliament was a strategic one, since the Rath Yatra and its aftermath
reveal the extent to which the party utilized the interim period as preparatory for
the final assault on the forces challenging Hindu consolidation.

Plebiscitary democracy: political outcome

The discussion carried so far brings out three points that require to be dealt with
more carefully to understand the emerging contours of India's democracy.

First, despite severe challenges from within and the consolidation and triumph
of forces opposed to democracy in the neighbouring states, India's experience with
democratic forms of politics and government is rather successful. Although the
British democratic tradition contributed immensely to India's democracy, equally
significant is the role of the Congress Party, which sustained the democratic spirit
at least institutionally since its inception. Not only did the Congress stalwarts
absorb the democratic values, they played a role in legitimizing democratic rule
as a whole. The general concern is not so much for the substance of political
authority as for the mechanisms entailing elections, representation and mandate
obtained through adult suffrage. They derive their sustenance from the 1950 Constitution, which provides for a specific structure of political life 'by allowing and
encouraging (within limits) popular participation in the political system within
a framework of rules, rights, structures and processes which must be broadly
respected by both rulers and ruled'.[23] Here probably lies the strength of India's
democracy, which has developed a different mode of legitimacy to consolidate
itself in the context of challenges from within and outside its boundaries.

Despite the pronounced socialist tilt of both Nehru and Indira Gandhi, the fact
that the party never identified itself with the left shows the extent to which the
centrist ideology prevailed over other considerations. Similarly, the argument that
the right-wing elements found in the party an effective instrument to champion
their goals also reveals the careful handling of the party's centrist image. In the
Indian context, centrism, according to an analyst, therefore means that:

> only those formation(s) which can appeal to a broad cross section of classes
> and castes could hope to come to power nationally. This has implied not the
> absence of ideology but a capacity for ideological flexibility, a general pro-
> gramme which seeks to be consensual and to avoid too close an identification
> with left or right.[24]

Second, in the context of a rapidly changing political scenario, the logic of
explaining the continuity of the Congress Party as a centrist force in terms of
its ability to carry the masses by offering a general consensual programme may
appear unacceptable because no longer is the contention valid that the Congress
vote-bank comprising the upper caste and the core minorities (Dalits, tribals and

Muslims) remains intact. There has been continuous efforts to wean the core voters away from Congress: the V. P. Singh-led Janata Dal has succeeded in creating a constituency among the backwards by offering to implement the controversial Mandal scheme; the BJP has consolidated its support among the upper castes through its well-designed campaign for the construction of a temple at the controversial site in Ayodhya – a demand that is likely to incite rabid Hindu fundamentalism. The Congress Party in order to occupy the centrist space in Indian politics incorporated new demands that were floated in the wake of Mandalism and Rath Yatra by adopting pledges in the election manifesto championing soft Hinduism, soft Mandalism and the Kapoori Thakur formula.[25] The process indicating the adaptation of the parties to the changing socio-political environment does not show a serious departure from an overall centrist perspective; instead, it has drawn our attention to the fact that 'the centre of gravity of Indian centrism has shifted from what it was and even now has not got fixed' primarily because the realignment of forces at the ground level has not yet been completed. And, therefore, the argument substantiating 'the decline of centrism' does not seem plausible because what has happened in the process 'is not the decline of centrism so much as its search for redefinition.'[26]

Finally, within the framework of plebiscitary democracy, individual leadership has become more important than both the party structure and the ideology it professes. This is largely true of the Congress Party, which in different incarnations presided over India's destiny, with two brief interludes since the 1947 transfer of power. With Gandhi throwing his weight behind Nehru, the leadership issue was decided amicably in his favour. As long as he was on the political scene, Nehru appeared formidable probably because of his ability to carry the masses with him. His rise as the only able and effective Congress leader was relatively easy because of the demise of his equally competent and charismatic colleagues, such as Vallabhbhai Patel. Congress victory in elections both at the national and provincial level under Nehru's stewardship made the party dependent on a single individual for his remarkable vote-catching ability. The party therefore looked redundant in the absence of a charismatic leader – this is the beginning of a process that assumed massive proportions with the passage of time. Although Nehru did not groom his daughter, Indira Gandhi, consciously as his successor, the mantle of Congress leadership had fallen on her owing to Lal Bahadu Shastri's untimely death. The Congress syndicate, comprising senior Congressmen such as Atulya Ghosh, K. Kamraj and S. Nijalingappa, accepted her as she would, they thought, serve their interests better than other contenders. Through a direct communication with the people, Indira Gandhi reduced the Congress Party to a mere name. Her emergence as a charismatic leader who swayed the masses brought victory to her party in the 1971 Lok Sabha elections. It was essentially a verdict of the people on her performance as a leader amidst crisis.

The 1971 electoral victory made Indira Gandhi's position invincible.[27] This election was also the beginning of plebiscitary politics, which 'opened direct relation between Indira Gandhi's personalized leadership and individual voters rather than of an issue-oriented politics that mobilized classes and interests in support of

Congress programmes and candidates'.[28] Indira Gandhi became Congress's most vital resource, the key to political power and personal advancement; the party and the person tended to become one. As a result, not only was the party reduced to 'an individual fiefdom', an attempt was also made to retain its leadership within the family by grooming her son, Sanjay Gandhi, as her probable successor. The young Gandhi was projected as the future prime minister by the party, which depended largely on Indira Gandhi for its survival. Within a brief period, Sanjay Gandhi appeared acceptable to the Congressmen irrespective of factions, show-ing probably the extent to which the Nehru–Gandhi lineage prevailed over other considerations so far as the leadership was concerned. A sizeable section of con-temporary politicians, both inside and outside the Congress (I), owed their rise in politics to Sanjay Gandhi. Since Indira Gandhi's capacity to sway the masses in her favour was enviable, there was not a single protest against her deliberate attempt to establish a dynastic rule by projecting her youngest son. Her defeat in 1977 was due more to the excesses of emergency than personalization of politics. Her victory in 1980 corroborates the plebiscitary democracy model. The slogan for stability acted favourably in view of the chaos experienced during the 1977–79 Janata rule.

The accidental death of Sanjay Gandhi, anointed as Indira Gandhi's successor, in 1980 created a break in the line of succession, which appeared temporary fol-lowing the induction of Rajiv Gandhi into national politics; so the Nehru–Gandhi lineage continued. The unanimous choice of Rajiv Gandhi as Indira Gandhi's successor following her tragic end in 1984 seems to have been drawn on the consideration that 'if the Congress remains the central fact of India, [the Nehru family] has become the central fact within it'.[29] Indira Gandhi's brutal killing and the rising tide of divisive tendencies made '*Desh bachhao*' the most effec-tive vote-catching slogan in the 1984 election. Rajiv was projected as a natural heir to the victory with an unprecedented 49 per cent of the popular vote to his credit, ensuring the importance of the individual leadership rather than the party in obtaining votes.

The sudden and tragic death of Rajiv Gandhi created an obvious vacuum in the Congress leadership. There were attempts to make his widow, Sonia Gandhi, the Congress president, which she declined. The move was probably prompted by one of two reasons or perhaps a combination of both: it may have been a strategic move to avoid an internal power struggle that was inevitable given the internecine feud within the party; second, it might have been a well-calculated endeavour to exploit a brutal killing for electoral gain on the promise that the slain leader's sorrowing wife would be an asset in the election campaign. Resolutions adopted by various provincial Congress committees supporting the suggestion seem to explain the deplorable state of affairs within the party, which gave the impres-sion that without the stewardship of Nehru–Gandhi family it looked completely disarrayed. The apparent bankruptcy of the party is probably obvious because, with organizational elections long overdue, it had become an organization of subservient camp followers. As a result, it became a fact of political life that the only people 'who shone at court were either those who had no home base to draw strength from, or flunkeys who were able to assist the leader in a secretarial capacity'.[30] Although the Congress cobbled together a majority by forming a coalition, it remained a minority coalition. A Congress-led minority government assumed power under the leadership of Narashima Rao, who was tipped by the Sonia-supported Congress High Command simply because he lacked a political base and hence would never become a threat to the party authority. Despite his being the prime minister of a Congress-led minority government, the Rao regime will be remembered in history for its failure to prevent the destruction of the Babri Masjid in 1992 by the Hindu right wing. Perhaps to regain the Hindu vote bank for the Congress, Rao seemed to have gone slow even after he had clear indications of the vandalism that was to follow on 6 December 1992.[31]

The Mandal recommendations

Just like the demolition of the Babri mosque, which radically altered the texture of Indian politics, the introduction of reservation in public employment for the Other Backward Castes (OBCs) brought about dramatic changes in conceptualizing the political in the Indian context. In what is euphorically described as 'deepening of democracy', the Mandal recommendations remained the most critical input. Recommending a quota for the OBCs, the 1980 Mandal Commission report is broadly a scheme for 'affirmative action' for socially underprivileged sections of society. By deciding to implement the Mandal Commission Report, submitted to the Government of India in 1980, the V. P. Singh government championed, as it were, the cause of 52 per cent of the population belonging to the OBCs. Although the recommendations were accepted by the government in 1990 there was a series of attempts at according reservation to what were defined as OBCs. To fulfil a constitutional obligation, as Article 340 suggests, the government of India appointed the First Backward Classes Commission, popularly known as the Kaka Kalekar Commission after its chairman, in 1953. The Commission submitted its report in 1955, listing about 32 per cent of the population as backward on the basis of caste identity. The Commission also identified 2399 castes as backward. However, Kalekar rejected the report when he presented it for presidential assent, saying that it would have been preferable to determine backwardness on 'principles' rather than 'caste'. The reservations seemed to have lost its momentum except that nearly all the states constituted their Backward Commission and legalized reservation in public services and educational institutions under state control. The Second Backward Classes Commission, known as the Mandal Commission, appointed in 1978, revived interest in formulating a national policy for OBCs.[32] The commission suggested that OBCs, who form 52 per cent of the country's population, require special concession to correct the social imbalance. But the Supreme Court ruled that reservations cannot exceed 50 per cent of the jobs. So the Commission reluctantly agreed to accept 27 per cent of jobs for the OBCs though they constitute more than half of India's population. There was also a rider because the commission also categorically stated that 'candidates belonging to OBCs recruited on the basis of merit in an open competition should not be adjusted against their reservation quota of 27 per cent'. By implication what it means is that, if the commission's recommendations are respected, half the posts in the public sector and universities will be filled by people who could not get in on merit, provided they belong to 'the right castes'. As is evident, the Mandal formula rests on two premises: (a) the OBCs comprise a very large segment of India's population and (b) their representation (only 5 per cent) in the public sector is abysmally poor.[33] Hence the recommendations ensuring 27 per cent reservations in central jobs and education for the OBCs appear revolutionary. In contrast with the Kalekar Commission, the Mandal Commission Report 'changed the original philosophy of reservations by clearly identifying the potential of cultural identity as a key strategy for enhancing political influences and thereby seeking subsidies and favours for the entire caste/group'.[34]

Reservations were born out of a concern to remedy injustices that deprived certain sections of an equal opportunity to raise themselves in the socio-economic hierarchy. In order to create 'an inclusive Indian identity', the post-independence Indian leadership favoured 'policies of discrimination' as instruments through which 'to offset the advantage, enjoyed by some, and to equalize opportunities at the starting line'.[35] As a political instrument, reservation is also 'a means by which the state, governing a polity divided into many communities, tries, instead of dissolving the communities into one, to construct a supplementary community by representation which will mediate the relations between the many communities that actually exist'.[36] Seeking to rectify the social imbalance due to the age-old economic deprivations, the Mandal formula seeks to give 27 per cent reservation to a total of 3743 OBCs in government jobs. What it therefore means is the promotion of the backward castes, who will also be entitled to a much bigger slice of 'an already meager employment cake'.[37] The violent student riots, led primarily by the privileged upper castes, that swept the entire north of India after the announcement seem explicable in view of the perceptible threat to the upper-caste hegemony in the white-collar world. South India was hardly affected probably because of the long tradition of non-Brahmin movement there.[38] The recent violence over the extension of the controversial scheme shows the extent to which the idea of reservation has itself become repulsive to the assertive section of the upper castes. In the immediate aftermath of independence reservation was mandatory for the scheduled castes and scheduled tribes as it is directed 'towards advancing social and economic equality'.[39] In 1977–78, the Bihar Chief Minister, Karpoori Thakur, introduced 26 per cent reservation for the OBCs. The formula,[40] which took into account the economic backwardness as a criterion for reservation, provoked a violent outburst in which 118 people were reported to have been killed. The Madhya Pradesh government raised reservation from 28 per cent to 32 per cent in 1985, which sparked off violent riots and arson. So widespread and alarming was the trouble that the government was forced to revoke its decision. Gujarat shared the same fate in 1985 when the Madhavsinh Solanki government fell following the introduction of reservation in promotions of posts in medical colleges. These illustrations draw out the fact that north India has not had a consensus of the kind evident in the south.[41] This probably explains why in north India 'the acceptance of the Mandal Commission Report has resulted in condemnation verging on hysteria'.[42]

Whatever advantages the Mandal formula may have, reservation for the backward castes and for the religious minorities is directed towards maintaining a balance of power in caste-divided India's social structure. As a scheme striving to strike a balance between the privileged upper castes and the hitherto neglected OBCs, the Mandal recommendations deserve appreciation. In reality, however, the better-off sections of the OBCs would reap the benefit at the cost of the more deserving sections within these castes. To substantiate the argument, let us draw our attention to the caste dynamics in north India. Till the 1950s, domination was enjoyed in the rural areas by the AJGAR (Ahir, Jats, Gujars and Rajputs) group.[43] They gained remarkably in material terms after the Green Revolution[44] and all of them moved well and truly into the modern sector. The intermediate castes, Kurmis, Koeris, Lodhas and others, also benefited but not uniformly, and therefore there is considerable social and economic heterogeneity in each of these castes. Hence, the Mandal definition of 'backwardness' does not appear plausible in view of its obvious limitation of having ignored social and economic heterogeneity among OBCs. As a result, the benefits meant for the backward of the OBCs are likely to be monopolized by the better-off and influential in these castes. In other words, 'the rhetoric of reservation is addressed to the mass of underprivileged, but their rewards are reserved for the affluent upper castes of the OBCs'.[45] M. N. Srinivas thus argues that 'when a certain caste has political clout it should be excluded from the backward class list; otherwise, the richer members of the higher groups among the backward classes . . . will hog the benefits which should have gone to the genuinely deserving backward classes'.[46]

The political imperatives behind reservations are thus apparent. What prompted the ruling elite to accept the Mandal recommendations is probably a well-calculated design aiming at mobilizing the support of the OBC elite. L. R. Naik, the only Dalit member of the Mandal Commission, refused to sign as he felt that the recommendations would placate the interest of the powerful landowning castes within the OBCs as against those who remained at the periphery within this social segment.[47] Despite clear economic gains for the OBCs, there is no doubt that what governed the V. P. Singh-led National Front government's decision to implement the recommendations were political calculations that surely hinge on the following:

a   a populist vote-catching device as the OBCs constitute the majority of the Indian population;

b   a move to upstage the Haryana leader, Devi Lal, who was threatening the V. P. Singh-led coalition with rural–urban polarization;

c   to shift the focus from the Ram Janmabhumi issue, which singularly created a solid vote bank for the BJP especially after the October (1990) Rath Yatra;

d   the realization that it was one issue on which none of the allies of the National Front (NF) would be able to openly oppose the government, if presented with a *fait accompli.*

By virtue of its unique status in OBC society, its wealth, its relatively high educational level and its hegemony in a majority of caste councils, the OBC upper crust is viewed as the most significant power brokers in the Hindi heartland. So the Mandal formula, designed to ensure social justice, is virtually a scheme for creating and sustaining a secure vote bank for the National Front government. And, since number counts in franchise today, parties irrespective of ideology strive hard to win the support of caste groups for electoral gains by promises whipping up caste sentiments. So, if caste has acquired a new lease of life in independent India, this is almost entirely because of the increasing use made of it in politics. The decision to implement the Mandal Commission report is just another effort to effectively draw on caste sentiments for victory in elections. The Commission is thus described as 'a caste commission' which is seen 'as a passport to power'.[48] Whatever the future of the reservation plan, the Mandal formula has polarized the contemporary political forces more sharply than before. So, a mere acceptance of modern secular political idioms does not ensure their sustenance in a society that draws on feudal sentiments and primordial loyalties. It is not therefore strange that elections are conducted on caste calculations, the candidates are nominated on a caste ratio and, as a consequence, patronage is likely to be distributed on a caste basis and public policies are also to be tilted in favour of the caste support base.

Despite sharp criticism and violent student fury directed against the Mandal Commission Report, the formula deserves serious attention as it strives to correct the immemorial injustice of centuries inflicted on the downtrodden in the name of the discriminatory *varna* system. Owing to the peculiar socio-economic transformation in India, which had a long colonial past, the benefits, meant for the genuinely backward, are likely to go to the relatively better-off sections within the OBCs. So, the Commission's aim of ensuring a greater equality for the OBCs as such is sure to be defeated under the present circumstances. The NF decision on reservation therefore appears 'mainly a tactful response of a desperate regime to the struggle for empowerment by the oppressed sections of [Indian] society'.[49] Unless it becomes a part of a comprehensive plan for development, the Mandal formula, despite B. P. Mandal's sincerity and devotion to the OBC cause, hardly makes sense in a situation in which the reservation plan is being utilized primarily for electoral gains. Yet none of the political parties can be critical of the reservation scheme perhaps because of 'adverse political implications and also the political costs of opposing it'.[50]

Mandal II: reservation for social justice or appropriation by the creamy layer?

Reservation in educational institutions is referred to as Mandal II. In August 2005, the Supreme Court abolished all caste-based reservations in unaided private colleges. On 21 December 2005, the Lok Sabha passed the Ninety-Third Constitutional Amendment Act, 2005, rolling back the Supreme Court judgment by introducing a new clause into Article 15 to allow for reservations for Scheduled Castes and Scheduled Tribes as well as other backward classes in private unaided educational institutions other than minority institutions. In 2006, the UPA government agreed to introduce 27 per cent reservations for OBCs in central government-funded higher education institutions such as Indian Institute of Management, Indian Institute of Technology, All India Institute of Medical Sciences and Central Universities. In other words, the proposed design is meant to introduce a 27 per cent 'quota' to all institutions of higher learning. This blanket guarantee for reservations stands in contradiction with the 1992 Supreme Court judgment in the case of *Indira Sawhney* versus *Union of India* delivered on 16 November 1992, which upheld 27 per cent reservations subject to the exclusion of socially advanced persons/sections (creamy layer) from amongst the OBCs. The Court also directed the government to evolve criteria for identification of this creamy layer. In response to the Court directives, the government appointed a committee which suggested that rules of exclusion applies to children of persons holding different constitutional positions, class I officers and defence personnel who hold the rank of colonel and above. Children of persons with annual income greater than Rs 100,000 were also to be excluded. The limit was later revised to Rs 250,000 in 2004. The recommendations were accepted and circulated among all ministries/departments of Union and state governments in September 1993, allowing reservations to come into force.[51]

Viewed in a long term perspective, Mandal II is a logical corollary of Mandal I. It takes forward 'the process of transfer of social and political power to majority communities'.[52] In the context of Mandal II, V. P. Singh characterized Mandal as 'a macro-process that has acquired its own dynamics. [Hence,] no matter which party forms a government, it has to take the process further'.[53] It would not be an exaggeration if one argued that the centre of gravity in Indian politics is now defined by 'quota politics'.[54] Whatever the implications, reservation through quota translates 'protective discrimination' into reality. In contrast with 'affirmative action' practised in the US, it is the combination of quotas and lower eligibility criteria that defines protective discrimination in India.

The Mandal II arguments

The state can adopt discriminatory measures[55] to favour one group of people against another in a multicultural society. In order to neutralize inequality, the state must provide resources to the underprivileged 'on non market principles – free education, assured income, nutritious food and health'.[56] The idea of 'recognition' is thus clearly political because it is justified keeping in mind a specific type of power relationship. Can 'reservation' be thus an appropriate scheme to accord 'recognition' to those who are disadvantaged for historical reasons? Perhaps yes. A politically 'liberal' society, however, does not endorse social discrimination because citizenship, conceptually speaking, is 'universal'. Hence 'ascribed' identities are completely disregarded in defining citizens. One may perhaps theoretically defend this position. But, given the peculiar evolution of societies in various socio-economic and political contexts, this position may not appear tenable simply because 'identical' rights for all are inadequate for protecting cultural minorities.

What we therefore require are 'special' rights for minorities who are identified as 'disadvantaged' groups. The argument that justifies discriminatory laws draws on the idea that, since citizens are 'differentiated' and thus 'unequal', for obvious reasons, different communities should have different rights as citizens. Based on this logic, theorists of multiculturalism articulate the notion of 'differentiated citizenship'. There are two significant implications of this conceptualization: (a) in contrast with universal citizenship of the liberal variety, differentiated citizenship clearly argues for discrimination in favour of cultural minorities as 'justified'; (b) by taking into account 'cultural distinctiveness' as a denominator, those championing differentiated citizenship challenge the ideologically charged attempts at 'homogenizing' communities with clear socio-cultural differences.

There is a historical dimension too. Different communities undergo different social churning processes. Hence some are 'privileged' and some are 'marginalized'. A society that rejects 'differentiated citizenship' and appreciates universal citizenship seeks to insist that the latter give up their identity and merge with the majority. This is how a society flourishes. From the multicultural point of view, this position smacks of 'cultural imperialism' because the prism through which a society is uniformly viewed insists on treating unequals equally. This is clearly a case of cultural imperialism because norms and values of the privileged majority acquire salience given their well-entrenched nature and therefore any opposition to them provokes consternation among those who tend to belittle the importance of historical processes in dividing humankind.

There are thus strong arguments in favour of reservation in a multicultural country such as India. But difficulty arises the moment groups or communities that deserve reservation are identified on the basis of ascribed identity, namely caste. Except in the 1931 census of India, caste was never a criterion in classifying Indian population. So, if caste is a defining category, the 1931 index remains critical. This is hardly persuasive because the 1931 census was guided by imperial priorities and may not have reflected India's actual demographic profile. Furthermore, since the criterion of 'backwardness' is historically conditioned it is doubtful whether it remains valid even in the twenty-first century.

Similarly, reservation in higher education seems to be an empty slogan in the light of the fact that seats for scheduled castes and scheduled tribes remain vacant for lack of applicants. Even after more than half a century of reservation for these communities, the number of beneficiaries is abysmally low. The reasons are not difficult to seek. As evident in the latest educational statistics, released by the Union Ministry of Human Resources Development, whereas 73 per cent of scheduled caste (SC) students quit school before taking the class X final examination, the figures for scheduled tribe (ST) students (79 per cent) are worse. Interestingly, the drop-out rates are not so high among the children within classes I–IV. Only 37 per cent of SC students discontinue whereas 59 per cent of the ST students fall under this category. If contrasted with the prevalent high Gross Enrolment Ratio, which is 83 per cent for the SCs and 86 per cent for the STs, the drop-out rates reveal the unfavourable socio-economic circumstances in which they are forced to take up odd jobs for mere survival. Since the majority of the SC and

ST population draw on agriculture for livelihood, these children are roped in for farming once they reach 10–12 years.

Given this reality, reservation in higher education makes no sense so long as drop-out rates in schools are alarmingly high. In order to translate the scheme into practice, what is thus required is to pursue 'the literacy mission' seriously especially among the downtrodden by creating conditions in which benefits for going to school outweighs the forced alternative of working in the field for mere survival. Otherwise, the benefits of reservation continue to be 'uneven' among those who can avail them. The well-placed group of the backward section would be better off with such reservation. It would help only the creamy layer to grab the advantages. Thus the social justice agenda will always remain a distant goal.

It is difficult to suggest a convincing scheme to get out of the imbroglio relating to the reservation issue.[57] In order to arrive at a solution one may begin by taking into account most seriously the creamy layer judgment of the Supreme Court, unless one reviews whether it is appropriate to extend reservation to the creamy layer generation after generation. It makes no sense if the children of the IAS officers, for instance, enjoy reservation simply because of their ascribed social status, even though they, despite their caste identity, are socio-economically better placed than their upper-caste counterparts. As the argument goes, 'to allow the undeserving to benefit from reservation is to deny protection to those who deserve to be protected'.[58] So, is the cause of social justice served well if reservation is confined to first-generation learners or further? Differentiated citizenship is a powerful device to achieve social justice. But it causes serious social distortion unless it is conceptualized in the affirmative action mould rather than extending a blanket licence to those who are differentiated merely by virtue of birth.

Assessment

Despite having stirred the sensibilities of both the socially advantaged and disadvantaged sections of society, the Mandal initiative is a powerful input that has brought about radical changes in Indian polity and society. The grammar of entitlement has become an integral part of the language of politics in contemporary India. Whereas the first phase of reservation under the Mandal Commission represented the politics of caste assertion or the politics of identity, the second phase is one in which castes are asserting their right to power. Mandal II is a well-argued statement demanding 'retooling of the normative subjectivity of formal democracy [that] involves critical reformations of the institutions of public and private life and requires altogether new frameworks for the accountability of the government to the people'.[59] This transformation is suggestive of 'a silent revolution' because 'power is being transferred, on the whole peacefully, from the upper caste elites to various subaltern groups [and] the relative calm . . . is primarily due to the fact that the whole process is incremental'.[60] There can be a debate on how to execute the decision, but all political parties are unanimous in accepting the logic and reality of the Ninety-Third Amendment Act (2005) confirming reservation in all institutions of higher learning. The appointment of the Oversight Committee in 2006 to suggest steps to expand the OBC quota without adversely affecting the equilibrium in admission to institutions of higher learning is a strategy to defuse social tension in the country.[61] Yet the 2006 controversy had also shown 'how entrenched social prejudices remain and how deep runs the hostility to change in areas where it matters the most'.[62]

Nonetheless, the Mandal debate marks an important shift in the public justification of reservations. After Mandal, caste, as a basis of collective struggle for gaining equality in positions and social status, became 'a term of respectable usage' among the marginalized. It is now being seen as 'an empowering device to enhance one's meager entitlements in society'.[63] The shift thus involved a reinterpretation of the nationalist goal of a more equal and just society by empowering the disadvantaged and recognizing the socially denigrated groups in addition to reduction of socio-economic disparities. The conceptual mechanism articulating the redefinition involved, argues Rochana Bajpai, 'a relocation of equality in proximity to democracy on the one hand, and by distancing (but not its dissociation) from national unity, on the other'.[64] However one characterizes the Mandal debate, the reservation policy has nonetheless become 'the fixed point of Indian political life' because different groups have different reasons to support it. It is a soft option for the political elites who, 'reluctant to carry out deep-rooted changes in society would rather opt to enlarge the constituency for reservations in a shrinking state sector and in a declining educational system, than transform ownership of resources in the country'.[65] In other words, by securing the numerically mandated quotas for the OBCs, Mandal II is a way of avoiding doing the things that really create access to opportunities. Bhikhu Parekh laments:

> [s]ocial justice has come to be defined almost exclusively in terms of reservations, and the massive programme of redistribution needed to tackle the deep roots of historically accumulated disadvantages has been marginalized. Rather than fight for such a programme, the scheduled caste, scheduled tribe, and OBC representatives in powerful positions use their constituents as a vote bank to promote their own careers.[66]

By deciding to implement the Mandal II reservation scheme, the primary aim of the Congress is, suggests a commentator, 'to lure back the traditional voter [and] reservation has [thus] dammed all to do with balancing society; it has everything to do with winning elections'.[67] The left-wing political parties extend support to the reservation scheme because, in the absence of the implementation of radical 'redistribution programme', it is best 'to stick to constitutionally guaranteed and politically accepted policy of reservation'. On account of peculiar socio-economic circumstances, the reservation policy not only enjoys 'a broad-based support' but has also become what Bhikhu Parkeh characterizes as 'a touchstone of social conscience and an integral part of Indian politics'[68] though 'the churning of Indian politics and society that followed Mandal has [largely] petered into an endlessly involuted conflict of one sub-caste with another [and] most anti-caste movements turn out to be . . . merely anti-upper caste movements [happily excluding] those below them'.[69]

The changing political parties

Indian politics is now far more complex than before. Both the Mandal formula and the Mandir agenda seem to be most critical in reconceptualizing Indian politics. Political parties holding 'the live wire' of representative liberal democracy can hardly be indifferent to the new ideological issues that figure prominently in contemporary India. The change seems to have begun with the breakdown of 'the federal and coalitional pillars of the Congress Party'[70] that contributed to the growth of other parties with regional roots. The process became very prominent especially in the 1990s when the electoral trend was towards a fractured mandate, as the results of succeeding national polls show. It is thus perfectly possible to conceive of circumstances when a particular social group/or class is represented by various political parties. Hence the argument drawn on 'a stable social base' for a party or a group of parties may not always be tenable. And also, conversely, it is perfectly logical to challenge the notion of 'traditional vote banks' when several parties are vying for the same vote bank championing more or less similar issues despite 'the ideological differences' among themselves. What is striking is the fact that not all of the parties jostling for social constituencies succeed uniformly and this is where the explanation lies of why one party 'shines' and others do not under specific circumstances. Coalition is perhaps the best possible theoretical construct to articulate this 'moment' in Indian politics when political processes do not appear to be 'uni-directional' at all. This is a moment that not only captures the trends towards redefining Indian politics but also identifies its determinants in the changed domestic and global social and economic milieu. Indian politics is both coalitional and regionalized. As the successive poll results show, gone are the days of a single-party rule. The thirteenth Lok Sabha is illustrative of the stupendous achievement of the National Democratic Alliance (NDA) in sustaining a spirit of consensus among as many as twenty-four heterogeneous parties which were united only in their basic opposition to the Congress. The process that began in the 1967 state assembly elections seems to have struck roots in the Indian soil in view of the success of the NDA government in completing a full term of five years in power despite occasional hiccups. The fourteenth Lok Sabha poll in 2006 confirms the trend with the formation of another coalition government, led by the United Progressive Alliance (UPA).

As evident, the growing importance of coalition in government formation suggests the failure of the parties to cobble together a majority on their own and hence coalition is the only available option; it also shows a tenacity of 'community identities, in the form of caste and religion, as groups struggle to construct majorities that rule at the Centre'. That these identities suddenly became significant in political alignment in the late twentieth century also underlines that they are products of modern politics and not 'residues of the past'.[71] Indian parties thus represent, argues Paul Brass, 'a unique blending of Western and modern forms of bureaucratic organization and participatory politics with indigenous practices and institutions'.[72] Thus it is not surprising, as the Rudolphs have shown, that a caste groups that is relatively homogeneous and cohesive but politically not well-represented tends 'to form a partisan attachment to a particular party [or even] to form and operate a political party of its own'.[73] This is one side of the story. The other side relates to the emergence of various outfits (which later may become independent parties) as the caste group becomes differentiated by class interests, and by differences in education, income, occupation and cultural characteristics.

The trajectory of Indian politics confirms the trend. In the first election in independent India in 1952, for example, the all-pervasive Congress Party was opposed at the pan-Indian level by four ethnic parties, namely the Ram Rajya Parishad, the Hindu Mahasabha and Bharatiya Jana Sangh, jostling for support of the Hindu 'majority', and the All India Scheduled Caste Federation seeking to draw on the support of those constitutionally recognized as scheduled castes. In view of their failure to garner adequate electoral support, three of these four parties disappeared. The Bharatiya Jana Sangh failed to emerge as an alternative to the Congress presumably because it was confined to north India and never succeeded in acquiring an all-India image.[74] The decline of the Congress Party created space for the rise of the ethnic parties. Seemingly seeking to capture the support of the Hindu 'majority' against the Muslims, the Bharatiya Janata Party was formed in 1984 by those who formed the core of the Bharatiya Jana Sangh. Later, the Bahujan Samaj Party and Janata Dal, among other, came into being to consolidate the backward castes and Muslims against the upper-caste Hindus. In course of time, however, most of these parties diluted their support base by being politically moderate and accommodative of the other groups that so far remained anathema for valid ideological reasons. The most striking example happens to be the BJP, which put all the contentious pro-Hindu and anti-Muslim agenda under the carpet for political expediency.

The scene is no different in the states, where the ethnic parties have grown in importance over decades. As Kanchan Chandra has shown,[75] first the Dravida Munnetra Kazagham (DMK) and later its offshoot, All India Anna Dravida Munnetra Kazagham (AIADMK), drew on ethnic solidarity to capture power in opposition to other contending parties. In Punjab, at the initial stage of its career, the Akali Dal survived and drew its electoral strength from Sikh ethnic identity. Similarly, the Shiv Sena in Maharashtra captured power in 1995 on Hindu cards by adopting a very strong anti-Muslim rhetoric, though it has underplayed its anti-Muslim stance to a large extent now presumably because of the realization that it would alienate even the moderate Hindus from the party. There is another dimension that is peculiar to Maharashtra, namely that the two dominant castes of Maharatta and Kunvi constitute a critical mass in elections. Hence the contending parties always vie for their support. The party that succeeds in drawing these ethnic blocs in its favour stands out in election. As the succeeding elections show, the Maharatta–Kunvi combination always remains critical to any party seeking to form a government. What is therefore paramount for the parties is not the ideology, but the articulation of the ideology in such a form as to draw maximum support from these ethnic groups that gets translated into votes.

Ethnification of party[76]

As is evident, the appeal to caste-based ethnic identity continues to remain critical in electoral politics in India. The story of Indian electoral democracy is thus one of paradox because political parties, despite their 'emphasis on policies related to economy in their respective manifestos, tend to rely on identity basis for mobilization'.[77] Even the Congress Party, which carried the legacy of the nationalist struggle, does not seem to be different. In most of the states, except perhaps the left-ruled Tripura, West Bengal and Kerala, every major party seeks to gain by appealing to the electorate on the basis of ascriptive categories. However, the politics of caste varies with context. In the 1960s, as the Rudolphs have shown, the continuity of the upper castes in positions of power was possible because of a quid pro quo arrangement between them and the numerically strong lower castes: upper castes needed the numerical strength that lower castes' support supplied and lower castes gained access to the resources and opportunities that support for upper-caste leadership could yield. Although with the introduction of secret ballot in elections the capacity of the upper caste to mobilize lower castes significantly declined, the former nonetheless held the key to political power presumably because there was hardly a threat from the latter.[78] The situation, however, dramatically changed in the 1990s with the growing consolidation of parties representing the numerically lower castes. As the evolution of the Bahujan Samaj Party in Uttar Pradesh shows, the rise of Mayawati is largely attributed to her ability to couch her appeal to the voters in clear ethnic terms.

The 2007 assembly election in the state of Uttar Pradesh is a watershed in India's recent electoral history for two reasons: first, the prediction that the election would result in a hung assembly did not come to pass – that the electorate voted against the incumbent government and accepted the Mayawati-led Bahujan Samaj Party (BSP) was perhaps a glaring example of how discerning Indian voters can be, flummoxing political analysts and pollsters alike. Second, it is clear that the Congress Party no longer remains a catch-all party capable of sustaining the rainbow coalition, drawn on the conceptual category of 'traditional vote banks'. It makes no sense to suggest that the middle castes and Muslims are favourably inclined towards Congress. Furthermore, their support for reservation for the OBCs has surely rattled the upper-caste voters who are already disillusioned with the Bharitya Janata Party (BJP) in Uttar Pradesh. Likewise, the Muslim vote bank of the Congress is now highly fractured and the Dalits are hardly with the Congress since they have found the messiah in Mayawati. The near decimation of the Congress in the 2007 assembly election is indicative of new electoral equations in the state. (See Table 3.1 for the poll outcome of the UP assembly elections in 2007 and 2002.)

It was clear from voter sentiment on the eve of the election that the BSP had a clear edge over other contending political parties in what is regularly referred to as India's 'most happening state': Uttar Pradesh. The BSP was a forerunner for two important reasons: first, the slogan, '*brahmon jodo*' (integrate Brahmins or the upper castes), was a master stroke that yielded dramatic results. In order to translate the slogan into reality, the first major step Mayawati undertook was the

Table 3.1 Poll outcome of the UP assembly elections in 2007 and 2002

Party	Seats in 2007 election (%)	Seats in 2002 election (%)
BSP	206 (30.46)	98 (23.06)
Samajwadi Party	97 (25.45)	143 (25.37)
BJP	50 (16.93)	88 (20.08)
Congress	22 (8.56)	25 (8.96)
Independent and others	27 (18.60)	49 (22.53)
Total	402	403

Source: *The Hindu*, 13 May 2007.
Note: figures in the parenthesis refer to the share of popular votes (in percentage) of each political party.

induction of the former advocate-general, Mr Satish Chandra Mishra, a Brahmin, within the party. By organizing Brahmin *mahasammelans* (massive congregation) at regular intervals, Mishra helped the BSP to make significant inroads among the Brahmins. While addressing these *mahasammelans*, Mayawati repeatedly assured the Brahmins that the BSP is against *Manuwadi* or the Brahminical discourse for lower castes, and not against Brahmins.

Similar *mahasammelans* were organized regularly to win back the other forward castes. These *mahasammelans* were largely well-attended though doubts were expressed whether this would tilt the outcome in favour of the BSP, as forward castes do not seem to be so easily amenable to change given the historical roots of caste barriers and also because of the resentment of the upper castes due to BSP's well-defined anti-*Manuwadi* platform. Nonetheless, the BSP's victory in most of the constituencies is largely due to its success in forging an alliance with castes and communities that are brought together by constructing a common history of exclusion. The second supportive factor was concerted attempts by the party workers to build an organizational network, widely spread across the state, the parallel of which can be found in West Bengal where the Left Front, supported by a well-entrenched organization, has achieved a political stranglehold of sorts. Unlike other political parties in the fray, the BSP began its election drill almost two years ago by selecting candidates for most of the constituencies and interacting with voters on the ground. Divided into twenty-five sectors (with ten polling booths in one sector), each constituency was closely monitored by the High Command. In tandem, each polling booth, hosting roughly 1000 voters, was made the responsibility of a nine-member committee including at least one woman to motivate and mobilize female voters. As the arrangement suggests, *Behanji* (sister), as Mayawati is popularly known in the state, left no stone unturned in her effort.

On the surface, the BSP's organizational effort seems to have paid dividends since a large chunk of forward castes supported the BSP. It is difficult to surmise whether this was positive support for the party, or it represented the best available option given the failure of BJP to deliver. What is clear, however, is a growing separation of the forward castes from the BJP. Their voice was more or less uniform in expressing disappointment with the BJP that conveniently put, as a school teacher in Allahabad pointed out, 'the Ram mandir *mudda* [the agenda] under the carpet'.[79] They were also upset with the incumbent state government, led by Mulayam Singh, who was accused of unnecessarily 'pampering' the Muslims.

In explaining the poll verdict, two broad arguments have been put forward: first, the triumph of the BSP is largely attributed to Mayawati's social engineering project – a euphemism suggestive of an alliance between the Dalits, Brahmins and to a lesser extent, the *Banias* (merchants). In other words, Mayawati's success can be attributed to 'a rainbow coalition', reminiscent of the Congress system that survived till 1967 in India, in spite of her inability to win the support of both the Muslims and OBCs to the extent the BSP supremo had expected. The second argument revolves around the popular inclination for a single party majority government since coalition governments failed to govern irrespective of caste, class or religion. Whether the poll verdict corresponds with an anti-coalition trend is difficult to say. But there is no doubt that an anti-incumbency factor played a critical role in BSP's favour. Given the genuine grievances of the common Uttar Pradesh voter, with a per capita income less than half the all-India average, the discontent was but natural.

Statistics reveal that one in four Brahmins in India lives in Utter Pradesh. Correspondingly, the state has the largest Dalit population (23 per cent) in India. Since the breakdown of the Congress-led social coalition in the first two decades after independence, the BSP political platform represents the first renewed attempt at unifying socially 'antagonistic' groups in the political arena. The BSP's new political mantra, which was critical of the Mandal reservation scheme for the OBCs and drew on Ambedkar-inspired principles, undoubtedly favoured the political aspirations of the party. This ideological package drew Dalits and forward castes together irrespective of their clearly different, if not antagonistic, location in the traditional social hierarchy of caste. The electoral appeal of intermeshing the pro-Dalit ideology of Ambedkar with the anti-Mandal stance of the BSP cemented a bond between castes which invariably became a deciding factor in the election.

Mayawati's success was also largely due to a peculiar caste chemistry that fermented the coalition between Brahmins and Dalits. By getting the traditional upper castes and the Dalits together, the BSP leader has done a lot more than just returning to the social pyramid that sustained the erstwhile Congress system. Whereas in the Congress system the upper castes remained the driving force, in Mayawati's social contract Dalits are the drivers of change. In this sense, the BSP victory is symptomatic of a paradigm shift in Indian politics. Mayawati has succeeded in building a social coalition that inverts the pyramid of caste/class hierarchy by building a rainbow alliance of social groups, now dominated by that greatest underclass of all, namely Dalits. Nonetheless, the BSP is hardly the party of its traditional ideological mould since its leader seems to have redefined its character by underlining the role of *Sarvjan* (Dalit–Brahmin combination), in staging a comeback. The triumph of the BSP cannot therefore be explained in terms of our conventional understanding of caste as a determining factor in Indian politics. The party did 'use caste but only as a metaphor to build innovative grassroots alliances, which demonstrated that the concerns of other communities mattered as much as those of dalits'.[80] Whether this formula will work elsewhere in India is debatable – it worked in Uttar Pradesh precisely because the Dalits were already a consolidated political force and the combination with the forward castes put the BSP in an unassailable position that none of the other political parties managed to challenge.

The BSP victory is not merely a change of guard in UP – it is also indicative of a new social coalition that is likely to be stronger in the days to come. By providing a unique formula bringing both the upper castes and so-called untouchables together, the BSP created a formidable social compact which, although heterogeneous by caste, is politically united. Neither the BJP nor Congress has succeeded in creating constituencies beyond its so-called traditional base. The new government in India's largest state (which sends the maximum number of parliamentarians to the national legislature) is also an articulation of a process highlighting a clear shift in the centre of gravity in Indian politics: power has been shifting lower and lower down the caste order. This is perhaps the process of a silent revolution that has taken place which neither the pollsters nor the strategists of the major political parties envisaged.

The BSP's political ascendancy is equated with India's 'silent revolution'. In explaining the phenomenon, Jaffrelot argues that the success is achieved not by resorting to a Marxist class struggle, but by 'returning to Ambedkar's project of uniting ascriptive groups which were victims of discrimination rather than only those who suffered from economic hardship'.[81] This has resulted in deep-seated changes in India's political panorama. With the fragmentation of social base, the appeal to a larger constituency seems to have lost its political appeal. The Indian state is fractured around caste, regional and religious considerations. Despite the political fluidity, a pattern seems to have evolved out of this kaleidoscope of political competition. Defending the argument for 'silent revolution', it is also being characterized as complementary to the 'maturing' of Indian democracy in the light of 'the high level of politicization' of the marginalized sections of the Indian masses.[82] There is however an exactly opposite point of view. Kanchan Chandra, for instance, provides a cynical interpretation by defining India as 'a patronage democracy'. According to her, the growing participation of the masses in electoral politics represents 'less a normative commitment or a spirit of celebration and more the intensification of a struggle over scarce resources provided by the state' where the stakes are high and the poll outcome makes an immediate difference to the lives of elites and non-elites alike.[83] In a patronage democracy, elections therefore become 'covert auctions in which basic services which should, in principle, be available to every citizen, are sold to the biggest bidder'.[84] In the first-past-the-post system of electoral democracy, majority matters and hence ethnic head counts acquire political salience. This is a double-edged device: on the one hand, numerically viable ethnic groups can never politically be excluded; it will also, on the other hand, lead to manipulation of the definition of ethnic categories given its clear positive gains.[85]

There is a related point here. Undoubtedly, the BSP and other parties representing marginalized groups radically altered India's political texture by involving those groups that hardly mattered in political decision making in the past. Here is a paradox because the parties seeking to democratize Indian political space seem to be most undemocratic internally for two reasons: first, the organization, highly individual-centric, remains confined to the centralized leadership and as a result it is not receptive to the democratic urges at the grassroots; second, as a result, the choice of candidates during elections is always made by the leaders in the upper echelons of the party hierarchy. Elected representatives thus become the mouthpiece of the leadership, largely ignoring their critical role in representative democracy. Hence there seems to be a disjuncture between the needs and aspirations of the people and 'high politics', articulated in the legislature.

Hindutva as an electoral agenda

There is no doubt that Hindutva, as an ideology, created a support base for the BJP by appreciating that the cultural heritage of the country should not be ignored or dismissed simply because it does not measure up to modern criteria.[86] India has a rich cultural heritage that needs to be critically evaluated and suitably mobilized because 'no country can build-up its self-confidence and self-respect by living on imported ideas alone'.[87] Instead of being xenophobic, Hindutva also defends the cultural ethos by seemingly integrating the best in our past with what it needs to learn from others. Three strategies on which Hindutva draws are those centred on 'places, areas and routes of synergy'. As Deshpande argues, these strategies remain most effective in charging Hindus emotionally since they draw on 'the sacred sites, loyalties [to religion, defined in a particular way], processions and pilgrimages'.[88] Nonetheless, its success is limited presumably because of Hindutva's homogenizing design. In fact, what is most negative in the entire conceptualization is the tendency to homogenize the Indian civilization and the texture of Indian identity. Hindutva does not seem to be designed to create a social coalition of diverse groups, but rather an aspiration to homogenize and construct a unity by submerging diversity. Indian civilization has drawn on various sources, including Hinduism. It is an outcome of a long-drawn interactions among civilizational values, making it not a homogeneous whole, but a loose federation of different systems of thought and practices. Hence any attempt to homogenize it therefore necessarily distorts and does grave injustice to it because Hindutva cannot, argues Bhikhu Parekh,

> unite all Indians because of its antipathy to minorities. It cannot even unite all Hindus because it stresses only one version of Hindu history and culture. Indeed it creates a deep division among them by classifying some as "good" or "true" and the rest as "pseudo" or "confused" Hindus.[89]

Hindutva can therefore never strike a chord with the people at large presumably because of the sociological constraint connected with the inherently pluralist character of Hinduism. Conceptually, Hindus cannot be nationalist, if nationalism is understood as an ideological device seeking to 'homogenize' a set of people on the basis of well-defined criteria. This is perhaps 'the gravest impediment to at least the more extreme items on its agenda'.[90] Yet it would be wrong to conclude that the Hindu nationalist influence is on the wane because it is located in a much broader space than that represented by the BJP. Because they overlap and blend with other key discourses on Indian society, culture and identity, 'these are ideas which are manifested in a wide range of political actions and articulations'. Hence the political impact of Hindutva needs to be measured, argues John Zavos, 'in terms of its continuing activism [in large parts of India involving the marginalized sections of society] where politics is manifested not in terms of formal state institutions, but as a contest for power in a network of localized institutions and practices'.[91] Simultaneously with the expansion of influence of Hindu nationalism, there is also the ascendancy of caste groups and caste-based parties especially in the 'Hindi heartland', which have gained enormous electoral clout in recent years. In fact, the process is so powerful that it has been characterized as 'a silent revolution' whereby power is being transferred from the upper-caste elites to various subaltern groups.[92]

How did the BJP gradually expand its base? Apart from avoiding the contentious issues – like the abrogation of Article 370 and imposition of the uniform civil code – the importance of the national agenda cannot be ignored in projecting the BJP in a different garb. To a large extent, the presence of its political allies has aided this process and the BJP has gained a foothold in new territories. The growing expansion of the BJP has been, as an analyst comments, 'intertwined with a distinct three-tiered growth in its social appeal'.[93] The first tier growth involves the growing success of the BJP in extending its sphere of influence beyond its traditional support base of upper-caste Hindus. In the Hindi heartland, apart from its core support base – the upper castes – the only other community that has been mobilized in this region is 'the scheduled tribe'. The second tier consists of the OBCs, which was another significant community that voted for the BJP presumably because of its poll alliance with those regional parties with strong organizational presence in those states. Here the alliance with these parties allowed the BJP to strike roots among the OBCs, which had so far remained peripheral in its agenda. The first victim of 'this confluence of lower caste mobilization and regional assertion [has been] the dominance of the Congress at the state-level'.[94] The most important segment of the BJP's growing social base relates to the scheduled castes and Muslims: the third tier of its support base. In the last national poll the secondary states, where the BJP hardly existed, became significant and the BJP through its allies got a foothold in these regions. Parties such as Telegu Desam, AIADMK, Trinamul Congress and to a lesser extent the Biju Janata Dal had the strongest organizational base in the regions to which they belonged, while the BJP remained a nonentity. The poll agreement with these political parties acted favourably for the BJP, which 'prospered by association and without [these parties] would most probably have been marginalised'.[95] Contemporary Indian politics therefore provides, argues an analyst, 'a dual framework' of analysis. On the one hand, the framework of backward caste politics gains remarkable salience, while the BJP and its frontal organizations (like the Viswa Hindu Parishad,

Bajrang Dal and above all the RSS) seek to draw political capital out of their old Hindutva line.[96] There is, however, on the other hand, another framework based on opposition to the major political parties, namely the Congress and BJP. Within this framework of reference, the coming together of the parties draws upon anti-Congress and anti-BJP sentiments.[97] In this process of coalition, regional parties seem to be playing a crucial role in initiating 'a democratic upsurge involving women, tribals, *dalits*, lower castes and rural voters'.[98]

As is evident, the BJP gained to a greater extent than any political party since the decline of the Congress Party as a dominant pan-Indian force and has also been able to project itself in new geographic areas and social segments as a result of holding power at the centre and increasing prominence within the national political scene. However, the extent of this geographic and social expansion is subject to continuous contestation at all levels of the political process. In this respect, the BJP is a class by itself seeking to reconstitute a new form of national hegemony by adopting a relatively elastic ideology. As an analyst comments, 'the strident rhetoric of Hindu nationalism seems to have died [and] instead of *mandir*, *masjid* and *mandal*, election campaign revolved around *bijlee* (electricity), *sadak* (road) and *pani* (water), which is indicative of a dramatic change in the Indian political mindset in fifty years'.[99] The pre- and post-poll agreement with regional parties notwithstanding ideological incompatibility is largely the outcome of a reinvented BJP, which is single-mindedly committed to remaining in power at the centre. So what may appear to be an ideological dilution seems to be a strategic calculation of the BJP to renegotiate with the rapidly changing India's socio-political and economic realities in a qualitatively different fashion. Rather than endorsing the ideological orthodoxy in which the party articulated its world view in the past, the BJP seems to have upheld a pragmatic approach appreciating the constantly changing national profile. It was not surprising therefore that the BJP, which suffered one of its most humiliating electoral reversal at the hands of Congress in 1984 election, emerged as a principal contender for the centrist position in Indian politics by the 1990s. In other words, with its wider organizational capacities for mass mobilization, the BJP sustained its 'moderate' image presumably because of its redefined ideological appearance within the constraints of coalition government. Not only has the effort paid electoral dividends to the party and its coalition partners, it has also translated into reality a search for a politically stable alternative to the Congress at the centre by reconstructing a national system of political hegemony. Two factors seem to be critical in the rise of the BJP as coalition's leading partner: the numerical importance of the regional parties given the failure of the national parties to muster a majority in parliament; and also the willingness of these parties to form an alliance with the BJP, which agreed to put the contentious issues under the carpet for coalition maintenance. What was therefore critical in the coalition was not ideological but programmatic compatibility. So the BJP, which was reportedly responsible for the demolition of the controversial Babri Masjid in Ayodhya in 1992, had succeeded in building a competitive bloc by adopting an agenda which was not clearly 'partisan' but politically meaningful in a multicultural milieu. If that be so, is it empirically correct to characterize the BJP in a stereotypical mould? The answer is perhaps no, although there is always a space for 'the hidden agenda' that seem to have sustained the core despite its apparent dilution on the surface for obvious political mileage. Hence the explanation for the steady rise of the BJP has to be couched in terms of politically meaningful 'anti Congressism', a euphemism that Rammanohar Lohia popularized in the 1967 Assembly elections when the Congress was completely routed in the Hindi heartland and West Bengal.[100]

Decline of the majoritarian ideology

The Hindutva brigade championing 'the majoritarian' claim thus seems to have lost 'its cutting edge', as the outcome of the 2004 national poll demonstrates.[101] Even for sustaining the national coalition government that came into being in 1999, the BJP, which drew on the Hindu nationalist agenda, had to considerably dilute its ideological fascination to cement a bond among the ideologically incompatible coalition partners. So the growing importance of coalition politics seems to have struck at the very foundation of Hindu nationalism. There is no doubt that, given the well-entrenched socio-political plurality in India, it is almost impossible for any political party with extreme views to capture power independent of partners. The National Democratic Alliance (NDA) was perhaps a powerful public statement on 'the non-threatening image of Hindutva'[102] that was largely 'cultural' and less 'political', as Subrata Mitra has shown in analysing the policies towards the minorities, especially the Muslims. Once in governance, the BJP, for instance, found it politically expedient to continue with the *Haj* subsidy presumably to change its image as an organization with clear anti-Muslim bias. Similarly, the critical importance of the regional parties in the NDA accounted for its appreciation of federalism as perhaps the most appropriate system of governance that, argues Katharine Adeney, took the constituent states as 'equal partners'.[103] In two areas, however, the BJP succeeded in redefining India's ideological goal in accordance with its priority. By adopting a policy of nuclearization, the NDA sought to carve out a distinct Indian position in the comity of nations.[104] Similarly, the regulated design of school textbooks was also drawn on an ideological motive of imparting a specific kind of knowledge supportive of a world view seeking to evolve 'a nation' on the basis of a majoritarian faith.[105]

Nonetheless, the Hindutva march was halted in the 2004 national poll despite its 'India shining' claim. As studies have shown, the 2004 defeat was not 'about endorsing or rejecting *Hindutva* and fundamentalism but principally about jobs, roads, water and electricity'.[106] The 2004 verdict is an articulation of 'revolt against economic reforms by India's voters'.[107] Furthermore, the decline of the BJP's numerical strength in the national parliament is also attributed to a fundamental difference between the core supporters and the pragmatic office seekers that certainly robbed the party of 'the organized *Sangh Parivar*'[108] responsible for protecting the foundational values of the party. The outcome of the 2007 election in Gujarat is illustrative of a situation when the Narendra Modi-led BJP secured a comfortable win for the party notwithstanding the opposition of its frontal organization, including the RHS and VHP. Whether this is an aberration is debatable, but the poll outcome in Gujarat provides a plausible explanatory framework drawn on individual charisma.

Concluding observations

Democracy survives in India in a reinvented form that is meaningful in a non-western context. Its sustenance presents us with a paradox that lies in the persistence of abysmal poverty along with serious democratic commitments on the part of the poor. There is hardly the well-developed civil society that is critical to democracy and yet democracy is flourishing.[109] By their ritual and seasonal involvement in the democratic process, Indian voters perform the assigned duties in elections. The formation of a minority government with support from other parties without ideological conformity is probably unfolding a new dimension of India's democracy, which puts forward the notion of 'coalition government' as a real possibility. In a subcontinent such as India, which is diverse on various counts, the idea that a single party or a single leader or a single issue will sway the county as a whole does not seem to be practical. Political diversity matching probably with India's multi-religious, multi-linguistic and multi-racial character epitomizes political maturity as well. Although it is still uncertain whether the process manifested in the election will form a pattern, it has nonetheless effected changes in India's political arithmetic: at one level, the process has challenged the hegemony of a single party in the constituent states, and has thus contributed to the rise of strong political forces highlighting socio-economic and political issues, relevant to the respective areas; at another, far more significant level, it has brought the state-level political forces to the centre stage of all-India politics and, in the absence of a clear verdict for the government, the ruling party needs to take them into confidence for mere survival.

That India's democracy is passing through a transition is evident from the breakdown of the vote banks, so important in the understanding of the 'Congress system'. One also traces the root of coalition governments to the fractured mandates in both the 1999 and 2004 national polls. This suggests, *inter alia*, the changing social constituencies of the parties. It is thus perfectly possible to conceive of circumstances when a particular social group or class is represented by various political parties. Hence the argument for drawing on 'a stable social base' for a party or a group of parties may not always be tenable. Conversely, it is perfectly logical to challenge the notion of 'traditional vote banks' when several parties are vying for the same vote bank championing more or less similar issues despite 'the ideological differences' among themselves. What is striking is the fact that not all of the parties jostling for social constituencies succeed uniformly and this is where the explanation lies for why one party 'shines' and others do not under specific circumstances. What is germane in this process is perhaps a new conception of democracy, as Rajni Kothari underlines. The gradual erosion of 'traditional vote banks' is certainly symptomatic of 'sustained attack on sources of internal decay and degeneration, [all of which] is reminiscent of the freedom struggle in which liberation and *swaraj* were sought not just from an external power but also from the enemy within'.[110]

What is significant is the vibrant nature of India's democracy, which constantly redefines its domain by throwing up issues of consequence. It is indeed a spectacular achievement unparalleled in known political history. And yet, as Amit Bhaduri laments, it remains 'a grossly flawed achievement'.[111] The failure has been the persistence of mass poverty and destitution even six decades after independence. B. R. Ambedkar, one of the main architects of the Indian Constitution, perhaps foresaw this when he noted that an incongruity between political equality and social and economic inequalities would effectively exclude sections of the populations from the democratic process. He thus expressed his feelings before the Constituent Assembly by stating that:

> on the 26th of January, we are going to enter a life of contradictions. In politics we will have equality and in social and economic life we will have inequality. In politics we will be recognizing the principle of one man one vote. In our social and economic life, we shall, by reason of our social and economic structure, continue to deny the principle of one man one vote. How long shall we continue to live this life of contradictions? How shall we continue to deny equality in our social and economic life? If we continue to deny it for long, we do so only by putting our political democracy in peril. We must remove this contradiction at the earlier possible moment or else those who suffer inequality will blow up the structure of political democracy which this assembly has so laboriously built up.[112]

Yet the political process or processes that make democracy function create a distinct space for various kinds of struggles to seek to correct the imbalance in available economic opportunities. Democracy is a struggle, argues Sunil Khilnani, 'whose protagonists are at once products of ancient habits and of modern ambitions, who have found in democracy a form of action that promises them control over their own destinies'.[113] The democratic process is thus 'the space that becomes available – contracting or expanding – for the range of resistance people are capable of'.[114] So, the functioning of democracy has not resolved the problems of economic imbalances and yet it has given rise to a new kind of 'democratic progress' constrained, of course, by the existent restricting socio-economic circumstances redefining primordial values in typical modern idioms. Electoral participation is certainly a powerful mode that is always being complemented by people's democratic involvement in processes that may not be directly linked with the poll, but may have consequences for its outcome.[115] The Indian model therefore adds new dimensions to theories of democracy. Despite being an aggregative model, the Indian version has also elements of deliberative democracy simply because, even after expressing their preferences through voting, the Indian voters participate in everyday struggles against an encroaching state.

4 Parliamentary federalism

Redefining the Westminster model

The most significant development in India's constitutional history is the consolidation of a parliamentary form of government that broadly corresponds with the Westminster model. What is equally striking is the growth of federalism in India in spite of parliamentary government that, in its classical form, flourished within a unitary system of government. Whereas Britain is identified as a classical model of parliamentary government, the United States is always referred to as an ideal form of federal government. Both these political systems have evolved specific constitutional practices in consonance with their ideological preferences and socio-economic requirements. What largely explains the emergence of specific types of governance in both the United Kingdom and United States is the peculiar historical circumstances in which they emerged as nation-states. In view of a gradual decline of monarchy in Britain, parliament became sovereign, reflecting popular aspirations, articulated through a well-devised system of elective democracy; whereas in the United States the decision of the constituent units to merge for a strong political system led to the rise of a union that held power to sustain the federal arrangement that emerged following the 1787 Philadelphia Conference. This is, however, not to suggest that there is a 'conflict' between parliamentary sovereignty and federalism as theoretical categories. Federalism does not necessarily imply 'divided' sovereignty, incompatible with the notion of parliamentary supremacy, any more than parliamentary government seeks to establish 'unfettered' majority rule. Historically speaking, in framing the Dominion Constitutions (for Australia and Canada) in the early 1900s, 'parliaments' were not made 'supreme'. Instead, it was the Constitution that enjoyed supreme authority, exercised through judicial review (by the Privy Council). This is a common pattern in parliamentary federalism, in which constitutional supremacy is perhaps the most effective device to avoid distortions in majority rule. Historically speaking, Canada was the first federation to incorporate a system of parliamentary responsible government in which the executive and legislature are fused. This combination of a federal and parliamentary system was subsequently adopted in Australia in its 1901 Constitution. The majoritarian character of parliamentary federal institutions has had tremendous impact on the dynamics of federal politics in both Canada and Australia.[1] While the former combined federal and parliamentary institutions, with responsible cabinet government operating at federal and state levels, as a parliamentary federation Australia evolved the institutions and processes of 'executive federalism' presumably because of the well-entrenched British heritage of parliamentary institutions and tradition of executive federalism.[2] The Constituent Assembly while deliberating on the form of government for independent India was in favour of executive federalism, which they presumed was appropriate for a stable political authority. Owing to radical changes in India's political texture in recent times, parliamentary federalism has metamorphosed to a significant extent and the growing importance of constituent states in governance at the national level has created conditions for 'legislative federalism' suggestive of equal and meaningful representation of the units in federal decision-making. It is therefore possible to articulate the story of India's parliamentary federalism as a dialectically constructed politico-constitutional scheme to provide meaningful governance in India that is socio-culturally plural and ideologically heterogeneous. There has thus been a clear shift from a predominantly parliamentary government under the Congress dominance to a considerably federalized system under a multi-party system with coalition government since 1989.

The aim of this chapter is to dwell on the evolution of a peculiar form of constitutional arrangement in India that is both parliamentary and federal at the same time. How did the founding fathers justify 'parliamentary federalism' despite the apparent contradiction between the two? Whereas parliamentary system is conceptually unitary, federalism is diametrically opposite. This is a puzzle that needs to be understood in a specific historical context. The British parliamentary model remained a major reference point to the Indian constitution makers. Federalism seemed to have provided an institutional arrangement to accommodate India's pluralist socio-political character. Despite being conceptually incompatible, the founding fathers were favourably inclined towards parliamentary federalism as perhaps the most appropriate institutional setup for governance in India. Parliamentary federalism is thus a creative institutional response to democratic governance suitable for India's peculiar socio-political milieu. Its resilience can be attributed to a series of adjustment to contextual requirements that built up and also strengthened its capacity to survive in adverse circumstances.

Demystifying the Indian polity

India has a hybrid system of government. The hybrid system combines two classical models: the British traditions, drawn upon parliamentary sovereignty and conventions, and American principles upholding the supremacy of a written constitution, the separation of powers and judicial review. The two models are contradictory since parliamentary sovereignty and constitutional supremacy are incompatible. India has distinct imprints in her constitution of both the British and American principles. In other words, following the adoption of the 1950 Constitution, India has evolved a completely different politico-constitutional arrangement with characteristics from both the British and American constitutional practices. The peculiarity lies in the fact that, despite being parliamentary, the Indian political arrangement does not wholly correspond with the British system simply because it has adopted the federal principles as well; it can never be completely American since parliament in India continues to remain sovereign. As a hybrid political system, India has contributed to a completely different politico-constitutional arrangement, described as 'parliamentary federalism', with no parallel in the history of the growth of a constitution.[3] Based on both parliamentary practices and federal principles, the political system in India is therefore a conceptual riddle underlining the hitherto unexplored dimensions of socio-political history of nation-states imbibing the British traditions and American principles. At the time of the framing of the Constitution, political institutions were chosen with utmost care. In their zeal to create a 'modern' India, the founding fathers seem to have neglected traditions entirely, taking the typical Enlightenment view of treating those values and practices as 'erroneous'. They also wrongly held the view that 'to rescue people from tradition, their intellectual and practical habitats, all that was needed was simply to present a modern option; people's inherent rationality would do the rest'.[4] As the actual political experience in India demonstrates, this was not the case and traditions reappear in various different forms in the political articulation of democracy. Thus, instead of disappearing with the introduction of elections based on universal suffrage, both caste and religion, for instance, continue to cement the bond among the voters both during the poll and afterwards. The principal argument that this chapter seeks to articulate is concerned with the complexity of the processes that finally led to the formation of a hybrid political system, influenced heavily by both the British tradition and American principles. In trying to understand the current complexities and future prospects of Indian political system, looking to European and American precedents is not therefore enough. Instead, it is necessary to understand the historical logic internal to this process. Given the ingrained constitutional peculiarities and their evolution, this chapter further underlines the importance of historical circumstances and socio-economic and cultural distinctiveness in shaping India's political system following the transfer of power in 1947.

Some theoretical inputs

The Westminster model is based on the sovereignty of parliament and the supremacy of the law of the land. As A. V. Dicey argues, 'the principle of Parliamentary Sovereignty means . . . that Parliament has, under the English constitution, the right to make or unmake any law whatever. [Furthermore] there is no person or body of persons who can, under the English constitution, make rules which override or derogate from an Act of Parliament or which . . . will be enforced by the courts in contravention of an Act of Parliament'.[5] There is no doubt, as Dicey underlines, that parliament, comprising the Queen, the House of Lords and the House of Commons, cannot be challenged even by the law courts because it is sovereign. In the concluding chapter of his *The Law of the Constitution,* Dicey reiterates that '[b]y every path we come round to the same conclusion that

Parliamentary sovereignty has favoured the rule of law, and that the supremacy of the law of the land both calls forth the exertion of Parliamentary sovereignty, and leads to its being exercised in a spirit of legality'.[6]

According to Dicey, parliamentary sovereignty and federalism are irreconcilable. The supremacy of parliament is ascertained by the fact that 'no person or body is recognised by the law of England as having a right to over-rule or set aside the legislation of Parliament'. Federalism, in Dicey's conceptualization, posits two sets of governmental authorities 'which were legally coordinate and a supreme constitution authoritatively interpreted by the courts'. As he argues,

> [a] federal state is a political contrivance intended to reconcile national unity and power with the maintenance of 'state rights'. The end aimed at fixing the essential character of federalism, for the method by which federalism attempts to reconcile the apparently inconsistent claims of national sovereignty and of state sovereignty consists of the formation of a constitution under which the ordinary powers of sovereignty are elaborately divided between the common or national government and the separate states . . . . Whatever concerns the nation as a whole, should be placed under the control of national government. All matters, which are not primarily of common interest, should remain in the hands of several states.[7]

Once the above principle is conceded, the governmental authority is federal. Under this constitutional arrangement, parliament is subservient to a written constitution, upheld by an independent judiciary. Dicey thus concludes:

> [f]rom the notion that national unity can be reconciled with state independence by a division of powers under a common constitution between the nation on the one hand and the individual States on the other, flow the three leading characteristics of completely developed federalism, – the supremacy of the constitution, the distribution among bodies with limited and coordinate authority of the different powers of government [and] the authority of the courts to act as interpreters of the constitution.[8]

What Dicey suggests is reinforced by Arend Lijphart. Underlining that the Westminster model of fusion of power within the cabinet is an inappropriate style of government for countries with wide geographical, cultural and linguistic differences, Lijphart argues for consensus models as the best possible options for pluralistic societies. In his opinion, not only does the consensus model 'establish constraints on majorities . . . but also preserve and affirm the rights of minorities'. Based on his theorization of 'consociational democracy', he further argues that 'the approach is not to abolish or weaken segmental cleavages but to recognize them explicitly and to turn the segments into constructive elements of stable democracy'.[9] While elaborating the model, Lijphart identifies the following features:

(a) executive power-sharing and grand coalitions; (b) separation of powers, formal and informal; (c) balance bicameralism and minority representation; (d) a multi-party system; (e) a multi-dimensional party system (a mix of parties which are distinguished one from another on many different bases, including ideology, geographical base, cultural and ethnic communication, class etc.); (f) proportional representation; (g) territorial and non-territorial federalism and decentralization; (h) written constitution and minority veto.[10]

Based on the premise that 'political power should be dispersed and shared in a variety of ways', Lijphart also warns that the consensus model 'is a more difficult model to apply than the simpler majoritarian model [though] it contains the great advantage that the consensus model can be adapted to suit the special needs of particular countries [by providing] the constitutional engineers the option of building onto existing legitimate traditions'.[11] For the Westminster model to strike roots in a diverse society, federalism seems to be most appropriate political arrangement for two important reasons. On the one hand, federal principles ensure segmental autonomy by formally recognizing the importance of the segments for the whole; they also, on the other, firmly establish the relative strength of the constituent units that can be undermined only at the peril of the federal state. For Lijphart, federalism is not merely a device of multi-layer governance, it is also 'a consociational method' by which a plural society can be organized in such a way as to meaningfully implement parliamentary federalism. What is significant in Lijphart's formulation is a clear possibility of the growth of an institutional structure drawing upon the British traditions of parliamentary democracy and federal principles. In other words, parliamentary federalism is a hybrid structure of governance and probably a unique constitutional arrangement to ascertain 'segmental autonomy'. As a hybrid system, it has features that are contingent on the socio-economic environment in which it strikes roots. So, the Indian political system is unique, as is its Canadian counterpart, with distinct features articulating the peculiar unfolding of its politico-constitutional structure that has roots in colonialism as well.

Nature of the Indian Union: the constitutional inputs

Owing to peculiar historical circumstances, the consensus that emerged in the Constituent Assembly was in favour of a union with a strong centre.[12] Arguments were marshalled for a parliamentary form of government and the colonial experience was a constant reference point. In devising the Union–State relations, the founding fathers were influenced by the principles underlying the Constitutions of Canada and Australia, which had parliamentary federalism, and the United States, which had a presidential system. The 1935 Government of India Act seems to have influenced the Assembly to a large extent though the 1950 Constitution was substantially different in spirit and ideology. As it finally emerged, the Constitution has important 'federal' features but cannot be characterized as federal in its classical sense. It is a unique document, which is, as Ambedkar had articulated, 'unitary in extra-ordinary circumstances such as war and other calamities and federal under normal circumstances'. Hence, India is described as 'a union of states' where the union is 'indestructible' but not the constituent states because their contour and identity can be 'altered' or even 'obliterated'. There emerged a consensus and the Assembly rejected a motion seeking to characterize India as 'a federation of states'. Challenging the motion, Ambedkar sought to expose the logical weaknesses and practical difficulties of imitating the classical federation such as the US by saying that,

> though India was to be a federation, the federation was not the result of an agreement by the States to join in a federation, and that the federation not being the result of an agreement, no State has the right to secede from it. The Federation is a Union because it is indestructible. Though the country and the people may be divided into different States for convenience of administration, the country is one integral whole, its people a single people living under a single *imperium* derived from a single source. The Americans had to wage a civil war to establish that the States have no right of secession and that their federation was indestructible. The Drafting Committee thought that it was better to make it clear at the outset rather than to leave it to speculation or to disputes.[13]

So federalism as a constitutional principle was articulated differently because of the historical context in which the Constitution was made. The Constituent Assembly, Jawaharlal Nehru and Vallabhbhai Patel in particular, 'worried that a more potent federalism in India would weaken feelings of national unity in the country and would make it harder for governments in the Centre to push ahead with the "social revolution" that was needed to secure economic development'.[14] As evident in the discussion in the Constituent Assembly, the framers refereed mainly to two traditions: the British and the American. But in the background was always a third stream – understandably downplayed by Ambedkar and other members – the ideas of Ian Coupland and K. C. Wheare, who appeared to have provided the foundational basis of the constitutional experiments in the British Dominions. It is, after all, to the 1935 Government of India Act that we owe not only the federal structure and the legislative acts, but also the continuance of the unified legal and financial systems, and such distinctive features as group rights, machinery for resolution of inter-state water disputes, state governors and Article 356. There had of course been strong opposition to the 'federal' provisions of the 1935 Act that envisaged the future accession of the princes, including the right of secession that figured unambiguously in the 1942 Cripps Mission proposals. The 1946 Cabinet Mission also endorsed the plan for a central government with very limited powers and relatively strong provinces having a considerable degree of autonomy with all the residuary powers. Despite inputs supporting a weak centre, the 1950 Constitution provided a scheme of distribution of power that was heavily tilted in favour of a strong centre. The decision to go for a strong centre even at the cost of regional autonomy was perhaps conditioned by pragmatic considerations of maintaining national integrity that received a severe jolt with the acceptance of partition.[15] Ambedkar echoed this feeling in his final report of the Union Powers Committee of the Constituent Assembly by saying that 'it would be injurious to the interests of the country to provide for a weak central authority which could be incapable of ensuring peace [and also] of coordinating vital matters of common concern'. Hence he was in favour of a strong Centre, 'much stronger than the Centre we had created under the Government of India Act of 1935'.[16] What determined the choice of the founding fathers was their concern for the unity and integrity of India. As Lokananth Mishra argued, 'it has been our desire and it has been the soul of the birth of freedom and our resurgence that we must go towards unity in spite of all the diversity that has divided us'.[17] The word 'federal' was therefore deliberately omitted in the final draft of the Constitution and India was defined as 'a union of states'. Nonetheless, the constitution endorsed the federal principle in 'recognition' of the multi-dimensional socio-political and geographical Indian reality by clearly demarcating the constitutional domain of the constituent states within the union. It is clear that the framers of the Constitution were in favour of a federation with a strong centre. To avoid friction between the centre and the constituent states in future, the Constitution incorporated an elaborate distribution of governmental powers – legislative, administrative and financial – between the Union and provincial governments. Despite a detailed distribution of power between the two levels of government, the Union government is constitutionally stronger simply because the framers wanted it so.

Parliament in India

In the history of India's constitutional development, the idea of parliamentary sovereignty was pre-eminent despite Gandhi's characterization of parliament as 'a prostitute'. In fact, Gandhi's intervention in the debate led to a search for an indigenous model of governance, more suited to the Indian traditions.[18] It had no imprint however in either the 1916 Lucknow pact or the 1928 Nehru Report. In the latter, an argument was made to defend 'the Dominion model of Parliament . . . and an executive responsible to that Parliament'. As the Report further underlines, 'what India wants and what Britain has undertaken to give her, is nothing less than Responsible Government [and] the assimilated tradition of England has become the basis of Indian thought' in this regard.[19]

The Nehru Report seems to have provided the foundation on which the discussion on India's constitutional future was based. Replacing the old central legislature, the Constituent Assembly, elected by members of Provincial Assemblies, it was to be a temporary legislature as well as framer of the future.[20] A brief scan of the debates on this question is useful to understand how the idea of parliamentary sovereignty was articulated by those who appeared to have been heavily influenced by the British tradition. Seeking to draw their attention to other constitutions, B. R. Ambedkar, the Chairman of the Drafting Committee, underlined, 'we have to look to countries other than Britain to be able to form a correct estimate of the position of a Constituent Assembly. I have no doubt [that] you will pay . . . greater attention to the provisions of the American Constitution than to those of any other'.[21] Apart from Ambedkar's prefacing remarks, the Objective Resolution, moved by Jawaharlal Nehru, had cast influence on the shape of the 1950 constitution. Nehru was unambiguous in his preference for a political system drawing its sustenance from people by saying that 'all power and authority of the sovereign Independent India, its constituent parts and organs of government are derived from the people'. What follows from this, as Nehru further argues, is that 'we stand for democracy [but] what form of democracy and what shape it might take is another matter . . . for this House to determine'.[22]

The Objective Resolution and Ambedkar's inaugural address continued to remain decisive in the deliberations on the making of India's constitution. The most clearly spelt-out argument in favour of parliamentary government was made in the reports of the two committees set up (in April 1947) to determine 'the principles of a Model Provincial Constitution' and 'the Principles of the Union Constitution'. Introducing the reports in Assembly, Patel clearly expressed that the members of those Committees 'came to the conclusion that it would suit the conditions of this country better to adopt the parliamentary system of constitution, the British type of constitution with which we are familiar. . . . The Provincial Constitution Committee has accordingly suggested that this constitution shall be a parliamentary type of cabinet.'[23] Endorsing Patel's sentiment, N. V. Gadgil, a member of the committee that determined the principles of the Union Constitution, argued that 'we have been brought up in an atmosphere which has been conducive to the establishment of what are generally accustomed to term Parliamentary Responsible Government. . . . The system of government in Britain must be followed here. That system could not be blamed for the strife in India; in fact, the trouble was that the system had, properly speaking, not yet been put in operation in India.'[24] As parliament was to be elected by adult suffrage, the Muslim members were critical of the reports, apprehending that the parliamentary sovereignty of the British type would invariably lead to 'the oppression of minorities' by the majority. What was articulated as the Muslim opinion was also fractured. Reflecting the general mood of the Assembly and also the division among its Muslim members, Hussain Imam seems to have been persuaded by the arguments in favour of parliamentary government. He thus confessed that 'opinion in India is so much in favour of the British model and that it is not practical politics to try to sing the praises' of other systems.[25] The reports were accepted as they were though the discussion in the Assembly clearly shows a clear division among its members.[26]

By November, 1947, the Draft Constitution was ready. Presenting it to the Assembly, Ambedkar identified its basic characteristics by announcing that:

> [t]here is nothing in common between the form of government prevalent in America and that proposed under the Draft Constitution. . . . What the Draft Constitution proposes is the Parliamentary system. . . . The president of the Indian Union will be generally bound by the advice of his Ministers . . . and the Ministers are members of Parliament. . . . The daily assessment of

responsibility which is not available under the American system is, it is felt, far more effective than the periodic assessment, and far more necessary in a country like India.[27]

Drawing on the Westminster model of democracy, Ambedkar elaborated the structure of the proposed form of governance in which parliament reigned supreme. The model seemed to be most suitable in India since 'experience with quasi-parliamentary institutions had become an essential part of Indian conditions'.[28] K. M. Munshi was more categorical when reinforcing Ambedkar's argument in favour of parliamentary government. 'We must not forget a very important fact', argued Munshi,

> that during the last one hundred years Indian public life has largely drawn on the traditions of English constitutional law. . . . For the last thirty or forty years some kind of responsibility has been introduced in the governance of this country. Our constitutional traditions have become parliamentary, and we have now all our provinces functioning more or less on the British model. . . . After this experience, why should we go back upon the traditions that have been built for over a hundred years and try a novel experiment framed 150 years ago and found wanting even in America?[29]

As is evident, there are two specific types of arguments to support the parliamentary form of government. First, given the experience of quasi-parliamentary institutions in India under the British rule, the founding fathers thought it appropriate to retain the system, suitably amended to fulfill free India's politico-constitutional goal; second, parliamentary government provides for a constant watch on the individual ministers through the principle of collective responsibility, which is completely absent under the American system. Although Ambedkar and his colleagues were persuaded,[30] the Gandhians characterized the adoption of parliamentary government as 'a slavish imitation of, nay much more, a slavish surrender to the West'[31] since the basic ideals on which the constitution was based 'have no manifest relation to the fundamental spirit of India'.[32] As Loknath Mishra laments, 'the objective resolution envisaged a federal constitution . . . [b]ut the Draft Constitution . . . is laying the foundation more for a formidable unitary constitution than a federal one. . . . [T]his constitution does give nothing to the individual, nothing to the family, nothing to the villages, nothing to the districts, and nothing to the provinces. Dr. Ambedkar has taken everything to the Centre.'[33] 'We wanted the music of Veena or Sitar', argued another member, 'but here we have the music of an English band.'[34] Even Ambedkar was accused of completely bypassing Indian values and traditions. A member pronounced that, 'if you look at the constitution, . . . it would be difficult for you to find anything Indian . . . . The British have departed but I regret to say that our countrymen have not [given up] the ways of their former masters. We will experience much more difficulty in bidding goodbye to the ways of the British than we experienced in bidding goodbye to the British themselves.'[35] One may sum up the arguments by quoting a perceptive remark of W. H. Morris-Jones, who, while seeking to grasp the organic roots of the Westminster model of parliamentary democracy in India, attributed the adoption of this form in independent India to 'an ideological commitment of many of India's rulers to the Westminster model'. The dedication is determined by the need 'to disprove . . . the old allegation that India could not be a home for responsible government' and 'the attachment to the institution' due to its historical existence in India was too strong to ignore.[36] Despite its imperial origin, parliamentary democracy of the Westminster variety emerged, thus goes the argument, as the best possible option for the nation because of 'the attachment to the familiar', which was more a matter of 'habit' than anything else.

The role of Rajya Sabha: a think tank or the states' voice?

That the framers were favourably inclined towards a strong centre is evident by the constitutionally guaranteed status of the second chamber of India's Parliament, the Rajya Sabha.[37] The composition and functions of the Rajya Sabha were designed to subserve the following purposes:

> (a) to secure, for the legislative process at the Union level, the thinking and guidance of mature and experienced persons, popularly known as 'the elders' who are disinclined to get involved in active politics and contest in direct elections to the Lok Sabha; (b) to enable the state to give effective expression to their viewpoints at the parliamentary level; (c) to ensure some degree of continuity in the policies underlying parliamentary legislation; and (d) to function as a House of Parliament which would more or less be coordinate with the Lok Sabha, with safeguards for speedy resolution of any conflicts between the two Houses on legislation.[38]

A perusal of the debates in the Constituent Assembly on the provisions relating to the second chamber reveals unanimity among the founding fathers. The Rajya Sabha was conceptualized as a second chamber providing 'checks and balances' to the functioning of parliamentary democracy in India. As Gopalaswamy Ayyangar characterized the Rajya Sabha:

> The most that we expect . . . the Second Chamber to do is perhaps to . . . hold dignified debates on important issues and to delay legislation which might be the outcome of passions of the moment until the passions have subsided and calm consideration could be bestowed on the measures which will be before the Legislature . . . this Second Chamber is only an instrument by which we delay action which might be hastily conceived and we also give an opportunity perhaps, to seasoned people who may not be in the thickest of the political fray, who might be willing to participate in the debate with an amount of learning and importance which we do not ordinarily associate with a House of People.[39]

Besides its traditional functions, Rajya Sabha as a second chamber has, as Morris-Jones articulates, 'three outweighing merits': (a) it supplies additional political positions for which there is demand, (b) it provides some additional debating opportunities for which there is occasionally need and (c) it assists in the solution of legislative timetable problems.[40] The Rajya Sabha was thus a 'watchdog' of the processes that usually inform the parliamentary system of government. Its role was that of 'a facilitator' and not 'a clog either to legislation or administration'.[41]

Apart from twelve nominated members, the members of the Rajya Sabha are representatives of the states, elected by the elected members of the legislative assemblies. As they are chosen on the basis of elections in which only the elected members of the assemblies participate, they represent a fair cross-section of the views of the parties elected to the State Legislative Assembly. Given its composition and the way it is formed, the Rajya Sabha becomes an instrument for the effective expression at the parliamentary level of the viewpoints of the states.

The Rajya Sabha is not as federal in character as the US Senate simply because the constituent states do not have equal representation in this second chamber. In the Constituent Assembly, drawing upon the practice in the US and Australia, an amendment was suggested to ensure that each state should elect five members to the Rajya Sabha by adult suffrage.[42] The amendment was not carried forward because it was not practicable to implement a uniform rule for all the Indian states when they are not uniform in area and demographic strength. Furthermore, unlike the constituent states that made up the USA in 1789, the British Indian provinces were not independent before India was decolonized. Hence, the Rajya Sabha 'was not envisaged to function primarily as a Federal Chamber of the classical type like the Senate of the USA'.[43] The Rajya Sabha was weakened by the decision that in case of a conflict with the lower chamber on a Money Bill the view of the Lok Sabha would prevail.

It is now evident that the Rajya Sabha in the 1950 Constitution is not a federal chamber in its classical sense. Its primary function is to coordinate with the Lok Sabha in discharging the parliamentary legislative functions. Only under circumstances, as stipulated in Articles 249 and 312, the Rajya Sabha supported by not fewer than two-thirds of the members present and voting is empowered to authorize the parliament to make laws with respect to any matter in the State List. For all practical purposes, the lower house enjoys 'hegemonic' powers and the upper chamber's authority is generally confined to ratifying the decisions already taken in the Lok Sabha. There are however occasions when the Rajya Sabha acted tough with the Lower House. Its partisanship was, for instance, demonstrated during the brief Janata interlude (1977–80) when the Congress-dominated Rajya Sabha thwarted a government-initiated constitutional amendment by refusing to endorse the move, for which a two-thirds affirmative vote was required. This is most likely to happen nowadays since the Congress has a majority in the Rajya Sabha and therefore there is no guarantee the elders shall approve that whatever is passed in the Lok Sabha, whereas in the days before 1967 the Rajya Sabha had hardly a significant role except to corroborate the views expressed in the Lower House. Following the installation of non-Congress governments in various states since 1967, the upper chamber seems to have acquired a definite, if not completely new, role in the governing processes.[44] Despite its growing importance due to peculiar circumstances, the changes in the composition of the Rajya Sabha will hardly make any difference simply because of the constitutional provisions supporting the role of the centre in radically altering the territorial boundaries of the constituent states that, in consequence, will have an immediate impact on the number of representatives for the Upper House. Furthermore, an amendment adopted in 2003 led to two basic changes in the election to the Rajya Sabha by (a) introducing open ballot and displacing secret voting and (b) removing the residential qualification for the candidate. Both these changes seem to be an affront on the democratic processes that go with the election. With the abolition of the secret ballot, election in the Rajya Sabha will be a farce and the party with a majority in the house will always be decisive in deciding the fate of a bill. The withdrawal of the residential qualification will weaken the representative character of this second chamber because anybody can be elected to the Rajya Sabha regardless of whether the candidate belongs to the state from which he/she is seeking election. Hence it has been sarcastically argued in the media that Council of States has become Council of Nominees.[45]

Federalism in India

The classical federations, such as the USA, Australia and Canada, are the outcome of the 'coming together' syndrome because the existing sovereign polities voluntarily enter into an agreement to pool their sovereignty in a federation, whereas most of the contemporary federations are illustrative of 'holding together' federations due to circumstances in which the centre agreed to 'devolve' power to hold the federal units together. India is a good example of this category because the Constituent Assembly, despite having defended a strong centre to contain lawlessness immediately after independence, was clearly in favour of decentralization of political authority as a clear guarantee for 'holding' India together.[46] As B. R. Ambedkar argued, 'the chief mark of federalism lies in the partition of the legislative and executive authority [and] between the centre and units of the constitution' though the constitution can be federal or unitary according to the requirements of time and circumstances. Yet the centre 'cannot, by its own will, alter the boundary of that partition. Nor can the judiciary . . . [because it] cannot assign to one authority powers explicitly granted to another.'[47] Generally speaking, whether a political system is federal is determined by these five criteria:

(a) dual or two sets of government – one at the centre, national or federal, and the other at state or provincial level;
(b) written constitution – list of distribution of powers, though the residuary powers generally rest with the federal government;
(c) supremacy of the constitution;
(d) rigidity of the constitution – the constitution can be amended by a special majority followed by ratification by at least half of the states, barring 'the basic structure' of the constitution;
(e) the authority of the courts as regards the interpretation of the constitutional provisions.

In the light of the above criteria, there was no doubt that the founding fathers preferred federalism in its true spirit and yet what emerged after the deliberations in the Constituent Assembly was a unique form, adapted to the Indian context. As Ambedkar argued, the draft constitution contained provisions that provide for both federal and unitary forms of government. 'In normal times, it is framed to work as a federal system', stated Ambedkar. But in times of war 'it is so designed as to make it work as though it was a unitary system. Once the President issues a Proclamation which he [*sic*] is authorized to do under the Provisions of Article 275, the whole scene can become transformed and the State becomes a unitary state.'[48] Ambedkar showed extreme caution when defending provisions for federalism. There was no doubt in his mind that Indian federalism was to be adapted to 'the local needs and local circumstances'. But this very diversity, 'when it goes beyond a certain point, is capable of producing chaos'. Hence '[t]he Draft Constitution has', argued Ambedkar, 'sought to forge means and methods whereby India will have Federation and at the same time will have uniformity in all the basic matters which are essential to maintain the unity of the country.' Three important means of holding the country together were thus identified: (a) a single judiciary, (b) uniformity in fundamental laws, civil and criminal, and (c) a common All India Civil Service to man important posts.[49]

There is no doubt that the founding fathers took great care in creating a constitutional arrangement that is 'federal' in a very specific sense. The system that emerged in India was hardly comparable with any of the extant federations. What was critical in their vision was perhaps the fact that federalism is not merely a structural arrangement for distribution and sharing of power between the federal partners, it is also a culture sustaining its very spirit. Its emergence and later consolidation in India is slightly paradoxical since it is the product of two conflicting cultures: one representing the national leaders' 'normative' concern for India's multicultural personality, shaped by its unique history and geography, and the other underlining their concern for unity, security and administrative efficiency. Whereas the former led to the articulation of federalism, as laid down in the 1950 Constitution, the latter resulted in the retention of the very state machinery that had consolidated the colonial rule in India. The net result was the articulation of a semi-hegemonic federal structure that drew largely upon the 1935 Government of India Act. Nonetheless, the federal system that supported unwarranted centralization of power appeared to be the most suitable option for nation-building in India. However, the situation radically changed following the articulation of new demands by hitherto peripheral socio-political groups. The aim here is to grasp the processes that contributed to this significant metamorphosis of India's federal system in the context of constantly changing domestic and global situation.

The federal arrangement: its evolution

The British colonial rule introduced federalism in phases partly in response to the nationalist demand for decentralization of power and partly to implement the liberal principle of 'self rule' in colonies. Despite its organic roots in colonialism, federalism was also an outcome of the growing democratization in India that the Gandhi-led nationalist movement facilitated. In short, the legacy of colonialism, partition and the vision of nation-building all contrived to create a centralized federation that hardly corresponds with its classical form. Two major constitutional inputs from the colonial past seem to be critical in the evolution of federalism in India. First, the 1918 Montague–Chelmsford Report on constitutional reforms and later the 1929 Simon Commission Report strongly argued for decentralization of authorities among the constituent provinces as perhaps the best administrative device in 'politically-fragmented and strife-ridden India'. In its report, the Simon Commission made a strong plea for a federal constitution by stating that 'the ultimate Constitution of India must be federal, for it is only in a federal constitution that units differing so widely . . . can be brought together while retaining internal autonomy'.[50] The second serious intervention happened to be the 1935 Government of India Act, which provided for the distribution of legislative jurisdictions with the threefold division of powers into federal, provincial and concurrent lists. The Act also led to the establishment of a federal court to adjudicate the disputes between units of the federation and also the appellate court to decide on the constitutional questions. On the fiscal front, the Act provided a detailed scheme of sharing of revenue that, in fact, laid the foundation of fiscal federalism in independent India.

Whereas for the colonial ruler federalism was politically expedient, for the nationalist it emerged as possibly the best constitutional arrangement for the country, which was socio-politically so disparate. The Congress developed its own federal scheme, being organized on linguistic lines. As early as 1928, the Indian National Congress unanimously decided in favour of regrouping of provinces 'on a linguistic basis [since] language as a rule corresponds with a special variety of culture of traditions and literature. In a linguistic area all these factors will help in the general progress of the province.' The second equally important consideration 'is the wishes of the majority of the people [because] people living in a particular area feel that they are a unit and desire to develop their culture . . . even though there may be no sufficient historical or cultural justification for their demand. . . . [A third consideration], though not of the same importance, is administrative convenience, which would include the geographical position, the economic resources and the financial stability of the area concerned. But the administrative convenience is often a matter of arrangement and *must as a rule bow to the wishes of the people*.'[51] What is striking in this 1928 report is the fact that the pluralist character of the Indian polity was a significant determinant in devising a constitutional arrangement for the country. The Congress leadership seemed to be appreciative of this principle and thus endorsed regional grouping on the basis of distinct cultural traits, including language.

With the above perspective in mind, let us dwell on the actual federal structure of governance as it evolved immediately after the transfer of power. For B. R. Ambedkar, the choice was categorical since

the draft constitution is a Federal Constitution in as much as it establishes . . .
Dual Polity [with] the Union at the centre and the States at the periphery, each
being assigned with sovereign powers to be exercised in the field assigned to
them respectively by the Constitution. The States in our Constitution are in
no way dependent upon the Centre for their legislative and executive authority. [T]he Centre and the States are co-equal in this matter. [I]t is therefore
wrong to say that the States have been placed under the Centre.[52]

Ambedkar's clear preference for a specific type of federal polity did not match
with the provisions of the 1950 Constitution, which were heavily tilted in favour
of the 1935 Government of India Act.[53] What probably conditioned the choice of
those who presided over free India's destiny was a pragmatic consideration of
transforming India into 'a Union out of the patch work quilt of [British Indian]
Provinces and Princely States'.[54] Given the large number of princely states that
enjoyed paramountcy during the colonial rule, the task of bringing them under
the union was difficult. Moreover, the decision of the Muslim majority provinces
of British India to constitute themselves into Pakistan aroused the apprehension
in the minds of the nationalist leadership in India that they might have to face
further attempts at secession from a future Indian union. As a result of this fear,
'the Gandhian notion of a truly decentralised and federal India did not receive the
serious attention in the debate on the Constitution which it otherwise deserved'.[55]
However, the very apprehensions that produced a desire for stronger central authority also led to a counter-tendency in the form of demands from several states
for greater autonomy. There were also members drawing inspiration from 'the
Gandhian tradition for greater decentralization of institutions . . . down to the
district and village level' who pressed hard for greater autonomy of the states as a
precaution against the growth of an authoritarian centre.[56]

There is another distinctive feature that clearly separates Indian federation
from its counterparts elsewhere. Indian federalism is a distinct case of 'asymmetrical' federalism, which characterizes a federation in which some of the units
are accorded weightage under the imperative of compelling historical or cultural
factors necessitating 'special constitutional recognition'. One comes across four
kinds of asymmetries in Indian federation. First, there is universal asymmetry
with regard to the constituent provinces because they are represented in the Rajya
Sabha on the basis of their demographic strength, unlike the American system
in which each state has two members in the Senate regardless of the strength of
population. Second, there are specific asymmetries as regards administration of
tribal areas, inter-state regional disparities, the law and order situation and fix-
ing the number of seats, as per Article 371 of the Constitution, in states such
as Maharashtra, Gujarat, Manipur, Assam, Andhra Pradesh, Arunachal Pradesh,
Sikkim and Goa. Third, the areas identified as Union Territories – seven in 2006
– enjoy special constitutional status. Finally, there is a stark asymmetry vis-à-vis
Jammu and Kashmir, Nagaland and Mizoram. While Article 370 accords 'special
status' to Jammu and Kashmir, Article 371 guarantees special privileges to Nagaland and Mizoram.[57]

As the discussion shows, Indian federalism, or for that matter any constitutional arrangement, is contextual and is thus relative to the polity in which it has evolved over a period of time. T. T. Krishnamachari, a member of the Constituent Assembly, thus argued that federalism 'is not a definite concept; it has not got any stable meaning. It is a concept the definition of which has been changing from time to time.'[58] Hence it is theoretically misleading and empirically wrong to characterize Indian federalism in a simple strait-jacketed formula. As a constitutional format, federalism is constantly reinvented and the governing principles are thus regularly redefined. In recent times, the federalization process has been augmented by the more active role of the new incumbents of federal institutions – the President, the Election Commission and the Supreme Court of India. The President and the Election Commission have become more watchful to ensure that the rules of the game in their restrictive constitutional jurisdictions are respected by the political and administrative authorities.

The Congress system

One of the factors that supported parliamentary federalism, as conceptualized by the framers of the constitution, was what is popularly described as 'the Congress system',[59] which thrived thanks largely to a homogeneous elite in roles of authority and decision making. In a functional sense, the Congress system was a mechanism of integrating new elites through vertical linkages in the existing 'spoils system' by assigning each new elite a place in the queue for leadership within each layer that produces a system of alternation between layers at different levels of the organization. In this way, the new elites were accommodated by 'distributing and subdividing probabilities of obtaining posts, rather than expanding the number of posts itself'.[60] The old Nehruvian order had provided a unique model of integration based on a coalition of diverse interests that the Congress Party had represented in the decades following independence. It was possible, argued Ravinder Kumar, because out of the mass aspiration for social and economic change Jawaharlal Nehru, the first Prime Minister of India, shaped a working coalition of social classes and communities that enabled Congress to dominate national politics for two decades and more. The coalition succeeded because it 'rested upon a discourse that entrusted largely to the State the responsibility of promoting the social and economic welfare of the people'.[61] Rajni Kothari described the Congress system as a huge, hierarchically structured party, broadly rooted throughout the countryside, apparently providing a mechanism whereby a plurality of elites, sub-elites and groups could both voice their claims and attempt to realize them. At the same time, Congress could adequately mediate and settle these multiple and often conflicting claims. If necessary, the Congress High Command could intervene to seal the final bargain. Within this system, the range of social groups represented in the ruling party was considered its most positive feature, making it possible for the opposition parties to forge links with like-minded Congress factions. Furthermore, two factors that appear to have strengthened the system were (a) the practice of intra-party democracy, and (b) socially rooted party and political leaders at the state and district levels. Broadly speaking, on account of its organizational strength, its ideological flexibility and its umbrella character as a broad social coalition, the Congress Party remained perhaps the most formidable electoral force, which reduced the elections to a process of confirming its popularity till at least 1967. One of the reasons for its long-term viability was probably the success of the post-independence political process in bringing wide sections of society within the political arena and exposing traditional and emerging elites to both 'the pedagogy and the practice of a democratic polity wedded to an egalitarian ideology'.[62] Underlying this, as the argument proceeds, lay the reasons for the relatively smooth functioning of federalism, which was never seriously threatened probably because of an effective mechanism of political communication involving various actors at different levels of the Indian polity.[63]

Like all ideal types, this schematic picture of consensual politics under the Congress system appeared to be divorced from a much more complex reality that was characterized by, *inter alia*, very low levels of political awareness among the lower castes and poor classes. With the continuation of the major political institutions that held the colonial power even after independence, it is, in fact, plausible to argue that politics in the Nehru era as a whole is basically 'a continuum with the Raj'. Whatever social configurations the Congress Party confronted in the various provinces, 'its leader, like the British before them, did not attempt to change the social order but to adapt to it'.[64] Furthermore, it is probably justified to argue that Indian politics in the first two decades after decolonization was built on a kind of consensus based primarily on elite accommodation. The system passed uncontested 'because of its nearness to the mobilization of the national movement, and the relation of implicit trust between its leadership and the masses'. It was a consensus of 'discourse rather than ideological positions'.[65] Soon after Nehru's demise, the system started breaking down – a process that became evident especially from 1969 onwards when Nehru's successor, Indira Gandhi, faced with increasing opposition strength, 'rejected the principle of consensus in favour of the majoritarian principle'.[66] Since she carried the masses with her, she ignored the party, which had lost its democratic mainspring. Furthermore, the choice of candidates by the leaders at the upper echelons of the party hierarchy made regional leadership absolutely redundant. As a result, most elected representatives became 'easy prey of party factions, various socio-economic groups with vested interest in influencing government policies in key areas in which they have vital stakes, money and muscle'.[67] The centralization of power within party's top leadership 'weakened the regional roots . . . [and] regional demands were no longer filtered through party channels, but began to be asserted with rising irritation against the central state'.[68] Centralization, which was once considered as 'an instrument of purposive interventions by a cohesive and disciplined elite', soon turned out to be 'suicidal to the prevalent party system and the federal structure and wider affiliations that were built through them'.[69] The outcome was most disastrous because the concentration of power choked the federal system by making the constituent states mere appendages to the centre. There were hardly debates and discussions involving the regional stakeholders, and articulation of regional demands was dismissed as 'anti-national' and as threats to 'national integrity'. Parliament truly became supreme and federalism was a casualty in the heyday of the Congress hegemony after the breakdown of the Congress system.

The deinstitutionalization of the Congress party contributed immensely to the erosion of India's federal system by 'dismantling the party's federal structure'.[70] Not only did this decay lead to a massive concentration of power in the central leadership, it also deprived the party of seasoned national and state party officials. What undermined the system significantly was the conscious endeavour of the top boss within the party to substitute 'loyalists and favourites at state and constituency level for party officials and candidates with local knowledge and support'.[71] Indira Gandhi could afford to ignore the party since she had established 'a direct and unmediated line with the people who had transposed enormous faith in her charisma and her image as deliverer and secular messiah'.[72] During the 1969–77 period, centre–state relations were practically reduced to a state of near non-existence and '[u]nitarism triumphed under the aegis of a strong state whose power was controlled by a ruling party which relied exclusively on its leader for its survival'.[73] The 1975–77 Emergency was probably the most serious affront to federalism since it led to the consolidation of a puissant centre presiding over a federation of thoroughly enfeebled states.[74]

So India's federalism had undergone a paradigmatic shift on the eve of the 1977 national elections, which replaced the Congress Party with a loose-knit Janata coalition representing various, if not contradictory, interests. During the brief interlude of the Janata regime (1977–80), probably because of its other pre-occupations, no serious attempt was made to counter the centripetal tendencies, which had, by then, firm roots in Indian politics. Indira Gandhi's style of functioning completely destroyed internal democracy within the Congress Party. With the disintegration of provincial Congress organizations, the state leaders became mere clients of the central organ of the party. As she became the key to political power and personal gain, there was hardly any challenge to her leadership and the party was reduced to almost a nonentity. The consequence was disastrous. The state tended to ignore the demands of the constituent units and favoured concentration of power simply because those who mattered in political decision making neither questioned centralization nor endeavoured to provide an alternative.

The breakdown of the consensus model led to the rise of various other structures, both political and non-political, that became formidable in the era of mass politics. Despite Nehru's limitation as a statesman, the Congress Party under his tutelage both absorbed new demands and strove to provide avenues for their fulfilment. With the collapse of the party as an effective institution and the inability of the system to create new institutional modes for dealing with newer demands, there emerged 'a new social class of mediators in the political process'.[75] Kothari draws our attention to the wider implications of this new development in Indian politics:

> The erosion of parliamentary, party and federal institutions and decline of authority of the State and of the national political leadership has also been

one of the reasons for the rise of new actors on the scene, new forms of political expression and new definitions of the content of politics.[76]

Historically, federalism in India has undergone radical changes in different phases of its evolution that are linked with the changing nature of the polity. For instance, the first phase is characterized by the single-party dominance or the Congress system (1947–66). Following the growth of regional parties, a different type of power relationships emerged between the states and the centre in the second phase, which continued till the rise of the Janata Party coalition in 1977. In the third phase (1978–97), fragmentation of parties brought about a significant impact on the nature of federalism that confronted new issues affecting the federal balance. Following the rise and consolidation of coalition government at the centre at the behest of the NDA in 1998, the fourth phase of the evolution of India's federalism seems to have begun. The paradox however is that, while the centre has steadily declined in the last two decades, the states have also become 'weaker'. A fragmented party politics is likely to give some states greater power depending on the nature of coalition, but the reliance of unstable multi-party coalitions in Delhi on regional parties, even factions, in the states seems to be leading to a crisis in the federal system. The system of 'cooperative federalism', envisaged by the Sarkaria Commission, with the Inter-State Council as the principal instrument, has failed to strike roots in the political processes.

The expansion of political participation in the last two decades has placed historically disadvantaged and marginalized groups at the centre of political system and governance at all levels. The rapid politicization and accelerated participation of groups such as OBCs and Dalits raises questions about inclusion, exclusion, varied patterns of empowerment and the impact of these patterns on the growth and consolidation of democracy.[77] One aspect of these changes has to do with the processes and strategies that have inspired the induction of marginal groups into the political decision-making process leading to politically empowering the disadvantaged groups. Though not unique to India, these struggles and contentions have overshadowed the idioms and ideologies that dominated and sustained the post-colonial agenda of social transformation. Many of these are expressions of discontent traceable to the anger of the subalterns against an elite that has cornered the benefits and privileges of post-colonial economic development; these expressions of discontent have significantly reformulated the political terrain.

Parliamentary federalism and the basic structure of the Constitution

Parliamentary federalism is a core value of the Constitution of India in two significant ways: first, by providing a definitive format in which governance is to be articulated, parliamentary federalism lays and sustains India's politico-administrative foundation. Second, despite the apparent incompatibility of the parliamentary form of governance with federalism, it emerged as perhaps the best possible structure in the context of the political situation arising out of the partition of the country and the integration of the states. Do federalism and the parliamentary system constitute 'the basic structure' of the Constitution? Given their politico-institutional importance in sustaining democratic structure in India there is no doubt that they are critical to Indian polity. Constitutionally significant, ideologically critical and politically meaningful, these values seem to have grown stronger presumably because of India's pluralist character. In this sense, despite the imperial origin because parliamentary federalism was conceptualized (though in a different from) in the 1935 Government of India Act, the combination of two apparently contradictory constitutional tendencies acquired salience largely because of the peculiar social texture of the Indian polity in which this constitutional format struck organic roots. 'Our defiantly democratic constitution', argues Amartya Sen, unfolds 'in defiance of the standard understanding in the world of what is or is not feasible in a country with such overwhelming poverty and massive illiteracy.'[78] As a living document, the constitutional provisions are being regularly revisited by the judiciary in response to the changing socio-economic milieu without disturbing its 'basic structure', which has never been articulated in clear terms. Presumably because of the obvious difficulty in exactly spelling out the basic structure of the Constitution, which is relative to the socio-economic circumstances, the judiciary seems to have avoided it. Nonetheless, in its various judgments, the Supreme Court of India has elaborated the concept keeping in view the contingent circumstances responsible for judicial intervention.

Defined as 'the bedrock of constitutional interpretation in India',[79] the basic structure debate that began with the 1973 Kesavananda Bharati case redefined the constitutional discourse in India. In this oft-quoted case, the Supreme Court of India restricted the parliamentary domain with the argument that any constitutional amendment, even if enacted under procedures laid down under Article 368 of the Constitution, could be declared invalid if it violated 'the basic structure of the constitution'. Through its judgment, the Supreme Court 'constructed a dyke', argues Arun Shourie, 'to shield the country and the citizen from the political class'.[80] This is a significant judgment in two respects: first, it reiterates the caution of the founding fathers that parliament in India is not as supreme as it is in the Westminster system of governance except during emergency; second, the critical principles that hold the Constitution in its true spirit can never be sacrificed in any circumstances. Parliamentary supremacy is appreciated within the political format of parliamentary democracy, which upholds 'federalism' as a lifeline of the Indian polity. One can tinker with these foundational values of the Constitution only at the cost of its basic structure.

There is a serious problem of interpretation of what constitutes the basic structure because the Supreme Court itself stressed that 'the claim of any particular feature of the Constitution to be a basic feature would be determined by the Court in each case that comes before it'.[81] So these basic features are not 'finite', although the Court identifies a number of features – such as the supremacy of the Constitution, parliamentary democracy, the principle of separation of powers, the independence of the judiciary and the limited amending powers of parliament – as basic features. What the doctrine therefore amounts to is that there are some features in the Constitution that are more 'basic' or 'fundamental' than others. Although the Constitution can be amended by following the stipulated procedures, these features which are basic to the Constitution can never be altered presumably because amendment to these radically alter the nature of the Constitution.

Two important points that emerge out of the discussion on the basic structure need to be addressed. First, the debate seeks to strike a balance between judiciary and parliament by redefining parliamentary supremacy as 'relative' to the circumstances. In no circumstances is the parliament empowered to challenge the foundational values since they are so integral to the evolution of India as a parliamentary democracy. Second, by seeking to provide a contextual interpretation of the basic structure, the apex court draws our attention to the organic nature of the Constitution that evolves in conjunction with the rapidly changing socio-economic and political circumstances. Conceptually, the idea of basic structure is not sacrosanct, but is amenable to change if circumstances so require. An example will suffice here. The federalism that the founding fathers preferred was articulated as a scheme of distribution of power between two layers of government – one at the union level and other at the provincial level. The Seventy-third and Seventy-fourth Amendment Act in fact altered the basic structure of the Constitution by introducing 'a third tier' besides the union and states and were therefore 'violative' of the basic structure. The introduction of a third tier is a striking distortion in the prevalent two-tier structure of governance because this change is 'in the direction of greater federalism' than what exists. However, these amendments were appreciated for having translated the notion of 'democratic decentralization' into practice and are thus reflective of the organic nature of the Constitution. Similarly, the introduction of such terms as socialism and secularism (though the former considerably lost its salience with the adoption of the 1991 New Economic Policy) did not disrupt the basic structure simply because these changes evidently commanded 'general assent'. What is thus critical is the fact that the values or the constitutional structure that are considered 'basic' or 'fundamental' are not entirely sacrosanct, but are amenable to change if it is absolutely necessary to keep pace with the social, political and economic milieu.[82] Although basic structure doctrine creates a contentious space it nonetheless has struck 'a balance, if an uneasy one, . . . between the responsibilities of parliament and the Supreme Court for protection of integrity of the seamless web [of constitutional democracy in India]'.[83] Nonetheless, supporters and detractors of the basic structure doctrine are clearly divided: critics see it as 'judicial usurpation of democratic sovereignty' and thus an assault on parliamentary supremacy while the supporters welcome the doctrine as 'a necessary check on parliamentary majorities bent on jeopardizing democratic freedoms and as a legitimate pressure on the state [to adopt] ameliorating policies for the vulnerable sections of society [conforming to] the Directive Principles of the Part IV of the Constitution'.[84]

Parliamentary federalism is not merely a constitutional structure, but also provides an ideological foundation to cement a bond among Indian constituent states, which are diverse on various counts. In this sense, it is basic to the politico-constitutional structure that has evolved in India since the Constitution was adopted in 1950. Especially in the coalition era, parliamentary democracy in India is redefined with the growing federalization that began with the decimation of Congress rule in various states in the 1967 state assembly election. The scene was completely different during the heyday of the 'Congress system' when the Congress Party controlled all the state governments and also the union. What was symptomatic in 1967 seems to be a well-entrenched pattern now with the clear political ascendance of the constituent provinces, governed mainly by parties with regional roots. The leading members of either of the major coalitions at the pan-Indian level can afford to ignore them only at their political peril. In India's changed political texture, parliamentary federalism seems to be a creative politico-constitutional response to a situation that is hardly comparable. Because of its historical roots, parliamentary federalism also provides perhaps the only mechanism that reconciles the seemingly contradictory tendencies between parliamentary and federal forms of government.

Concluding observations

India's political system is in constant flux. Parliamentary federalism is a unique form of governance that is context-driven. Adapting the colonial model of centralized governance designed to sustain 'a revenue-based-law-and-order federal structure',[85] independent India favoured a powerful centralized bureaucracy as critical for securing nation's unity and planned development. Yet parliament is neither supreme nor sovereign as in the Westminster model of parliamentary democracy. The adoption of the federal principles seems to have 'tempered the unlimited power of Parliament'.[86] Yet the ruling party, if it musters a stable majority in parliament, can become an absolute authority under specific circumstances in which the legislature will simply act as a ratifying agency. Supported by three major institutions – the Finance Commission, the Planning Commission and the All India Services – the central government may substantially alter the federal balance in its favour. Furthermore, under the changed circumstances of liberalization, the constitutionally guaranteed rights of the constituent states have been significantly eroded. One area that has created consternation among the member states of the union is whether the centre is constitutionally authorized to sign treaties with other countries without consulting the affected states.[87] This has become relevant at a time when trade and other international agencies – like those under the Uruguay Round of the General Agreement on Trade and Tariffs (GATT) are being created in ways such that national barriers and sovereignty of the nation state are being assailed. The new GATT is a special instance in question because it is concerned with not just trade in goods but also services (General Agreement on Trade and Services), investment (Trade Related Investment Measures), intellectual property (Trader Related Intellectual Property Rights) and various other aspects of the economy. Apprehending that GATT is likely to curb their power that has been guaranteed by the Constitution, three States, Tamil Nadu, Rajasthan and Orissa, filed suits in the Supreme Court in 1994 against the Union of India 'raising a federal dispute that the new GATT affects their exclusive powers given to them by the Constitution and forces them to share power with the Union in ways that violate the basic structure of the Constitution'.[88] Though the court verdict is inconclusive, the step is indicative of a new trend according to which the provinces no longer remain the 'silent' observers. Whatever one may think of the desirability of GATT there is no doubt that it effectively redefines the centre–state relations in the context of restrictions imposed by the international agencies. This is one dimension of federalism in its new form. The other dimension is about the changing nature of centre–state relations in the changed environment of the twenty-first century. For instance, the state governments are not dismissed the way they were in the 1970s and 1980s, but they have declined in a situation where the centre has surreptitiously taken many of the states' powers. Whatever one may think of the desirability of India's signing up to the WTO, there is no doubt that it has tilted the balance in favour of the union government because the centre is authorized to endorse an economic treaty that affects things on the state list (taxation, agriculture) without serious consultation of the states. Nonetheless, the fact that in many cases international organizations deal with state governments directly – at times bypassing the union government – is indicative of the rising importance of states in federal India. A network with the global capital has thus contributed to the consolidation of 'a federal market economy' fast replacing 'the Nehruvian centralized command economy in the country's economic imagination and practice'.[89] It is not therefore surprising that the World Bank negotiated separate structural adjustment packages with Andhra Pradesh, Karnataka and UP since 1998. The World Bank also recognized that 'a reorientation of its strategy' was necessary in view of the changing texture of federalism in India. Hence it declared, '[w]hile continuing to support nation-wide programs in health and education, the Bank has reoriented its strategy to focus on reforming States'.[90] At an uncritical level, this was welcome and the World Bank support was well appreciated. The World Bank showcase of Andhra Pradesh with its glitter of information technology based industries was hailed as 'the brightest star' in the skyline of the 'shining India' campaign by the erstwhile NDA government. There were constant reports in the media of suicides of indebted farmers, but the market-friendly policies of inviting foreign investment continued. With the electoral defeat of the incumbent state government, it became apparent that 'investment without a human face' might not be politically expedient. And a government, argues Amit Bhaduri, 'whose eyes and ears are turned to the market, fails to see the poor, and hear their voice' may not succeed in a situation where the political is constantly redefined.

Federalism is thus no longer a constitutional format of distribution of power, but a process that is being constantly reinvented in view of the rapidly changing socio-economic and political circumstances in which it is rooted. The growing assertiveness of major political institutions holding the federal balance, such as the Supreme Court, the President and the Election Commission, have radically altered the centre of gravity. In the famous 1994 Bommai judgment, the Supreme Court quashed the decision of the union government to impose president's rule in Karnataka under Article 356 by underlining that

[d]emocracy and federalism are essential features of the Constitution and are part of its basic structure. . . . States have an independent existence and they have as important role to play in the political, social, educational and cultural life of the people as the Union. They are neither satellites nor agents of the Centre.[91]

The unanimous judgment by the nine-judge constitutional bench held that any proclamation under Article 356 is subject to judicial review. The judgment further endorsed that Article 74 (2) does not bar the court from summoning the material that guides the cabinet in deciding in favour of imposition of president's rule in a state. This path-breaking ruling radically altered the centre–state relations by 'the federal compact of a new institutional force'.[92]

There is one final point concerning the gradually changing nature of the structure of governance, as it has emerged in India retaining the 'basic' structure of the 1950 Constitution. As a hybrid political system, India is neither fully parliamentary nor federal. The 1950 Constitution has devised an elaborate system of distribution of powers. So, it is federal following the principles enshrined in the American Constitution. It is not federal because the Constitution has failed to acknowledge the need to make the central institutions of government fully federal through bicameralism.[93] Instead, the Constitution is clearly in favour of 'an obsolescent' Westminster model of parliamentary government that is clearly 'unitary'. Yet the script of Indian federalism is being constantly rewritten given the changing nature of its context. For instance, the radical departure from the established federal arrangement happens to be the recent local government amendments of 1992, which require the states to devolve power and resources permanently to the control of three-tier local panchayats from grassroots to district levels. Furthermore, the political processes however have led to the gradual but steady increase in importance of inter-governmental agencies, such as the National Development Council (NDC) and Inter-State Council (ISC). Identified as 'federal' agencies, these structures are clearly those with potential for radically altering the governance format.[94] However, at present these institutions do not appear to be effective in the context of economic liberalization when there is a clear shift from 'inter-governmental cooperation' to 'inter-jurisdictional competition'. Although there are institutions like the NDC or ISC to tackle the former, there is no formally constituted agency except the ad hoc conferences of chief ministers and the inter-state Water Commission to grapple with the emerging tensions arising out of centre–state relations. In the light of the increasingly competitive patterns of federal relations, this absence creates 'a problem for the horizontal integration of the states in India'.[95]

There is no doubt that India's politico-constitutional structure has undergone tremendous changes to adapt to changing circumstances. Parliament continues to remain supreme, at least constitutionally, though it has considerably lost its authority probably because of the decline of the single-party rule and the critical importance of the regional parties in governance in contemporary India, which itself is, argues Granville Austin, 'symptomatic of increased national unity, not of integrity threatened'.[96] Under the changed circumstances, what is evident is a clear shift of emphasis from the Westminster to federal traditions, more so in the era of coalition politics when no single political party has an absolute majority in parliament. For practical purposes, the scheme the framers had adopted to bring together diverse Indian states within a single authority was what is known as 'executive federalism' – a structure of division of powers between different layers of governmental authorities following clearly defined guidelines in the form of 'Union', 'State' and 'Concurrent' lists in the Seventh Schedule of the Constitution of India. Owing to compulsions of circumstances arising out of coalition politics, the constituent states do not remain mere instruments of the union; their importance is increasingly being felt in what was earlier known as 'the exclusive' domain of the centre. Although India has an executive-dominated parliamentary system, backed by powerful all-India services dominating the over-centralized governance, a process seems to have begun towards 'legislative federalism' in which the upper chamber representing the units of the federal government is as powerful as the lower chamber. Drawn upon the American federalism, in which the Senate holds substantial power in conjunction with the House of Representatives, legislative federalism is an arrangement based on an equal and effective representation of the regions. The decisions taken at the union level, appear to be both democratic and representative given the role of both the chambers in their articulation. In other words, legislative federalism in its proper manifestation guarantees the importance of both the chambers in the decision-making process, which no longer remains the 'exclusive' territory of the lower house for its definite representative character. Not only will the upper chamber be an effective forum for the regions, its role in the legislative process will also be significant and substantial. If properly constituted, it could be an institution that represented the regions as such, counterbalancing the principle of representation by population on which the lower house is based. It will also be a real break with the past since India's politico-constitutional structure draws upon the Westminster model with a strong centre associated with unitary government.

Whether 'bicameralism' with a reconstituted Rajya Sabha enjoying equal authority with the Lok Sabha would be desirable is debatable. If the political climate undermines the spirit of coalition it would increase governmental impotence because what is likely to govern the decisions of the parliamentarians is a design to stall the motions that may not have been inspired out of solicitude for states' rights. So the changed composition of Rajya Sabha may not be a politically appropriate device to creatively fashion the federal balance in India, though there have been occasions when the Rajya Sabha has been tough with the lower house. Its partisanship was, for instance, demonstrated during the brief Janata Party interlude (1977–80) when the Congress-dominated Rajya Sabha thwarted a government-initiated constitutional amendment by refusing to endorse the move, for which the support of two-thirds of the house was required. The divide between the two houses has become more prominent of late. The Congress majority in the Rajya Sabha appears to have preempted several attempts to adopt legislation to fulfil the government's agenda, whereas in the days before 1967 the Rajya Sabha hardly played a significant role except to corroborate the views expressed in the lower house. Following the installation of non-Congress governments in various states since 1967, the upper chamber seems to have acquired a definite, if not completely new, role in the governing processes.[97] The rejection of the Prevention of Terrorism Ordinance (POTO) in early 2002 is an example showing that the Rajya Sabha had asserted its independence by rejecting the Ordinance, already endorsed by the lower house. In terms of its numerical strength the upper chamber is not simply equipped to stall the acceptance of any bill when the Lok Sabha has adequate numbers to push whatever decisions it adopts. In the case of POTO, the ruling coalition openly challenged the Rajya Sabha that turned down the legislation already approved by the directly elected representatives.

Parliamentary federalism is a unique hybrid system of governance in which the apparently contradictory tendencies are sought to be managed. What has emerged in India during the course of more than half a century does not correspond with any of the classical models of government. The Indian political structure is neither strictly unitary nor purely federal; it is a form in which the elements of both are traced and evident.[98] Distinct from the classical types for obvious reasons, Indian political system offers a unique model drawing upon both the British tradition of parliamentary sovereignty and the American federal legacy in which regions seem to be prior to the centre. This is essentially a hybrid system of governance that has emerged from a peculiar unfolding of socio-political processes in the aftermath of India's rise as a nation state. Parliamentary federalism is therefore not merely a structural device for distribution of powers between different layers of government; it is also an articulation of a basic philosophy accommodating diverse regional interests in the name of a nation.

5　The chaotic 1960s

Decade of experiments and turmoil

There is no doubt that the Congress system sustained one-party dominance in India till the 1967 election to the state assemblies. What was basic in the Congress system was the hegemonic role of the Indian National Congress in conducting public affairs almost without resistance from parties outside the Congress fold. Sorting out the opposition internally, the earlier Congress leadership never allowed challenge from within to destroy its viability both as a party of governance and as a machinery to resolve conflict involving regional issues. This was a time-tested device and the Congress Party sustained its hegemony on the Indian political scene almost uninterrupted till 1967. The Congress wave was halted, as it were. What was significant was not so much the failure of Congress to maintain its rule in the states but that the consolidation of the parties with their strong presence posed a serious challenge to the Congress Party. It is also true that most of these regional parties did not differ much ideologically from the Congress party; in fact, the roots of most of these parties can be traced back to Congress. Opposed to Congress, these parties articulated a unique political voice that assumed significant dimension presumably because of a conducive political environment in which the anti-Congress political sentiments were meaningfully translated into votes.

Furthermore, what brought the regional parties to centre stage in the provinces were perhaps the anti-Congress sentiments. Barring the 1957 Kerala experiment, this is the first occasion when the non-Congress parties formed coalitions in as many as nine states in opposition to Congress.[1] This was largely a region-dictated political phenomenon in the sense that the issues that figured in both the formation of coalition and its continuity were dictated largely by regional interests. The rise of the regional parties as a combined force bidding for power at the centre is possibly due to the following factors: first, the decline of the Congress as an institutionalized party representing various and also conflicting socio-economic interests. It lost its hegemony because of, *inter alia*, the departure of the nationalist generation, demise of internal democracy and the emergence of personalized mass appeal of the top leadership.[2] No longer did Congress remain a party capable of accommodating conflicting social interests and fulfilling the individual ambitions of those involved in its expansion at the provincial and local levels. Second, with successive elections, new social groups and strata are being introduced to the political processes. Since the entrenched groups in the dominant party tended to impede their entry to the political processes these new entrants found it easier to make their debut through non-Congress parties or occasionally even founded new parties. So, the emergence of new parties outside the Congress fold to articulate hitherto neglected socio-political interests seems to be a major factor that contributed to the consolidation of a coalition with different ideological perspectives.

The aim of this chapter is to focus on the 1967 elections, which catapulted the regional parties to centre stage of Indian politics. In fact, it would not be wrong to argue that the 1967 elections are clearly a break with the past in the sense that several regional parties realized the importance of a coalition of the like-minded political organizations to pursue ideological goals that remained peripheral in the Congress agenda. This chapter will therefore be a synthetic study of this phenomenon in the context of a new wave of coalition politics in India. Building on the argument that coalition is both ideological and politically expedient, the chapter will probably lay the foundation for the future experiments of similar types when coalition becomes an integral part of Indian political existence. In other words, the 1967 experiment directs our attention to a twofold process: on the one hand, this election indicates a clear crack in the Congress base in the regions; the 1967 poll outcomes also reflect, on the other, the beginning of a significant process whereby the splintered regional parties were united on the basis of distinctly regional interests, which the Congress failed to adequately represent.

The fourth general elections to the Lok Sabha and the state assemblies elections in February 1967 had radically altered India's political landscape. The Congress lost its hegemony in as many as nine states. Except in the case of Madras, where DMK won an absolute majority and C. Annadurai became chief minister, governments were formed in other states through a coalition of several parties. What brought them together was perhaps the opposition to Congress, which had held power in these states uninterruptedly till 1967. In order to sustain the coalition, a common minimum programme was framed that avoided as far as possible contentious issues. So, the most significant feature of the 1967 elections was the coming together of non-Congress parties when the Congress system seemed to have shown massive cracks due to a complex unfolding of socio-economic circumstances. However, the coalition did not appear to be stable presumably because they were neither ideologically cohesive nor programmatically uniform. The only common factor that cemented the bond among these regional parties was their anti-Congress sentiments. Thus in Bihar, a Samyukta Vidhayak Dal was constituted by the SSP, the PSP, the Jana Sangh, the Jan Kranti Dal (which later merged with the Bharatiya Kranti Dal) and the CPI. With majority support in the Bihar Assembly, the SVD elected Mahamaya Prasad Singh of the JKD as the first non-Congress chief minister. In Punjab, those with non-Congress sentiments – the Akali Dal (Sant group), the CPI(M), the CPI, the Jana Sangh, the Akali Dal (master group), the SSP and the Republican Party – came together and formed the Popular United Front, and Gurnam Singh of the Akali Dal (Sant group) became chief minister.

In West Bengal, the two non-Congress governments were formed in the aftermath of the 1967 elections. Whereas the CPI(M) was the leading partner in the first experiment, the second one was led by the Bangla Congress. Ajoy Mukherjee of the Bangla Congress was the first non-Congress chief minister in West Bengal. In Kerala, a United Front ministry, headed by E. M. S Namboodiripad of the CPI(M) held power. In Orissa, the dissident Congressmen, led by the former chief minister, H. K. Mahatab, joined with the Swatantra Party – a party mostly of former princes – to constitute the government in Bhubneshwar.

In the Hindi heartland, particularly Uttar Pradesh and Madhya Pradesh, the non-Congress sentiments were articulated by those who left the Congress before the 1967 elections. In Uttar Pradesh, the Congress ministry headed by C. B. Gupta collapsed within three weeks of its formation and was later replaced by Charan Singh-led SVD ministry following latter's defection from the Congress. In Madhya Pradesh, the Congress lost its numerical strength following the desertion of Vijay Raje Scindia and the government of D. P. Mishra was defeated. Later, a G. N. Singh-led SVD ministry comprising the Scindia group, the Jana Sangh, the SSP and the PSP came to power. The situation in Haryana was slightly different where the Congress lost its numerical majority in the assembly following a large-scale defection of the dissident Congressmen. A United Front was formed and Rao Birendra Singh became its leader and chief minister.

As evident, the 1967 elections heralded a new era in Indian politics. This was the beginning of an era of coalition whereby parties with anti-Congress sentiments came together. That these coalitions largely drew on anti-Congress sentiments was both their strength and weakness: strength because anti-Congress feelings crystallized the desire for a political bond in opposition to a political 'foe'; weakness simply because the oppositional sentiments were not strong enough to sustain the bond the moment there were clashes of interests among the constituents. As a result, the coalition evaporated as soon as crises engulfed the partners and no mechanism was available to defuse the situation before it became disastrous. So, the story of coalition is one of both success and failure. Although it failed to sustain the spirit in which it was constituted, the ephemeral existence of coalition governments in the states clearly spells out a new political wave challenging the conventional faith in the Congress system. Reflective of the unrivalled cultural diversity of the country, this was a process that was rooted in the growing regionalization of politics in India. The 1967 elections were therefore a watershed in Indian politics in the sense that these assembly elections epitomized a struggle between regionalizing and centralizing political forces. In other words, the 1967 poll outcome clearly suggest a metamorphosis in Indian politics that 'produced a tendency in the form of demands from several states for greater regional autonomy and in somewhat more feeble, but recurrent proposals from politicians who continue to draw inspiration from the Gandhian tradition for greater decentralization of institutions in India down to the district and village level as well'.[3]

The Congress decline and crystallization of a new wave

The 1967 mid-term poll in February 1967 in West Bengal, Uttar Pradesh, Bihar and Punjab is undoubtedly an articulation of a new wave in Indian politics. That the Congress lost miserably in these states demonstrates its failure to accommodate the conflicting socio-political interests of the voters that remained the main source of strength of the earlier Congress system. The lesson was unambiguous: no party was capable of having an independent majority on the floor of legislature. The variety of interests, ideas and ambitions was larger than a single political party, including Congress, could possibly accommodate. To share or not to share power was 'a dilemma when the alternative to sharing power [was] perhaps to lose it'.[4] What it shows is the possibility of an alternative structure of power on the basis of considerations that were politically expedient. Ideology did not seem to play an important role in bringing together disparate political forces. In circumstances where the anti-Congress sentiments were high and clearly articulated, the situation seemed favourable for the non-Congress parties to come forward for a front by underplaying ideology and other related considerations. So, coalitions were nothing but translations of a contextual logic that largely drew on the opposition to the Congress.

The transition from Congress hegemony to 'multi-partyism' was translated into coalition governments. The example of the United Front government in West Bengal is unique in the sense that it had fourteen parties within its fold. The combination of clearly ideologically incompatible parties was due to the exigency of the situation when it was possible for the front partners to keep Congress out of power. The prominent factor that brought these ideologically disparate parties together happened to be anti-Congress sentiments that were 'an expression of the mood of the times and the pattern [appeared] to have come to stay'.[5] Given the instability of the Front government, it would not be wrong to argue that the decline of the Congress created a vacuum within the state and was not filled until 1977 when the CPI(M) emerged as the new ruling party.

Coalition in West Bengal

The West Bengal coalition was a part of the experiments of non-Congress governments in other states. What was unique was the decision of the Communist Parties to merge with their ideologically opposite counterparts? Defending their decision to join the coalition, a CPI(M) document suggests:

> The UF governments that we have now are to be treated and understood as instruments of struggle in the hands of our people, more than as Government that actually possess adequate power that can materially and substantially give relief to the people. In clear class terms, our party's participation in such governments is one specific form of struggle to win more and more people and more and more allies for the proletariat.[6]

Discarding its ideological catholicity, the CPI(M) leadership further appreciated the importance of coalition against an organizationally mighty Congress by even justifying their participation in governance even with the so-called communal parties. As it was further reiterated:

> A dogmatic, sectarian and wrong attitude towards political parties like the DMK, Akalis, and Muslim League persisted in the once united Communist party. . . . Our Party correctly took the lead in discarding this erroneous attitude and boldly fought for electoral agreements, adjustments, united fronts and finally, even for participation in United Front Governments with parties on an agreed government programme.[7]

It is clear that the CPI(M) participated in such an experiment of governance for a specific political goal. On the one hand, it was a design to bring in the like-minded political parties in opposition to a major political party since it would, on the other hand, strengthen their efforts at people's well-being by adopting pro-people socio-economic programmes.[8] A resolution to this effect was adopted to explicitly state the objective of such a decision on the part of the CPI(M). In an unambiguous way, the Party leadership thus declared:

> Our Party's representatives in the state governments of Kerala and West Bengal should take the lead in the matter, prepare certain land and other agrarian bills, and strive to get them enacted by the representative UF Governments. In order to strengthen the hands of these ministers and also to arrest possible vacillations and wobbling among the other partners and groups in the ministries, independent mass mobilization for such legislations and around them is to be undertaken without delay.[9]

The common minimum programme was probably the response to such a design whereby parties with contradictory ideological stances came together under one central leadership in so far as government was concerned. There are other factors that contributed to the decline of Congress and later the formation of a coalition in the state. By the mid-1960s, the nationalist leaders passed away. The political leaders of the stature of B. C. Roy and Atulya Ghosh kept the factional fights in the organization within control and they therefore never became a serious problem for the party. As result, Congress gained enormously by drawing on its nationalist role in successive elections. Factional fighting led to a split – the Bangla Congress emerged – even before the all-India Congress was divided. Second, two consecutive droughts in the mid-1960s resulted in severe food shortages that posed a serious difficulty to the Congress government. The situation was precarious in West Bengal because of the influx of refugees from East Bengal after the 1947 partition. The state suffered on a double count: (a) it accommodated more refugees than any other states in India, which put unprecedented pressure on the state exchequer for obvious reasons; and (b) the state failed to meet this pressure because its demands for extra central grants were not always favourably viewed especially after the death of B. C. Roy in 1962 when the Congress government in West Bengal lost its bargaining power considerably. Furthermore, the growing strength of the left parties in West Bengal also contributed to the Congress decline. As the poll outcomes show, there had been a gradual, but steady decrease of Congress seats in the legislature, from 150 seats in the 1952 elections to 127 in the 1967 elections, while the left political parties had registered a significant increase, from 42 seats in 1952 to 72 in 1967. One of the factors that certainly enhanced the electoral presence of the left parties was the crisis due to food shortage in the state that the Congress government failed to combat. Furthermore, strikes in factories added to the economic misery of the people. The recurrence of riots in the state indicated the weaknesses of the government in the field of the maintenance of law and order.

In the aftermath of the 1967 elections,[10] the United Front government came to power with the left parties – CPI, CPI(M), Forward Bloc and Revolutionary Socialist Party – joining hands with the dissident Congressmen forming the Bangla Congress. Although it signalled a new era of coalition in state politics, its track record was not, however, very worth emulating. The UF government was formed when the state was in the throes of a variety of crises. The food shortage was the Achilles heel for the government. Apart from this insurmountable problem, the government was divided internally by party feuds among the constituents. One of the major factors was certainly the unbridgeable gulf between the two principal communist parties – CPI and CPI(M). As an expert unequivocally comments:

> The only permanent antagonism within the UF was that between the two communist parties. Not that the two parties did not sit in the same group to resolve conflicts within the UF, but such periods of harmony were short. Either old disputes revived or new ones cropped up to vitiate their relations.[11]

What it suggests is the obvious difficulty a coalition confronts when its partners fail to appreciate the significance of 'togetherness' in a situation of chaos and crisis. It also probably shows a lack of maturity among those constituting the coalition. That is probably the reason why the pre-coalition feud within what was known as the CPI figured prominently in the UF government, disrupting the normal functioning of the government. The anti-Congress sentiments that brought them together, were not strong enough to sustain the coalition when a serious crisis broke. In other words, neither the Bangla Congress nor other constituents, including the two leading communist parties, ever submerged their distinct identities within the government for the sake of the coalition, which was perhaps most fragile from the outset owing to drought, recession, inflation and labour unrest. Yet the Ajoy Mukerjee-led Front government brought about some radical changes in the spheres of irrigation, distribution of land among landless peasants, public relations, increase of seats in degree colleges and also the relations between judiciary and executive by being respectful to the judicial verdicts. However, there was always a tightrope walk for the Front since its majority was so fragile and its constituents, especially the communists, were never comfortable with the coalition that brought the two major communist parties – CPI and CPI(M) – under one platform given their ingrained animosity in the aftermath of the 1964 split between CPI and CPI(M).

The Front suffered a death blow not from the communists but from the dissident Congressmen who broke away to form a Progressive Democratic Front under the leadership of P. C. Ghosh, the food minister in the erstwhile government. The Governor dismissed the ministry with the plea that the Front had lost its majority and had no *locus standi*. In November the Ghosh ministry was sworn in with the help of the Congress Party, which had remained aloof from the Front ministry. However, by February, the honeymoon with the Congress was over and the Ghosh-led Progressive Democratic Front (PDF) ministry lost its legislative majority. The President's rule was proclaimed and the chapter of coalition politics came to an end.

Although the experiment was short-lived it nonetheless provided an alternative theoretical conceptualization of government formation. In contrast with the model of one-party dominance, the coming together of disparate parties was undoubtedly a significant step towards building coalition governments in a situation when a single party majority was inconceivable. The other point of significance was the growing importance of 'defection' as a mode of mobilizing support for a coalition. That there were two governments in less than a year in West Bengal shows the failure of the coalition to sustain its viability. Whereas in the first Front the opposition to the Congress cemented the bond, the PDF was formed as a counter to the Ajoy Mukherjee-led government. In both these cases, it was not ideological distance but personal predilections of those who mattered in these fronts that seemed to have governed the choice. This also underlines the importance of defection when the legislative majority was illusory to the parties constituting coalitions. So, what the West Bengal experiment suggests is a paradox because, although there was a clear possibility of coalitions even in circumstances when the constituents were hardly interconnected ideologically, the very lack of ideological compatibility led to the collapse of coalitions on both occasions.

Coalition in Uttar Pradesh

The 1967 poll outcome radically altered the texture of politics in Uttar Pradesh (UP).[12] Congress lost its electoral majority and failed to form a government in the state. Although Congress lacked the numerical majority, it was still the single largest party in the UP assembly. The space created by the declining influence of Congress was occupied by the two principal opposition parties, *viz.* the socialists and the Jana Sangh. Of these, the rise of the Jana Sangh was meteoric since the party, which had only 6.3 per cent of the votes in the first general election, obtained 21.6 per cent of the votes in the 1967 elections. The Sanyukta Socialist Party (SSP) also gained at the cost of Congress. As the 1967 election results show, Congress lost its electoral support in comparison with its tally in the third general elections in 1962 (see Table 5.1). Given the fractured opinion, the non-Congress parties held several meetings to explore possibilities of forming a coalition

Table 5.1 Election results in Uttar Pradesh

Name of party	Seats won 1962	Seats won 1967
Indian National Congress	273	199
Bharatiya Jana Sangh	45	98
Samyukta Socialist Party (SSP)	35	44
Communist Party of India	13	14
Communist Party of India (Marxist)	1	1
Swatantra Party	12	12
Praja Socialist Party (PSP)	9	11
Republican Party of India	6	9
Independents	25	37
Total	419	425

Sources: 1962 figures from M. S. Verma, *Coalition Government: UP's First Experiment*, Lucknow: Department of Public Administration, Lucknow University, 1971, p. 43; 1967 figures from *Hindustan Times*, 2 April 1967.

government. The idea appealed to all those parties opposed to the Congress. What however prevented them from coming together was the uncertainty over whether the Jana Sangh and the communists could share power in view of their serious ideological differences. Furthermore, there were doubts whether such disparate groups could evolve a common minimum programme to guide the coalition. Once the Jana Sangh and the communists were united in Bihar under the leadership of Mahamaya Prasad Singh, who became the first non-Congress chief minister there, their respective UP counterparts agreed to form a coalition in the state.

While there were attempts by the non-Congress parties to forge an alliance, Congress also left no stone unturned to constitute a government in the province. The vacuum created by the defeat of a veteran Congress leader Kamalapati Tripathy was filled by C. B. Gupta, who was elected leader of the Congress legislative party with the support of independents in preference to Charan Singh, an equally strong contender for the leadership. Annoyed with the Congress High Command, which preferred Gupta, Charan Singh refused to join the ministry. Gupta's ministry was therefore crippled from the very outset because a large number of MLAs with allegiance to Charan Singh and his confidante Jai Ram Verma remained aloof. Within a fortnight after Gupta was sworn in as chief minister, Congress was split on 1 April 1967 and the breakaway group under the leadership of Charan Singh formed Jana Congress. Characterizing the defection as 'a historic turn in our lives', Singh defended his action as 'most appropriate' by saying that:

> Today the people are unable to understand why prices come down in those states where non-Congress governments were formed and not in [UP]. . . .
> Public service is the main instrument of a political party. We had cherished certain ideals and principles of political life. We find [that] we cannot work

for those ideals if we remain within the Congress and we feel [that] we would be able to follow them by going out.[13]

With this defection of Congress members, Gupta lost 'the no confidence' motion and his eighteen-day-old government collapsed. As in Bihar, the non-Congress members of the UP legislative assembly formed the Samyukta Vidhayak Dal (SVD) comprising Jan Congress, Jana Sangh, SSP, PSP, Swatantra, Communists, Republican Party and independents. The SVD was a combination of heterogeneous elements with clear ideological differences among the partners. What brought them together were anti-Congress sentiments that appeared to have lost their edge once the main objective of ousting Congress from power was fulfilled. Charan Singh was unanimously elected leader of the SVD on 3 April 1967 and was sworn in as chief minister of the first coalition government in UP, which was also known as the SVD government.

True to the spirit of coalition, the SVD ministry accommodated the partners in proportion to their strength in the ruling group. Unlike other governments where the chief minister generally recruits the cabinet colleagues, in case of the SVD government, the party chiefs were authorized to send their representatives. However, the representation of the constituents in the cabinet was decided on the basis of their proportional strength in the SVD though there were departures from this principle, as Table 5.2 shows.

In order to sustain a coalition of ideologically incompatible partners, a common minimum programme was formulated avoiding the contentious issues. The common minimum programme, also known as the nineteen-point programme, enunciated a list of governmental measures aiming at improving UP's socio-economic profile. Seeking to serve the interests of government employees and the agricultural sector, the nineteen-point programme underlines the following points: (a) abolition of land revenue, tax on land and buildings and profession tax;

Table 5.2 Representation of the various constituents in the Charan Singh ministry and their ratio in the SVD (%)

Political party	Ministry*	Share in the SVD
Jana Sangh	28.3	41.9
SSP	17.5	19.1
Jan Congress	28.3	8.0
PSP	4.3	4.7
Swatantra	4.3	4.7
CPI	6.5	5.9
Republicans	4.3	3.0
Independents	6.5	11.4

* When deciding the proportional share in the ministry, a principle was devised that the chief minister was equivalent to two ministers and two deputy ministers were taken as one cabinet minister.

Source: Computed from the figures available from *Hindustan Times*, 4 April 1967, and *National Herald*, 5 and 6 April 1967.

(b) introduction of equal pay for equal work for teachers of aided schools with their counterparts in the government schools; (c) linking up the dearness allowance with the cost of living index and acceptance of the government employees in this regard; and (d) enunciation of a well-defined policy for effecting stability in the prices of food grains, agricultural produce and consumer goods.

Although these programmes were laudable, the chief minister and Jan Congress, which later became Bharatiya Kranti Dal (BKD),[14] did not endorse these programmes. In fact, in his maiden speech in the legislative assembly as chief minister, Charan Singh categorically refused to commit himself to these demands as they were 'impractical'. According to him, these suggested measures were nothing but 'recommendatory' in nature. He further elaborated that it was one thing 'to demand cut in taxes and increase in wages of government servants while in opposition but quite another matter to implement all this from treasury benches'.[15] So, the UP coalition government was handicapped from the very outset and, despite persuasion, the Jan Congress (and later the BKD) did not reverse its stance in this regard.

The euphoria over the non-Congress coalition was short-lived as the internal differences within the SVD became apparent. Insisting on 'the abolition of land revenue',[16] Rammanohar Lohia, the SSP leader, threatened to withdraw from the SVD unless this demand was conceded by the government. Apart from division on ideology, the SVD partners were also divided over the role of Jana Sangh in the government. Political parties with a clear anti-Jana Sangh stance – such as PSP, SSP, CPI and Republican Party – were critical of the role of the Jana Sangh for 'its utilization of government machinery in spreading its influence in as many spheres of life as possible'.[17] By July 1967, the fission within the SVD was evident and Charan Singh submitted his resignation to the secretary of the SVD for the first time on 16 August 1967. It was not possible for him to continue as chief minister, Singh argued, because of 'the unreasonable attitude of the constituents of the coalition government'.[18] Later, however, he withdrew his resignation on the assurance of cooperation by the coalition partners. This was a temporary breather for the SVD coalition. Dissension within the ruling coalition went beyond control. With the withdrawal of CPI from the SVD and Jana Sangh's decision to remain neutral in case of a no-confidence motion against the government, the Charan Singh government was left with no alternative but to resign. Following Charan Singh's resignation on 17 February, Article 356 was promulgated in the state on 24 February 1968.[19]

In the 1969 election, the fractured opposition enabled Congress to come back to power.[20] Although short-lived, the SVD coalition government ushered in a new phase in India's political history. Not only was the Charan Singh government a significant departure from the past, it also created possibilities of a political alternative to Congress. In a way, the emergence of the coalition of ideologically dissimilar political parties was an outcome of the disintegration of the Congress system that had sustained the Congress hegemony since the 1952 elections to the UP legislative assembly. Undoubtedly, the breakdown of the Congress system led to a fragmented and politically unstable party system. Yet the 1967 elections redefined the electoral map in UP by challenging the Congress hegemony in areas that were traditionally its strongholds. As evident, the dissident Congressmen played a key role in the weakening of the party, which lost its hold in UP once the opposition parties were united irrespective of ideology to contain Congress electorally. The SVD was therefore a unique experiment in coalition of parties that failed to outlive the internal contradictions owing largely to ideological incompatibilities among its constituents.

Coalition in Madhya Pradesh

Although the coalition experiment was a failure in West Bengal, its counterpart in Madhya Pradesh (MP) completed a full term of five years in three different incarnations. MP had two SVD coalitions, followed by a third – a Congress-led one. There were a series of coalitions that survived the entire term despite occasional hiccups. Thus an expert comments that the MP experiment 'provides a remarkable example of an uneasy, inchoate alliance, surviving one ministerial crisis after another, and gaining a fresh lease of life "for the time being" on each agonizing occasion'.[21] Like what had happened in West Bengal, the coalition governments collapsed on account of defections. Congress was the victim and the Congress dissidents seceded to form a breakaway group that provided the required numerical strength in the legislature. Given the fragile nature of three different coalitions, there is no doubt that what brought the dissidents together was the desire to keep specific groups away from power by any means. This seems to be logical because the dissidents not only were former Congress members but also broke away from the parent body simply in opposition to the factions that held hegemony within the provincial Congress.

The first stroke was the defection of Govind Narayan Singh and his Congress colleagues from the party led by the chief minister, D. P. Mishra. Once the short-lived Congress ministry was toppled, G. N. Singh constituted a coalition ministry with thirty-six ministers: of these, nineteen were from the G. N. Singh-led Lok Sevak Dal, and also supported by Vijayaraje Scindia of Gwalior, seven from the Jana Sangh and rest from other splinter groups. As evident, the Mishra ministry collapsed since it lost legislative majority with the defection of the factions led by G. N. Singh and Vijayaraje Scindia. The media attributed the fall of the ministry to the personal rivalry between the erstwhile chief minister, D. P. Mishra, and Scindia.[22] Here what mattered was not ideological difference but sheer personality clashes between two former members of the provincial Congress. This ministry with G. N. Singh as its chief minister lasted for twenty-one months and it survived as a result of an efficient balancing between those within its fold and the detractors. Singh promised the post of chief minister to Raja Naresh Chandra Singh on the assurance of the latter's defection from Congress. The promise was kept since, after his resignation, Singh proposed the Raja as his successor. The SVD coalition was already fragile with frequent threats from those who constituted the party. The politics of intrigue seemed to have reached a peak when Singh himself broke away along with his colleagues from the SVD to return to Congress. On 19

March 1969, Raja's ministry lost the majority and had no alternative but to leave the fort, as it were. So Congress gained in the process. However, the euphoria was short-lived since the Congress legislative party leader, D. P. Mishra, was censured by a judicial verdict and had to step down. This necessitated a leadership change and S. C. Shukla was chosen as leader of Congress. With Shukla at the helm of affairs, a new coalition was formed with support from the Progressive Legislators' Group of twenty. The coalition remained fragile simply because it had to depend on a variety of political groups within the legislature for survival; yet, unlike that in West Bengal, it completed its term. So the MP experiment is illustrative of the new wave of coalition, which survived in different political forms despite constant threats to its existence. In explaining this, one may attribute the continuity of the coalition to the fact that it was basically a factional fight within Congress and a majority of factions cooperated with one another in order to keep certain other factions out of power on the basis of personal dislike of leaders. In other words, the three different ministries were actually Congress fragments, each of which became significant under specific coalitions. What accounted for the growth of these coalitions was largely factional feud in which the individual priorities prevailed over the party and the ideology for which the party stood. Whereas the lack of ideological commitment explains the fragility of coalitions in MP, the fact that the coalitions lasted longer than expected also suggests the importance of a broad ideological affinity among those who were politically baptized by the Congress. Despite factional rivalries, those who contributed to three different coalitions were all former Congress members. There were perhaps sentimental bonds that acted favourably under certain circumstances. This was what brought the factions together for certain well-defined goals, including the desire to keep certain groups away from power.

The Haryana experiment

As shown, coalitions drew on dissidence and defection. Congress was the first victim. By the 1960s, Congress seemed to have lost its accommodating capacity to defuse conflicting interests before they became disastrous for the party. Moreover, the party leadership created a support base by the individual contributions of the leaders to the growth and consolidation of the party. So, the decline of Congress seems to have been historically conditioned. A perusal of the coalition experiment in Haryana reveals the extent to which political circumstances conducive to coalition evolve owing to historical weakness in Congress, which failed to retain its social base. Dissidence that was managed internally became devastating in course of time presumably because of Congress's inability to dissolve crisis by conferring 'patronage'. Those who had a support base or were influential in the organization threatened to secede to gain capital out of the difficulty the factions in power confronted. So, dissidents sought to gain by defecting from the parent body to form a new party or by joining the leading factions to pursue their interests.

The story of Haryana repeats the familiar pattern. The ministry headed by Bhagawat Dayal Sharma came to power following the 1967 poll. It lasted for only a fortnight when Rao Birendra Singh, who broke away from Congress along with fourteen MLAs, constituted a Front government in the province. It was a tit for tat. Because Sharma was alleged to have contributed to the defeat of large number of Congress candidates loyal to Singh, the incumbent chief minister was taught a lesson this way. The Rao ministry failed to muster majority support because of the opposition of the Sharma group. It was more or less expected and the Rao government therefore never tried to prove its majority on the floor of the legislature. After weeks of precarious existence, the Governor dismissed the ministry and was unable to constitute an alternative ministry with the plea that 'the state administration had been paralyzed and no alternative government was possible with a large number of legislators rapidly changing their loyalties'.[23]

The mid-term poll in Haryana did not provide any respite from governmental instability. The new face in Congress was Bansi Lal. Sharma was not allowed to contest, but financially supported a large number of winning Congress candidates who expressed loyalty to him. Bansi Lal was in a precarious condition with hardly any power to influence the newly elected members of the legislative assembly. Sharma supported Lal in the hope that he would defend the former's bid to become the president of the provincial Congress. This did not happen because Lal was reluctant to stand behind Sharma, who by then had become the leader of a factional segment within the legislature, called the United Front. With strong Jat support, Lal managed to scuttle the efforts of Sharma, who had a very narrow support base among the upper castes, especially the Brahmins, who never had a significant numerical presence within the caste groups in Haryana. So, the strong caste majority and the SVD opposition's fear of losing its support base acted in Lal's favour and the possibility of a showdown by the opponents against the ministry was nipped in the bud. In other words, the Haryana coalition is a story of two clear possibilities: on the one hand, the first two experiments of the SVD were familiar articulations of coalitions as a politically expedient exercise. The fragility of these coalitions was noticeable from the very outset thanks largely to the uncertainty in garnering adequate numerical support in the legislature. The other story, articulated by Bansi Lal, demonstrates, on the other hand, the extent to which a strong social base deters the dissidents when there is no guarantee for their electoral victory. In fact, the Congress system survived simply because it had created a social base by projecting its multi-cultural characteristics. The groups that left Congress to form separate political units or parties sought to appropriate the social base that they represented when in Congress. In Haryana, both Sharma and Rao Birendra Singh represented upper castes that had neither a strong support base nor popularity among the masses. As a result, their appeal was restricted, but was always supplemented by the financial support they extended to those in the election fray. It had a positive result so long as the base of politics was not democratized. Given the complex evolution of coalition governments in Haryana, it is now clear that the era of single-party majority was coming to an end and, true to Indian's multi-cultural personality, coalition governments were nothing but examples of new experiments in the political arena. In other words, a unique process seemed to have unfolded whereby the failure of the Congress Party to articulate diverse interests led to the growth of various parties and groups seeking to create a viable support base by their appeal to class, caste or regional interests.

Coalition experiment in Kerala

Following the dismissal of the democratically elected communist government in Kerala in 1959, a new phase began in its political history.[24] The CPI-led single-party government was a victim not to any internal dissension or loss of majority in the assembly but to its own failure to come to terms with the demands of the conflicting interests of the dominant caste groups.[25] Socio-politically unique, this southernmost state of India is distinct in its demographic profile. Not only are there Hindus, but Muslims and Christians have significant shares in Kerala's population. The politics of Kerala is in fact 'the making of permutations and combination of the four communities'[26] of Ezhavas (22.1 per cent), Christians (22.1 per cent), Muslims (19.1 per cent) and upper-caste Hindus belonging to the Nair community (14.4 per cent).[27]

The different religious groups are not evenly distributed through the state. Muslims are, for instance, concentrated in north Malabar, especially in the Malappuram district, whereas Christians are numerically preponderant in south central Kerala (Ernakulam, Kottayam and Idukki districts). This peculiar demographic arithmetic is important in conceptualizing coalition politics in Kerala. Since Muslims are a preponderant minority, they not only hold the electoral balance in the district but also provide the required numerical support to a coalition of parties endorsing their demands. As the electoral outcome shows, this district has been represented continuously by the Muslim League in different forms. Similarly, the Christians also act as a solid vote bank, divided between the Congress and other splinter groups representing the 'sons of the soil'.

Since 1967, Kerala has been ruled by two different coalitions of parties: the CPI(M)-led Left Democratic Front (LDF) and the Congress-dominated United Democratic Front (UDF). Besides the three major communist parties, CPI(M), CPI and Revolutionary Socialist Party (RSP), the LDF also included the Mani and Pillai faction of the Kerala Congress, the rebel Muslim League and the vacillating Congress (Urs) so long as it existed. Like the LDF, the UDF is equally heterogeneous because, apart from the Congress, the other constituents were the Muslim League, a faction of the Kerala Congress, the Janata Party, the Praja Socialist Party, the (Nair) National Democratic Party and the (Ezhava) Socialist Revolutionary Party. Although the major parties in both these conglomerations remained firm, the constituents kept changing affiliations for political expediency. Kerala's peculiar communal profile, with no religion or caste groups ever being numerically dominant and the obvious conflicting interests of different social groups, seemed to have contributed to the multiplicity of political parties that perhaps made coalition government inevitable.

The disintegration of the Congress system in 1967 coincided with the formation of the non-Congress government in Kerala. Under the leadership of E. M. S. Namboodripad, the United Front came to power. Defending the United Front as ideologically most appropriate, B. T. Randive argued that the necessity of a united front including a united front ministry, arises out of the needs of class struggle, out of the awareness of the people that without their combined efforts they cannot move forward. Leaders of opportunist parties may look upon the United Front as an electoral machine, but the masses attach more basic importance to it as their weapon of struggle.[28]

In order to ensure smooth functioning of the coalition government, a coordination committee was set up by representatives from the coalition partners including the CPI(M). From the very outset, the Namboodripad ministry had to sail through rough weather. The United Front's essential problem rose primarily from internal rivalries that in turn provoked conflicts within as well as between its constituents. The coordination committee failed to mitigate the tensions within the coalition and its existence virtually became ornamental. Its failure was attributed to the prevalence of conflicting opinions that never led to a consensus. There were three shades of opinions: the chief minister had his views, which invariably represented that of CPI(M) of which he was a leader; the cabinet decisions, which reflected the diverse views of the constituent partners; and finally the views of the partners, usually representing the socio-political constituencies they held.[29] So the coordination committee was practically ineffective. One of the reasons for its gradual decline was the reluctance of the major partner, CPI(M), to endorse the decisions arrived at after deliberations in the committee. For instance, the CPI(M) openly opposed decisions of the committee regarding the procurement of the entire surplus of paddy from those holding more than ten acres of land and vesting the responsibility for the wholesale trade in food grains in the Food Corporation of India. Such a clear violation by the major partner created a fissure within the ruling coalition.

Corruption was rampant. The government was hardly effective in this regard presumably because of the rivalry between the CPI and CPI(M). It was a tragedy, argues a Kerala expert, that 'the government that pledged to provide a clean administration finally went down on charges of corruption against all the thirteen of its ministers'.[30] The role of the Coordination Committee was insignificant. In fact, it was alleged that the Committee always acted as a shield for the CPI(M) since it was headed by a member of this party. This was the reason for its virtual non-existence. The discussion in the Committee was thus merely academic with hardly any consequence. As a result, the coalition partners were always suspicious of one another and the government machinery was utilized to improve their political fortunes rather than strengthening the coalition government in the interest of the people. Even the major partners, CPI and CPI(M), seemed to have less attention to administration since, according to them, 'nothing could be done under the present bourgeois framework of the Indian constitution'.[31]

What drove the coalition government was not the spirit of accommodation and consensus, but compromise, on most occasions. In view of the acrimonious relationship between CPI and CPI(M), the Muslim League, which was key to the coalitions' survival, managed to squeeze maximum benefits in exchange for its support. In order to isolate the CPI, the League emerged as the most acceptable strategic partner to the CPI(M) in its opposition to the former. In the process, the League gained most and the government conceded its demand for a Muslim majority district in Malappuram and a new university at Calicut. The non-League partners in the coalition characterized this as 'abject surrender to the communal demand of the Muslim League'.[32] Given its numerical strength in the assembly, the League's support was crucial for coalition's survival. It was therefore strategically suicidal for the CPI(M) to ignore the League. This is what made the League indispensable for the coalition. The position of the CPI(M) was most vulnerable when the League joined hands with other coalition partners in demanding an interim enquiry into corruption charges against CPI(M) ministers. The chief minister declined and suggested to move a no-confidence motion against the government. The motion was carried and Namboodripad resigned. His calculation that the Governor would impose Article 356 was wrong and the CPI leader Achutha Menon was invited to form a minority ministry comprising the Muslim League, Indian Socialist Party and Kerala Congress, supported by the RSP, and tacitly by Congress. The Menon ministry was a unique example of coalition in which the CPI(M) was totally excluded.[33]

The CPI(M) seemed to have been edged out by the CPI and other non-CPI(M) political parties. On the eve of the historic 1977 assembly election, the CPI(M) forged an alliance of seven parties – with the Janata Party, the Congress Radicals, the Opposition Muslim League, the RSP National, the Kerala Socialist Party and the Kerala Congress (Pillai) – that came together in their hostility to Indira Gandhi. Because of its impressive track record when in power, the Congress-led Ruling Front won 'handsomely with fifty three percent of the votes and 111 of the 140 Legislative Assembly seats'.[34] The worst sufferer was CPI(M), which was reduced to seventeen seats in the Assembly and managed only 22 per cent of the votes.

Since 1982, a pattern of coalition seems to have emerged in Kerala in which two specific types of coalition of parties figure prominently. On the one hand, there is the United Democratic Front with Congress as its dominant partner; and on the other side of the spectrum remains the CPI(M)-led Left Democratic Front. Except the respective dominant partners in the Fronts – Congress and CPI(M) – the constituents have crossed the floor more than once. It would not be wrong to suggest that what was initiated in the 1967 with the formation of the United Front under Namboodripad's stewardship has become an important feature in political articulation in Kerala. The Fronts have gradually become more ideologically oriented and less politically expedient. Hence, by 1987, the CPI(M)-led LDF decided not to include the Muslim League because of its 'explicit' communal ideology to develop 'a fairly genuine LDF, [based on] the socialist ideas of coalition-building'.[35] Notwithstanding the ideological metamorphosis of the respective Fronts, their importance in redefining Kerala politics in coalition terms can never be underplayed. The assembly elections since 1982 corroborate the trend, as Table 5.3 shows.

Unlike other states in India where the coalition experiment did not last beyond 1969 – except perhaps West Bengal, where an ideologically inspired coalition

Table 5.3 Election results in Kerala, 1982–2001

Front	1982 Assembly	1984 Lok Sabha	1987 Assembly	1989 Lok Sabha	1991 Assembly	1991 Lok Sabha	1996 Assembly	1996 Lok Sabha	1999 Lok Sabha	2001 Assembly
UDF contested	140	20	138	20	140	20	140	20	20	140
Won	77	17	60	17	92	16	59	10	11	99
% of votes	48.2	50.9	43.6	49.3	48.1	48.6	48.6	46.6	46.7	49.0
LDF contested	140	20	140	20	140	20	140	20	20	140
Won	63	3	78	3	48	4	80	10	09	40
% of votes	47.2	42.3	45.0	44.4	45.9	44.3	46.7	44.6	43.7	42.2

Note: In the 2001 assembly election, Congress won 62 of 88 seats contested whereas the CPI(M) gained only 23 of 77 seats contested. *The Hindu*, 14 May 2001.

Source: James Chiriyankandath, 'Bounded nationalism: Kerala and the social and regional limits of Hindutva', in Thomas Blom Hansen and Christophe Jaffrelot (eds), *The BJP and the Compulsions of Politics in India*, Delhi: Oxford University Press, 1998, p. 223. Figures for 1999 Lok Sabha poll and 2001 assembly poll: *Indian Express*, 14 May 2001.

has survived since 1977 – Kerala is the only state continuously governed by a coalition of parties irrespective of ideology. Crucial to coalition in this densely populated state on the south-western coast of India is not ideology but the success of the political parties/groups in mustering support of the major communities of Ezhavas, Nairs, Christians and Muslims. The growing decline of 'the left and right ideologies' seems to have created a vacuum in which the community-based choices have gained in importance both in the formation of ministry and its survival. It is therefore not surprising that the Catholics, despite being ideologically opposed to the atheists, support the Communist-led coalition. Similarly, both the Congress and the Communists forge alliances with the Muslim League notwithstanding its communal character. The class-based ideology seems to have lost its resilience and political parties tend to be community-based presumably because of the importance of communities in the assembly and Lok Sabha elections.

The possible outcomes

These different experiments, though inchoate, suggest a new political trend in Indian politics. An age of coalition seemed to have begun. As evident, by and large regional parties and those with a strong local base became the beneficiaries of the decline of the Congress system. In the 1967 provincial elections, local issues appeared to have gained centrality in the poll campaign and also in its aftermath. The governments, once installed in the state capital, pledged to fulfil the local demands on priority. Now, was this a situation when national perspectives seemed to have taken a backseat and local issues determined the political articulation in the changed environment? The answer seems to be difficult because the political indications were not very clear. At best, one can argue that the coalition experiments were perhaps an articulation of an answer with reference to the fluidity of socio-political circumstances in which provinces were placed following the breakdown of the Congress system. On the surface, the growing importance of regionalization did not appear to have matched with the concern of the constitution makers as it apparently challenged the unified central authority. It was probably most appropriate when the Constitution was inaugurated in 1952 for the young nation that suffered partition. The Constitution does not remain static. In its organic evolution over more than five decades, the Constitution is constantly redefined to articulate new dimensions, meaningful in the changed environment. So, the apparent contradiction with the goal, the Constitution devised at the outset, is misleading unless the supreme law of the land is interpreted in literal terms without reference to its changing nature in response to the obvious socio-economic metamorphosis of the context. What is argued here is that the Constitution, as an organic system of thought, is to reject the old conceptualizations and welcome the new waves to reinvent its goal as is most appropriate at a given point of time. As will be shown below, what was just a trend in the 1967 election became gradually a settled fact. And coalition was probably the only response to a situation when the notion of a single-party majority was merely academic.

The most unique feature of this experiment was a clear political polarization in the states. It is true that the Congress was polarized in several interest groups and its continuity is attributed to its capacity to accommodate the diverse, if not conflicting, interests. Now, the parties, however ephemeral, had emerged to ostensively represent 'the neglected' socio-economic interests, though there was hardly a uniform pattern in this regard. For instance, the United Front government in West Bengal was exceptional in the sense that it sought to project a completely different ideological combination presumably because the communists dominated the coalition. It was a qualitatively different political formation, pledged to protect the interests of the downtrodden, especially the workers and landless agricultural labour. Given their ideological belief, the other major partner, the Bengal Congress, was not comfortable with this governmental agenda, but had to swallow the bitter pill to avoid the disintegration of the Front. The Punjab situation is also illustrative here. So long as the Congress was in power, it always drew upon its strategy of balancing the conflicting Hindu and Sikh interests in the state. The new Akali–Jana Sangh coalition in Punjab was reflective of a new politics of adjustment that was inevitable, as Balraj Madhok conceptualized as early as 1964 by saying that, 'if parties remain separate, strains and stresses are bound to be there. So, in the long run complete merger and setting up of a national democratic party is the only solution which can provide an alternative pole to the people.'[36] By 1967, what was just an idea became a reality; coalition governments came into existence and parties with ideological differences merged to justify the formation of coalition governments by non-Congress parties where no single party had been able to obtain a clear majority. In a resolution adopted in a meeting of the Central General Council, the Jana Sangh defended its participation in these coalitions by underlining that

> the formation of these governments has been in deference to the popular sentiment, and fully in conformity with democratic traditions. Despite its ideological and policy differences with the other opposition parties, the Jana Sangh has agreed to join the governments with them on the basis of a minimum common programme.[37]

So, the period between 1962 and 1967 therefore had shown 'the first signs that the Jana Sangh's young leaders who had taken control of the party in 1955 were beginning to weigh up the relative advantages' of alliances with parties that stand for 'social justice, reduction of inequalities [and] changing of the status quo'.[38] So, the Jana Sangh seemed to have given up political catholicity in regard to selection of its allies except the communists for their uncritical acceptance of 'totalitarian governance' as inevitable for social change. By agreeing to support and join, on occasions, the coalition governments in various states, the Jana Sangh became an integral part of the coalition experiments in India. In Bihar, the Mahamaya Prasad Sinha cabinet included two Jana Sanghi ministers; in Punjab, the chief minister, Gurnam Singh, persuaded the Jana Sangh leader, Baldev Prakash, to join the United Front government. In Haryana, the Jana Sangh extended support from outside to both the Sharma and Bansi Lal ministries. In Uttar Pradesh, the formation of the Jana Congress ministry, led by Charan Singh, who broke away from Congress, was possible with the support of Jana Sangh, who had five ministers and three deputy ministers in his cabinet. These instances exemplify the new trend in which the coming together of various non-Congress parties, including the Jana Sangh, translated into reality an alternative model of governance in which Congress as a party hardly figured.[39]

Although the coalitions were indicative of a remarkable trend in India politics, they did not last long presumably because of the lack of congruity among the constituents. In fact, apart from the parties, the dependence on so many independent legislators was also a serious weakness of these formations. Illustrative of this is Bihar, where the chief minister, Mahamaya Prasad Sinha, devoted most of his energy to keeping this large number of independents in good humour largely because their support on the floor of legislature was crucial. With a large number of indeterminate incompatible loyalties almost 'every coalition [had] too many internal incompatibles to be durable and effective'.[40] The phenomenon of '*aya ram* (those coming to the coalition) and *gaya ram* (those defecting) seemed to have acquired notoriety because of the frequent disintegration of ruling coalitions.[41] So the possibility of coalitions created a paradox: before 1967, the opposition parties were terribly frustrated because of the hegemonic presence of the Congress Party and in consequence their endless exile. With the capture of power in the states, they became excessively important in government formation. Given the fragile nature of these coalitions, the constituent parties failed largely to meet their aspirations and the coalitions broke on flimsy personal grounds. It was easier to make ministries than to sustain and nourish them as politically viable formations. Governance was the victim because of so many splinter groups constituting the government. Like its ingrained multicultural existence, Indian politics is fragmented: each state is a unique political formation in itself.

In the frequent breakdown of coalitions, the politics of defections gained tremendous significance. The floor-crossing was so frequent that none of the coalition governments in a state ever had stability and they were always in the throes of crisis. As contemporary figures show, many of the government changes in the northern states were the result of defection or floor-crossing by individual legislators, both party members and independents. Floor-crossing was 'pretty regular' and there remained 'a defector market'.[42] Congress suffered most because defectors flowed both ways, both into and out of Congress. More flowed out, however, than in, causing the fall of the Congress governments in UP, Madhya Pradesh and Haryana.[43] Corrupt legislators 'indulged in horse-trading and freely changed sides, attracted mainly by the lure of office or money'.[44] Between 1967 and 1970, nearly 800 legislators crossed the floor and nearly 155 of them were rewarded with ministerial office. Party discipline was thus the first casualty, except perhaps in the communist parties and Jana Sangh. There was no respite because defection turned out to be a safe instrument for upward mobility for the legislators, who suddenly became important for the survival of the coalition by providing the adequate numerical support on the floor of legislature. It was only with the acceptance of the defection law by the Congress government in 1986 that defection lost its importance.

Concluding observations

Whatever the assessment, the 1967 experiment brought about far-reaching changes in Indian politics in two fundamental ways. First, the days of the single-party majority were over and replaced by a coalition of parties not purely on the basis of ideological compatibility but for a desire to push the Congress Party out of power. In the formation of coalition, defection was an important ingredient and most of the parties were adversely affected, except that those parties to the far right and left maintained their organizational integrity through discipline and ideological consistency. So, the period 1967–69 proved a transitional stage or interregnum in politics illustrating the rise of a new phase when coalition of parties became an inescapable phenomenon. Second, anti-Congressism gained ground with the 1967 elections and the idea that the Congress Party was invincible seemed to have exhausted its potential. Anti-Congressism was defined in a very vague manner so as to catch on with all the parties opposed to Congress. This was probably how the major communist parties, including CPI(M) and CPI, shared the platform with the dissident members of Congress when forming the United Front government in West Bengal. What drove them to support even the ideologically incompatible partners was perhaps the national democratic ideology of diverse class interests in order to trounce a major political foe, Congress. Whatever the theoretical justification, the primary goal was to rout Congress. The high-priest of anti-Congressism was Rammanohar Lohia, who, as Kothari argued, 'devoted himself of destroying the Congress monopoly of power by uniting all anti-Congress forces in the country'.[45] Lohia succeeded in his mission and the Indian polity was clearly divided into two opposite camps: those supporting Congress and those who were opposed to it. Any group, any party and any leader who declared itself/himself in opposition to the Congress were deemed to be politically correct and worthy of admiration. Whatever the reason, the Lohiaite anti-Congressism made electoral tactical sense because parties with an anti-Congress stance booted Congress out only when they were united. But this was not always put into practice because highly antagonistic contradictions among the non-Congress parties were rooted in the social realities of rural India. Unfortunately there was no cohesive opposition and, despite having won power in the 1967 elections in as many as nine states, no durable coalition was formed. A new phase had begun when both Congress and opposition parties sought to redefine themselves in the changed environment. No longer was it possible for Congress to reap electoral gains simply by its role in the freedom struggle and achievement during the Nehru era. For the opposition parties, although the anti-Congress sentiments catapulted them to the centre stage of Indian politics, they failed to ensure stability of coalition government without substantial socio-economic programmes.

This was an era of possibilities. Congress lost power and, for its revival, it had to renew itself keeping in mind the changed nature of Indian polity. Similarly, the opposition parties translated the sentiments against Congress into an opportunity whereby Congress was pushed out of power in a majority of Indian provinces (nine of sixteen states). Yet its euphoria at electoral victory over Congress was short-lived. So this was also an era of political uncertainty in which none of the major political parties was sure of its fate in future India. Characterized by uncertainty and chronic political instability, the period 1967–69 therefore represented a clear break with the past by creating a definite space for coalition politics as opposed to monocentric single-party rule. The event of coming together of parties with diverse interests was thus a part of wider democratic processes whereby a new wave was crystallized with a far-reaching impact and significant consequences on future political articulation. And coalition is inevitable because the basic shift that has occurred in Indian politics cannot be glossed over.

6 The Left Front and the 2006 assembly elections in West Bengal

Marxism reinvented

The continuity of the Left Front government in power in West Bengal for the last thirty years is a record not only in India but also in the context of electoral politics anywhere in the world. The reasons are not difficult to seek. Besides augmenting steady agricultural growth with effective land reforms, the left coalition maintained its strong presence in the state through a carefully managed organizational spread of disciplined left parties and their increasing mass base across the state. West Bengal is thus a unique example of democratic governance where political stability has not been the result of low levels of political mobilization,[1] but an outcome of sustained organizational efforts involving stakeholders in both urban and rural areas. Parallel to the prevalent bureaucratic structure of the government, these organizations became facilitators for almost all public provisions, from admission to hospitals to selection of beneficiaries in targeted government schemes. People, too, approached these organizations to settle private, even familial, disputes. It is therefore impossible to understand the durability of the government without appreciating the spread of the Left organizations in the arteries of West Bengal's social sphere. While it gave society a sense of coherence, it also made the Left – in its anxiety to be acceptable – socially conservative.[2] Nonetheless, the Left Front had won all the state assembly elections in a row from 1977 to 2006, which itself is an exception in India's contemporary political landscape. The juggernaut of the Left Front seems to be unstoppable and the 2006 poll outcome is a continuation of the trend that began in 1977 when it captured power in the state for the first time. Besides almost completely eliminating the opposition in the state, the Left Front constituents, especially its leading partner, CPI(M), have made significant inroads in Calcutta and other peripheral towns across various age groups. This election is a watershed in West Bengal politics with far-reaching political consequences not only for the Left Front leadership but also for the state, which seems to have eschewed the orthodox Marxist state-directed development paradigm. In theoretical terms, the Left Front is closer to the West European social-democratic path as some major policy decisions regarding industrial revival in the state by the newly elected government clearly indicate. This has not, by any chance, happened overnight. The aim of this chapter is to dwell on the changing nature of the Left Front leadership and its ideology, which is not exactly classical Marxism but its reinvented form.

Conceptual points

By translating *vox populi* or the voice of the people into 'decisions', elections have become a basic creed of democracy, giving the will of the people 'divine authority'. Citizens remain supreme so long as the fate of the election is undecided. Once the election is over and the results are out, they accept the verdict as 'divinely ordained' regardless of whether or not the process is actually 'democratic'. Nonetheless, elections are significant milestones in liberal democracies for the following interconnected reasons. First, elections provide an opportunity for the voters to evaluate the incumbent political authority. In this sense, it is also an occasion for auditing the performances of the ruling parties in governance. Second, elections are an index of the importance of the issues that gain prominence during the campaign for votes. In view of the breakdown of 'the vote banks', elections have largely become issue-based. It is true that there always remain some major issues that tend to galvanize the voters regardless of age and social locations. But the crucial shift in voting is generally attributed to area-specific issues or issues that sway specific sections of population rather than the rest. Third, elections are also commentaries on the electoral viability of the political parties and their leadership. It is obvious that the electoral outcome is critical for the future of the political parties that participate in the elections; it is equally significant for the leadership, which, if it fails to capture the popular imagination, is likely to fade away. In other words, political leadership is a crucial component in the electoral battle, just like the party organization, which by projecting a specific type of leadership seeks to gain politically in competitive situations. Fourth, the electoral outcomes are also indicative of the changing nature of the political parties involved in elections. Just like the leadership, parties cannot survive if they are not amenable to change in terms of the ideology they prefer to project both during the election campaign and also otherwise. In other words, unless political parties are organic to the system in which they are located, the chances of their survival are low, if not bleak. What it suggests is that political parties need to reinvent themselves in tune with the surrounding social, political and economic milieu simply because they, in a liberal democracy, are the most time-tested vehicle for articulating new values, ideas and perspectives. The British Conservative Party is known for clinging to 'orthodox' values and yet its nature has undergone radical changes in contrast with what it was in the past. Similarly, the Congress Party in India, which was so enthusiastic about 'socialist values' in the past, began appreciating 'neo-liberal' values in the 1990s. Even in the 2004 national elections, the importance that Congress gave to 'economic liberalization' clearly suggests that the party is seeking to shake off its earlier ideological mould. Fifth, elections are important 'moments' for the country in two specific ways: first, in a diverse 'third world' situation, it is impossible, if not difficult, to identify issues that will gain political salience in elections. In the 2004 Lok Sabha poll, both the pan-Indian political parties in India, the Congress and Bharatiya Janata Party (BJP), raised more or less similar issues packaged in a calibrated response to economic liberalization. The outcome was not dramatic in the sense that both the parties were more or less evenly poised in terms of Lok Sabha seats. In extraordinary circumstances, however, the election results are most likely not to conform to what is projected. The outcomes of the 1977, 1984 and 1991 Lok Sabha polls in India are illustrative here because the peculiar circumstances that arose in the aftermath of the 1975–77 Emergency or the assassination of Indira Gandhi in 1984 and Rajiv Gandhi in 1991 radically altered the electoral behaviour that manifested in the results. These elections, characterized as 'plebiscites', though exceptional, reflect a particular moment of the national mood that was translated into votes. Second, elections are also moments when the organizational strength of the political parties is tested and assessed. It is true that 'swing' is a critical factor in elections in the first-past-the-post system though organization is what sustains the party regardless of whether it wins or not. Organization is 'the lifeline' of political parties in any ideological set-up. One of the reasons for the growing decline of the Congress Party is certainly 'the weakening' of its organization since the breakdown of the Congress system of the earlier days. A contrasting example of the Left Front that ruled West Bengal for almost three decades will suffice here to show the importance of organization in consolidating its position in the state. The leading partner of the Left Front, CPI(M), is perhaps the most organized party in India, remaining politically viable, if not invincible, by regularly reinventing its ideology taking into account the changing social, economic and political circumstances. It would not have been possible for the Front to translate its redefined ideology into votes without a well-entrenched organization that gradually evolved in West Bengal. What is thus significant, as the West Bengal example demonstrates, is the fact that ideology becomes a powerful vehicle for electoral mobilization provided there exists a strong organization with tentacles at the grassroots. Sixth, the poll results also indicate the growing importance of new segments of society that hardly mattered in politics before. In this sense, election provides a mechanism for social mobility. As is evident in most of the recently conducted elections in India, the decline of the upper/forward castes' dominance follows the ascendancy of the OBCs in political decision making. The emergence of these hitherto peripheral segments of Indian society has brought about radical changes at the grassroots. The increasing importance of OBCs and scheduled castes in contemporary Indian politics redefined the political discourse, which remains largely unidimensional presumably because of the centrality of the dominant castes in its articulation. Indian elections – whether at the national or provincial level – seem to be symptomatic of social transformations in the sense of the rise and fall of caste groups in various forms. Seventh, elections seem to articulate a process of interaction between civil society and state. The so-called anti-incumbency wave can, for instance, be conceptualized as civil society's backlash against the state. Similarly, following Gramsci, the Italian Marxist, one can also argue that civil society also acts as a buffer for the party holding state power. Election results are illustrative of whether the civil society is a buffer for or against the prevalent political authority. The recently concluded state assembly elections in Kerala and West Bengal demonstrate that, whereas the civil society in urban West Bengal supported the incumbent Left Front government, in Kerala the support was not forthcoming for the ruling party. Finally, elections are also an occasion when the federal balance of the Indian polity is clearly tilted in favour of the Union government in various ways. The growing importance of the Election Commission in elections in India reduces the role of state-centred governmental agencies, including the police. With its non-controversial image, the Election Commission is readily accepted by the voters and its role in conducting free and fair elections is highly acclaimed. Whether the intervention of a supra-state agency is conducive for federal practices that are being refashioned in a newly emerged coalitional context is debatable. But there is no doubt that the revamped Election Commission has changed the complexion of election in India in recent times by its pro-active role. Whereas the poll outcome in the 2005 Bihar election is largely attributed to the role played by the Election Commission in containing the poll malpractices, in West Bengal the Commission's intervention was condemned as 'unwarranted' for indulging in 'practices' that provoked mass consternation in both urban and rural West Bengal. Nonetheless, in view of the well-entrenched malpractices in elections, the Election Commission is perhaps the most significant constitutional machinery that has meaningfully defined elections in India.

These theoretical points are drawn out of the elections held in India over a period of time. In a sense, these are the points abstracted from the electoral practices that evolved historically. The outcome of the 2006 West Bengal assembly election may not be dramatic in the sense that the incumbent Left Front government recaptured power. What is however most striking is the growing popularity of the Left Front in Kolkata and its satellite towns where its electoral presence was negligible in the 2001 Assembly election. By redefining its ideology in the changed socio-political context, the left parties have gained enormously in electoral terms. The new voters endorsed the reinvented Left Front presumably because they felt that, in the absence of an alternative competitive bloc, it would contribute to their well-being by creating opportunities for them. This is undoubtedly an achievement for the Left Front, which always remained invincible in rural West Bengal largely because of the effective implementation of land reform schemes. The present Left Front is a conglomeration of political activists who despite their critical faith in a Marxism-inspired value system are not exactly averse to market-drawn neo-liberal ideologies so long as they contribute to the economic well-being of the rather backward state of West Bengal.

The context of the poll

The 2006 West Bengal Assembly election is not at all different from the earlier ones since the electoral outcome remains identical. The Left Front returned to power with a comfortable majority. Yet, this election is perhaps most dramatic in a number of ways. First, the Election Commission (EC) took charge of the election in the state in an unprecedented manner. The state government was largely, if not completely, bypassed for its alleged partisan role in election. Two reasons account for such 'an abusive role': first, the incumbent Left Front government was charged with manipulating the voters' list; second, the party cadres threatened reportedly anti-government voters and hence the intervention of the EC was hailed by those opposed to the ruling authority. One of the charges that gained currency was the inclusion of 'bogus' voters. The EC found a large number of them in various districts. During the clean-up operation, the observer found 1.3 million false names[3] in the list of voters, and struck them off. Hence the charge seemed authenticated and the media thus attributed the sustained electoral victory of the Left Front to 'the bogus voters'. The stringent measures that the Commission undertook, however, alienated a large number of people who found the intervention 'unwarranted' and 'undemocratic' as well because, in the name of correcting the voters' list, the Commission acted in a 'high-handed' manner. Thus a commentator remarks:

> the state was virtually under the control of the EC. Imported police and para-military personnel penetrated all parts of the state; route marches by them were organized in every constituency, sometimes twice a day.[4]

The EC was made to believe that the law and order situation in West Bengal was as bad as that of Bihar. Given its remarkable success in Bihar, the Commission resorted to the same strategy to contain 'electoral malpractices' that appeared to have contributed to the continuous Left Front victory.

The second factor that made this election different from the earlier-ones was linked with the 'pro-active role' of the Election Commission. In order to hold a free and fair poll, the Commission decided to conduct the poll over five widely dispersed dates stretching almost two months. Again, the Bihar formula was accepted in the sense that the election was held under strict surveillance of the coercive instrument of the state. The Commission requisitioned police and paramilitary forces from outside the state simply because the state police did not appear to be reliable. Because the dates were dispersed, it was possible to get an adequate number of them to supervise the voting on the election days. The state was under siege, as it were. It is true that, thanks to their presence, this election was almost free from electoral violence involving any of the contending political parties. Voters cast their votes without any threat. What disturbed the voters was, however, the difficulty that they underwent to accommodate a large contingent of these forces before election. A large number of public buildings, including schools, colleges and libraries, were taken over, disturbing the normal life of the areas in which elections were held. Even the National Library was not spared. Instead of raising hopes, the very presence of such a huge contingent of coercive forces caused consternation and anger among the common voters. In fact, the existence of these forces was never appreciated by the voters. The very idea of disciplining them by force did never sit well with Bengali sensibilities, as an on the spot survey reveals. The voters expressed resentment on the ground that 'the entire Bengali *jati*' was blamed for the misdeeds of a handful of miscreants.[5] The high-handed manner in which the Election Commission dealt with the poll preparation created an impression that it considered the people of West Bengal 'a suspect species'. Perhaps this also contributed to the close to 7 per cent increase over 2001 in the number of people who voted. They voted, as Ashok Mitra euphorically suggested, 'with their feet against the innuendoes dropped by the commission'.[6]

Following the discovery of 'bogus voters' in various parts of the state, the apprehension of manipulation in preparing the voters' list gained ground. It was also found out that, in its enthusiasm for a free and fair poll, the Commission also struck off names of a large number of genuine voters. This surfaced only during the election.[7] How was it possible for the Commission to emerge as 'a messiah' in a state that is politically conscious and largely free from prejudices linked with ascriptive identities? One of the reasons was surely 'the media hype' that arose once the Commission-appointed observers emerged on the scene. Wherever the observers went, the leading newspapers gave extensive coverage to their discoveries of 'bogus voters'.[8] The purpose was to authenticate the allegation of 'manipulation' of the voters' list. By so doing, the media actually upheld the charges of the parties in opposition that the sustained electoral popularity of the Left Front was largely possible because of 'extraordinary corrupt practices at all levels' that made 'scientific rigging', as it is euphemistically described, possible. The local bureaucracy was held responsible. As a former bureaucrat argues, 'either they slipped up negligently or more probably they connived stealthily with the interested political groups to manipulate the voters' list in their favour'.[9] The 2006 assembly election is thus a clear break with the past.

The poll outcome

This election is historic because, if nothing else, 'the zeal shown by the Election Commission in monitoring this election lends the result a special meaning'.[10] There were three major coalitions of parties in the electoral fray. Besides the Left Front, the other two coalitions of parties were the Trinamul-led alliance and the conglomeration that formed around Congress. As the results show, the Left Front is far ahead of other contending political parties both in terms of the number of legislative seats and also the share of votes. In fact there has been a steady increase in these counts since 1996 (Table 6.1). Unlike the Left Front, the opposition experienced 'a poll debacle' because of the dramatic decline both in numerical legislative strength and share of votes, as Table 6.2 illustrates.

As the tally of seats and percentage of the share of popular votes reveal, the Left Front victory is most impressive, though the most spectacular win happens to be the 1987 assembly election when, in a tally of 251 seats for the Left Front (out of a total of 294 assembly seats), the CPI(M) won as many as 187 seats. Yet the 2006 poll results evoke surprise because of the dramatic decline of the opposition parties. There is hardly an opposition worth the name.

Table 6.1 Seats and percentage share of votes in West Bengal assembly elections, 1996–2006

Name of coalition	1996	2001	2006
Left Front	203 (46.7%)	199 (48.4%)	235 (50.2%)
Trinamul-led alliance	n/a	60 (30.7%)	30 (26.3%)
Congress conglomeration		26 (7.9%)	21 (15%)

Sources: *Anandabazar Patrika*, 12 May 2006; *The Telegraph*, 13 May 2006.

Table 6.2 The 2006 West Bengal assembly election results (in contrast with the 2001 outcome)

Parties	Seats won 2001	Seats won 2006	Percentage of votes 2001	Percentage of votes 2006
Left Front	199	235	48.4	50.2
CPI(M)	143	176	36.6	37.0
CPI	7	8	1.8	2.1
AIFB	25	23	5.6	5.7
RSP	17	20	3.4	3.7
WBSP	4	4	0.7	0.7
RJD	0	1	0.7	0.1
DSP	0	1	0.4	0.1
Independent (LF)	0	2	0.4	0.1
Congress	26	21	7.9	15.0
Trinamul Congress	60	30	30.7	26.3
GNLF	3	3	0.5	0.1
JKP(N)	0	1	0.2	0.2
Independent	9	4	5.0	3.8

Sources: *The Hindu*, 16 May 2006; *Frontline*, 2 June 2006, p. 6.

The possible explanation

The poll outcome in West Bengal was not dramatic in the sense that it was more or less anticipated. The stringent measures of the Election Commission to ensure 'a level playing field for all' in the state – resulting in the highest voter turnout – denied the opposition the chance 'to explain away the defeat by pointing to the election malpractices'.[11] From the point of view of the Left Front, the verdict is, as commonly defined, both a change and continuity. Given the retention of power in the Writers' Building, the 2006 poll is clearly continuity. But with the growing importance of the new leadership in the Front, this election has also endorsed its new face.

The Brand Buddha[12] in rural Bengal

The achievement of the Left Front in the rural areas in particular – its land reform measures, the registration of sharecroppers (*operation barga*), the panchayati system – has ushered in a significant process of radical changes in the political layout of the state.[13] Much of the economic change in rural West Bengal since 1977 has been made possible because of a significant political process, initiated and carried forward by the Left Front government. Important here has been the devolution of power – including considerable financial powers – to the elected panchayats. This step together with a strong political commitment to implementing land reforms, has ensured a process of genuine democratic participation by the rural poor in the remaking of their lives and their socio-economic environment. Although the enactment of the Seventy-third Amendment Act is a significant step towards revamping the panchayati institutions in the country, the Left Front initiated the process as early as 1977–80 by giving *panchayats* substantial power for local development.[14] Since the programmes for poverty alleviation sponsored by New Delhi or other agencies have been closely supervised through the party hierarchy, they are better implemented in West Bengal than in any other states. Such a supervisory role has developed and sustained a constant interaction with the people at the grassroots which, *inter alia*, accounts for the consolidation of the Left Front in rural Bengal. Furthermore, with its long tradition of political mass mobilization, the Left Front has not only sustained but also gradually expanded its organizational network within the State. As Table 6.3 shows, the Left Front appears invincible in rural Bengal.

This is one side of the coin. The story of the Left Front ascendancy can also be told in a different way. The fact that the ruling party candidates win unopposed in a large number of panchayat constituencies (Table 6.4) is indicative of a dangerous political trend that hardly allows opposition to crystallize simply because they would not dare 'to provoke a situation in which they would face the combined wrath of the [party] cadres and police'.[15] Furthermore, contrary to the Left Front claim, as a study reveals, the downward devolution of power has given way to the rising middle sections of the rural society who now control the panchayats. As a result, these bodies have become 'synonymous with the elected popular bureaucracy'.[16] What it suggests is that the panchayats seem to be crippled by

Table 6.3 Share of the Left Front votes in the panchayats and zila parishads

Year	Gram Panchayat	Panchayat Samiti	Zila Parishad
1978	70.3	77.0	71.5
1983	61.2	66.2	62.2
1988	72.3	79.0	73.5
1993	64.4	72.8	65.7
1998	56.1	67.1	58.1
2003	65.8	74.1	67.2

Source: computed from the data available in *Paschim Banger Panchayat Nirvachan Tathya O Samiksha* (1978–2003), Bharater Communist Party, Paschim Banga Rajya Committee.

Table 6.4 Left Front candidates elected unopposed

Year	Number of seats uncontested	Percentage of total seats
1978	338	0.73
1983	332	0.74
1988	4200	8.00
1993	1716	2.81
1998	600	1.35
2003	6800	11.0

Source: D. Bandyopadhyay, 'Caucus and masses: West Bengal Panchayats', *Economic and Political Weekly*, 15–21 November 2003, p. 4826.

rigid party control in the name of ushering in an era of participatory democracy in the real sense. Despite the overwhelming electoral and organizational presence of the poorer sections of rural Bengal, the process seems to be strengthened presumably because of the rigid party control over these rural centres of democratic administration. Governed by what is known as the 'political-organizational perspective', the CPI(M), for instance justifies hegemonic control of the party in terms of ideological goal of 'democratic centralism'. That the party cannot be bypassed is clearly spelt out by the CPI(M) state committee, saying that

> democratic participation [does] not mean acting at will. It means [that] the activation of panchayats in accordance with the principles of and ideals of the party. The basic issue involved here is giving party leadership to panchayats. This leadership consists of (a) political leadership and (b) organizational leadership. . . . The political leadership of the party is established only when people in their own experience, accept the political perspective of the party as their own. Even though decisions may be correct, they are not automatically translated into actions. We need to activate our activists and the masses for carrying out our decisions. . . . The party has a definite aim. Panchayat activities should be conducted in such a way that they conform to the basic goals of the party.[17]

There is thus no doubt that the panchayats in West Bengal are governed by the party in power. In order to translate the party perspective, the CPI(M) State Committee constituted, at the level of panchayats, a guiding cell (*parichalan committee*) that is entrusted with the task of steering the panchayats in accordance with the directives of the party high command. The party therefore commands that

> [a]ll elected party members of panchayat samiti and zila parishad will act under the respective committees. Generally the local and zonal committees of the party will look after the gram panchayat samitis. The final decision at each level will be taken by the Parichalan Committee of the party, although the elected members of the party may offer views if they are not satisfied with the decision.[18]

The growing hegemony of the party provides, on the one hand, organizational strength to the panchayats; it also, on the other hand, strengthens the party functionaries, who, despite being 'outsiders', continue to remain significant in the panchayat bodies simply because of their assigned role in the party directives. So, centralization of power actually strikes at the very root of devolution of power. What thus emerges gradually is the politics of patronage and populist policies. Furthermore, because political parties compete in panchayat elections and the winner has direct control over the substance of the village level plan and the selection of the beneficiaries, 'the panchayat system [invariably] indulges in politicization of the planning process and the implementation of the public projects'.[19] This probably explains the story of death and malnutrition in Amlasole in West Midnapur, in the tribal belts of Purulia, Nadia and the eastern part of Murshidabad, in tea-garden areas of Cooch Bihar and the fringe areas of Dinajpur. Panchayats failed and the party functionaries appropriated these grassroots institutions to fulfil their selfish goal, as an important Left Front cabinet minister confessed: 'the local panchayat leaders squandered the Central government funds for development to buy liquor and build club houses'.[20] Yet, the juggernaut of the Left Front seems unstoppable, as the poll verdict suggests. In fact, the Left Front has further consolidated its position in rural Bengal. In the economically backward districts of Bankura and South Dinajpur, the Left Front trounced other contending parties by winning all the thirteen and five seats respectively. Even in the district of Burdwan, which always remains the centre of left consolidation, the poll verdict hardly makes a dent in the left support base. By using the state power for the social transformation of the marginalized classes, a commentator argues, 'the government has created a climate of security [for these classes] and has provided more for the poor than other Governments have'.[21] What explains the continuity of the Left Front is the success in integrating the government's ameliorating pro-people policies with the strategies of political mobilization. By contextualizing the Marxist ideology, the CPI(M)-led coalition shifted its social base from 'being a party of the industrial proletariat' to that of marginal farmers, sharecroppers and the landless poor. This class base was 'carefully stitched together for a coalition of socially marginalized groups that included Dalits, Adivasis and Muslims'. The sustained viability of the Left Front for more than three decades can be attributed to 'this unique class–community coalition' that makes the Left Front invincible in rural Bengal.

The Brand Buddha in urban Bengal

The 2006 poll outcome is illustrative of the success of the Brand Buddha in expanding the Left Front support bases even among those who never stood by the left. The results in Kolkata demonstrate that the poll verdict is clearly tilted in favour of the beleaguered left. Kolkata was never the left stronghold and the anti-incumbency factors always remained critical in voters' preference. This time, the Front victory in ten constituencies in Kolkata and its suburbs reflects its growing popularity among the urban voters. Similarly, in results in the industrial belts of Howrah and Hooghly the overwhelming majority of the Front tells an identical story. In Howrah, the Front won fourteen of sixteen seats, of which CPI(M) captured eleven. Of the nineteen seats in Hooghly, the Left Front obtained seventeen, of which the CPI(M)'s share is thirteen.

There is no denying the importance of the party organization in the Left Front victory. What is new in the 2006 election is the pro-active role of the Chief Minister, Buddhadeb Bhattacharjee, the new face of the Front and symbol of continuity and change. The efforts at industrialization and securing investments for the state by Bhattacharjee seem to have paid electoral dividends to the Front that he leads. The message that the new leadership gave by focusing more on industrialization, urban infrastructure and urban middle classes has 'kindled the hopes and aspirations of the new voters'.[22] In fact, the principal aim of the new government is to adopt policies and programmes for developing both the rural and urban Bengal to arrest the economic degeneration of the state, which was the industrial hub of the country in the recent past.

While delineating his priorities as the chief of the Front government, Bhattacharya provided a blueprint for the future, which he prefaced by saying that 'the message that the people have given us with their verdict is that we have to give even more importance to what we are doing and we have to succeed'.[23] In this press conference, he identified three important tasks that the Front has to accomplish to fulfil the expectation of the voters: first, to continue to accord importance to the agriculture sector because that is what sustains the economy in a big way; second, to match the improvement in agriculture by similar growth in the industrial sector, which is possible if equal importance is given to industrial growth and investment in industries that create jobs and also contribute to state's overall economic growth; third, to ensure overall growth in the state and also to take care of those who are still below the poverty line.[24]

It is a tightrope walk for the Chief Minister, who is clearly following an ideological path that resembles European social-democratic practices. By adopting a guarded approach to liberalization, Bhattacharjee seems to be striking a balance between those hardcore supporters who dismiss 'economic liberalization' as a bourgeois conspiracy and those revisionists willing to endorse the neo-liberal ideology so long as it contributes to the economic well-being of the state. This was evident in the first press conference that he addressed after the announcement of the poll results. Emphatically arguing that 'not everything about liberalization is right', Bhattacharjee further elaborated that 'we are against the policy of hire and fire of labour and arbitrary privatization'. Despite his firm commitment to socialism, that he is a pragmatic leader was evident when he mentioned that 'we cannot avoid liberalization because we live in a time where we have to work according to the market conditions'.[25] He is in favour of inviting 'private capital' for industrial rejuvenation of West Bengal because 'this is the mandate [which] the Left Front cannot ignore'.[26] He is critical of 'isolationism', which was, according to him, responsible for the breakdown of the former Soviet Union. In conformity with 'the Chinese reformist ideology', Bhattacharjee never found any contradiction between the private or even the foreign sector and the state sector when the primary mission is to 'ensure economic well-being of the people'. Besides his social-democratic economic stances, he is favourably inclined towards multi-party democracy, which is, according to him, most appropriate in a diverse society like India. Believing in the dictum of 'let a hundred flowers blossom', the Chief Minister redefines the CPI(M) ideology by being critical of 'rigidity and parochialism' in the party.[27] It is too early to predict the consequences of these stances in favour of 'restricted' liberalization. What is, however, clear is the success of the Brand Buddha in garnering new support base in urban Bengal. As the poll results show, in greater Kolkata, out of a total of forty-eight seats, the Left Front increased its tally to thirty-three in contrast with its tally of twenty-two seats in the 2001 election. The main loser happens to be the Trinamul Congress, which was routed in as many as twelve constituencies where it had won in the 2001 election. Now, the Mamata-led Trinamul Congress retains only eleven seats from greater Kolkata. One of the reasons for such a reversal is certainly a clear vote swing away from the Trinamul Congress.[28]

There is thus no doubt that the Brand Buddha reinvented the CPI(M)-led Left Front by seeking to adapt the governmental ideology to the changed environment.[29] This electoral victory is a significant turning point for the Left Front, which cannot afford to be an ideological monolith in the radically altered global circumstances with the apparent triumph of 'the end of history phase'. The Front's ascendancy is also indicative of peculiar state-centric social, economic and political processes that perhaps explain why only one state has been able to remain insulated from the strong storms of anti-incumbency that swept the rest of the country.[30] Also, the unassailable popularity of Buddhadeb Bhattacharjee is also evident by the fact that he created history by trouncing his opponent by a massive margin of 58,130 votes, which also shows the growing importance of the Brand Buddha in West Bengal politics.

The election machinery

Furthermore, the success of the Left Front parties in elections is also attributed to a well-tuned election machinery.[31] The CPI(M) nurtures a strong organization with a wide network to maintain a firm grip on the cadres and voters. Furthermore, employees in the formal sector constitute an important source of strength for the Left Front, especially CPI(M). There are approximately 3 million industrial workers belonging to the CPI(M)-led Centre of Indian Trade Unions (CITU). The frontal organizations – the All Bengal Teachers' Association, West Bengal College and University Teachers' Association, and the West Bengal Government Teachers' Association – control the teaching profession in the state. The Coordination Committee is one of the biggest and perhaps the most powerful trade union organization controlling the government employees. By securing benefits, these frontal organizations have gained enormous respect among their supporters. Furthermore, Krishak Sabha with its huge membership among the peasantry constitutes the lifeline of the CPI(M) support base in rural West Bengal. Unlike other contending parties, which are revitalized once the poll dates are announced, these frontal organizations always remain active in their respective fields. By linking the government and the governed, they provide inputs to the policy makers that may not be otherwise available. The government thus never remains a distant agency to those at the grassroots, which undoubtedly consolidates the ruling party's support base.

Whereas the Left Front draws on the support of the frontal organizations in normal times, during election campaigns the following structure, as elaborately shown in Table 6.5, is created to effectively mobilize voters for the Left Front. This structure is probably unmatched in any other electoral democracy in the world. Managed by the full-time party cadres, these committees play crucial roles

Table 6.5 Election committee for assembly segment

Urban areas	Rural areas
Ward committees	Area committee
Booth committees	Anchal committee
Station or sub-station	Branch committee
Street-in-charge	Booth committee
Campaign workers	Campaign units for groups of households

Source: District Committee, South Calcutta.

both in the selection of the candidates for the assembly segments as well as in the campaign during the election. Operating within specified geographical boundaries, the activities of these committees are coordinated by the district committee, the apex body in the district, which is put under the state-level committee, located in Calcutta. Although during the elections their activities are geared towards the elections, they continue to function even after elections as permanent local units of the Left Front parties, involved in the day-to-day life of the people living in particular localities. In other words, they continue as the link between the localities and the provincial party machinery, which provides the basic input to the Left Front government in adopting the appropriate policies. The table shows how the election machinery works by linking various sectors of the state, by linking them with 'the election cell' in the party headquarters, which also runs a propaganda cell for publicizing the views of the party on various social, economic and political issues.

The left bastion has thus been well-maintained over the years thanks to a well-entrenched election machinery. This is certainly a significant factor in its consistently impressive electoral performance. Neither the Trinamul Congress nor the Indian National Congress has succeeded in evolving an organization to match the Left Front. Whereas for the others political mobilization begins and perhaps ends with the election, the Left front is engaged in a continuous dialogue with the voters that is perhaps translated into votes during the election.

The fragmented opposition

The left juggernaut seems to be invincible because there is hardly an organized opposition to match the cast-iron organization, supported by trained cadres and an election machinery with its tentacles even in the remote areas of rural Bengal. Apart from remaining divided, the anti-Left political parties have neither any leader worth the name nor any organization capable of competing with 'the mass fronts of the parties constituting the Left Front'.[32] The decline of the opposition began in the 2004 Lok Sabha election when out of a total of forty-two parliamentary seats the Left Front won thirty-five, Congress captured six (14.6 per cent of the votes) and the Trinamul Congress one (21 per cent of the votes). The explanation has to be located in the failure of the opposition parties to come together against perhaps the most organized political party in India. As against a fragmented opposition, the Left Front is a homogeneous unit willing to brush differences under the carpet for the sake of the coalition. The outcome of the 2006 assembly election was thus predictable. It is not surprising that the Left Front secured more than 50 per cent of the popular vote, which is better than any of the contending parties. While the Trinamul Congress obtained 26 per cent of the popular vote, the share of Congress and the BJP remained 15 per cent and 2 per cent respectively. So the fragmented opposition was no match for the organized left. A study reveals[33] that one of the principal reasons for the Left Front victory is surely the vote split among the voters who supported the opposition against the left. Had there been no division of opposition votes, the number of the Left Front seats in the legislative assembly would certainly have been less. In a number of constituencies, the Left Front candidates won by default since votes were divided among the parties opposed to the ruling conglomeration. If there had been 'a *mahajot*' (grand collation) of the three major anti-Left Front political parties, namely Congress, the BJP and the Trinamul Congress, the CPI(M)-led coalition would have seen reversals in a large number of constituencies. This argument can be substantiated by the index of opposition unity, which also shows that the opposition registered victory because the level of unity among those opposed to the Left Front was very high, as Table 6.6 demonstrates.

Of sixty constituencies in which Left Front candidates lost, there are six constituencies – Darjeeling, Kandi, Bow Bazaar, Chowringhee, Serampore and Kharagpur Town – in which the opposition unity was very low and yet the opposition parties had won presumably because (a) a massive split of votes due to infighting among both the ruling and opposition parties decided the fate of the candidates by a very marginal swing of votes and (b) 'the sons of the soil' argument might have favoured the candidates who had won as against the 'imported candidates' who hardly had any organic roots in the constituencies. Besides these six constituencies, the table merely confirms that a high level of opposition unity – in terms of either seat adjustment or fielding a common candidate – is what explains the victory of the anti-Left Front candidates in circumstances in which the left juggernaut seems 'unstoppable'.

Given the fractured opposition, it is fair to attribute the massive Left Front victory to lack of unity among the opposition parties. Hence the victory of the Front candidates is not indicative of pro-left sentiments, but an inevitable outcome of lack of unity and factional squabbles among the contending parties. In fact, the failure to form an electoral coalition against the Left Front cost the opposition parties as many as seventy seats because votes split between the Trinamul and Congress candidates enabled the Left Front candidates to win. Whether one can attribute this poll debacle of the anti-left political parties to 'a serious strategic failure' is debatable. But there is no doubt that the opposition parties in West Bengal are largely crippled by internal feud and the whimsical nature of the leadership. Of the three major parties, the Trinamul Congress emerged as an alternative, though it, argues a commentator, self-destructed, thanks to its creator, Mamata Banerjee, who destroyed 'the hopes by her whimsical behaviour that hardly inspires a great deal of confidence'.[34] Furthermore, though she is 'an

Table 6.6 2006 assembly election in West Bengal; index of opposition unity

Constituency	Winning party	Index of opposition unity
Sitai	Congress	84.6
Dinahata	Trinamul	80.0
Jalpaiguri	Congress	79.2
Kalimpong	GNLF[b]	61.8
Darjeeling[a]	GNLF[b]	59.9
Kurseong	GNLF[b]	69.0
Goalpokhar	Congress	87.5
Raiganj (SC)	Congress	73.6
Kharba	Congress	88.7
Araidanga	Congress	91.4
Englishbazar	Congress	85.1
Suzapur	Congress	87.1
Farakka	Congress	87.1
Lalgola	Congress	89.1
Naoda	Congress	90.7
Berhampore	Independent	80.0
Kandi[a]	Independent	52.1
Nakashipara	Trinamul	82.6
Nabadwip	Trinamul	91.3
Santipur	Congress	89.6
Bagdaha (SC)	Trinamul	93.4
Bongaon	Trinamul	93.6
Gaighata	Trinamul	89.0
Kultali (SC)	Independent	90.8
Joynagar	Independent	70.6
Bhangar	Trinamul	89.2
Behala West	Trinamul	89.5
Garden Reach	Congress	79.4
Budge Budge	Trinamul	91.3
Satgachia	Trinamul	84.2

Constituency	Winning party	Index of opposition unity
Cossipur	Trinamul	72.5
Jorasanko	Trinamul	67.4
Bow Bazaar[a]	Congress	56.6
Chowringhee[a]	Trinamul	58.3
Kabitirtha	Congress	82.4
Alipore	Trinamul	82.1
Rashbehari Avenue	Trinamul	68.3
Tollygunge	Trinamul	86.7
Ballyguange	Trinamul	84.6
Sealdah	Congress	79.2
Burtola	Trinamul	80.9
Belgachia West	Trinamul	83.8
Sankrail (SC)	Trinamul	80.9
Shyampur	Trinamul	88.0
Serampore[a]	Trinamul	58.1
Singur	Trinamul	89.9
Bhagabanpur	Trinamul	92.5
Contai South	Trinamul	90.8
Egra	Trinamul	90.4
Sabang	Congress	90.3
Kharagpur Town[a]	Congress	53.2
Binpur (ST)	JKP(N)[c]	93.5
Jhalda	Congress	80.3
Kulti	Trinamul	88.7
Nadanghat	Trinamul	88.5
Katwa	Congress	88.0
Rampurhat	Trinamul	81.9
Hansan (SC)	Congress	89.1

Notes
a Constituencies with low opposition unity.
b Gorkha National Liberation Front.
c Jharkhand Party (Naren).

Source: calculated from the website of the Election Commission of India (www.eci.gov.in/).

excellent rabble rouser', underlines another analyst, 'she is unable to think or execute any coherent programme for either the administration or the state [simply because] she is too temperamental'.[35] Besides her own folly, the organization that she leads has shown serious cracks due largely to factional fights among her colleagues. Furthermore, what disturbed the Bengali sensibilities was perhaps her fickleness in selecting coalition partners. At one point of time it was the BJP, at another it was Congress. Congress is a weak link because of its failure to rise above factional fights[36] and the BJP lacks the organization and also the popular support that project the party as a formidable contender besides its failure to strike a chord with the politically baptized Bengalis presumably because of its endorsement of the so-called communal ideology. In contrast with all these contending parties, 'the Left Front vote bank remains stable – with the Bengali electorate left with no option but to accept the [Front] as something better than others'.[37] And the new leadership seems to have swayed the majority of the voters by appropriate socio-economic programmes for rejuvenating the state economy and revamping its infrastructure. It is therefore not surprising that the Trinamul Congress lost its grip largely on account of a significant vote swing away from the party, as is evident in Table 6.7.

Although the vote swing of 1.2 per cent in favour of the Left Front is not terribly significant, the Trinamul Congress, as the table shows, undoubtedly suffered a serious setback in West Bengal. The voters re-endorsed the Left Front for another term presumably because it is perhaps the only conglomeration that is capable of providing a stable government with reasonably persuasive economic programmes and political agenda, which both the major contending parties miserably lack. Hence, an enthusiastic supporter of the Left Front sarcastically concludes that, 'to ensure free a fair elections in West Bengal, it was not enough to import poll personnel, poll observers and paramilitary security guards from elsewhere, one must also import voters from other states!'[38] There is no denying that in some constituencies the Front contained reversals by gaining new constituencies of support. The Left Front, especially its leading member, CPI(M), seems to have acquired the characteristics of 'a catch-all party' that is willing to adopt 'reconciliatory stances' (even at the cost of its core ideological beliefs) to expand its support base. Whether this will rattle the 'core supporters' or adapt them to the reformed party is not easy to evaluate, at least now when the euphoria over electoral victory is high.

Table 6.7 Electoral performance of Trinamul Congress, 2006

Region	Seats won	Swing
Greater Kolkata	12	−5.7
North Bengal	1	−6.5
South East	8	−2.4
South West	9	−3.4
Total	30	−4.3

Source: computed on the basis of data available from *The Hindu*, 16 May 2006.

Concluding observations

Democracy, if not marginalized, is certainly a casualty in West Bengal in the light of the last poll outcome. This is an obvious conclusion given the large-scale, if not complete, undermining of the opposition in the state. By winning 235 seats in the newly constituted state assembly, the Left Front is far ahead of both the Trinamul Congress (thirty seats) and Congress (twenty-one seats). Given the failure of the opposition parties to even win the required number of seats to gain the status of 'an opposition' in the assembly, it would not be wrong to suggest that members of the ruling party need to discharge the role of a responsible opposition. Will 'democracy' thus be a casualty? The copy book answer is yes simply because of the absence of a sizeable opposition checking the governmental excesses. In other words, with the absence of 'a responsible opposition' in the assembly, the government can easily get away with whatever decisions it adopts. This is highly unwarranted because the assembly floor is a space where serious debates take place on the merit of the governmental decisions, which receive adequate publicity in civil society through print and visual media. So opposition is not merely a group of people holding views contrary to that of the government; it also represents a politically vibrant section of society that is the first to be exposed to the government's decisions on the floor of the house. There is no denying the fact that the opposition will surely raise its voice though it is likely to be feeble given the massive numerical strength of the ruling party. Since 'the majority principle' governs the legislative practice in a liberal democracy the opposition can, at best, register its protest by recording 'a note of dissent'. The role of the parties opposed to the government is thus considerably marginalized.

Is the West Bengal situation just a revival of the Congress system that sustained the Congress Party's rule for almost two decades after independence? In the light of the absence of a numerically strong opposition and the hegemonic presence of the ruling party in the legislature, this contention may not be without substance. There was hardly an opposition to the Congress Party either in the national parliament or in state legislatures till 1967. The old Nehruvian order, drawn from a coalition of diverse interests, succeeded because it 'rested upon a discourse that entrusted largely to the State the responsibility of promoting the social and economic welfare of the people'.[39] This was further supported by the emergence of what Rajni Kothari characterized as the Congress system,[40] which provided a mechanism whereby a plurality of elites, sub-elites and groups could both voice their claims and attempt to realize them. At the same time, Congress could adequately mediate and settle these multiple and often conflicting claims. Underlying this was the reason for the relatively smooth functioning of the creatively defined Westminster model of parliamentary democracy, which was never seriously threatened probably because of an effective mechanism of political communication involving various actors at different levels of the Indian polity.[41]

The debilitation of the opposition is also a source of weakness for the Left Front government unless it imbibes 'self introspection' in its true spirit. The party representatives forming the government need to be critical despite being part of the Left Front. Unless a mechanism of 'checks and balances' is internalized, the

Front government is likely to drift away from the ideological goal that accounts for a massive popular mandate in its favour. There is also the fear of 'ideological distortion' given the unassailable majority of the ruling coalition; there is also the tug-of-war between those following the 'orthodox' line of thinking and their counterparts redefining Marxism underlining the Trotskyite observation that 'socialism cannot strike roots in one corner of the country'. There is no doubt that the West Bengal chief minister has captured the lost ground in urban areas on the dream of what a liberalized economy can bring to the state. Now he has to sell this brand of 'economics' to those 'hardcore' members of the party who are still critical to the organization. Furthermore, the opposition of the CPI(M) labour union, CITU, to 'economic reforms' is undoubtedly a deterrent to the electoral promises that the chief minister made to the voters. The Left Front government seems to be caught in a serious dilemma. Although in its rhetoric and positioning the command economy of the Nehruvian state had offered the Left enough room to be critical of private capital, in the context of the neo-liberal economic reforms that most states in India appear to have zealously accepted the state-led development paradigm does not seem to be very promising. How to align with capitalist globalization and accrue its advantages without compromising its distinct ideology by appearing as its votary seems to be a serious political challenge to the Left.[42] With a missionary zeal for rapid industrialization, the chief minister sought to bypass the political process and engage the government directly with the people. In a way, he was undoing what the Left Front had done for more than two decades. He misread the massive verdict of the 2006 assembly poll as approval for his ways, and scrambled for acquisition of fertile agricultural land purely by bureaucratic means for the industrialists seeking to invest in West Bengal. Nonetheless it would be wrong to suggest that 'the Left Front in West Bengal [had] mounted the proverbial bandwagon of neo-liberalism', as the chief minister himself made it clear that, on account of 'the severe fiscal squeeze applied to the state by a dominant capitalist national and international economic system', his government agreed to 'capitalise on new-found opportunities'.[43] This is undoubtedly a tightrope walk for the communist leadership in West Bengal, which seeks to weave elements of capitalism into its reinvented form of Marxism.

The recent controversy over acquisition of land from the farmers in West Bengal for industries clearly suggests that the bottom-up mode of governance is hardly effective in India's most politically mobilized state. The chief minister's zeal for quick industrialization not only provoked strong criticisms from his Left Front partners but also allowed the opposition parties to bolster their anti-government campaign. According to those critical of the decision to forcibly acquire land for a car factory in Singur in the vicinity of Kolkata or for the Special Economic Zone (SEZ)[44] in Nandigram (in the district of Medinipur), it has alienated a significant section of grassroots supporters who were drawn to the Left Front primarily because of the radical land reform measures that the government undertook since it came to power. The leading partner of the Front, CPI(M), gained from 'operation *barga*', which appears to have taken a back seat given Bhattacharjee's enthusiasm for rapid industrialization. As a bewildered supporter articulates his disenchantment, 'the only party we have known all our life is CPI(M). For years, we heard leaders spew anti-industry speeches. Now, there is a sudden turnaround. I don't understand.'[45] Bewilderment led to anger when the state police resorted to violence, killing fourteen protestors in Nandigram on the occasion of a protest march opposing SEZ on 14 March 2007. Justifying SEZ as perhaps the only effective device to 'reverse the process of de-industrialization',[46] the Left Front leadership dismissed the incident as 'a stray one, engineered by outsiders'. The situation, however, took a radical turn when the Nandigram firing hogged the limelight and also caused a fissure among the Front partners. None of the constituents, including the three major partners, Revolutionary Socialist Party, CPI, and Forward Bloc, supported the government's uncritical endorsement of SEZ. Describing the incident as 'unexpected, unbelievable and traumatic', the CPI, for instance, squarely blamed Bhattacharjee for running the Left Front government as 'a government of CPM [*sic*] alone keeping the allies in the dark'.[47] The state government, however, defended the decision by underlining that industrialization would provide new sources of livelihood to the people of the area where the income from land has considerably shrunk for a variety of reasons, including massive fragmentation of land. So, Nandigram as an SEZ would have fulfilled the twin goals of contributing to the economic wealth of the state in addition to providing alternative sources of income to the local population. The argument did not make sense to those for whom it was underwritten, the rural folk, resulting in turmoil that brought together the government's political foes under one platform, namely the Bhumi Ucched Partirodh Committee (Land Eviction Resistance Committee), regardless of ideology.

The Bhattacharjee-led Left Front government was in a tight spot because of its failure to secure land for the proposed Indonesian chemical hub. This not only threatened to dishearten prospective investors, but also extended a moral boost to the coalition of forces that came together to scuttle the government's blueprint for the rapid industrialization of the state. Given its numerical hegemony in the Left Front government, the CPI(M) did not seem to swallow 'the defeat', as what followed in Nandigram in November 2007 confirmed. The well-planned 'recapture' of Nandigram from anti-land acquisition forces by armed cadres was clear testimony to how ruthless a party could be in spite of leading a government with more than a two-thirds majority in the legislative assembly. Justifying the intervention of the armed cadres and the refusal to call in the police, government sources contended that 'the police was not sent for fear of a repeat of the 14th March incident'. The consequences were disastrous, leading to killing of many innocent people and also forcing those who were opposed to the SEZ to leave Nandigram. Bhattacharjee, the chief minister, seemed to be happy when these armed cadres barged into the village to 'reclaim' the lost ground because the protesters, as he emphatically stated, 'have been paid back in their coin'.[48] The People's Tribunal that looked into the police firing on 14 March 2007 in Nandigram also came out sharply against the government by insinuating that 'the motive behind this massacre seemed to be the ruling party's wish to teach a lesson to the poor villagers by terrorising them for opposing the proposed SEZ'.[49]

Nonetheless, the CPI(M) cannot afford to give up its commitment to the industrialists, as the SEZ is widely agreed to represent the passport for rapid industrialization in the state. And Buddhadeb Bhattacharjee also received accolades from Indian big business as 'a brave and reformist chief minister fighting a lonely but modern battle to shift the paradigm of an archaic ideology'. If the party cadres had not acted in Nandigram, then the entire process of industrialization would have stalled. It would not have been possible for the government to acquire land for industrial purposes and no new factories could have come up because the landowners and the activists would have resisted the acquisition of land for this purpose. So as far as the CPI(M) was concerned, there was no alternative to the violent operation that allowed the ruling authority to 'regain' control of Nandigram although the chemical hub had already been shifted to another place.[50] This has happened in the state of West Bengal, which returned the Left Front to power just over a year ago. Is this thus indicative that the support-base of the ruling parties is perhaps dwindling?

The Left Front Government won the first round of the battle by following what can only be described as a quintessentially Stalinist formula in settling the Nandigram problem. Even those sympathetic to the Left Front found it difficult to accept that the CPI(M), long regarded as a friend of the poor, could have been so ruthless. More appalling was the application of brute force that was applied to make some of India's poorest people surrender the piece of land which gave them identity.[51] Seeking to redefine its ideological priority in the changed circumstances of globalization, the Left Front government seems to have charted a new course of action despite significant opposition to it, both in West Bengal and elsewhere in the country. The battle between the CPI(M) and its opposition has gone beyond the original struggle of landholders against the state's forcible acquisition of land for SEZs. Not only has the Nandigram controversy brought out the dark side of economic reforms, it has also articulated the changed ideological preferences of the left parties in West Bengal, which, instead of rejecting it, seem to have opted for the capitalist path of development as perhaps the only way to achieve adequate economic growth in the country. How will the Left Front, especially its leading partner, CPI(M) resolve this contradiction while engaging with the neo-liberal charter of SEZ-led investment? This is too serious a contradiction to sweep under the carpet and the sooner the Front addresses the contradiction the better; otherwise, the euphoria that translated into votes for the Left Front in the 2006 election will evaporate in no time.

7 Coalition politics in India
Cultural synergy or political expediency?

Coalition building has invariably been an integral part of democratic politics and governance. In its broadest sense, coalition building implies initiation of measures to secure consensus among diverse social groups and communities in the pursuit of a common minimum programme. By this definition, in the competitive environment of democratic society, several agencies including broad mass movements and political parties as well as the governments are constantly involved in building coalitions. When a single political party fails to achieve a clear majority in the legislature, coalition government becomes an authentic mode of managing interactions between legislature and executive. In the process, the executive is able to gather staying power on the basis of winning key votes in the legislature. The politics of coalition as well as the functioning of the multi-party coalition governments have matured and stabilized in the context of several European countries.[1] Coalition seems to have become intrinsic to the Indian polity. This chapter concentrates on its evolution in a historical perspective underlining the critical role of the socio-political processes in shaping its nature. Coalition is not merely the coming together of political parties to capture power; it is also reflective of the fragmentation of social interests at the grassroots. The questions that this chapter thus seeks to address are (a) whether coalition is the culmination of a process that might have begun once the Congress Party ceased to become an umbrella organization and (b) whether coalition is a convenient mode of coagulation of parties, regardless of ideology, for capturing power.

Historical roots

The roots of coalition politics in India can be traced back to the nationalist movement and especially in the Gandhian conceptualization of *Swaraj*. It is true that the non-western leaders involved in the struggle for liberation were deeply influenced by European nationalist ideas. They were also aware of the limitations of these ideas in the non-European socio-economic context due to their alien origin. So while mobilizing the imagined community for an essentially political cause they began, by the beginning of the twentieth century, to speak in a 'native' vocabulary. Although they drew upon the ideas of European nationalism they indigenized

them substantially by discovering or inventing indigenous equivalents and investing these with additional meanings and nuances. This is probably the reason
why Gandhi and his colleagues in the anti-British campaign in India preferred
Swadeshi[2] to nationalism. Gandhi avoided the language of nationalism primarily
because he was aware that the Congress flirtations with nationalist ideas in the
first quarter of the twentieth century frightened away not only the Muslims and
other minorities but also some of the Hindu lower castes. This seems the most
pragmatic idea one could possibly conceive of in a country such as India that was
not united in terms of religion, race, culture and common historical memories of
oppression and struggle. Underlying this is the reason why Gandhi and his Congress colleagues preferred 'the relaxed and chaotic plurality of the traditional Indian life to the order and homogeneity of the European nation state [because they
realized] that the open, plural and relatively heterogeneous traditional Indian civilization would best unite Indians'.[3] Drawing on values meaningful to the Indian
masses, the Indian freedom struggle developed its own modular forms, which are
characteristically different from that of the west. Although the 1947 Great Divide
of the subcontinent of India was articulated in terms of religion, the nationalist
language drawing upon the exclusivity of Islam appeared inadequate to sustain
Pakistan following the creation of Bangladesh in 1971.

As an idea and a strategy, *Swaraj* gained remarkably in the context of the
nationalist articulation of the freedom struggle and the growing democratization
of the political processes that had already brought in hitherto socio-politically
marginal sections of society. So *Swaraj* was a great leveller in the sense that it
helped mobilize people despite obvious socio-economic and cultural differences.
This is what lay at the success of *Swaraj* as a political strategy. Underlining its
role in a highly divided society like India, *Swaraj* was defined in the following
ways: (a) national independence; (b) political freedom of the individual; (c) economic freedom of the individual; (d) spiritual freedom of the individual or self
rule. Although these four definitions are about four different characteristics of
Swaraj they are nonetheless complementary to each other. Of these, the first three
are negative in character whereas the fourth one is positive in its connotation.
Swaraj as 'national independence', individual 'political' and 'economic' freedom
involves discontinuity of alien rule, absence of exploitation by individuals and
poverty respectively. Spiritual freedom is positive in character in the sense that it
is a state of being that everyone aspires to actualize once the first three conditions
are met. In other words, there is an implicit assumption that self rule is condi-
tional on the absence of the clearly defined negative factors that stood in the way
of realizing *Swaraj* in its undiluted moral sense. Even in his conceptualization,
Gandhi preferred the term *Swaraj* to its English translation presumably because
of the difficulty in getting the exact synonym in another language.[4] As the discussion shows, the coalition of forces that Gandhi brought together drew largely
on *Swaraj*, which provided the ideological glue, as it were, to the nationalist
campaign. It further demonstrates the importance of a process whereby ideology gets articulated in a particular fashion underlining the significance of India's
multicultural socio-economic environment. Coalition is therefore an ideology of

multicultural existence with varied manifestations in different historical phases of Indian history.

Institutional roots of coalition politics in India

Coalitions are articulated within an institutional framework. There are two specific ways in which this has been concretized in Indian constitutional laws and practices. The Constitution is illustrative of various devices to create and sustain norms, values and practices that are integral to the multicultural Indian reality despite the fact that it has the imprint of the 1935 imperial Constitution. However, a clear change is visible in the working of the constitutional institutions presumably because of the changing ideological character of the polity in which they function and translate the democratic ethos of the polity in the aftermath of the 1947 transfer of power in India. Despite its imperial roots, the Constitution served a useful purpose in sustaining India's multicultural personality. Second, the prevalent socio-economic context in which the British governmental practices were enmeshed seems to be an important influence in this process. The Constitution's greatest success, as a constitutional expert comments, 'lies below the surface of government. It has provided a framework for social and political development, a rational, institutional basis of political behaviour. It not only establishes the national ideal, more importantly it lays down the rational, institutional manner in which they are to be pursued – a gigantic step for a people committed largely to irrational means of achieving other-worldly goals.'[5] One of the institutional devices borrowed from the British system is the *first-past-the-post system*, which largely accounts for peculiar electoral outcomes that are favourable for coalition. Under this system, those parties that have a widespread following are disadvantaged in comparison with those whose support is narrowly concentrated. For instance, regional parties with lots of votes in a small number of seats do extremely well compared with those parties whose votes are widely scattered in many constituencies. In this system, a candidate or a party wins by obtaining the largest number of votes. None of the parties that captured power at the union level had ever had majority support at its disposal. The Rajiv Gandhi-led Congress party made history when it obtained 44 per cent of the popular vote. In the last Lok Sabha poll in 2004, the NDA's share was 35.5 per cent while the ruling UPA was just 1 percentage point ahead by obtaining 36.5 per cent of the popular votes. So, it is perfectly plausible to argue that the incumbent ruling authority in New Delhi is not representative at all simply because of the lack of support of the majority. This principle also undermines the democratic processes in a context where coalition seems to be critical in the formation of governments. It is most likely that parties based on ideology that have a widespread base may not succeed while those drawing on regionalism and casteism will perform better because their votes are concentrated in specific constituencies. And in the formation of coalition governments it is the regionalists and casteists who become decisive because they have numbers. The collapse of majority governments and the consolidation of coalition of convenience have thus, warned an analyst, 'promoted casteism, regionalism and communalism'.[6] One possible way out is certainly a system of proportional representation (PR) in which a party can have a presence in the legislature on the basis of its overall popular support, regardless of whether or not the party can win seats on the basis of the largest number of votes.[7] The advantage of the system is that it is more genuinely representative and that it accurately captures the mood of the nation. Small parties with concentrated support will no longer have an unfair advantage.

Besides the first-past-the-post system, the institutional set-up that the Constitution confirmed seems to have contributed to coalition culture presumably because it was based on (a) consensus and (b) the principle of accommodation. The first is a manner of making decisions by 'unanimity' or 'near unanimity'; the latter refers to the ability to reconcile or harmonize. With accommodation, concepts and viewpoints, although seemingly incompatible, stand intact. They are not simply bypassed or entirely ignored, but are worked out simultaneously. Accommodation is therefore a matter of belief and attitude. As explained by a commentator, 'the most notable characteristic in every field of Indian society . . . is the constant attempt to reconcile conflicting views or actions, to discover a workable compromise, to avoid seeing the human situation in terms of all black or all white'.[8] The Indian constitutional structure is a good example of consensus and accommodation as the proceedings in the Constituent Assembly and the evolution of constitutional practices in independent India clearly demonstrate. The institutional foundation that the Constitution provides was supportive of the Congress system[9] so long as it remained an umbrella party representing myriad social interests.

The success of the Congress system was attributed to its 'central role in maintaining and restructuring political consensus'. The system continued almost uninterrupted till the 1967 elections when the non-Congress governments came to power in several states, setting a new trend of coalition politics in India. In explaining this phenomenon, a perceptive political analyst argues:

> the socio-economic and demographic profile of the polity is changing rather fast. . . . The mobilization of new recruits and groups into the political process . . . has given rise to the development of new and more differentiated identities and patterns of political cleavage. [This gave rise to] the expectation of freer political access . . . and a greater insistence on government performance. Intermediaries and vote banks, while of continuing importance, have become increasingly circumvented as citizens search for more effective participation in the political market place and develop an ability to evaluate and make choice.[10]

The breakdown of the federal and coalitional pillars of Congress reinvigorated regional politics. The centralization of power within the party from the early 1970s weakened the regional roots of the party and 'unleashed disastrous potentials'. Regional demands were no longer 'filtered through party channels, but began to be asserted with rising irritation against the centre'. Initially these demands were confined to those endorsing their identities as distinct socio-cultural entities in the polity; but later they were articulated as demands for 'full scale autonomy and separatism', as evident in Punjab and Kashmir. So, centralization and neglect of federal channels 'incited strident regionalism; the substitution of a "national" electorate and the redefinition of democracy forced Congress into inviting local identities into the national arena, which worked to the advantage of those who claimed to represent more directly and intimately these groupings of religion and caste'.[11] It was not therefore surprising that by the 1996 national poll there were as many as twenty-eight different parties with strong regional roots. Asserting their regional identities, these parties left significant marks on the national scene. Economic reforms initiated in 1991 by the minority Congress government of Narasimha Rao assigned 'greater powers to regional governments and provoked greater competition for control over them'. The intensity of political competition 'produced a generation of regional leaders with remarkable skills' and ability to resort to novel ways of flattering 'popular cultural sensibilities'.[12] In fact, the success of the erstwhile Bihar chief minister, Laloo Prasad Yadav, is largely attributed to his capacity to sway the masses by clinging to local dialects and illustrations that are meaningful to the people at the grassroots.

There is no doubt that India's politico-constitutional structure has undergone tremendous changes to adapt to changing circumstances. Parliament continues to remain, at least constitutionally, supreme though the constituent states have become more powerful than before.[13] Under the changed circumstances, what is evident is a clear shift of emphasis from the Westminster to the federal tradition, more so in the era of coalition politics when no single political party has an absolute majority in parliament. For practical purposes, the scheme the framers had adopted to bring together diverse Indian states within a single authority was what is known as 'executive federalism' – a structure of division of powers between different layers of governmental authorities following a clearly defined guidelines in the form of 'Union', 'State' and 'Concurrent' lists in the Seventh Schedule of the Constitution of India. From compulsions of circumstances arising out of coalition politics, the constituent states do not remain mere instruments of the Union; their importance is increasingly being felt in what was earlier known as 'the exclusive' domain of the centre. A process seems to have begun towards 'legislative federalism', in which the upper chamber representing the units of the federal government is as powerful as the lower chamber. Drawing upon American federalism, in which the Senate holds substantial power in conjunction with the House of Representatives, legislative federalism is an arrangement based on an equal and effective representation of the regions. The decisions, taken at the Union level, appear to be both democratic and representative given the role of both the chambers in their articulation. In other words, legislative federalism in its proper manifestation guarantees the importance of both the chambers in the decision-making process, which no longer remains 'exclusive' territory of the Lower House for its definite representative character. Not only will the upper chamber be an effective forum for the regions; its role in the legislative process will also be significant and substantial. If properly constituted, it could be an institution that represented the regions as such, counterbalancing the principle of representation by population on which the Lower House is based. It will also be a real break with the past since India's politico-constitutional structure draws upon the Westminster model with a strong centre associated with unitary government.

The expansion of political participation in the last two decades has placed historically disadvantaged and marginalized groups at the centre of the political system and governance at all levels. The rapid politicization and accelerated participation of groups such as other backward classes (OBCs) and Dalits raises questions about inclusion, exclusion, varied patterns of empowerment and the impact of these last on the growth and consolidation of democracy.[14] One aspect of these changes has to do with the processes and strategies that have inspired the induction of marginal groups into the political decision-making process. The rise of coalition governments is thus a manifestation of the widening and deepening of democracy in India. Different regions and different social groups have acquired a greater stake in the system, with parties that seek to represent them winning an increasing number of seats, usually at the cost of Congress, which no longer remains truly a national party. Though not unique in India, these significant political changes, reflective also of social churning, have overshadowed the idioms and ideologies that dominated and sustained the post-colonial agenda of social transformation in the post-colonial world. Many of these are also expressions of discontent traceable to the anger of the subalterns against an elite that has cornered the benefits and privileges of post-colonial economic development; these changes have significantly reformulated the political terrain.

Coming together syndrome in Indian politics

As shown in Chapter 5, the evolution of alliances began in 1967 in various Indian provinces with the formation of coalition governments by the parties opposed to the Congress. Inspired by Rammanohar Lohia,[15] several parties formed coalitions that drew primarily, if not exclusively, on anti-Congress sentiments. Lohia was emphatic in his belief that a continued alliance among the parties would enable them to come closer despite being ideologically dissimilar. A question was raised whether an opposition consisting of parties like Swatantra and Jana Sangh at one end and the communists at the other could ever govern. Given a clear ideological demarcation among them, the scepticism about their viability as a group did not appear to be unfounded. In response to this charge, Lohia argued: how could 'a motley Congress' with Krishna Menon at one end and S. K. Patil at the other remain united? Presumably because the Congress despite its diversities and contradictions had 'inherited the habit of working together and shared loyalty to the Nehru–Gandhi family'. Although doubt persisted in his mind about the feasibility of anti-Congress parties, Lohia found in attempts at opposition unity a creative political process seeking to relocate the non-Congress parties as well. As he argued, 'such a combination might not achieve anything spectacular but it would at least inspire the confidence that the country could get rid of the Congress rule at the Centre'.[16] Despite being ephemeral, the non-Congress governments that captured power in 1967 in nine states rewrote history by replacing the Congress

Party in the provinces. This was the beginning of an era of 'non-Congressism' that had not fully blossomed presumably because of the lack of a well-knit organizational network of the opposition parties across the length and breadth of the country. Notwithstanding the organizational weaknesses, the anti-Congress coalitions, known as Samyukta Vidhayak Dal, formed governments in a majority of the states following the 1967 assembly elections. The euphoria over the formation of non-Congress governments was short-lived with the quick disintegration of these governments presumably because of a lack of ideological and programmatic compatibility. The untimely death of Lohia also left a void as there was no comparable figure that could carve out another grand coalition of the opposition parties. The subsequent split in the Congress Party, the 1971 war with Pakistan and the 1975–77 Emergency greatly retarded the opposition consolidation in the forthcoming decades.[17]

Indian politics had undergone a paradigmatic shift on the eve of the 1977 national elections, which replaced the Congress party by a loose-knit Janata coalition representing diverse, if not contradictory, interests. During the brief interlude of the Janata regime (1977–80), probably because of other preoccupations of the regime, no serious attempt was made to counter the centripetal tendencies that had, by then, firm roots in Indian politics. Indira Gandhi's style of functioning completely destroyed internal democracy within the Congress Party. With the disintegration of provincial Congress organizations, the state leaders became mere clients of the central organ of the party. As she became the key to political power and personal gain, there was hardly any challenge to her leadership and the party was reduced to almost a nonentity. The consequence was disastrous. The state tended to ignore the demands of the constituent units and favoured concentration of power simply because those who mattered in political decision-making neither questioned centralization nor endeavoured to provide an alternative.

Stable pan-Indian coalitions: trends and patterns

The first real coalition at the level of the Union government was formed in 1977, three decades after independence, when the Janata Party came to power. A coalition of several pre-poll allies, the Janata Party consolidated the alliance on the issue of opposition to the 1975–77 Emergency, imposed by the erstwhile Indira Gandhi-led Congress regime. In view of intra-party rivalry, the Janata government collapsed within two and a half years of its inception and Congress swept back to power in the 1980 national poll. The next coalition government at the Union level was formed in 1989 by the Janata Dal, led by V. P. Singh, a former Congressman who defected from the party because of his disagreement with its leader, Rajiv Gandhi. A no-confidence motion in the Lower House knocked the government from power and was followed by a breakaway group of the Janata Dal, known as the Janata Dal (Samajwadi), forming a government with outside support from Congress, which was the single largest party in Lok Sabha. After the May 1996 elections, which followed the end of Narasimha Rao's tenure, India saw four coalition governments that also did not last the full term of the eleventh

Lok Sabha. Led by the BJP, the first of these four coalition governments lasted for only thirteen days once it was clear that the government would lose the vote of no confidence on the floor of the house. This was followed by the United Front government under the stewardship of H. D. Dave Gowda and was supported by the Congress. The United Front was a post-poll conglomeration of thirteen parties. Congress threatened to withdraw support from the United Front government unless the incumbent premier was replaced because of his failure to amicably settle 'inter-state disputes' over Cauvery water. This led to the formation of another Congress-supported United Front government, which elected I. K. Gujral as its premier. With its collapse following the withdrawal of Congress support, a mid-term election was announced in February–March 1998. This election was distinct in India's recent political history for two important reasons: (a) the BJP secured pre-poll tie-ups with as many as thirteen big and small regional parties spread over nine major Indian states; (b) the BJP was drawn to the coalitional strategy because of its failure to sustain beyond thirteen days in 1996 due to lack of numerical support in the lower house. As the election results show, this strategy worked favourably for the BJP, which emerged as the single largest party in the twelfth Lok Sabha in 1998 with 182 seats. With its electoral allies, it had 258, still falling short of the halfway mark of 272. Since it was the largest conglomeration of parties, the alliance was invited by the president to form the government at the Union level. Nonetheless, the alliance never became stable, with one partner or another threatening to quit the coalition at frequent intervals. Its fate was sealed following the withdrawal of the AIADMK, though the rest of the partners of the BJP-led coalition remained together. So the fourth coalition government met the same fate as the others in just over two years. Although these four different experiments of coalition government at the Union level failed because they did not last full terms, they nonetheless are indicative of significant changes in India's political landscape. From now on, not only the BJP but also its competitor, Congress, favoured pre-poll alignment with partners even, on occasions, by underplaying the ideological compatibility when selecting allies.

The thirteenth general election, held in September–October 1999, was a watershed in India's recent political history for at least two reasons: first, for the first time, a pre-electoral alliance – the National Democratic Alliance – was able to win a majority in the Lok Sabha. Although the BJP lost 2 per cent of its share of the popular votes, its earlier tally of 182 seats in the Lok Sabha remained intact. Contrarily, the Congress share of votes had gone up by 3 per cent, though it lost thirty seats presumably because of the 'first-past-the-post' principle of election. Formed in 1999, the BJP-led NDA, which completed its term of five years, clearly shows the viability and strength of a mega-political formation across the country. With the formation of another coalition government at the centre following the 2004 election to the Lok Sabha, the trend that began in 1999 appears to have continued. Led by Congress, the United Progressive Alliance (UPA) government is constituted by regional and state-based parties with outside support from the left parties and Samajwadi Party. What accounts for the rise of coalition government is the failure of the pan-Indian parties to secure a majority in parliament on their own. The reasons are complex and rooted in the radical social churning at the grassroots. Nonetheless, the idea of coalition has historical roots in India. The National Congress was, for instance, a grand social coalition under Gandhi's stewardship and reaped rich electoral dividends till the fourth general elections in 1967. During the regime with Mrs Indira Gandhi at the helm, the trend seems to have discontinued and she steered India to what is conceptually identified as 'plebiscitary' politics, which turned out to be the nemesis of the Congress party. Though efforts at conjuring up a political coalition at the national level were made from the days of the Janata Party and followed by various 'fronts' led by the Janata Dal (in 1989, 1996 and 1997), the BJP is perhaps the first political party to have understood the importance of creating a nationwide political coalition. Ideological disagreements with the BJP apart, the party must be given its due in seriously attempting power-sharing with diverse allies. Illustrative of this is the gradual expansion of the NDA from an eighteen-party coalition to a twenty-four-party broad-based coalition.

The 2004 national poll is similar to the 1999 Lok Sabha election in at least one way. Both the pan-Indian parties – BJP and Congress – have failed to secure a majority and hence are unable to form a government at the centre on their own. The obvious upshot of such poll outcomes is the importance of the regional and state-based parties in providing the magic number to the parties seeking to constitute the government. These splinter parties have become an integral part of governance in view of the changing complexion of the parliament, which is no longer dominated by a single party. There has been a fundamental change in the role of parliament since the emergence of multi-party coalitions as 'a regular form of government' in India. What has changed in recent years is that the majority of members providing numerical support to the government belong to a large number of parties, inside and outside the ruling coalition. The survival of the government depends on the support of one or more parties which have different ideologies and different support bases. Several of them, while united at the Centre, are deeply divided at the regional and state levels.[18] The dependence of the government on the support of parties that are otherwise opposed to it has had several unintended consequences for the functioning of Parliament and other vital pillars of India's democracy. The ruling coalition may not always be free to adopt policies in accordance with its priorities unless there is a consensus among the partners that are critical for its survival. An important consequences of this is the growing importance of 'behind the scenes' agreements among different sets of party leaders, both within and outside the government. So long as the government enjoys the backing of leaders with majority support, there is no threat to its continuity and it can get parliament to do whatever it proposes to do.[19]

One of the factors that contributed to the rise of these smaller parties is certainly the breakdown of Congress and also its failure to represent the myriad social and economic interests at the grassroots. So, political coalition, at the level of government formation, seeks to articulate the neglected voice by bringing in to the centre stage those parties which are not exactly 'centrist'. In this sense, coalition is a great leveller of interests. With their crucial role in the government for its performance and continuity, these parties with limited geographic spread also forced the bigger parties to redefine their roles in the changed socio-economic and political reality. So coalition is not merely a cementing device; it has also ushered in a new era of constant dialogues among those competing for power regardless of size and depth of organization.

The definite decline of the national parties is also indicative of their failure to effectively address issues of contradictory social classes. In most cases, regional parties are constituted with specific socio-economic agenda. In other words, these are political formations drawing on specific social and economic interests that largely remain unrepresented. They thus are not only useful in involving the hitherto neglected sections in the democratic processes, but also change the nature of the political by redefining its contour. So, political coalition at the centre draws on the social coalition at the grassroots. Regional parties representing various kinds of social coalition seem to provide a link between the national and the local. Given their crucial role in the continuity of the government in power, they cannot be ignored, let alone wished away. Hence, the socio-political and economic issues relevant to those sections of society they represent are likely to be important in so far as policies at the national level are concerned. In this sense, the regional parties act as an ideological bloc according 'corrective steps', as it were, to the national government by providing a correct perspective to the governmental policies and programmes. So, coalition is a grand opportunity for the national decision makers to adopt socially meaningful and economically ameliorating programmes in view of the inputs from the grassroots that are possible thanks largely to the involvement of the regional and state-based political actors.

Both the thirteenth and fourteenth elections to the national parliament seem to have set a pattern shaping the outcome of the poll and thus the nature of the government. Because coalition is organically constituted in India in the sense that a complex social coalition leads to a political coalition, there is no doubt that the days of the single party majority are gone. The reversal of the trend is simply inconceivable because of a serious social churning at the grassroots involving marginalized sections of Indian society. Not only are these socially peripheral and economically backward sections significant players in political choice, they are represented by organized parties with well-entrenched networks of support certainly in one, if not more states. So, coalition government is not merely an arrangement based on ad hoc political alliances; it is perhaps inevitable given the radical socio-economic changes in rural India since the late 1980s. The former NDA government and its successor under the aegis of the UPA are illustrative, though ideological affinity may not always have acted in cementing the bond among the constituents of the coalition. But, once a part of the government, the coalition partners regardless of their numerical strength remain important forces that can be wished away only at the peril of the government. Hence coalition creates a situation whereby the government, in order to avoid threats to its existence, is forced to accept the constituent regional parties as 'equal partners' and not merely appendages to the party/parties leading the coalition because of their numerical might. By accepting coalition as inevitable, political parties competing for power at both the national and state levels are also involved in a critical way in a process whereby the India's political system and its ideological contours are being dramatically altered and thus redefined.

Despite the commonly held views of the Indian political experience as a single dominant party system splintering into a multi-party coalition, the modern Indian polity has thus emerged as an example of coalition politics *par excellence*. Not only was the single dominant party a social as well as ideological coalition, even the cabinet government in the initial years was constituted on coalition principles. It is important to remember that the bulk of the Indian party system has emerged owing to a gradual erosion of this coalition. It reached its peak in 1967 when, as an impact of this erosion, political coalition emerged at the state level as well. The decades of the 1970s and 1980s witnessed experiments by the Indian electorate with coalition and one-party rule. Indira Gandhi transformed Congress from a coalition of groups into a centralized party absolutely under her control.

The 1990s were a decade of slowly but surely nurturing coalition culture in India. Despite the red herring drawn by the advocates of stability across the path of conglomerating coalition, the completion of a five-year term by the NDA and the assumption of power by the UPA have established beyond doubt the prospects of a stable government even under a coalition of parties. Though it is impossible to play down principles, the patterns and priorities of making or sustaining coalitions anywhere and in any situation are governed by perceived political convenience and expediency. The emerging patterns of coalescence in a society provide insights into weaknesses that lead to unstable political coalition.

Apart from centrism as a binding force in any conglomeration of parties, there are certain other factors that are peculiar to the articulation of coalition in India as a conceptual category. In other words, the formation of coalition governments is premised on certain distinctive characteristics of the Indian socio-political reality that appear to have informed the theoretical search concerning this phenomenon. Prominent among these are as follows:

Coalition is a region-dictated political phenomenon. Despite being ideologically heterogeneous, regional parties agree to come together on the basis of programmatic compatibility. As illustrated by the NDA, the regional parties had a significant say in its consolidation and continuity at the centre. What brought them together was a common minimum programme. Even in the formation of the United Progressive Alliance (UPA) after the fourteenth Lok Sabha poll in 2004, the cementing factor is undoubtedly a common minimum programme in which the regional parties had significant inputs. Seeking to accord constitutional sanctity, the post-election fourteen-party United Front (1996–97), for instance, formulated a common minimum programme committed to the principles of political, administrative and economic federalism. In pursuit of this goal, the programme suggested a dual strategy: (a) true to its commitment, the Front proposed to implement the major recommendations of the 1984 Sarkaria Commission to ensure greater autonomy to the states to enable them to determine their own plan priorities within the framework of the national five-year plans; and (b) the United Front government also promised to appoint a powerful committee to review and update the recommendations of the Commission and to examine the devolution of financial powers to the state governments.

The 1989 poll outcome reveals the extent to which the patterns of electoral response became increasingly 'regionalized' and 'fragmented'. The Mandal recommendations[20] have also contributed to the regionalization of Indian politics by utilizing the region-specific caste configurations of those belonging to the OBCs. The pattern remained unchanged in the 1996 elections. As an observer comments, 'there is no nationwide wave for or against any political combine. Yet, there are mini-waves at the local level which are dominated by local issues as in the case of Tamil Nadu, Bihar, West Bengal or Madhya Pradesh.'[21] The formation of the United Front government at the centre in 1996 clearly demonstrated that the regionalization of the Indian polity even at the national level was now a reality. The Indian parliament formed in 1996 contained twenty-eight different parties, more than ever before, with roots in the regions. Following the breakdown of the federal and coalitional pillars of Congress, 'the proliferating regional parties had set their own stamp on the national political imagination'.[22] Given the strong roots of the constituents of the Front in the regions, it is therefore necessary to take into account the 'state' and 'region-specific issues'. For example, the decline of the Janata Dal, an important constituent of the first Third Front government at the centre, was possibly due to withdrawal of support of 'regional lords' such as Mulayam Singh Yadav and Laloo Prasad Yadav and Naveen Pattanaik who carved out an unassailable position in UP, Bihar and Orissa respectively. Their electoral victory can be attributed to their success in building up winning caste coalitions of demographically preponderant castes (Yadavs in UP and Bihar and Karans in Orissa), Muslims and Dalits. The social constituency for the third force had therefore clearly expanded, but it remained 'fractured and divided between diverse regional and sectional parties'.[23] So, coalition is also an articulation of a process of an increasing fragmentation of the party system along regional and ethnic lines that is linked with a process of 'creolization' or 'vernacularization' of Indian politics seeking 'to develop shared protocols with the preexisting language of the people'.[24] In other words, the influx of lower orders into the field of democratic contestation has radically altered the vocabulary of this contestation, for the new entrants brought with them their beliefs as well. For the first time, 'the borrowed high ideological spectrum' was disturbed by 'homespun ideological fragments'. The raw narratives of 'social justice', articulated by Kanshi Ram or Laloo Prasad Yadav and Mayawati, achieved what Lohia's sophisticated philosophy of history failed to do three decades earlier, namely, 'to make it respectable to talk about caste in the public-political domain'.[25]

This situation – the growing fragmentation of political parties as well as the changing nature of their support base – has been theoretically conceptualized by Alfred Stepan in a twofold classification of parties of (a) politywide and (b) centric-regional parties.[26] The politywide parties are ones with a strong organizational, electoral and emotional presence in all, or virtually all, the member units of a federation whereas the centric-regional parties are those that receive almost all their votes in one unit or geographic space in the federation. If the political system is parliamentary, the centric-regional parties provide adequate numerical support to a politywide party to form a government in which they are both crucial and decisive. The growing importance of these centric-regional parties in the governing coalitions at the centre in India also suggests the increasing regionalization of the parties that owe their sustenance, if not existence, to the regions. In interpreting India's coalition experience, which is long and rich at the state level, it is theoretically important to underline that the regional parties have gained massive salience at the national level presumably because of the relative decline of the politywide parties. The centric-regional parties have prospered more than the so-called national parties, indicating a process, perhaps nebulous now, highlighting their invincible role in forming coalitions. They cannot be ignored simply because the pan-Indian parties no longer represent the centrist space in Indian politics in its entirety, which the Congress did because of the success in accommodating diverse regional interests. The quick disintegration of the pre-NDA coalitions since the 1977 Morarji Desai government was always highlighted to argue that these experiments, though reflecting the intense democratic churning at the grassroots, failed to generate confidence in their governance capability. They were 'stigmatized by their opponents as dominated by regional leaders preoccupied with regional interests, and the sceptre of disintegration was freely brandished'.[27] Those who are critical of the rise of regional parties as integral to national coalitions tend to argue that 'the entire ethos of regional parties is to magnify local interests and ignore those of the rest of the country. So, far from creating a happier country, the rise of regional parties could spell more tensions.'[28] Given the NDA's success in completing the term of five years, the argument seems to have lost its viability and there is hardly scope for scepticism because of the evolution of a healthy coalition culture, based on a creative interaction among the constituents on the basis of a common minimum programme.

The coalition has come to stay and gone are the days of the single-party majority in the parliament. As Table 7.1 shows, the decline of parliamentary seats of the politywide parties has created a situation in which coalition is inevitable in view of the importance of the regional parties in providing the required numerical majority in the legislature by their support. The table is illustrative of a clear decline of the national parties and the rise of those parties with regional roots. As evident, the regional parties contributed almost 42 per cent of seats in the thirteenth Lok Sabha. And it was reflected in the NDA's composition – there were as many as twenty-four parties, which came together to form a stable coalition. Indicative of a significant change, the NDA is also unique in providing stable governance, which was the first casualty in the past experiments with coalition governments in India. So it is a trend-setter in Indian politics by showing that coalition government is inevitable when the pan-Indian parties fail to represent, let alone accommodate, the plurality of interests. There is no doubt that the growing importance of the regional parties in the formation of coalitions since 1989 has accelerated the process of federalization of India's parliamentary system of governance, which during the Congress system bordered on the centre's hegemony disregarding regional interests to a large extent.

Table 7.1 Lok Sabha elections, 1989–2004: poll results for six national elections

Election year	1989	1991	1996	1998	1999	2004
Total number of seats	529	511	543	543	543	543
Indian National Congress	197 (39.5%)	227 (36.5%)	140 (28.8%)	141 (25.8%)	114 (25.8%)	145 (26.4%)
BJP	85 (11.5%)	119 (20.1%)	161 (20.3%)	182 (25.6%)	182 (25.6%)	138 (22.2%)
Janata Party/Janata Dal	143 (17.7%)	56 (11.8%)	46 (8.1%)	6 (3.2%)	22[a] (3.2%)	8[b] (3.0%)
Communist Party (Marxist)	33 (6.5%)	35 (6.2%)	32 (6.1%)	32 (5.2%)	33 (5.2%)	43 (5.7%)
Communist Party of India	12 (2.6%)	13 (2.5%)	12 (2.0%)	9 (1.8%)	4 (1.7%)	9 (1.3%)
Total five national parties	470	450	391	370	355	343
% of total seats	88.9	88.1	72.0	68.1	63.1[c]	62.1
Major regional parties	30 (15.5%)	42 (15.1%)	110 (23.6%)	168 (23.6%)	182 (24.3%)[d]	190 (24.6%)

Notes

a   Janata Dal (U) 21, Janata Dal (S) 1.
b   Only the seats obtained by the Janata Dal (U).
c   Parties other than the national parties obtained approximately 41.05 per centage of seats in the thirteenth Lok Sabha.
d   Data for regional parties (1989–1999) are from Nagindas, Usha Thakkar, 'Regionalization of Indian politics', *Economic and Political Weekly*, Vol. 35 (6), 12 February, 2000, p. 517.

Sources: Computed from the data available from the following sources: for 1989 and 1991, Subrata K. Mitra and James Chiriyankandth, *Electoral Politics in India*, New Delhi: Segment, 1992, pp. 270–2, and Election Commission Reports, 1996, 1998 and 1999; for 2004, National Election Study, *Economic and Political Weekly*, 18 December 2004, pp. 5539–43.

As is evident, the rise of the regional parties as a combined force bidding for power at the centre is possibly due to the following factors: first, the decline of Congress as an institutionalized party representing various and also conflicting socio-economic interests. It lost its hegemony by, *inter alia*, the departure of the nationalist generation, the demise of internal democracy and the emergence of personalized mass appeal of the top leadership. No longer did Congress remain a party capable of accommodating conflicting social interests and fulfilling the individual ambitions of those involved in its expansion at the provincial and local levels. The vacuum created by 'the progressive self-destruction' of the Congress Party has been filled in different ways in different parts of the country, though invariably by the parties that draw on the support of the OBCs and other lower castes. This has further deepened regionalism, underlining the growing importance of 'region-specific' issues in national politics. Indicative of a new political trend, regionalism has also ushered in a certain democratization involving the hitherto neglected sections of socio-political groups. Second, with successive elections, new social groups and strata are being introduced to the political processes. Since the entrenched groups in the dominant party tended to impede their entry to the political processes these new entrants found it easier to make their debut through non-Congress parties or occasionally even founded new parties. So, the emergence of new parties outside the BJP and Congress fold to articulate hitherto neglected socio-political interests seems to be a major factor that contributed to the consolidation of a coalition with a seemingly different ideological perspective. Third, the critical importance of regional parties in coalition government seem to have favoured the economic reform process that began 'by stealth' without admitting the paradigmatic shift in 1991. Two interlinked reasons may be offered to plausibly explain the support that the coalition partners provide to the reform process: the first is the emergence of regional parties in national politics with 'neutral economic ideology'. Their critical role for the stability of the coalition governments and their participation in government 'out of the opportunistic motives [has brought] upfront the need to step up economic growth that reforms try to push'. The second reason revolves around 'the growing and widespread acceptance [by the regional parties] of the need for a very rapid economic growth that can be served by the market-oriented reforms'.[29] Even the Left Front, including its leading partner, CPI(M), which vehemently opposed economic reforms in the past, are now favourably inclined even at the cost of losing its base in rural West Bengal by insisting on especially creating special economic zones (SEZ) for rapid industrialization in the state. The political repercussions are difficult to predict. Nonetheless, there are indications that the benefits of economic reforms have, for obvious reasons, not percolated down to the grassroots, waiting perhaps to translate the simmering discontent into forms that may not be comprehensible in the context of euphoria for 'rabid consumerism'.

Concluding observations

Indian politics is now regionalized and coalition governments have become an important ingredient of political articulation reflecting the socio-political and cultural diversities of the country. What appeared to be a mere trend in 1967 when several Indian states saw the formation of coalition governments seems to have become a pattern. So, the formation of stable coalition government in New Delhi is the culmination of a process. Is India therefore heading towards a bi-party system in the classical sense? The answer is perhaps no given the consolidation of the two competitive blocs around two major pan-Indian parties, namely the BJP and Congress. Although they failed to capture a majority in the national legislature their critical importance makes them 'nodal' in the formation of the coalition government. This will perhaps lead to the rise of a 'bi-nodal' party system in which the regional parties, despite their inevitable role in government formation, will remain 'politically insignificant' independent of these two major parties. Nonetheless, the regional parties that provide the required numerical legislative strength seem to hold the balance of power in a political situation in which none of the so-called national parties has the magic number of parliamentarians to justify their independent claim. So, despite their distinct identities, the national parties hardly remain as decisive as before in the environment of coalition politics; they cannot afford to ignore the regional parties entirely. This is suggestive of unique socio-political processes whereby regional issues gain immense importance in governance at both the central and provincial levels. On occasions, this results in a tightrope walk for both the regional and national parties where the support of the regional parties is absolutely crucial for the survival of the coalition. Under such circumstances, political blackmailing by the coalition partners cannot be ruled out to squeeze advantage when the coalition is most vulnerable. The collapse of the 1996 United Front government is illustrative here because the withdrawal of Congress support led to its loss of majority in parliament. This is not the situation, however, if the leading partner holds a majority in the legislature and thus can survive even if the partners withdraw support. For instance, the Left Front governments owe their stability largely to the adequate strength of CPI(M) in the state assemblies. Here, the political existence of the partners is better protected within the coalition and hence the differences are usually sorted out through meaningful dialogues and discussions. These two different varieties of coalitions articulate two different theoretical positions: on the one hand, ideological congruity among the partners provides greater possibilities for the coalition to coagulate better for a stable formation; its lack, on the other hand, simply weakens the coalition unless the partners appreciate the importance of coming together in opposition to a common political 'foe' or to fulfil a common political agenda prepared by those constituting the coalition. The success of the BJP-led NDA in completing its term of five years is illustrative here. Glued by the common minimum programme avoiding contentious issues, the NDA survived drawing on a clear understanding between the numerically strong BJP and other smaller regional parties. Articulating a new wave in Indian politics, the NDA is perhaps the most successful experiment in India's recent political history of a coalition of apparently ideologically incompatible but politically congruent partners due largely to acceptable common minimum programmes. The formation of another coalition government, led by the Congress, is a continuation of the trend that began in 1999. Whereas the NDA was a majority coalition in the sense that its constituents had a majority in parliament, the United Progressive Alliance government, of which the Congress is a leading partner, owes its survival in case of a 'no-confidence' motion to the 'outside support' provided by the CPI(M) and Samajwadi Party with a tally of ninety-seven seats in total. Like its predecessor, the present UPA is consolidated with common minimum programmes. Apart from programmatic compatibility among its constituents, the compulsion of pushing the BJP and its allies away from power has cemented the bond despite serious ideological differences among them.

Conclusion

India's existence as a democratic state has been a puzzle for a variety of reasons. Foremost among them is certainly gradual, but firm, changes in the articulation of the political that cannot be comprehended, let alone conceptualized, within the Euro-centric theoretical format. Moreover, the political is constituted and reconstituted. There are three processes involved in the articulation of the political: a reasoned attention to the historical context out of which the political emanates; the specific sequence of processes; and in particular the idea that articulation of the political is not governed by a blind imitation of western history or institutions, but a self-conscious process of reflexive construction of society that rationally assesses principles from all sources and improvises institutions suitable for specific socio-economic realities. As a modern nation, India is 'simply *sui generis*'. It stands on its own, different and distinct from the alternative political models on offer – be these Anglo-Saxon liberalism, French republicanism, atheistic communism or Islamic theocracy.[1] India has 'a well-established reputation', argues Robert Dahl, 'of violating social scientific generalizations'.[2] Though rooted in the Westminster model of parliamentary democracy and post-Enlightenment philosophy of the western variety, India as a system of governance thus provides a unique model in which the political is enmeshed in the wider social, economic and cultural matrix. So models seeking to articulate the complexities of the political in India in 'received wisdom' appear to be theoretically sterile and intellectually restrictive. What is critical in any understanding of the political in India (or for that matter in socio-economic circumstances similar to that of India) is the multiple axes (in social, economic and cultural terms) in which the political both revolves and evolves. In a nutshell, the political is both an articulated language and a process reinventing its ingredients regularly on the basis of inputs from the reality. Indian experiments are thus translated into perhaps the most exciting model of constant politicization of a fragmented social structure through a penetration of the political in terms of values and ideologies that, on most occasions, appear puzzling, if conceptualized within the derivative discourse of the western lineage. The principal argument that the book supports is linked with the idea that, given that the political is contextual (and also historical), one simply cannot capture, let alone comprehend, the complex evolution (besides its nature) of Indian politics in the globalized world within the ethno-centric liberal democratic framework. That the political is context-driven is illustrated by the fact that despite having shared 'a common critical juncture'[3] or disjuncture, namely decolonization, democracy failed to strike roots in Pakistan, for instance. Also, the well-entrenched ethnic diversity, instead of being a retarding factor, provides useful resources for democratization by bringing in the pluralistic ethos in the domain of the political. Indian politics always remains a puzzle because it hardly bears any resemblance to either textbook accounts of representative democracy or parliament-led models of democracy existing elsewhere. The sixty-year-old democracy invented and harnessed a wide range of new devices for 'publicly monitoring and checking the exercise of power'. Defined by various older and newer means of 'public contestation of power' upholding citizens' rights and interests, Indian democracy resembles 'the multi-trunk banyan tree' with interlinked aerial roots and branches that grows throughout the subcontinent.[4]

Growing democratization

Democracy is a guarantee of adult suffrage in India. This has unleashed a process that has gone beyond mere voting by empowering people in a manner that radically changed the contours of Indian politics. The process is translated as rage and revolt, making India 'a country of a million little mutinies'.[5] But these mutinies created a tangible space for the democratic aspiration to flourish. Also, they make the state available for those who have hitherto remained peripheral to any political transactions.[6] The process is significant for another related reason: democratic empowerment of the lower strata of society and formerly excluded groups led to articulation of voices that always remained 'feeble' in the past. Since these groups interpreted 'their disadvantage and dignity in caste terms, social antagonism and competition for state benefits expressed themselves increasingly in the form of intense caste rivalries'.[7] So the growing importance of caste in contemporary Indian politics is essentially a modern phenomenon and not 'a throwback traditional behaviour'. This is theoretically puzzling since caste action in India, articulated in modern political vocabulary, cannot be comprehended within the available liberal democratic parameters unless one is drawn to the empirical context that radically differs from the typical liberal society in the west.

Politicization and democratization seem to be dialectically interlinked. As a result, the outcome of this intermingling may not be predictable. In a typical western liberal context, deepening of democracy invariably leads to consolidation of 'liberal values'. In the Indian context, democratization is translated in greater involvement of people not as 'individuals', which is a staple of liberal discourse, but as communities or groups. Individuals are getting involved in the public sphere not as 'atomized' individuals but as 'members of primordial communities' drawn on religious, caste or *jati* (sect within a caste) identity. Similarly, a large section of women is being drawn to the political processes not as 'women' or individuals, but as members of a community holding a sectoral identity. Community identity seems to be the governing force. It is not therefore surprising that the so-called peripheral groups continue to maintain their identities with reference to the social groups (caste, religion or sect) to which they belong while getting involved in the political processes despite the fact that their political goals remain more or less identical. Nonetheless, the processes of steady democratization have contributed to the articulation of a political voice, hitherto unheard of, which is reflective of radical changes in the texture of the political. The expanding circle of democratic participation since independence has thus transformed 'the character of politics as previously subordinate groups have gained a voice'.[8] By helping to articulate the political voice of the marginalized, democracy in India has led to 'a loosing of social strictures' and empowered the peripherals to be confident of their ability to improve the socio-economic conditions in which they are placed.[9] This is a significant political process that has led to what Christophe Jaffrelot describes as 'a silent revolution'[10] through a meaningful transfer of power from the upper-caste elites to various subaltern groups within the democratic framework of public governance. Rajni Kothari captures this change by saying that 'a new democratic process' seems to have begun 'at a time when the old democracy is failing to deliver the goods [leading to] a new revolution representing new social churnings that are already under way . . . in the electoral and party processes, as also within the deeper arenas of the non-party political processes'.[11]

Secularism

The Indian variety of secularism[12] is a mixed bag in the sense that it hardly corresponds to the conventional wisdom on the phenomenon.[13] It was creatively articulated underlining the complexities of typical non-western contexts. Secularism was thus not an ideology for Nehru. For him, it was nothing but civilized behaviour practised by all but a few contemporary states in the modern world. He thus denied it was a big deal or that

> by saying that [since] we are a secular state we have done something amazingly generous, given something out of our pocket to the rest of the world, something which we ought not to have done, so on and so forth. We have only done something which every country does except a very few misguided and backward countries in the world. Let us not refer to the word in the sense that we have done something very mighty.[14]

As it is clear, Nehru's strategy could be dubbed as one 'that sought to transcend cultural differences, accommodate conflicts arising out of them, combat parochial and militant Hindu nationalist forces and get on with the business of state as he saw it'.[15] It would be thus appropriate to argue that Nehru saw 'the agenda of the modern state in terms of the transformation of Indian society from one regulated by *dharma* to one of law and instrumental rationality'.[16] This was evident in his argument against the Hindu Code Bill, which sought to impose a uniform civil code for the country. Division within the Congress Party forced the withdrawal of the bill, which ultimately led to the resignation of B. R. Ambedkar from the

Union ministry. In its place, the Hindu Marriage Bill was proposed, suggesting a uniform civil code for the Hindus. While criticizing those opposed to the Bill, Nehru emphatically pronounced,

> it is only the women who have to behave like Sita and Savitri [Hindu mythical characters famous for their feminine virtues], the men may behave as they like. . . . You cannot have a democracy, of course, if you cut off . . . fifty percent of the people and put them in a separate class apart in regard to social privileges. They are bound to rebel against that.[17]

His opposition to the Indian Cattle Preservation Bill, 1955, was also grounded on his faith in 'tolerant pluralism', 'cultural diversity' and 'egalitarianism'. Although the bill was finally shelved because, procedurally, the subject belonged to the state legislature, Nehru argued strongly to knock down the arguments in its favour. Those who supported the bill on religious grounds because of the importance of the cow in Hinduism lost their ground once Nehru intervened by saying 'the combination of religion and politics in the narrowest sense of the word, resulting in communal politics is – there can be no doubt – a most dangerous combination and must be put an end to. It is clear . . . that this combination is harmful to the country as a whole; it is harmful to the majority, but probably it is most harmful to any minority that seeks to have some advantages from it.'[18]

The critical point that emanates from Nehru's intervention on these two bills is linked with his broader ideological vision of a modern state that draws on tradition, but tempered by modern liberal values. Persuaded by Leninist statecraft, he believed in a strong state capable of guiding human existence in accordance with definite plans. The state emerged as a focal point of social, political and economic transformation. Nehru's historical success therefore lay not in the dissemination of democratic idealism, but in 'its establishment of the state at the core of India's society'.[19] The state remained strong so long as Nehru reigned presumably because of the nationalist sentiments that survived.

In the articulation of secularism, the role of the Supreme Court has always been decisive simply because of (a) its obvious changing nature and (b) the constitutional authorization of the apex court to interpret the idea in accordance with the transforming socio-political milieu. There does not appear to be consistency in what the Supreme Court holds as secularism. As a recently published work has shown, what was defined as secularism in the 1994 Bommai judgment stands in contradiction to its pronouncement in the 1994 'Hindutva' case and also the 2002 NCERT school textbook controversy. In the Bommai verdict, the Court held the opinion that secularism (which is part of the basic structure) meant a clear demarcation between the religious from political. By justifying the dismissal of the BJP-led state governments of Uttar Pradesh, Rajasthan, Madhya Pradesh and Himachal Pradesh following the demolition of the Babri Masjid in 1992 since use of religion for political gain was unconstitutional, the Court redefined the political as independent of considerations that should remain in the private domain. There is however a clear difference between the Bommai judgment and what the Court

decided in the *Ismail Faruqui* versus *Union of India* (1994) case, which is also
known as the Ramjanmabhumi case. In this judgment, which is also famous as
the Hindutva judgment because it dealt with the Ramjanmabhumi controversy,
the Court drew on the Hindu scriptures while defining secularism. Characterizing
secularism as *sarv dharma sambhava* (tolerance of all religions), the Court seems
to have attributed the strong roots of secularism in India to 'the tolerance of the
Hindus', who are demographically preponderant. The judgment is based on two
assumptions that are proved to be false at least in the light of the articulation of the
political. The first assumption, that tolerance is linked with ancient Hindu scriptures and hence Hindus are civilizationally tolerant, may not be at all consistent
with the recent political developments in India. By implication Hindus are, as the
second assumption underlines, instinctively appreciative of difference within the
cultural resources that Indian civilization has already created. Drawn on the cultural logic, reflective of the Savarkarian *pitribhumi–punyabhumi* formula, these
two assumptions feed the Hindu sectarian claim of accommodating diversity for a
pan-Indian identity. These assumptions also contribute to the view that 'secularism
as tolerance is steadfast with Hindu interests, which subsumes other faiths within
its philosophy'.[20] This leaves no space for 'plural values' as it privileges one set
of values over others. In the 2002 judgment on the textbook issue, the Supreme
Court seems to have favoured 'a majoritarian view' by glossing over the pluralistic Indian ethos. The argument is that, in essence, there is hardly a difference
among various religious faiths: what differ are practices. So, secularism is clearly
practice-linked. So far, the Court had been insistent on 'tolerance', whereas in this
judgment it appeared to have endorsed the spirit of assimilation, which stands in
contradiction with the basic notion of Indian pluralism. There is an implicit aim
of 'creating oneness' rather than allowing 'a definite space for social and political
diversity'. In other words, differences need to be respected with a view to creating
space for interreligious dialogues. This judgment, by seeking to assimilate differences into one, seems to have endorsed the Hindutva judgment by apparently
subsuming the majoritarian spirit in its articulation.

Gender as a critical component

In the context of growing democratization, issues such as women's empowerment
and gender rights have gained massive importance in contemporary political discourse though the founding fathers devoted a great deal of attention even while
evolving consensus on the gender issues in the Constituent Assembly and also
framing laws on these in independent India. B. R. Ambedkar proposed the Hindu
Code Bill seeking to protect some basic women rights, *viz.* the right to divorce,
outlawing polygamy, granting of inheritance rights and recognition of intercaste
marriage, among others. The Bill was knocked down in the lower house of parliament, despite Nehru's vehement support, presumably because it threatened 'the
patriarchal social framework'.

Two contemporary issues, namely a uniform civil code and reservation of
seats for women in national parliament and state legislatures, have redefined the

contour of feminist politics in India. Defending the spirit of the uniform civil code, Ambedkar argued strongly that the subjects of the Indian state shall have the right 'to claim full and equal benefit of all laws and proceedings for the security of persons and property as is enjoyed by other subjects regardless of any usage or custom based on religion and be subjected like punishment, pains and penalties and to none other'.[21] The Constituent Assembly was clearly divided on the issue of personal laws. On the one hand, there was a powerful lobby to protect religious freedom, especially minority interests, and on the other, to have a uniform civil code for all, based on the basic liberal view of citizenship. Unable to arrive at a consensus, personal laws of minorities – the whole gamut of family, property, marriage, divorce and adoption rights – were left within the domain of their respective religious strictures. Debates on these issues have also brought out the deep divisions within the women's movement following schism along lines of caste, class and community. Whatever the political aims of those pushing these two issues, there is no doubt that both these efforts articulated women's rights as citizens of a modern secular state by challenging particularistic and traditional values of family, religion, culture and community.

The controversy over the uniform civil code began with the 1985 Supreme Court judgment granting financial support to Shah Banu (who, once divorced, demanded alimony from her husband) under a provision in secular criminal law.[22] This verdict provoked the Muslims, who characterized this intervention by the Supreme Court as having fiddled with their personal law. The violation of personal law became a rallying point for Muslim political identity. To defuse the crisis, the Rajiv Gandhi-led Congress government hurriedly approved the Muslim Women (Protection of Rights in Divorce) Act in 1986 more or less along the lines endorsed by the Muslim leaders, ignoring other dissenting voices. The resolution of the controversy through a legal intervention amicably settled the uncertainty. But the issue of gender equality was hardly addressed. One of the powerful arguments for not taking the controversy to its logical conclusion was informed by the concern for communal amity. The code is a political question and needs to be settled politically. Laws could be an aid, perhaps powerful, once the decision is negotiated at the political level. Otherwise, a mere intervention of the Court is too weak to bypass the hegemonic patriarchal social framework.[23]

Like the uniform civil code debate, the arguments over the reservation of seats for women in the legislature focus on issues of political equality of women. The introduction of the Eighty-First Amendment Bill in 1996 by the United Front government brought back the gender issue to the centre stage of Indian politics. Women need to be empowered and reservation through a legal enactment is perhaps the most effective device to bypass the patriarchy. Besides settling the issue of gender parity at the political level, women intervention in the formal world of institutionalized politics is equally critical in translating the empowerment slogan into a reality. Reservation is justified on grounds of democracy, political equality and representation. Interestingly, these are the values that also inform the arguments challenging the reservations scheme in its present form. For instance, the demand for OBC sub-reservation is the result of the fear of appropriation of the quota by the upper-caste women. So one has to take into account both caste and community before making it a rule. The introduction of cleavages along caste and community suggests that women are clearly not a homogeneous collectivity. They are socially fractured and hence it would be conceptually misleading and empirically wrong to conceive of a situation in which women at various social strata articulate a single voice because of their uniformity in gender terms.

As is evident, in the construction of the political in contemporary India, gender is a significant component. The debates over the uniform civil code and reservation of seats for women clearly indicate the difficulty of conceptualizing feminism in India in a straitjacketed manner. The drive towards uniform civil code continues to remain a vacuous slogan unless it is debated at the grassroots; otherwise, the legal intervention from the top will always run the risk of being dubbed as engineered by motivated forces. Similarly, the reservation bill cannot ensure political equality for all; it merely seeks to expand the number of women in political decision-making. Nonetheless, these debates are symptomatic of a new politics underlining the critical importance of gender in conceptualizing the political. In other words, the feminist dialogue is as significant as the rise of the OBCs and Dalits in redefining 'democracy', 'equality' and 'representation' in contemporary India. Women therefore no longer remain 'just a voice', but a critical voice challenging the conventional outlook on social, economic and political issues while providing creative inputs to conceptualizing the political afresh.[24]

Growing importance of political institutions

Unlike her South Asian neighbours, political institutions have developed organic roots in India. There has been, however, a clear deterioration of the Indian parliament in its role in view of the decline of 'the moral credibility' of the elected representatives. Not only has the quality of the debate on policy issues gone down but the parliamentarians also tend to lose their dignity even on the floor of parliament once they are challenged by their colleagues. While attributing the steady decline of parliament in India to the general moral decadence and also growing importance of extra-constitutional factors in elections, Sumanta Banerjee explains this phenomenon by underlining the lack of (a) common adherence to the basic norms of parliamentary democracy and (b) a sense of awareness of the line between the responsible exercise of the right to freedom of speech and unrestricted license of speech within the walls of parliament.[25]

The parliamentary decline seems to be matched by the ascendancy of other political institutions of Indian democracy. For instance, the President, the Supreme Court of India and the Election Commission have, among others, shown a remarkable resilience in upholding some of the intrinsic liberal values.

India's President no longer remains an ornamental head of the state. In the context of the decline of single-party rule, the first citizen of the country seems to have redefined his/her constitutional role by being more 'pro-active' than before. Article 53 of the Constitution vests 'the executive power of the Union . . . in the President'; as constitutional head of state he/she is expected to act as an agent of the political executive, namely the council of ministers or cabinet. The rise of coalition government and the spread of corruption – in the political executive, legislatures and civil services – have created a legitimate space for other constitutional functionaries, including the presidency, 'to act as guardians of fairness and constitutional balance'.[26] That the President was not a mere 'rubber stamp' was evident when the late K. R. Narayanan prevented the Uttar Pradesh governor, Ramesh Bhandari, from arbitrarily dismissing the Kalyan Singh-led BJP government and replacing it with Jagdambika Pal's Congress–Samajwadi coalition. Bhandari dismissed the Singh government without giving the chief minister an opportunity to prove his majority on the floor of the assembly, which Narayanan thought was both 'unconstitutional' and also 'partisan', designed to help the ruling United Front–Congress in the forthcoming election.[27] A landmark Supreme Court judgment 'reinstalled' the BJP government, justifying K. R. Narayanan's intervention for constitutional propriety since there was 'widespread disenchantment . . . with the excessive use of President's rule for partisan purposes'.[28] Similarly, Narayanan's reluctance to endorse the decision of V. C. Pande, the Bihar governor, to appoint the Nitish Kumar-led minority government immediately after the 2000 state assembly election would have led to a serious constitutional crisis had Nitish Kumar not resigned. The fact that the Rabri Devi-led RJD coalition won the vote of confidence 'intensified the clamour against the governor's precipitous and apparently partisan action'.[29] Recently, President A. P. J. Abdul Kalam's refusal to approve the 2006 office of profit bill when it was sent to him after its endorsement by both the houses of parliament redefined the role of this institution in the changed socio-political environment. Although the President had no alternative but to grant assent once the bill was approved by the parliament second time, the episode is nonetheless reflective of the growing independence of India's highest constitutional authority. Three important principles were consolidated in the wake of this controversial office of profit episode: first, the underlying principle debarring the holder of an office of profit under the government from being a member of parliament is drawn on a foundational principle of the doctrine of separation of powers, namely that there should be a demarcation of authority and power between executive and legislature to avoid 'misappropriation of authority and power' by these two wings of government. The famous 1973 Kesavananda Bharati judgment of the Supreme Court endorses this principle as part of the Basic Structure of the Constitution of India. Second, the President's reluctance to approve the bill is also suggestive of the fact that there should be uniformity in interpreting the law as regards the office of profit. In fact, given the Supreme Court ruling on this, there is no scope for different interpretations and, as an apex judicial institution in the country, the Supreme Court is constitutionally authorized to enforce uniformity in this regard. Finally, by sending the bill back to Parliament for reconsideration, the President also upheld the judicial sanctity of the criteria that the Supreme Court devised to settle the controversy. These criteria are: (a) it must be a post created by and under the control of the government; (b) the appointee of the post should also be under governmental control; (c) the holder of the post must be entitled to some profit or benefit other than compensatory allowance, whether he/she takes it or not; and (d) the power/authority attached to that position that can be exercised by the holder.[30] It is true that the controversy was finally resolved not by following the judicial wisdom, but by political considerations. Nonetheless, this episode has established beyond doubt a healthy trend, which is constitutionally creative and politically challenging in so far as the institutions of governance are concerned. The bill was therefore a significant intervention in redefining the political, which is located in the institutions that had also creatively responded to the issues that perhaps were linked with deepening of democracy by meaningful participation of 'the people' in the political processes.

Similarly, the Supreme Court in the famous Bommai judgment of 1994 also radically altered the complexion of the debate on the basic structure of the constitution. Critical of the indiscriminate application of Article 356 to dismiss the duly elected state governments, the Supreme Court came out heavily against the Union government. B. R. Ambedkar was confident, as his statements in the Constituent Assembly endorse, that emergency provisions in the Constitution of India would rarely be invoked and, as Indian democracy matured, the need to do so would be less compelling, reducing Article 356 to 'a dead letter'. However, by 1994 this provision had been applied more than ninety times, the Supreme Court noted, and thus made this article 'a death letter', rather than 'a dead letter', as the founding fathers foresaw. The judgment put to rest all speculations regarding the 'delicate balance of powers in a federal polity' by saying that 'federalism envisaged in the Constitution is a basic structure. . . . The state *qua* the Constitution is federal and independent in its exercise of legislative and executive power.' It is true that the Constitution prefers an arrangement that is tilted in favour of the centre. But that does not mean that 'the States are mere appendages of the Centre. Within the sphere allotted to them, States are supreme. The Centre cannot temper with their powers.' Simultaneously, by clarifying the constitutional status of the states, the judgment also redefined the role of the President, who is not a mere stooge of the Union government, by underlining that

> the provision require that the material before the President must be sufficient to indicate that unless a proclamation (under article 356) is issued, it is not possible to carry on the affairs of the state as per the provisions of the Constitution. It is not every situation arising in the State but a situation which shows that constitutional government has become an impossibility, which alone will entitle the President to issue the proclamation.[31]

B. R. Ambedkar was right when he suggested that growing democratization will make the Emergency Provision redundant. The Supreme Court is certainly an important component in this process. By creatively interpreting the constitutional provisions, the apex court contributed to the redrawing of the basic contours of Indian federalism, which has, with its roots in the 1935 constitutional structure, evolved organically out of an engagement with the constantly changing social, economic and cultural milieu. The Bommai judgment is a watershed, perhaps the most significant, in the evolution of an organic federalism in India that is surely a break with the past.

The revival of the Election Commission as a political watchdog is a remarkable development supporting the growing democratization of Indian politics. Established in 1950, the Election Commission was set up as a constitutional agency and entrusted, according to Article 324 of the Constitution, with the task of superintendence, direction and control of all national and state-level elections.[32] The Commission holds substantial power so far as the procedural aspects of the elections are concerned. In fact, it derives its strength from the code of conduct formulated by the political parties participating in the election generally by consensus. There is no doubt that by its sincere involvement in the processes of elections, starting from the preparation of voters' roll to the declaration of the poll outcomes, the Commission has played a critical role in redefining the political in today's India. The role of the Commission in the recently concluded state election in West Bengal in 2006 is illustrative here: with the announcement of the dates of elections, the Commission took control of the election machinery of the state in an unprecedented manner. First, it took ample care to revise the voter's roll since the incumbent Left Front government was charged with manipulating the voters' list. The Election Commission found a large number of them in various districts. During the clean-up operation, the observer found 1.3 million false names[33] in the list of voters, and struck them off. Hence the charge seemed authenticated and the media thus attributed the sustained electoral victory of the Left Front to 'the bogus voters'. Second, following its success in Bihar in holding a free and fair election under the strict surveillance of the state-controlled coercive forces, the Commission decided to conduct the poll on five evenly dispersed dates stretching almost two months. The Commission requisitioned police and paramilitary forces from outside the state simply because the state police did not appear to be reliable. Because the dates were dispersed, it was possible to get an adequate number of them to supervise the voting on the days of the election. It was a remarkable election in West Bengal, which was held under the strict control of the Election Commission, that implemented its authority strictly in accordance with its constitutional obligation to Indian democracy.[34] Although the electoral outcome brought back the incumbent Left Front government to power, unlike in Bihar where a new government was installed replacing the government that had held power for more than fifteen years, the Commission provided critical inputs to the processes of democratization by empowering the ordinary voters, who now become part of 'the movers and shakers' of Indian democracy, which can be ignored only at the cost of the political parties seeking political power. In other words, the voters are not merely seasonal participants; they have also been made to feel their importance in the political processes that hardly mattered so far in their everyday life.

Adulthood of Indian states or decline of umbrella parties?

The recently concluded elections in 2006 in five different states in India confirm that the texture of Indian politics has undergone radical changes. What we saw in the 2004 Lok Sabha poll seems to have set a pattern from which there is no escape. An era of coalition has begun and gone are the days of single-party majority rule. Neither of the two pan-Indian political parties, Congress and its *bête noir*, the Bharatiya Janata party (BJP), is capable of mustering a majority in any of the recently held elections to the state legislature, just like the last national election when they failed to win a majority of seats in the Lok Sabha. Except in Pondicherry, where Congress won twenty out of a total of thirty assembly seats, the electoral outcome is clearly in favour of coalition of parties. The juggernaut of the Left Front seems to have swayed both the urban and rural voters in West Bengal. Besides almost completely wiping out the opposition in the state, the Left Front constituents, especially its leading partner, CPI(M), have made significant inroads in Calcutta and other peripheral towns across various age groups. In Kerala, the Left Democratic Front replaced the Congress-led United Democratic Front by following the rules of musical chairs, as it were. The voters' preference was for a coalition government, led by the LDF, in the 2006 assembly election. In Tamil Nadu, the DMK-led conglomeration, which included Congress as well, swept the poll, reducing the ruling coalition's numerical strength in an assembly of 234 seats to only 69. The story was no different in Assam, where the Congress-led alliance defeated the competing alliance, led by the AGP. There is no doubt that the poll outcome cannot be grasped in a uniform way. Because the socio-political and economic context differs from one state to another, explanations also vary. What however remains constant is the growing importance of coalition as probably the most critical factor in electoral victory.

It is doubtful whether the Left Front will gain in strength at the centre simply because of its thumping majority in West Bengal and its electoral success in Kerala. The reasons are threefold: first, in terms of electoral dividends, the landslide victory in West Bengal does not seem to add much to its political clout in Delhi because the 2006 election simply reinstalls the Left Front government that has survived for almost thirty years. That the Kerala victory surely adds to its clout is hardly significant because the left forces cannot afford to lose the Congress as an ally in Delhi in a situation when the other alternative happens to be 'the communal' BJP. Second, the left parties do not seem to have an alternative, but to remain within the UPA, which is reflective of 'the frog-in-the-well strategy'. These parties do not want to venture into the unknown and bigger world for fear of losing their bases in West Bengal, Kerala and Tripura since their overwhelming significance in national politics in the aftermath of the fourteenth Lok Sabha poll in 2004 derives directly from these states. Third, the continuous support for the UPA seems to be ideologically governed. By being in coalition with the ruling party, but not taking cabinet positions, the left political parties retained their role as 'a critical opposition' to the government. This fits in well with their wider concern for pushing the BJP-sponsored political forces out of the mass reckoning. The coalition era has thus fundamentally redefined the ideological contours of the left forces in India. By adopting a less catholic and clearly a pragmatic ideological vision, the left constituents of the UPA seem to have carved space for 'consensus politics' by avoiding contentious issues and agendas.

The 2006 poll outcome seems to have contributed to a process of genuine federalization of the Indian polity that began with the destruction of Congress rule in various states in the 1967 state assembly election. The growing importance of the regional parties, including the CPI(M), which, despite its national existence, at least ideologically, is still confined to three Indian states, led to the decline of the pan-Indian parties, namely the BJP and Congress. The scene was completely different during the heyday of the 'Congress system' when the Congress Party controlled all the state governments and also the Union, the success of which was attributed to consolidation of 'the clientelistic arrangement'[35] that became gradually intrinsic to the party. What was symptomatic in 1967 seems to be a well-entrenched pattern now with the clear political ascendance of the regional parties. The leading member of either of the major coalitions at the pan-Indian level can afford to ignore them only at their political peril.

Following the rise of the regional parties as formidable partners in governance, the constituent states in federal India are growing strong gradually and steadily. Not only are they now capable of articulating their demands effectively, but they have on occasions become decisive in policy-making. Politically, it seems to be a sign of 'adulthood of Indian states', which may create a con-federal polity with strong units and a centre as a mere monitoring instrument. This may lead to a situation in which 'the writ of the centre does not run as authoritatively as it once did'[36] especially when the ruling party in the state is not the same as (or at least sympathetic to) the ones holding power at the centre. Nonetheless, the adulthood of states is not at all a romantic conceptualization of growing importance of Indian states, but is premised on a particular variety of 'political consciousnesses', drawn from inherent diverse socio-cultural realities of India as a 'nation'. There are instances that may be cited to argue that adulthood disrupts national integrity and hence is despicable. But a thorough study of the so-called 'disruptive movements' championing regional autonomy may reveal that the outcome would have probably been otherwise had they been dealt with differently at the outset. To put it bluntly, the carefully crafted tendency to 'essentialize' multicultural Indian identity boomeranged and the sooner it is understood by those who preside over India's political destiny the better it is for the country. This apart, there is a fairly strong opinion to suggest that politics in India continues to be governed by traditional idioms and values. This is probably true if we interpret the growing importance of caste and other primordial loyalties literally without comprehending their articulation in conjunction with the socio-economic and political reality. Caste or religion is representational; hence its importance in political mobilization. And, apart from consolidating a group identity, caste and religion provide a critical meaning to the individuals, located in a wider collectivity. So the idioms that may be mistaken as 'traditional' are actually modern presumably because they are rooted in processes linked with the growing democratization of the political in its most complex form. It would therefore be wrong to suggest that the increasing importance of primordial loyalties in conceptualizing political in India leaves no scope for modern politics to strike roots. What is correct to argue, however, is that modernity[37] in Indian politics is a very complex admixture of various influences, drawing on the past as well as present experiences and there is therefore no straightforward way to easily delimit its domain. This is where the challenge lies.

Glossary

adivasi	tribal
ahimsa	non-violence/absence of desire to harm a living being
ahir	Hindu agricultural caste associated with cattle-rearing
Akhanda Bharata	Undivided India
Arya Samaj	Arya Society – Hindu reform organization
ashram	Hindu retreat (both spiritual and educational)
Bakr-Id	Islamic festivals involving sacrifice
bania	trader, moneylender
bhadralok	gentlefolk, refers mostly to upper castes with English education in Bengal
bhakti	Hindu devotionalism
Bharat	India
Bhumihar	land-owning caste mainly of Bihar
Brahmin	individuals belonging to upper castes
chamar	low caste, often associated with leather work and tanning
Chandala	a Hindu derogatory term for a Muslim
charkha	hand-held spinning wheel
crore	ten millions
Dal	party, corps
Dalit	oppressed (former untouchable)
desi	indigenous
dharma	duty, implying sacred moral law in Hinduism
garib	poor
goonda	hooligan, thug, lout
gram sabha	village assembly
Granth Saheb	the holy book of the Sikhs
Gujar	agricultural caste
harijan	people of God; Mahatma Gandhi's interpretation of scheduled castes of India
hartal	cessation of work as an expression of popular protest against the authority
hat	market in villages

Hindu Rashtra	Hindu nation-state
hinduraj	rule by Hindus, sovereignty of Hindus over themselves and others
Hindutva	Hindu cultural nationalism
jati	case, cluster, sub-caste
jatra	folk theatre
kayastha	caste of scribes, generally upper castes
khadi/khaddar	coarse/homespun cloth
Khattri	administrative and commercial caste
kirtan	devotional song
kisan	cultivator, farmer
kshatriya	Hindu upper caste of martial or royal status
Kurmi	agricultural caste
lakh	one hundred thousand
lathi	stick/bludgeon
Lok Sabha	lower house of Indian parliament
Mahabharata	Hindu epic
mahila mandal	women's group
majlis	Islamic religious meeting or gathering
mandir	temple
masjid	mosque
matribhumi	motherland
maulvi	Muslim priest or learned man
Moharram	Islamic festival
naxalite	CPI(ML) militant group in favour of armed insurrection following Mao's political ideology
panchayat	traditional village council
pitribhumi	fatherland
puja	worship
punyabhumi	holy land
Rajya Sabha	upper house of Indian parliament
Ram Rajya	the state governed by the mythical Ram, implying ideal state
Ramayana	Hindu epic depicting the lives of Ram and Sita and the battle of Ram with Ravana
sabha	association, society, council, assembly, congregation
sach/satya	truth
sadhu	Hindu ascetic or mendicant
samiti	committee
Sanatani Hindu	one who believes in Vedas, Upanishads and Puranas
sangathan	movement for organization or consolidation, usually of a community
sangh	association/organization
sanyasis	ascetics
sarpanch	head of a panchayat
sarvadaya	uplift of all

satyagraha	insistence on truth/non-violent resistance
scheduled tribe	advasis or tribals given special concession in the Constitution of India in recognition of their disadvantaged status
seva/sewa	service
shakha	branch of a political party
sharia	Islamic religious law
Shiv Sena	name of a political party that is Maharashtra-based
shuddhi	purification of Hindu reconversion movement
Shudra	an individual occupying the bottom of the Hindu four-tier caste hierarchy
sunni	one of the two branches of Islam, accepting the authority of Sunna
swadeshi	of one's own country (also a 1905 political campaign for home rule)
swaraj	self-rule
talukdar	landowner
Tanzeem	religious movement for the unity and organization of Muslims
thakur	landowning caste
thana/thaneder	police station/officer of the police station
untouchables	those not belonging to the four-tier caste hierarchy in Hinduism, people so low as to be placed outside the pale of normal physical contact
Upanishad	theological and argumentative part of the Vedas
vaishya	upper castes, usually traders and commercial groups
vakil	lawyer, representative
Vandemataram	Bengali hymn, written by the novelist Bankim Chandra Chattopadhyay, also adopted as India's national song
Vedanta	system of beliefs drawn on the philosophy of Sankara
Vedas	ancient Indian religious texts
vidyapith	university/place of higher learning
Yadav	Hindu agricultural caste associated with cattle rearing
zamindari	landed estate, landed property; land or estate, held by zamindar; the office or tenure of a zamindar; landlord-based system of revenue collection
Zila Parishad	district council

Annotated bibliography[1]

An attempt at surveying the literature on politics in India is faced with a peculiar problem of delimiting the domain of the subject, for the idea of politics in India is so all encompassing and overwhelmingly interdisciplinary that anything and everything written on the life of the people as a community with some bearing on the state and government can arguably be a tract on the theme. Hence, the best way out is to concentrate on those writings only that have their central theme located in one or the other aspects of the state and government. However, with the advent of the social movements in the country, the sphere of politics in India has expanded to include the writings on behavioral aspects of the Indian political system. This is not an exhaustive bibliography, but indicative of broad trends in academic discourses on Indian politics. It will serve a useful purpose for beginners and also those involved in unraveling the complex dynamics of Indian politics. In preparing this bibliography, I have included, as far as possible, both book-length monographs as well as major articles on the subject. Having categorized them under clear subheadings, I have also endeavoured to capture the multiple dimensions that one should not lose sight of while dwelling on the evolution of Indian society and politics since independence in 1947.

Constitution of India

The early writings on Indian politics tried to decipher the broad contours of the system by providing a critical interpretation of the constitution of India on the one hand and discovering the true nature of the state in India on the other. Thus, the classics on the Constitution of India include D. D. Basu, *Introduction to the Constitution of India* (Delhi: Prentice Hall of India, 1961), Granville Austin, *The Indian Constitution: Cornerstone of a Nation* (London: Oxford University Press, 1966), V. N. Shukla, *The Constitution of India* (Allahabad: Kitab Mahal, 1967) and M. V. Pylee, *An Introduction to the Constitution of India* (New Delhi: S. Chand and Company, 1960). Five decades of the working of the Indian Constitution has prompted some of the writers to assess the functioning of the Statute. Hence, Granville Austin's *Working a Democratic Constitution; The India Experience* (New Delhi: Oxford University Press, 2002) brings out the functional dynamics of the Indian Constitution. Similarly, Zoya Hasan, E. Sridharan and R. Sudarshan (eds), *India's Living Constitution: Ideas, Practices, Controversies* (Delhi: Permanent Black, 2002) analyses the theory and practice of the constitution by pointing out the controversial issues dogging the constitution and the polity. M. V. Pylee's *Our Constitution, Government and Politics* (Delhi: Universal Publishing Co., 2000) contextualizes the Indian Constitution with the functioning of the government and politics in post-independence times.

Nature of Indian state

The favourite theme of the scholars writing on India has been to unravel the true face of the state in India – a trend starting in the 1950s and 1960s and continuing to date. Thus, W. H. Morris-Jones, *The Government and Politics of India* (London: Hutchinson University Library, 1964) set the tone for the liberal-structural functional approach to the study of Indian politics. A precursor of even Morris-Jones happens to be Norman D. Palmer's *The Indian Political System* (Boston: Houghton Mifflin Co., 1961); Rajni Kothari's *Politics in India* (Boston: Little, Brown and Company, 1970), harped on the notion of dominant political centre to convey the autonomy of political processes in the country.

The liberal political economy approach providing a serious critique of development planning in India was evolved by Francine Frankel's *India's Political Economy 1947–2004* (Delhi: Oxford University Press, 2005). Lloyd Rudolph and Susanne Rudolph's *In Pursuit of Lakshmi: The Political Economy of the Indian State* (New Delhi: Orient Longman, 1987), exposes the paradoxical traits of the Indian state, e.g. weak-strong centre, command and demand polity.

The Marxian perspective on the Indian state has been provided by A. R. Desai's *State and Society in India: Essays in Dissent* (Bombay: Popular Praksahan, 1975), which views state in India as an instrument of class-domination. Achin Vanaik's *The Painful Transition* (London: Verso, 1990) looks at the Indian state as a relatively autonomous entity. The economic critique of the state in India is provided by Pranab Bardhan's *Political Economy of Development in India* (London: Oxford University Press, 1984). Among others, Atul Kohli's *State and Poverty in India* (Cambridge: Cambridge University Press, 1987), adopts a state-oriented focus in his comparative study of politics of reform in the three Indian states of UP, Karnataka and West Bengal.

In contemporary times, the dominant focus of writing on the Indian state is on the economic reorientation of the state apparatus. Hence, a number of works have been produced in recent times to locate the political motivations of economic reforms in India. Such works include Jos Mooij's (ed.), *The Politics of Economic Reforms in India* (New Delhi: Sage, 2005), Meghnad Desai's *Development and Nationhood: Essays in the Political Economy of India* (New Delhi: Oxford University Press, 2006) and Pranab Bardhan's *Scarcity, Conflicts and Cooperation: Essays in the Political and Institutional Economics of Development* (New Delhi: Oxford University Press, 2006). Further, Masaaki Kimura and Akio Tanabe (eds), *The State in India: Past and Present* (New Delhi: Oxford University Press, 2006) and Lloyd Rudolph and J. K. Jacobson (eds), *Experiencing the State* (New Delhi: Oxford University Press, 2006) deal with the changing perspectives of the state in India.

Politico-constitutional institutions

Various institutions of governance in India have been the theme of a number of scholarly works. Subhash Kashyap's *Our Parliament* (New Delhi: National Book Trust, 1989) and his *Parliament in India: Myth and Reality* (New Delhi: National, 1990) provide an outline of the structure and functions of the national legislature. A. Surya Prakash's *What Ails Indian Parliament* (New Delhi: HarperCollins Publishers, 1995) attempts at diagnosing the ills that plague the Parliament. J. M. R. Biju's *Parliamentary Democracy and Political Change in India* (New Delhi: Kanishka Publishers, 1999) looks at the dynamics of parliamentary democracy to act as the harbinger of political transformations in the country.

The writings on the Indian Executive differ in having their focus on a particular component of the whole. The works on the Indian President are dated and include M. L. Ahuja's *The Presidents of India and Their Constitutional Portrayal, 1952–1977* (Faridabad: Om Publications, 1977); B. C. Das's *The President of India* (New Delhi: S. Chand and Company, 1977) and Valmiki Chaudhary's *President and the Indian Constitution* (New Delhi: Allied Publisher, 1985).

On the office of Prime Minister, one book that stands out is that of L. N. Sharma's *The Prime Minister of India* (Delhi: Macmillan, 1976). Two scholarly works on the functioning of the cabinet government in India, dealing with two distinct phases, are R. J. Venkateswaran's *Cabinet Government in India* (London: George Allen and Unwin, 1967), which fathoms the situation till 1966, and V. A. Pai Pannandikar and Ajay K. Mehra's *The Indian Cabinet: A Study in Governance* (New Delhi: Konark Publishers, 1996), which stretches the analysis till the decade of the 1990s. On the changing nature of Indian administration, Kamala Prasad's *Indian Administration: Politics, Policies and Prospects* (New Delhi: Pearson and Longman, 2006) is an interesting tract.

Party system in India

The writings on the party system in India reflect the dominant trend of their time. After the path-breaking essay of Rajni Kothari on 'The Congress in India', *Asian Survey*, 4 (2), 1964, a number of scholarly writings appeared focusing their attention on the Congress Party. Two important writings in this category are Myron Weiner's *Party Building in a New Nation: The Indian National Congress* (Chicago: University of Chicago Press, 1967) and Stanley Kochanek's *The Congress Party of India: The Dynamics of one Party Democracy* (Princeton: Princeton University Press, 1968). M. P. Singh's *Split in a Pre-dominant Party: The Indian National Congress in 1969* (New Delhi: Abhinav Publications, 1988) narrates the events that led to the split in the Congress Party in 1969. Paul Brass and Francine Robinson's *The Indian National Congress and Indian Society: 1885–95* (New

Delhi: Chankya Publications, 1987) is an analysis of early social configurations of the Congress Party during the stipulated period.

Once the dominance of the Congress Party on the Indian political system had dissipated, a number of writing emerged to trace the contours of the new party system in India. Thus, Horst Hartman's *Political Parties in India* (Meerut: Meenakshi Prakashan, 1982) is a general survey of the main features of party system in India. Paul Brass's *Castes, Faction and Party in Indian Politics* (Delhi: Chankya Publications, 1984) analyses factionalism in the parties in India. Pradeep K. Chibeer's *Democracy without Associations: Transformation of the Party System and Social Cleavages in India* (New Delhi: Vistar Publications, 1999) is a study of the emerging societal fragmentations on the basis of caste and religion in the country.

The rise of BJP to power in India inspired two sets of writing: one trying to grasp the factors lying behind the rise of the Hindutva and the BJP, and the other providing a critique of Hindutva and Sangh Parivar. The precursor of writings that looked at the rise of Hindu nationalist parties is Bruce Graham's *Hindu Nationalism and Indian Politics: The Origins and Development of Bhartiya Jana Sangh* (Cambridge: Cambridge University Press, 1993). The other publications on Hindu nationalism and the BJP include Christophe Jaffrelot's *Hindu Nationalist Movement and Indian Politics, 1952 to the 1990s* (New Delhi: Viking, 1996), T. B. Hansen and Christophe Jaffrelot (eds), *The BJP and the Compulsions of Politics in India* (New Delhi: Oxford University Press, 1998) and Y. K. Malik and V. B. Singh's *Hindu Nationalists in India: The Rise of the BJP,* (New Delhi: Sage, 1995).

A critique of Hindu nationalism and the RSS is the theme of Tapan Basu, Pradip Datta, Sumit Sarkar, Tanika Sarcar and Sambuddha Sen, *Khaki Shorts and Saffron Flags: A Critique of the Hindu Right* (Delhi: Orient Longman, 1993), Christophe Jaffrelot (ed.), *The Sangh Parivar: A Reader* (New Delhi: Oxford University Press, 2005), P. R. Kanungo's *RSS Tryst with Destiny* (New Delhi: Manohar, 2004) and Edna Fernandes's *Holy Warriors: A Journey into the Heartland of Indian Fundamentalism* (New Delhi: Penguin, 2006).

The rise of the political parties championing the peripheral sections of society is one of the core areas of studies on party system in India in recent scholarship. Two important books have drawn attention to the processes of India's 'silent revolution': Christophe Jaffrelot, *India's Silent Revolution: The Rise of the Low Castes in North Indian Politics* (New Delhi: Permanent Black, 2004) and Kanchan Chandra, *Why Ethnic Parties Succeed: Patronage and Ethnic Headcounts in India* (Cambridge, Cambridge University Press, 2004).

Indian federalism

The tracts on Indian federalism cover a diverse range of issues stretching from the preliminary explorations into the centre–state relations to assessing the nature of Indian federalism in the new millennium. The standard writings on centre–state relations are found in such books as K. M. Kurian and P. N. Verghese (eds),

Centre–State Relations (New Delhi: Segment Book Distributors, 1990); the perennial issues in centre–state relations have been examined in Amal Roy's *Tension Areas in India's Federal System* (Calcutta: World Press, 1991).

The issue of ethnic identities as a factor in the Indian federal system is presented in A. S. Narang's *Ethnic Identities and Federalism* (Shimla: Indian Institute of Advanced Study, 1995). The adverse implications of the Supreme Court decisions impacting Indian federalism are the theme of Pran Chopra (ed.), *The Supreme Court versus the Constitution: The Challenge to Federalism* (New Delhi: Sage, 2006). A micro-level study of the intra-institutional dynamics of federalism at the central level is in Akhtar Majeed's *Federalism within the Union: Distribution of Responsibilities in Indian System* (New Delhi: Manak Publications, 2004). A reconceptualization of the Indian federal system is the central focus of a number of works, the most important among which include Rasheeduddin Khan's *Federal India: A Design for Change* (New Delhi: Vikas, 1992) and his *Rethinking Indian Federalism* (Shimla: Indian Institute of Advanced Study, 1997), and Akhtar Majeed's *Federal India: A Design for Good Governance* (New Delhi: Manak Publications, 2004).

The Indian federal system has been examined in comparison with other important federal systems, in a few important publications. Phillippe Gervais-Lambony, Frederic Landy and Sophie Oldfield (eds), *Reconfiguring Identities and Building Territories in India and South Africa* (New Delhi: Manohar, 2005) presents an interesting reading of the similar impact on the federal systems of the two countries of assertion of identities to seek spatial representation; Rekha Sexena's *Situating Federalism: Mechanisms of Intergovernmental Relations in Canada and India* (New Delhi: Manohar, 2006) deals with the structural-functional orientations in the intergovernmental interactions in the two federal systems; Ian Copland and John Rickard (eds), *Federalism: Comparative Perspectives from India and Australia* (New Delhi: Manohar, 2006) covers the whole range of issues having a bearing on the theory and practice of federalism in Indian and Australia; K. Shankar Bajpai (ed.), *Democracy and Diversity: India and the American Experience* (Oxford University Press, New Delhi, 2007) also deals with federalism in a comparative perspective.

A deep-seated analysis of the economic dimension of federalism in India, with reference to the development dynamics so far, is found in M. Govind Rao and Nirvikar Singh's *Political Economy of Federalism in India* (New Delhi: Oxford University Press, 2005). The contextualization of the Indian federalism in relation to twenty-first century imperatives has been provided in B. D. Dua and M. P. Singh (eds), *Indian Federalism in the New Millennium* (New Delhi: Manohar, 2003).

Coalition politics

The dawn of the intensive phase of coalition politics at the national level from late 1980s inspired a number of scholarly works on the theme. The precursor of the writing on coalition politics in India is S.K. Chatterjee (ed.), *The Coalition*

Government (Madras: The Christian Literature Society, 1974) followed by Subhash Kashyap (ed.), *Coalition Government and Politics in India* (New Delhi: Uppal Publishing House, 1977).

Of recent publications, Akhtar Majid's *Coalition Politics and Power Sharing* (New Delhi: Manak Publications, 2000) analyses the coalition politics in terms of convenient power sharing amongst various contender of power. Bidyut Chakrabarty's *Forging Power: Coalition Politics in India* (New Delhi: Oxford University Press, 2006) argues for situating the dynamics of coalition politics in the broad spectrum of socio-economic churning taking place in the country, as a result of which newer classes are emerging to stake their claim on the pie of political power. Finally, M. P. Singh and Anil Mishra (eds), *Coalition Politics in India: Problems and Prospects* (New Delhi: Manohar, 2006) focuses on the critical analysis of the operationalization of coalition politics in order to find out the problems and prospects of the same for the country.

The theoretical aspects of the coalition government and politics are elucidated in a number of scholarly works produced mainly outside India. Notable among such writings include William H. Ricker, *The Theory of Political Coalitions* (New York: Yale University Press, 1962); Swen Greenings, E. W. Kelly and Michael Leiserson (eds) *The Study of Coalition Behaviour* (New York: Holt, Rinehart and Winston, 1970); F. A. Ogg, 'Coalition', in Edwin R. A. Seligman (ed.) *Encyclopaedia of Social Sciences*, Vol. 3 (New York: Macmillan, 1963); James Bryce, *Modern Democracies*, Vol. 1 (New York: Macmillan, 1921); Maurice Duverger, *Political Parties* (Landon: Methuen, 1951); Jean Blondel, *An Introduction to Comparative Government* (New York: Prager Publishers, 1969); and M. Leiserson, *Coalition in Politics: A Theoretical and Empirical Study* (unpublished PhD dissertation, Yale University, 1966). Coalitions in parliamentary systems are the focus of attention in Lawrence G. Dodd, *Coalition in Parliamentary Government* (Princeton: Princeton University Press, 1976); John Stuart Mill, *Considerations on Representative Government* (New York: Liberal Art, 1958); Harold Laski, *Parliamentary Government in England* (New York: The Viking Press, 1938); and Lars Rudebeck (ed.) *When Democracy Makes Sense* (Stockholm: Akut, 1992). The experiences of particular individual countries in coalition are discussed in Michael Lover and Norman Schofield, *Multi Party Government: The Politics of Coalition in Europe* (London: Oxford University Press, 1990); Arnold Lijphart, *Democracy in Plural Societies: A Comparative Exploration* (Bombay: Popular Prakashan, 1989); G. L. Lowell, *Governments and Parties in Continental Europe*, Vol. 1 (Cambridge: Harvard University Press, 1896); W. L. Middleton, *The French Political System* (London: Ernest Benn, 1932); A. L. Lowell, *Greater European Governments* (Cambridge, MA: Harvard University Press, 1918); and A. Hermens Ferdinand, *Democracy or Anarchy* (Notre Dame: Notre Dame University Press, 1941).

The advent of coalition politics in India was initially experienced in certain provinces during 1967–69. A description of the state of things in the different provinces may be found in M. S. Verma, *Coalition Government* (New Delhi: Oxford, 1971); E. J. Thomas, *Coalition Game and Politics in Kerala* (New Delhi:

Intellectual Publishing House, 1985); John P. John, *Coalition Governments in Kerala* (Trivendrum: Institute for the Study of Public Policy, 1983); Sukadev Nanda, *Coalition Politics in Orissa* (New Delhi: Sterling, 1979); and Iqbal Narain, *Twilight or Dawn: The Political Change in India, 1969–1971* (Agra: Laxmi Narain, 1972). On the critical elections of 1967, see Rajni Kothari, 'The political change of 1967', *Economic and Political Weekly*, 15 February 1969; Harry Blair, 'Caste and British census in Bihar: using old data to study contemporary political behaviour', in Gerald Barrier (ed.), *The Census in British India* (New Delhi: Manohar, 1981); Walter Hauser and Wendy Singer, 'The democratic rite: celebration and participation in Indian elections', *Asian Survey*, 26 (9), 1986; Sudipta Kaviraj, 'The general elections in India', *Government and Opposition*, 32 (1), 1997; M. P. Singh and Douglas V. Varney, 'Challenges to India's centralized parliamentary federalism', *Publius, the Journal of Federalism*, 33 (4), 2003; Oliver Mendelson, 'The transformation of authority in rural India', *Modern Asian Studies*, 4, 1993; on coalition politics, E. Sridharan's 'Electoral coalitions in 2004 General Elections: theory and evidence' (*Economic and Political Weekly*, 18 December 2004) is a useful intervention. Ajay K. Mehra's 'Indian elections, 2004: multiple transformations' (*Think India Quarterly*, 7 (3), 2004) deals with this phenomenon.

The inauguration of coalitions in the country especially in the post-1989 phase has produced a huge literature in the form of books and articles in both journals and newspapers.

Important articles on the subject that have appeared in the newspapers include Pravangshu Dutta, 'Coalition politics: the Indian experiment', *Assam Tribune* (30 June 2001); Shibani Dasgupta, 'Coalition politics; treading on thin ice', *Assam Tribune* (15 June 2001); Hari Jaisingh, 'Importance of national consensus in a fractured polity', *Tribune* (30 March 2001); Mohit Sen, 'Power game', *Hindustan Times* (9 October 2000); C. P. Bhambri, 'Uneasy federal relations', *Observer* (20 September 2000); K. K. Katyal, 'Consensus in the mantra', *The Hindu* (26 March 2001); Ajit Kumar Jha, 'Junk ideology, talk numbers: the new grammar of coalition politics', *Indian Express* (9 March 2001); C. P. Bhambri, 'Coalition times are here again', *Financial Express* (30 June 1991), 'Coalition politics: mixed experiences', *The Hindu* (16 June 1996) and 'Coalition and governance', *Hindustan Times* (31 May 1996); B. G. Deshmukh, 'Coalition governments at the centre', *The Hindu* (7 December 1996); Nikhil Chakrabarty, 'Coalition compulsions', *The Hindu* (27 July 1996); A. Eswara Reddy, 'Coalition governments: the Indian experience', *The Hindu* (9 July 1996); A. S. Abraham, 'Coalition politics: federal system is inevitable', *The Times of India* (29 May 1996); Harish Khare and B. Muralidhar, 'Coalition and controversies', *The Hindu* (30 November 1997); Rekha Saxena, 'Viable coalitions', *The Pioneer* (1 April 1998); A. Surya Prakash, 'Dharma of coalitions', *The Pioneer* (13 December 2001); P. M. Kamath, 'Is coalition government inevitable?', *Free Press Journal* (28 February 2000); K. P. Srivastava, 'Seamier side of coalitions' (*National Herald*, 13 August 2000); Praful Goradia, 'Art of managing impossible', *The Pioneer* (19 May 2000); Sucheta Dalal, 'Coalition politics and damage to probity', *Deccan Herald* (10 May 2000);

Mahesh Rangarajan, 'Games coalition play', *The Telegraph* (5 May 2000); Sita Kaushik, 'Coalitions and contradictions', *The Pioneer* (28 April 2000); Subhash C. Kashyap, 'Coping with coalitions: coalitions can work provided . . .', *Freedom First* (July–September 1999).

Amongst the articles in journals, the more important ones include: Walter Anderson, 'Election, 1989 in India: the dawn of coalition politics', *Asian Survey*, 30 (6), 1990; M. P. Singh, 'Indian national front and united front coalition governments: a phase in federalized governance', *Asian Survey*, 41 (2), 2001; Aditya Nigam, 'India after the 1996 elections: nation, locality and representation', *Asian Survey*, 36 (12), 1996; E. Sridharan, 'Coalition politics', *Seminar*, 437, 1996; Chandan Mitra, 'Unholy alliances', *Seminar*, 454, 1997; S. C. Malik, 'Coalition governments', *Seminar*, 215, 1977; J. S. Bali, 'The new coalition experiment: Indian metamorphosis', *Politics India*, 1 (1), 1996; Rekha Saxena, 'Coalition experiments: problems and prospects', *Mainstream*, 25 April 1998.

The important books on coalition include D. Sunder Ram (ed.), *Coalition Politics in India: Search for Political Stability* (New Delhi: National Publishing House, 2000); K. P. Karunakaran (ed.), *Coalition Governments in India: Problems and Prospects* (Simla: Indian Institute of Advanced Studies, 1975); Akhtar Majeed (ed.), *Coalition Politics and Power Sharing* (New Delhi: Manak Publications, 2000); S. P. Agarwal and J. C. Agarwal, *The History of Rise and Fall of Non-Congress Governments of India* (New Delhi: Shipra Publications, 1991); Bhabani Sangupta, *India: Problems of Governance* (New Delhi: Konark Publications, 1996); and Madhu Limaye, *Birth of Non-Congressism: Opposition Politics, 1947–1975* (New Delhi: B. R. Publishing Corporation, 1985). Articles written in books include E. Sridharan, 'Principles, power and coalition politics in India: lessons from theory, comparison and recent history', in D. D. Khanna and Gert Keuck (eds), *Principles, Power and Politics* (Delhi: Macmillan, 1999); Balveer Arora, 'Coalitions and national cohesion', in Francine Frankel, Zoya Hasan, Rajeev Bhargava and Balveer Arora (eds), *Transforming India: Social and Political Dynamics of Democracy* (New Delhi: Oxford University Press, 2000); and Alladi Kuppuswamy, 'Coalition politics: trends and problems', in D. Sunder Ram (ed.), *Coalition Politics in India* (New Delhi: National Publishing House, 2000). On the Indian coalition experiment, Paranjay Guha Thakurta and Shankar Raghuraman in their *A Time of Coalitions: Divided We Stand* (New Delhi: Sage, 2004) have provided a contextual interpretation of the phenomenon.

Indian democracy at work

The conceptualization and execution of a democratic system of governance in India have provided an endless source of intellectual stimulation to scholars from the beginning to date to produce voluminous works on the subject. As the democracy is deepening in Indian society and unleashing hitherto suppressed forces to have adequate articulation of their interests, the corpus of literature on the subject is also multiplying rapidly.

The early writings on Indian democracy tried to grasp the institutional interactions to provide for the checks and balances in the system. Important among them are A. H. Hanson and Janet Douglas, *India's Democracy* (New Delhi: Vikas Publishing House, 1972); Myron Weiner, *The Indian Paradox: Essays in Indian Politics*, edited by Ashutosh Varshney (New Delhi: Sage, 1989); and S. A. H. Haqqui (ed.) *Indian Democracy at Cross-Roads* (New Delhi: K. M. Mittal Publications, 1986). Rajni Kothari's prominent works such as *Politics in India* (Boston: Little, Brown and Co., 1970), *Politics and the People: In Search of a Humane India* (2 vols, Delhi: Ajanta Publication, 1989) and *State against Democracy: In Search of Humane Governance* (Delhi: Ajanta Publication, 1990) examine the functioning of democracy in India at different times and with different orientations.

The onset of the 1990s heralded a number of path-breaking trends in Indian politics, e.g. the irredeemable decline of the Congress system, the emergence of Hinduism as a formidable force in the form of the BJP, the rise of Dalit assertion in the politics of North Indian states, and the introduction of economic reforms. These epoch-making trends inspired a number of writers to juxtapose them on the broader canvas of India democracy, thereby producing valuable volumes on the subject. Thus, Paul R. Brass's *The Politics of India since Independence* (Cambridge: Cambridge University Press, 1992) is an exploration of the deepening of democracy in India. Hari Har Das's *India: Democratic Government and Politics* (Bombay: Himalayan Publishing House, 1991) and M. P. Singh and Rekha Sexena (eds) *Ideologies and Institutions in Indian Politics* (New Delhi: Deep and Deep Publications, 1998) are efforts at examining the functioning of democratic institutions in the traditional mould. Upendra Baxi and Bhikhu Parekh (eds) *Crisis and Change in Contemporary India* (Delhi: Sage Publishers, 1995) analyses the traumatic upheaval that marked Indian politics at that time. Similarly, the scholarly works of Myron Weiner seek to capture 'the paradox' in Indian politics, especially in his *The Indian Paradox: Essays in Indian Politics*, edited by Ashutosh Varshney (New Delhi: Sage, 1989); see also Satish Deshpande, *Contemporary India* (New Delhi: Penguin, 2004); Dipesh Chakrabarty, Rochona Majumdar and Andrew Sartori (eds), *From the Colonial to the Postcolonial: India Pakistan in Transition* (New Delhi: Oxford University Press, 2007).

Jayant Lale and Rajendra Vora (eds) *State and Society in India* (New Delhi: Chankya, 1990) is a collection of essays mapping socio-political transformations during the 1980s. A. K. Jana (ed.) *Indian Politics at Crossroads* (New Delhi: Common Wealth Publishers, 1998) tries to grapple with the issues facing Indian democracy. Sudipto Kaviraj (ed.) *Politics in India*, (New Delhi: Oxford University Press, 1997), is a Marxian intervention in the discourse on Indian politics. Partha Chatterjee (ed.) *State and Politics in India* (New Delhi: Oxford University Press, 1997) is a compendium of essays providing a holistic perspective on Indian politics. S. D. Sharma's *Development and Democracy in India* (Boulder: Lynne Rienner Publishers, 1999) looks at democracy in India as the stimulus for development owing to the assertion of people's aspirations through political channels. Aseema Sinha also dwells on this in her *The Regional Roots of Developmental Politics in India: A Divided Leviathan* (Bloomington: Indiana University Press,

2005; Oxford University Press, Delhi, has also brought out an Indian edition). On the same theme, John Echeverri-Gent's *The State and the Poor: Public Policy and Political Development in India and the United States* (Berkeley: University of California Press, 1993) examines the issues of political development leading to democratic culture in the comparative perspective of India and America

The issues having strong bearings on democratic governance in India have been highlighted in Bhabani Sen Gupta's *India: Problems of Governance* (New Delhi: Konark, 1996). Similarly, Francine Frankel, Zoya Hasan, Rajeev Bhargava and Balveer Arora (eds) *Transforming India: Social and Political Dynamics of Democracy* (Delhi: Oxford University Press, 2000) also examines the tumultuous changes that were sweeping India in the 1990s. Ramashray Roy focuses on the transformation in Indian democracy in *Democracy in India: Form and Substance* (New Delhi: Shipra, 2005). Philip Oldenburg (ed.) *India Briefing – 1995* (Boulder: Westview Press, 1995) reads like a chronicle of contemporary political developments in India. Atul Kohli (ed.) *India's Democracy: An Analysis of Changing State–Society Relations* (Delhi: Orient Longman, 1991) is also a collection of essays examining the newer trends in the societal response to the deepening of democratic ethos in the country. Niraja Jayal Gopal concentrates on the changing nature of 'representation' in India in her *Representing India: Ethnic Diversity and the Governance of Public Institutions* (London: Palgrave, 2006).

Sunil Khilnani's *The Idea of India* (London: Hamish Hamilton, 1997) presents a beautiful exposition of the multicultural, composite and accommodative culture and ethos that forms the foundation stone of the democratic way of life in the country. Ayesha Jalal (ed.) *Nationalism, Democracy and Development: State and Politics in India* (New Delhi: Oxford University Press, 1997) analyses the functioning of democracy in India in the context of the issues of nationalism and development as articulated through the various claims on the Indian states. The latest in this genre is Ramchandra Guha's *India after Gandhi: The History of the World's Largest Democracy* (London: Picador, 2007).

The inception of the new millennium saw a number of scholarly works on Indian democracy: Niraja Gopal Jayal (ed.) *Democracy in India* (New Delhi: Oxford University Press, 2001) and her authored book *Democracy and the State: Welfare, Secularism and Development in Contemporary India* (New Delhi: Oxford University Press, 2001) closely examine the changing nature of democracy in India owing to the pressures brought on it by factors such as market orientation in economy, rise of communalism in new guise and claims and counter-claims of various sections of the society. S. K. Chaubey and Susheela Kaushik (eds) *Indian Democracy at the Turn of the Century* (New Delhi: Kanishka Publishers, 2003) is a reflection on the state of the functioning of democracy in India with focus on the unconventional issues coming into prominence. Rajendra Vora and Suhas Palshikar (eds) *Indian Democracy: Meanings and Practices* (New Delhi: Sage Publications, 2004) contains essays that look at the reconceptualization of democracy with the purpose of making it meaningful for the country. Ramashray Roy's *Democracy in India: Form and Substance* (Delhi: Shipra Publishers, 2005) is again an attempt to evaluate the notion of democracy in India with a view to reformulate the same.

Madhu Purnima Kishwar's *Deepening Democracy: Challenges of Governance and Globalization in India* (New Delhi: Oxford University Press, 2006) is obviously an exploration into the issues generated by the demand for governance and unavoidable globalization, which have numerous side-effects for democracy in India. Ram Puniyani's *Indian Democracy, Pluralism and Minorities* (New Delhi: Global Media Publications, 2006), critically presents the predicament of Indian democracy to safeguard the pluralist ethos of the country and guarantee a dignified life to the minorities in the face of growing religious fundamentalism among the majority people. A. G. Noorani's *Constitutional Question and Citizen's Rights* (New Delhi: Oxford University Press, 2006) also assesses the issues of citizen's rights, albeit from the perspective of the constitutional framework rather than the political perspective.

A remarkable feature of democracy in India is the reach of democracy at the grassroots level through the means of Panchyati Raj institutions. For a look at the state of things before the Seventy-Third Constitutional Amendment, G. Ram Reddy's *Patterns of Panchayati Raj in India* (Delhi: Macmillan, 1977) would be excellent reading. L. C. Jain's *Grass without Roots* (New Delhi: Sage Publications, 1985) provides an insightful assessment of the farce of Panchayati Raj. For the role political expediency has played in stifling the growth of Panchayati Raj institutions, George Mathew's *Panchayati Raj: From Legislation to Movement* (New Delhi: Concept, 1994) makes good reading. The state of affairs in urban local governance in India has been examined in Niraja Gopal Jayal, Amit Prakash and P. K. Sharma (eds), *Local Governance in India: Decentralization and Beyond* (New Delhi: Oxford University Press, 2006).

Area-specific dynamics of democracy in India has been the theme of a number of books. Ashutosh Varshney's *Democracy, Development and the Countryside: Urban–Rural Struggles in India* (Cambridge: Cambridge University Press, 1995) analyses the problem of what has come to be known as the paradox between India and Bharat. Harold A Gould's *Grassroots Politics in India: A Century of Political Evolution in Faizabad District* (New Delhi: Oxford and IBH, 1995) provides the historiography of grassroots politics in an Indian district. G. K. Lieten's *Development, Devolution and Democracy: Village Discourse in West Bengal* (New Delhi: Sage, 1996) narrates the intricacies of village-level democracy in India.

The forces unleashed by the deepening of democracy in India have led to an apparent crisis of governance in the country, which has been reflected in a number of books. Atul Kohli's *Democracy and Discontent: India's Growing Crisis of Governability* (Cambridge: Cambridge University Press, 1990) is one of the early works to raise the issue. In current times Subrat K. Mitra's *The Puzzle of India's Governance: Culture, Context and Comparative Theory* (London: Routledge, 2006) deals with the intricacies of governance in India with cultural factors providing the context. Avinash K. Dixit's *Landlessness and Economics: Alternative Modes of Governance* (New Delhi: Oxford University Press, 2006), analyses the problem of the breakdown of administrative machinery hindering the proper performance of the market and suggests market models of governance for the country.

Communalism and secularism

The literature on communalism and secularism is vast and varied. K. N. Panikkar (ed.) *Communalism in India: History, Politics and Culture* (New Delhi: Manohar Publisher, 1991) is the basic reader on the subject of communalism in India. Ashgar Ali Engineer's *Communalism and Communal Violence in India* (New Delhi: Ajanta Publications, 1989) provides an analytical approach to Hindu–Muslim conflict to trace the causes of communal violence in India. S. Gopal (ed.) *Anatomy of a Confrontation: The Ramjanambhoomi Babri Masjid Dispute* (Delhi: Penguin India, 1991) brings out the veracity or falsity of the two parties to the dispute based on historical evidences. Gyanandra Pandey (ed.) *Hindus and Others: The Question of Identity in India* (Delhi: Viking, 1993) contains essays that examine the issues of identity of various communities in India in the context of their position vis-à-vis the majority community. K. N. Panikkar (ed.) *The Concerned Indian's Guide to Communalism* (Delhi: Penguin, 1999) puts forth the dangerous portents of communalism in India and calls upon people to have the right perspective on the issue. Shikha Trivedy, Shail Mayaram, Achyut Yagnik and Ashish Nandy's *Creating a Nationality: The Ramjanambhoomi Movement and Fear of Self* (New Delhi: Oxford University Press, 1996) is a sociological analysis of the efforts to fan the passions of the people in the name of a non-existent issue to gain a false nationhood.

D. L. Sheth and Gurpeet Mahajan (eds) *Minority Identities and the Nation-State* (New Delhi: Oxford University Press, 1999) is a collection of essays locating the *problematique* of minority identities in the inclusive domain of the nation-state. Achin Vanaik's *Communalism Contested: Religion, Modernity and Secularization* (New Delhi: Vision, 1997) joins in the argument against communalism by putting faith in the value of secularization of the polity in the wake of modernity and subsidence of religion in the society. Zaheer Baber's *Secularism, Three Essays* (New Delhi: Collective, 2006) focuses on the role of intellectuals in society to contain the wave of communalism. Dietrich Reetz's *Islam in the Public Sphere: Religious Groups in India, 1900–1947* (New Delhi: Oxford University Press, 2006) is an analysis of the formation and consolidation of the religious groups in India with special reference to the Muslim groups. Ram Puniyani's *Contours of the Hindu Rashtra: Hindutva, Sangh Parivar and Contemporary Politics* (New Delhi: Kalpaz Publications, 2006) examines the programmes and strategies of the Sangh Parivar to gain mileage in contemporary politics owing to fluid political situations.

The theory and practice of secularism has been the focus of Rajeev Bhargava's *Secularism and its Critics* (New Delhi: Oxford University Press, 1997). Neera Chandhoke's *Beyond Secularism: The Rights of Religious Minorities* (New Delhi: Oxford University Press, 1999) argues for action beyond the rhetoric of secularism to acknowledge and safeguard religious minorities' rights. Aditya Nigam's *The Insurrection of Little Selves: The Crisis of Secular-Nationalism in India* (New Delhi: Oxford University Press, 2006) brings out the maladies in terms of the parochial affinities of people, which endanger the rubric of secular nationalism in India. Shriram Yerrankar (ed.) *Secularism in India: Theory and Practice* (New Delhi: Adhyanyan Publishers and Distributors, 2006) brings out the contemporary issues in the functioning of the secular polity in the country. Rajita Mohanty and Rejesh Tandon (eds) *Participatory Citizenship: Identity, Exclusion, Inclusion* (New Delhi: Sage, 2006) focuses on the choices and constraints of the people in coming to the mainstream of the political life in the country.

Election studies

Election studies form the empirical database of the political reality in Indian politics. Of the more recent works, Harold A. Gould and Sumit Ganguly (eds) *India Votes: Alliance Politics and Minority Governments in the Ninth and Tenth General Elections* (Boulder: Westview Press, 1993) is a mapping of the beginning of alliance politics in India. David Butler, Ashok Lahiri and Prannoy Roy (eds) *India Decides: Elections 1952–1995* (Delhi: Books and Things, 1995) is a useful, though dated, database on the subject. Subrata Mitra and V. B. Singh's *Democracy and Social Change in India: A Cross-Sectional Analysis of the National Electorate* (New Delhi; Sage, 1999) is a attempt at dissecting the underlying features of electoral politics in India.

Ramashray Roy and Paul Wallace (eds) *Indian Politics and the 1998 Election: Regionalism, Hindutva and State Politics* (New Delhi: Sage Publications, 1999) follows the trends unleashed by the landmark elections of 1998. Two recent works that seek to analyse the issues of electoral reservation and social change through elections in India are Alistair Macmillan, *Standing at the Margins: Representations and Electoral Reservation in India* (New Delhi: Oxford University Press, 2005) and Stephanie Tawa Lane-Rawal (ed.) *Electoral Reservations, Political Representation and Social Change in India: A Comparative Perspective* (New Delhi: Manohar, 2005).

Social movements

Social movements have always been the core content of writings on sociology of politics in India. The trendsetting writings on the subject come from M. S. A. Rao, whose edited volume *Social Movements in India* (Delhi: Manohar, 1978) and authored book *Social Movements and Social Transformation: A Study of the Backward Class Movement in India* (Delhi: Macmillan, 1979) stand out prominently. Another pioneer in studies on social movements is Ghanshyam Shah, whose *Protest Movements in Two Indian States* (Delhi: Avoanta, 1977) is one of the early accounts of social movements in India. Paul Brass's *Language, Religion and Politics in North India* (Cambridge: Cambridge University Press, 1974) also discusses the factors of language and religion as the medium of mass mobilization in the Hindi heartland.

The major and voluminous literature on the subject of social movements started appearing in the 1990s coinciding with the upsurge of caste-based mobilization in north India. Ghanshyam Shah (ed.) *Social Movements in India: A Review of*

Literature (New Delhi: Sage, 1990) provides a bird's-eye view of valuable works till the upsurge of new social movements. T. K. Oommen's *Protest and Change: Studies in Social Movements* (Delhi: Sage, 1990) talks about social movements from a sociological perspective. T. V. Satyamurty (ed.) *Religion, Caste Gender and Culture in Contemporary India* (Delhi: Oxford University Press, 1996) is a collection of essays seeking to assess the interplay of factors such as religion, caste, gender and culture in influencing and moulding the state of things in the 1990s. The other works on social movements of the 1990s include Subrata K. Mitra, *Culture and Rationality: The Politics of Social Change in Post-Colonial India* (New Delhi: Sage, 1998), Manoranjan Mohanty, P. N. Mukherjee and Olle Tornquist (eds) *People's Rights: Social Movements and the State in the Third World* (New Delhi: Sage, 1998), Atul Kohli and Amrita Basu (eds), *Community Conflicts and the State in India* (New Delhi: Oxford University Press, 1998), Gail Omvedt, *Reinventing Revolution: New Social Movements and the Socialist Tradition in India* (New York: M. E. Sharp, 1994) and Amrita Basu, *Two Faces of Protest: Contrasting Modes of Women's Activism in India* (Delhi: Oxford University Press, 1993). The other important tracts on the social movements in India include Raka Roy and Mary Fainsad Katzenstein (eds) *Social Movements in India: Poverty, Power and Politics* (Lanham: Rowman and Littlefield, 2005) and P. Sundarayya, *Telangana People's Struggle and its Lessons* (New Delhi: Foundation Books, 2006).

In recent times, the lower castes movements in India have inspired a host of writers to produce voluminous writings. Important among them are Buta Singh, *The Dalits and Dalits Awakening in India* (New Delhi: Gyan Books, 2005); Gopal Guru (ed.) *Atrophy in Dalit Politics* (Mumbai: Vikas Adhyayan Kendra, 2005); Christophe Jaffrelot, *India's Silent Revolution: The Rise of Low Castes in North Indian Politics* (New Delhi: Permanent Black, 2003); Kanchan Chandra, *Why Ethnic Parties Succeed: Patronage and Ethnic Headcounts in India* (Cambridge: Cambridge University Press, 2004); Vivek Kumar, *Dalit Leadership in India* (New Delhi: Gyan Books, 2005) and *India's Roaring Revolution: Dalit Assertion and new Horizons* (New Delhi: Gagandeep Publications, 2006); Johannes Beltz, *Mahar, Buddhist and Dalit: Religious Conversion and Socio-Political Emancipation* (New Delhi: Manohar, 2005); and Prakash Louis, *The Political Sociology of Dalit Assertion* (New Delhi: Gyan Books, 2005).

Notes

Introduction

1 Jawaharlal Nehru's 'Tryst with destiny' speech, delivered at the dawn of independence in India in 1947 – quoted from B. Shiva Rao (ed.), *The Framing of India's Constitution: Select Documents*, Vol. 1, New Delhi: Universal Law Publishing Co., 2004 (reprint), pp. 558–9.

2 Ian Copland, 'The imprint of the past: reflections on regime change with particular reference to "middle India", *c.* 1947–50', in Dipesh Chakrabarty and Rochna Majumdar (eds), *From the Colonial to the Post-colonial: India and Pakistan in Transition*, New Delhi: Oxford University Press, 2007, p. 303.

3 Rajnarayan Chandravarkar, 'Customs of governance: colonialism and democracy in the twentieth century India', *Modern Asian Studies*, 41 (3), 2007, p. 448.

4 Dipesh Chakrabarty, 'In the name of politics: democracy and the power of the multitude in India', in Dipesh Chakrabarty and Rochna Majumdar (eds), *From the Colonial to the Post-colonial: India and Pakistan in Transition*, New Delhi: Oxford University Press, 2007, p. 36.

5 D. A. Low, *Britain and Indian Nationalism: The Imprint of Ambiguity, 1929–1942*, Cambridge: Cambridge University Press, 1997.

6 Subrata Mitra, 'Constitutional design, democratic vote counting and India's fortuitous multiculturalism', Working Paper, November 2004, South Asia Institute, Heidelberg University, pp. 29–34.

7 Ashis Nandy, *The Intimate Enemy: Loss and Recovery of Self under Colonialism*, Delhi: Oxford University Press, 1989 (reprint).

8 Nandy, *The Intimate Enemy*, pp. 10–11.

9 W. H. Morris-Jones, *The Government and Politics of India*, New Delhi: BI Publications, 1974 (reprint), pp. 15–48.

10 Ramchandra Guha, *India after Gandhi: The History of the World's Largest Democracy*, London: Picador, 2007, p. 756.

11 Supportive of liberal democracy of the Western variety, Amartya Sen thus argues that democracy is always preferable because there is a plurality of virtues: first, the intrinsic importance of political participation and freedom in human life; second, the instrumental importance of political incentive in keeping governments responsible and accountable; and third, the constructive role of democracy in the formation of values and in the understanding of needs, rights and duties. Amartya Sen, *Development as Freedom*, Delhi: Oxford University Press, 1999.

12 Guha, *India after Gandhi*, p. 757.

13 Subrata Mitra, 'Constitutional design', p. 29.

14 Sarbani Sen, *Popular Sovereignty and Democratic Transformations: The Constitution of India*, New Delhi: Oxford University Press, 2007, p. 112.

15   Paul Brass, 'The strong state and the fear of disorder', in Francine Frankel, Zoya
     Hasan, Rajeev Bhargava and Balveer Arora (eds), *Transforming India: Social and
     Political Dynamics of Democracy*, Delhi: Oxford University Press, 2000, p. 60.
16   Granville Austin, *The Indian Constitution: Cornerstone of a Nation*, New Delhi:
     Oxford University Press, 1999, p. 21.
17   The 1946 Cabinet Mission, however, articulated a constitutional design by taking
     into account the principle of accommodating diverse socio-religious groups. Torn
     between the desire to preserve India's political unity and satisfy the strident demands
     of the Muslims for adequate safeguards in a Hindu-majority state, the Cabinet Mis-
     sion provided a constitutional scheme, adequately fit and politically appropriate for
     'divided India' in the following way: (a) there should be a Union of India, embracing
     both British India and the States, which should deal with Foreign Affairs, Defence
     and Communications and should have the powers necessary to raise the finances for
     the above subjects; (b) all subjects other than Union subjects and all residuary pow-
     ers should vest in the provinces; (c) the states should retain all subjects and powers
     other than those ceded to the Union; (d) any province could by majority vote of its
     Legislative Assembly call for the reconsideration of the terms of the Constitution after
     an initial period of ten years and at ten-year intervals thereafter. Cited in Mohit Bhat-
     tacharya, 'The mind of the founding fathers', in Nirmal Mukarji and Balveer Arora
     (eds), *Federalism in India: Origins and Development*, New Delhi: Vikas Publishing
     House, 1992, pp. 92–3.
18   Paul Brass, 'India, Myron Weiner and the Political Science of Development', *Eco-
     nomic and Political Weekly*, 20 July 2002, p. 2132.
19   B. R. Ambedkar, *Federation versus Freedom*, Poona: Gokhale Institute of Politics and
     Economics, 1939.
20   *Constitutional Assembly Debates* (*CAD* hereafter), Vol. 1, p. 102.
21   *CAD*, Vol. V, Report of the Union Powers Committee, 20 August 1947, p. 58.
22   *CAD*, Vol. V, p. 79.
23   *CAD*, Vol. XI, p. 839.
24   Bhattacharya, 'The mind of the founding fathers', p. 89.
25   Austin, *The Indian Constitution*, pp. 17, 317.
26   Austin, *The Indian Constitution*, pp. 311–21.
27   Austin, *The Indian Constitution*, chapter 12 ('Language and the constitution: the half-
     hearted compromise'), pp. 264–307.
28   *Hindustan Times*, 27 November 1949.
29   *CAD*, Vol. V, p. 974.
30   Shiva Rao (ed.), *The Framing of India's Constitution*, Vol. V, New Delhi: Universal
     Law Publishing, 2004, p. 835.
31   Austin, *The Indian Constitution*, p. 315.
32   Rajni Kothari, *Politics in India*, New Delhi: Orient Longman, 2005 (reprint), p. 107.
33   Rajendra Prasad's press statement, *Hindustan Times*, 29 December 1949.
34   Rajendra Prasad's statement, made after the Constitution was inaugurated on 26 Janu-
     ary 1950, *The Times of India*, 29 January 1950.
35   Bhattacharya, 'The mind of the founding fathers', p. 103.
36   Prakash Sarangi, 'Voters, institutions and governance: a theory and evidence from
     Indian elections in 2004', Working Paper no. 30, South Asia Institute, Heidelberg
     University, 2007, p. 10.
37   Technically one can trace back the roots of coalition government to 1946 when in the
     interim government under the British Cabinet Mission plan both the Muslim League
     and Congress participated under Jawaharlal Nehru's stewardship.
38   T. V. Sathyamurthy, 'State and society in a changing political perspective,' in T. V.
     Sathyamurthy (ed.), *Class Formation and Political Transformation in Post-colonial
     India*, Vol. 4, Delhi: Oxford University Press, 1996, p. 446.

39 For details of this argument, see Pralay Kanungo, *RSS's Tryst with Politics: From Hedgewar to Sudarshan*, New Delhi: Manohar, 2002, pp. 184–5.

40 James Manor, 'Parties and the party system', in Atul Kohli (ed.), *India's Democracy: An Analysis of Changing State–Society Relations*, New Delhi: Orient Longman, 1991, p. 74.

41 This paragraph draws upon James Manor, 'Parties and the party system', pp. 74–5.

42 Bipan Chandra, Mridual Mukherjee and Aditya Mukherjee, *India after Independence*, New Delhi: Penguin, 2000, p. 264. George Fernandes, in an interview with the author on 18 January 2004, endorses this by attributing the collapse of the Janata Party to (a) ideological incompatibility and (b) personal rivalry.

43 In fact, by drawing attention to the overwhelming influence of the Jana Sangh on the Janata Party, Y. B. Chavan, the opposition leader in the Lok Sabha, characterized the Janata party as 'nothing but the Jana Sangh, a political wing of the Rashtriya Swayamsevek Sangh'. According to Chavan, the RSS 'had sent the Jana Sangh as its emissary to the Janata Party and both were waiting in the hope that the Janata Party would one day disintegrate and they would be able to capture power on their own'. Y. V. Chavan was quoted in the *Times of India*, 18 July 1977.

44 Jyotirindra Das Gupta, 'The Janata phase: reorganization and redirection in Indian politics', *Asian Survey*, 19 (4), 1979, pp. 390–403, quoting p. 390.

45 The Janata Party's election manifesto for the Lok Sabha poll of 1977 made a number of promises of which the core was the programme for restoration of democratic freedom. The highlights of this programme were: (a) lifting of the two Emergency proclamations of December 1971 (proclaimed during the 1971 war with Pakistan) and June 1975; (b) repeal of the Prevention of Objectionable Matter Act and restoration of the Publication of Parliamentary Proceedings (Protection) or Feroze Gandhi Act; (c) release of political detainees; (d) repeal of the Maintenance of Internal Security Act (MISA); (e) rescinding of the anti-democratic forty-second amendment; and (f) making news agencies completely independent of the government and abolishing the *Samachar* monopoly. Madhu Limaye, *Janata Experiment: An Insider's Account of the Opposition Politics, 1975–77*, New Delhi: DK Publishers, 1994, p. 295.

46 Ashok Kumar Behera, 'Regions become equal partners', *The Statesman*, 15 October 1999.

47 Rajni Kothari talks about this in greater detail in his 'The democratic experiment', in Partha Chatterjee (ed.), *Wages of Freedom*, New Delhi: Oxford University Press, 1998, pp. 33–5.

48 Atul Kohli expressed doubt because the BJP-led coalition 'does not command a parliamentary majority, the partners are disparate, and, more fundamentally, the BJP itself is trapped between its Hindu-nationalist core and the moderation that it must assume (whether sincerely or not) to govern peacefully and effectively'. See his 'Enduring another election', *Journal of Democracy*, 9 (3), 1998, p. 11.

49 The coalition government that came into existence in wake of the 1996 national elections did not last long probably because of the inability of the coalition partners to rise above 'petty' interests apart from 'personality clashes' that manifested in an ugly form following the resignation of H. D. Dave Gowda as Prime Minister. While writing about the nature of coalition in the context of India, E. Sridharan draws our attention to some of these features, likely to plague the coalition. See his 'Coalition politics', *Seminar*, 437, January 1996.

50 For instance, the erstwhile V. P. Singh-led Janata Dal became, in the post-Mandal phase, a party of the backward castes. Similarly, the Samajwadi Party that was formed following a split within the Janata Dal also spoke of 'social justice' to compete for the same social base. Although their ideological goal seems to be national they are largely confined to north Indian provinces, also known as Hindi heartland. For details of this argument, see Aditya Nigam, 'India after the 1996 elections: nation, locality and representation', *Asian Survey*, 36 (12), 1996, pp. 1163–4.

51 For an elaboration of the concept of banalization of nationalism, see M. Billing, *Banal Nationalism*, London: Sage, 1996, p. 7, quoted in Mitra, 'Constitutional design', p. 34. Billing, however, cautions by saying that 'it would be wrong to assume that banal nationalism is benign because it seems to possess a reassuring normality, or because it appears to lack the violent passions of the extreme right. . . . In the case of Western nation states, banal nationalism can hardly be innocent: it is reproducing institutions which possess vast armaments. As the Gulf and Falkland wars indicated forces can be mobilized without lengthy campaign of political preparations. The armaments are primed, ready for use in battle. And the national populations appear to be primed, ready for supporting the use of those armaments.'

52 W. H. Morris-Jones dwells on these three languages in Indian politics at length in his *The Government and Politics of India*, New Delhi: BI Publications, 1974, pp. 52–64.

53 J. S. Mill, *On Liberty, Representative Government and the Subjection of Women*, London: Oxford University Press, 1971 (reprint of the 1861 publication), p. 382.

1 Setting the scene

1 W. H. Morris-Jones, *The Government and Politics of India*, New Delhi: BI Publications, 1974, p. 27.

2 Gyanendra Pandey, 'The prose of otherness', *Subaltern Studies*, Vol. 8, Delhi: Oxford University Press, 1994, p. 215.

3 As the Lahore resolution goes, 'the areas in which the Muslims are numerically in a majority in the North-Western and Eastern Zones of India should be grouped to constitute "independent states" in which the constituent unit shall be autonomous and sovereign'. See the resolution, adopted by the twenty-seventh session of the Muslim League on 23 March 1940, in S. S. Pirzada (ed.), *Foundations of Pakistan: All India Muslim League documents*, Vol. 2, Karachi: National Publishing House, no date, p. 337.

4 Even the Viceroy, in his appreciation of the political situation, underlined the importance of the Lahore resolution. According to him, 'though the scheme for a vivisection of India has been bitterly denounced by Hindus of all parties, . . . there is a growing consciousness of the strength of Moslem opinion behind the League; and even the Congress would like, if they could, to appease Moslem suspicion of majority rule'. See IOR, L/PJ/8/787, Telegram, the Viceroy to the Secretary of State, 19 April 1940.

5 Jinnah's statement in the *Dawn*, 21 September 1945. According to Jinnah, 'no attempt will succeed except on the basis of Pakistan and that is the major issue to be decided by all those who are well-wishers of India and who are really in earnest to achieve real freedom and independence of India, and the sooner it is fully realised, the better.'

6 IOR, R/3/1/105, V. P. Menon to Even Jenkins, the Governor of Punjab, 20 October 1945.

7 IOR, R/3/1/105, Wavell to Pethick-Lawrence, 25 October 1945. Reporting on Jinnah's election campaign to the Secretary of State, Pethick-Lawrence, Wavell had expressed his 'uneasiness' about the confidence the Muslims had shown in securing Pakistan in the aftermath of the 1946 elections.

8 IOR, R/3/1/105, the Governor of Punjab to Wavell, 16 August 1945. Jenkins, the Punjab Governor, was 'perturbed about the situation because there is a very serious danger of the elections being fought, so far as Muslims are concerned on an entirely false issue. Crude Pakistan may be quite illogical, undefinable and ruinous to India and in particular to Muslims, but this does not detract from its potency as a political slogan.'

9 Only a privileged 12.5 per cent of the total population and a mere 11 per cent of Muslims had the actual right of political choice. See Ayesha Jalal, *The Sole Spokesman: Jinnah, the Muslim League and the Demand for Pakistan*, Cambridge: Cambridge University Press, 1985, p. 149.

10 Anuradha Kumar, 'Partition, Congress secularism and Hindu communalism', *Economic and Political Weekly*, 29 July 2000, p. 2732.

11 Sucheta Mahajan, *Independence and Partition: The Erosion of Colonial Power*, New Delhi: Sage, 2000, p. 388.

12 In his analysis of the Bengali tract *Chhere Asha Gram*, Dipesh Chakrabarty argues that, although the Bengali Hindus had been the victims of Muslim communalism, in their home, the non-Muslim League Muslim – who did not demand Pakistan – was always 'a valued guest'. See Dipesh Chakrabarty, 'Remembered villages: representation of Hindu-Bengali memoirs in the aftermath of the partition', *Economic and Political Weekly*, 10 August 1996, p. 2150. A review of the contemporary literature shows, as Sisir Das reports, that the Hindu–Muslim bitterness was often underplayed presumably not to aggravate the situation further. (Interview with Sisir Das of the University of Delhi, 11 January 2001.)

13 The east Bengal refugees looked upon themselves as 'the victims of partition' and, as Bengalis, regarded it as their basic right to seek refuge in that part of Bengal which now lay in India. Having faced persecution and intolerance in east Bengal, they believed that 'it was their legitimate claim to seek rehabilitation within West Bengal, which they now felt was their natural habitat'. Tan Tai Young and Gyanesh Kudaisya, *The Aftermath of Partition in South Asia*, London: Routledge, 2000, p. 146. Attributing the continuous flow of refugees in West Bengal even after fifty years of independence to this 'feeling', Joya Chatterjee argues that, 'unlike those from the west, refugees from the east did not flood into India in one huge wave; they came sometimes in surges but often in barely perceptible trickles over the five decades of independence'. Joya Chatterjee, 'Rights or charity: the debate over relief and rehabilitation in West Bengal, 1947–50', in Suvir Kaul (ed.), *The Partition of Memory: The Afterlife of the Division of India*, New Delhi: Permanent Black, 2001, p. 74.

14 As Ian Copland describes, '[t]he year 1947 witnessed a significant closure (the end of colonial rule in South Asia), two significant beginnings (the birth of India and Pakistan as nation-states) and massive social upheaval (dispossessions, migrations and relocations)'. Ian Copland, 'The imprint of the past: reflections on regime change with particular reference to "middle India", *c.* 1947–50', in Dipesh Chakrabarty and Rochna Majumdar (eds), *From the Colonial to the Postcolonial: India and Pakistan in Transition*, New Delhi: Oxford University Press, 2007, p. 287.

15 Articles 38 and 39 spell out the sentiments. Article 46 underlines the concern for the weaker sections, including scheduled castes and scheduled tribes.

16 Suresh D. Tendulkar and T. A. Bhavani, *Understanding Reforms: Post 1991 India*, Delhi: Oxford University Press, 2007, pp. 18–19.

17 Francine R. Frankel, *India's Political Economy, 1947–2004*, New Delhi: Oxford University Press, 2007, p. 85.

18 Tendulkar and Bhavani, *Understanding Reforms*, p. 24.

19 Partha Chatterjee, 'Development planning and the Indian state', in Partha Chatterjee (ed.), *State and Politics in India*, Delhi: Oxford University Press, 1997, pp. 271, 279.

20 Aseema Sinha, *The Regional Roots of Developmental Politics in India: A Divided Leviathan*, Bloomington & Indianapolis: Indiana University Press, 2005, p. 277.

21 Quotations from *Hindustan Standard*, 27 September 1934.

22 I have dwelled on this aspect of the freedom struggle in my 'Jawaharlal Nehru and planning, 1938–41: India at the crossroads', *Modern Asian Studies*, 26 (2), 1992, pp. 275–87.

23 Jawaharlal Nehru on planning (a press release), *Hindustan Times*, 17 August 1963.

24 Meghnad Desai, *Development and Nationhood: Essays in the Political Economy of South Asia*, New Delhi: Oxford University Press, 2005, p. 121.

25 Desai, *Development and Nationhood*, p. 139.

26 Desai, *Development and Nationhood*, p. 137.

27 Desai, *Development and Nationhood*, p. 157.

28 Jagdish N. Bhagwati, 'Indian economic policy and performance: a framework for a progressive society', in his *Essays in Development Economics*, Cambridge, MA: MIT Press, 1985, quoted in Ramchandra Guha, *India after Gandhi: The History of the World's Largest Democracy*, London: Picador, 2007, p. 469.

29 Desai, *Development and Nationhood*, p. 158.

30 Desai, *Development and Nationhood*, p. 161.

31 Desai, *Development and Nationhood*, p. 175.

32 Desai, *Development and Nationhood*, p. 189.

33 Desai, *Development and Nationhood*, p. 196.

34 Rob Jenkins, *Democratic Politics and Economic Reform in India*, Cambridge: Cambridge University Press, 1999, pp. 172–207. Since economic reforms were not 'strategy-based' but 'crisis-driven' Indian had hardly had a choice and was thus more or less forced to accept 'the conditionalities' imposed by the donor agencies.

35 Suresh D. Tendulkar and T. A. Bhavani, *Understanding Reforms: Post 1991 India*, New Delhi: Oxford University Press, 2007, p. 85.

36 Aseema Sinha, 'The changing political economy of federalism in India: a historical institutional approach', *India Review*, 3 (1), 2004, p. 51.

37 Sinha, 'The changing political economy of federalism in India', p. 55.

38 Francine R. Frankel, *India's Political Economy, 1947–2004*, New Delhi: Oxford University Press, 2005, p. 625.

39 Ibid.

40 Joseph Stiglitz, *Making Globalization Work: The Next Steps to Global Justice*, London: Allen Lane, 2006, p. 292. This argument was forcefully made by Margit Bussmann in his 'When globalization discontent turns violent: foreign economic liberalization and internal war', *International Studies Quarterly*, 51 (1), 2007, pp. 79–97.

41 Amit Bhaduri and Deepak Nayyar, *The Intelligent Person's Guide to Liberalization*, New Delhi: Penguin, 1996, p. 159.

42 For a detailed account of the civil service in India during the British rule, see Philip Mason, *The Men who Ruled India*, Calcutta: Rupa, 1997 (reprint).

43 As the Report underlined, '[h]enceforth, an appointment to the civil service of the Company will not be matter of favour but matter of right. He who obtains such an appointment will owe it solely to his own abilities and industry.' The Macaulay Committee Report (1854) in *The Fulton Committee Report*, Vol. 1, London: HMSO, 1975, p. 125.

44 Quoted in *The Fulton Committee Report*, p. 125.

45 George Trevelyan, *The Competition Wallah* (second edition), London: Macmillan, 1907, pp. 6–7, quoted in Bernard S. Cohn, *An Anthropologist among the Historians and Other Essays*, Delhi: Oxford University Press, 1990, p. 545. Given their stake in the British administration, it is but natural that, whatever they did, they were simply acting in the imperial interests and in the process preserving or enhancing their superior positions. However, there is a school of thought that the imperial logic never appeared crucial in administration since 'the ICS [was] Jeremy Bentham's prototype of the benevolent social guardian committed to achieving the common good'. For details, see Eric Stokes, *The English Utilitarians of India*, Oxford: Oxford University Press, 1959, p. 159.

46 While explaining the nature of the British civil servants Bernard S. Cohn developed this argument further by drawing upon their post-recruitment training first at the Haileybury School and later in Oxbridge colleges that hardly took into account the rapid socio-structural shifts in India during the colonial rule. Cohn, *An Anthropologist among the Historians*, pp. 500–53.

47 Lloyd George was quoted in Mason, *The Men who Ruled India*, p. xv. Duffrin was probably more categorical in appreciating the role of the Indian civil service. According to him, '[t]here is no service like it in the world. If the Indian civil service were not [as they are], how could the government of the country go on so smoothly? We have

250 million subjects in India and less than 1,000 British civilians for the conduct of the entire administration.' Duffrin's statement was quoted by Jagmohan in his 'Riveting the steel frame of the ICS', *Hindustan Times*, 1 November 1998.

48 For a succinct account of the evolution of the Civil Service in India both during and after British rule, see B. Shiva Rao *et al.*, *The Framing of India's Constitution: Select Documents*, Vol. V, New Delhi: IIPA, 1968, chapter 23 (pp. 708–23).

49 Shibban Lal Saksena's statement in *CAD*, Vol. X, 10 October 1949, p. 46. Prominent among those who criticized the decision to retain the ICS was M. Ananthasaynam Ayyanger, who failed to understand the logic of providing 'guarantee to those persons who have played into the hands of others [and] cared only for money and the salaries they got'. Ayyangar's statement in the debate, ibid., 10 October 1949, p. 42.

50 Quoted in S. R. Maheshwari, *Indian Administration*, New Delhi: Orient Longman, 1984 (reprint), p. 211.

51 Vallabhbhai Patel's speech in the Constituent Assembly. See *CAD*, Vol. X, 10 October 1949, pp. 48–52. Seeking to persuade his colleagues in the Constituent Assembly, he further argued, 'if these service people are giving you full value of their Services and more, then try to learn to appreciate them. Forget the past. We fought the Britishers for so many years. I was their bitterest enemy and they regarded me as such . . . . What did Gandhiji teach us? You are talking of Gandhian ideology and Gandhian philosophy and Gandhian way of administration. Very good. But you come out of jail and then say, "These men put me in jail. Let me take revenge." That is not Gandhian way. It is going far away from that'. Ibid. p. 52.

52 Extracts from the letter from the Home Minister, Vallabhbhai Patel, to the Prime Minister, 27 April 1948, reproduced in B. Shiva Rao (ed.), *The Framing of India's Constitution: Select Documents*, Vol. 4, Delhi: Universal Law Publishing Co., 2004 (reprint), p. 332.

53 As late as 1934, Nehru characterized the Indian civil service as 'neither Indian nor civil nor service [and] it is thus essential that the ICS and similar services disappear completely'. Jawaharlal Nehru, *An Autobiography: With Musings in Recent Events in India*, London: John Lane the Bodley Head, 1941 (reprint), p. 445.

54 Jawaharlal Nehru's speech in the Constituent Assembly. See *CAD*, Vol. I, 1947, pp. 793–95.

55 For a detailed discussion in the Constituent Assembly during the preparation and finally acceptance of Article 311, see B. Shiva Rao (ed.), *The Framing of India's Constituion: A Study*, New Delhi: IIPA, 1968, pp. 713–23.

56 While explaining the continuity of the steel frame for almost two hundred years, Philip Mason stated that the administration in India 'had the immense advantage over those in the later African territories that it was possible to set up the framework of government before the invention of the electric telegraph and close control of England. Use was made of Akbar's machinery and whatever local institutions could be adapted. The whole was controlled by a cadre of district officers, rigorously picked, but trained almost wholly by doing what in fact they were learning to do. Because they were so few they had let their subordinates do their own work. Confidence that they would be backed up from above was the hall-mark of their profession and they acquired a confidence in themselves and a confidence that they would be obeyed, which meant that they were obeyed. Few administration can have ruled so many with so slight use of force. Everything was done through Indians and by Indians to whom power was delegated.' Philip Mason, *The Men Who Ruled India*, pp. 345–6.

57 P. C. Alexander, 'Civil service: continuity and change', in Hiranmoy Karlekar (ed.), *Independent India: The First Fifty Years*, Delhi: Oxford University Press, 1998, p. 62.

58 R. Sudarshan, 'Governance of multicultural polities: limits of the rule of law', in Rajeev Bhargava, Amiya Kumar Bagchi and R. Sudarshan, *Multiculturalism, Liberalism and Democracy*, New Delhi: Oxford University Press, 1999, p. 111.

59   B. P. R. Vithal, 'Evolving trends in the bureaucracy', in Partha Chatterjee (ed.), *State and Politics in India*, Delhi: Oxford University Press, 1997, p. 224.
60   For an interesting, though slightly dated, account of the panchayati system in West Bengal, Uttar Pradesh and Karnataka, see Atul Kohli, *The State and Poverty in India: The Politics of Reform*, Cambridge: Cambridge University Press, 1987; and for studies of urban government of Delhi, see Ajoy K. Mehra, *The Politics of Urban Development: A Study of Old Delhi*, New Delhi: Sage, 1991.
61   Kuldeep Mathur, 'Strengthening bureaucracy: state and development in India', *Indian Social Science Review*, 1 (1), 1999, p. 22. According to Mathur, '[t]he success of the Seventy-Third and Seventy-Fourth Amendments making decentralised structures part of the Constitution has yet to be seen – not only because they were only instituted in 1993, but also because the states have shown little evidence of implementing the requirement through their own statutes'.
62   Rajni Kothari, *State against Democracy: In Search of Human Governance*, Delhi: Ajanta, 1988, p. 287.
63   The process, known as 'deinstitutionalization', invariably leads to a non-policy government that 'operates by means of spoils and preferment that take into account the particular situations of persons and communities'. Very common in sub-Saharan Africa, 'such government tends to be "private government" both in the sense that government offices are treated as private property and in the sense that spoils, unlike policies, must be managed in a discreet and even clandestine fashion. They cannot be advertised, nor can they be publicly debated.' See Goran Hyden, 'Democratization and administration', in Axel Hadenius (ed.), *Democracy's Victory and Crisis* (Nobel Symposium no. 93), Cambridge: Cambridge University Press, 1997, p. 252.
64   Anil Bhatt, 'Colonial bureaucratic culture and development administration: portrait of an old-fashioned Indian bureaucrat', *Journal of Commonwealth and Comparative Politics*, 17 (3), 1979, p. 259.
65   Bhatt, 'Colonial bureaucratic culture', p. 281.
66   *The Report of the Fifth Central Pay Commission*, Vol. 1, New Delhi: Government of India, 1997, p. 117.
67   *Report of the Fifth Central Pay Commission*, Vol. 1, 1997, p. 95.
68   Ibid.
69   *Report of the Fifth Central Pay Commission*, Vol. 1, 1997, pp. 95–6.
70   *Report of the Fifth Central Pay Commission*, Vol. 1, pp. 122–23.
71   *Report of the Fifth Central Pay Commission*, Vol. 1, p. 175.
72   *Report of the Fifth Central Pay Commission*, Vol. 1, p. 150.
73   *Report of the Fifth Central Pay Commission*, Vol. 1, p. 151.
74   *Report of the Fifth Central Pay Commission*, Vol. 1, p. 157.
75   *The Times of India,* 25 May 1997. For details of the recommendations, see *Annual Reports, 1997–98*, New Delhi: Ministry of Personnel, Public Grievances and Pensions, 1998, pp. 65–9.
76   'The State in a changing world', *The World Development Report (Summary), 1997*, Washington, DC: The World Bank, 1997, p. 14.
77   According to the 1997 World Development Report (summary), there are three ways in which civil service can be radically reformed: (a) a recruitment system based on merit, not favouritism, (b) a merit-based internal promotion system and (c) adequate compensation. 'The State in a changing world', p. 9.
78   Atul Kohli, *State-Directed Development: Political Power and Industrialization in the Global Periphery*, Cambridge: Cambridge University Press, 2004, p. 285.
79   Woodrow Wilson, 'The study of administration', *Political Science Quarterly*, June, 1887, pp. 197–222.
80   Katharine Adeney and Andrew Wyatt, 'Democracy in South Asia: getting beyond the structure–agency dichotomy', *Political Studies*, 52 (1), 2006, pp. 9–10.
81   Francine Frankel, 'Decline of a social order', in Francine Frankel and M. S. A. Rao

(eds), *Dominance and State Power in Modern India: Decline of a Social Order*, Vol. 2, Delhi: Oxford University Press, 1990, p. 502.

82 Sudipta Kaviraj, 'On state, society and discourse in India', in James Manor (ed.), *Rethinking Third World Politics,* London: Longman, 1991, pp. 87–8.

83 Rakhahari Chatterjee, 'Democracy and opposition in India', *Economic and Political Weekly*, 17, 23 April 1988, p. 847.

84 Rajni Kothari, *State against Democracy: In Search of Human Governance*, Delhi: Ajanta, 1988, p. 30.

2 Shaping Indian politics

1 Given the growing salience of 'identity' in the academic discourses, Linda Martin Alcoff characterizes identity as 'a growth industry in the academy since generic Man has been overthrown by scholars and researchers who have realized the importance of taking identity into account. The constitutive power of gender, race, class, ethnicity, sexuality and other forms of social identity has finally, suddenly been recognized as a relevant aspects of almost all projects of enquiry'. Linda Martin Alcoff, *Visible Identities: Race, Gender and Self*, New York: Oxford University Press, 2006, p. 5.

2 Bhikhu Parekh, 'National identity in a multicultural society', in Mohmmad Anwar and Ranjit Sondhi (eds), *From Legislation to Imagination*, London: Macmillan, 1999, p. 197.

3 A. J. Cascardi, *The Subject of Modernity*, New York: Cambridge University Press, 1992, p. 3. For Cascardi, the tension and incommensurability among various sphere of values at the extreme where they claim autonomy appear not as an external difficulty for the individuals but as a series of contradictions within the subject itself. It is therefore obvious that, in circumstances where individuals had little access to the wider political arena and even less access to other identities, the situation appears less complicated than those in which individuals constantly confront with separate, if not conflicting, spheres of values.

4 Amartya Sen, *Reasons before Identity*, Delhi: Oxford University Press, 1999, p. 20.

5 Critical of the orientalist discourse seeking to essentialize the so-called fundamental characteristics of Indian society, Ronald Inden argues that European subjugation of India was facilitated by European-trained writers who successfully defined Indian society in terms of various essences that kept India essentially ancient and passive. Inden, speaking of the cognitive categories that the tradition of Indology has generated, gestures towards the political flaws of that particular intellectual vision that freezes the temporal and spatial dimensions of Indian society. It is true that the contributions of the Indologists who exercised a powerful hold on the sociological imagination have done much to capture and freeze Indian society in terms of her essences such as caste, Hinduism, villages and sacred kingship. Ronald Inden, *Imagining India*, Oxford: Basil Blackwell, 1990.

6 Tapan Raychaudhuri, *Perceptions, Emotions, Sensibilities: Essays on India's Colonial and Post-colonial Experiences*, Delhi: Oxford University Press, 1999, p. 4.

7 This is what made the basis of Indian nationalism so fragile. G. Aloysius argues that, '[i]n the absence of actual change within society, in our case, the destruction of the Brahminic social order, nationalism's relation to the potential nation becomes ambiguous at best. Here the process of *invention* is displaced by one of *prevention*: when imagination is limited to a minority of the elite, it turns out be an illusion to the masses – the nation.' G. Aloysius, *Nationalism without a Nation in India*, Delhi: Oxford University Press, 1997, p. 225 (emphasis added).

8 Underlining the importance of caste identity in south India because of peculiar historical circumstances, Andre Beteille sought to explain the continuity of caste quotas in public employment in terms of what began in the form of opposition to the Brahmin hegemony. Andre Beteille, 'Resistance to reservations: some north–south differences',

in his *The Backward Classes in Contemporary India*, Delhi: Oxford University Press, 1992 (reprint), pp. 100–6.

9   For details, see Shibanikinkar Chaube, *Constituent Assembly of India: Springboard of Revolution* (second edition), Delhi: Manohar, 2000, pp. 146–55; Gurpreet Mahajan, *Identities and Rights: Aspects of Liberal Democracy in India*, Delhi: Oxford University Press, 1998, pp. 149–58.

10 The notion of identity therefore involves both negation and difference. Post-structuralists such as Derrida, argues Eli Zaretsky, 'problematized identity for example by arguing that identity presupposes differences, that it involves the suppression of difference or that it entailed an endless process of deferral of meaning'. Post-structuralists therefore contributed to identity politics 'by introducing what is sometimes termed a politics of difference, a politics aimed less at establishing a viable variety for its constituency than at destabilizing identities, a politics that eschews such terms as groups, rights, value and society in favour of such terms as places, spaces, alterity and subject positions, a politics that aims to decenter or subvert than to conquer or assert'. Eli Zaretsky, 'Identity theory, identity politics: psychoanalysis, Marxism and post-structuralism', in Craig Calhoun, *Social Theory and the Politics of Identity*, Oxford: Blackwell, 1995, p. 200.

11 Tapan Raychaudhiri, *Perceptions, Emotions, Sensibilities: Essays on India's Colonial and Post-colonial Experiences*, Delhi: Oxford University Press, 1999, p. 18.

12 Raychaudhiri, *Perceptions, Emotions, Sensibilities*, p. 19.

13 Ibid.

14 T. K. Oommen, *State and Society in India: Studies in Nation-Building*, New Delhi: Sage, 1990, p. 39.

15 Ravinder Kumar argues: 'any nationalist transformation of Indian civilization, which rested upon a dozen and more well articulated regional and linguistic cultures, could not be easily compared to the emergence of the European Nation-States, which grew out of the consolidation of disaggregated polities, or a breakdown of composite empires'. Ravinder Kumar, 'India: a "Nation-State" or a "Civilization-State"?', Occasional paper on perspectives in Indian development no. VIII, New Delhi: Nehru Memorial Museum and Library, 1989, p. 22.

16 For Benedict Anderson, historical experience of nationalism in western Europe, America and Russia had supplied for all subsequent nationalisms a set of modular forms from which the nationalist elites of Afro-Asian countries had chosen the ones they liked. Benedict Anderson, *Imagined Communities: Reflections on the Origin and Spread of Nationalism*, London: Verso, 1983.

17 Partha Chatterjee, *The Nation and its Fragments: Colonial and Post-colonial Histories*, Delhi: Oxford University Press, 1994, p. 5.

18 *Swadeshi* is an Indian expression, popularized with loaded meaning in the course of the freedom struggle, which meant (a) collective pride, (b) ancestral loyalty and (c) communal integrity or amity.

19 Bhikhu Parekh, 'Ethnocentricity of the nationalist discourse', *Nations and Nationalism*, 1 (1), 1995, p. 39.

20 This is particularly true of the Muslims engaged in redefining their religiously informed cultural identity in the face of modernity underwritten by the fact of British sovereignty. Ayesha Jalal argues: '[c]ontinued recourse to the colonial privileging of religious distinctions thwarted many well-meaning attempts at accommodating differences within a broad framework of Indian nationalism'. Ayesha Jalal, 'Nation, reason and religion: Punjab's role in the partition of India', *Economic and Political Weekly*, 8 August 1998, p. 2183.

21 Charles Taylor, 'The dynamics of democratic exclusion', *Journal of Democracy*, 9 (4), 1998, p. 144.

22 Charles Taylor, *The Ethics of Authencity*, Cambridge: Harvard University Press, 1991, p. 48.

23 Ibid.

24 Gail Minault argues that, although the 1919–21 Non-Cooperation–Khilafat Movement did not succeed in forging a permanent Hindu–Muslim nationalist alliance, it certainly created 'a self-conscious and unified Indian Muslim political constituency'. Gail Minault, *The Khilafat Movement: Religious Symbolism and Political Mobilization in India*, Delhi: Oxford University Press, 1999 (reprint).

25 One of the major constraints of the Gandhi-led freedom struggle, writes M. N. Roy, is due to the fact that 'it rests on the reaction against a common oppression. This negative basis, however, renders the national liberation movement inherently weak [because it failed to combat] the dividing forces, generated and nurtured by nationalism itself'. M. N. Roy, *India in Transition*, Bombay: Nachiketa Publications, 1971, p. 150.

26 India Office Library and Records, London (hereafter India Office Library), L/P&J/8/689, Rahmat Ali, Md. Aslam Khan, Sk. Mohammad Sadiq and Inayat Ullah Khan, 'Now or never: are we to live or perish for ever?' Although the proposal defending a separate Muslim land was not placed before the second Round Table Conference, it was circulated among some of its participants.

27 One of the concerns that appeared to have haunted Rahmat Ali was perhaps the fear that Muslims were likely to be marginalized, if not assimilated, by the Hindus on account of their sheer demographic preponderance. That probably accounts for the high value he placed on orthodoxy, because it maintains identity of a community as against other communities and prevents an assimilation that could lead to the community disintegrating and being absorbed by others. See India Office Records, London, L/P&J/8/689, Rahamat Ali to the Secretary of State, 8 July 1935. It was more or less accepted by the government that the difference between Hindus and Muslims, as the report of the Joint-Select Committee on Indian Constitutional Reform (1934) shows, 'is not only one of religion in the stricter sense, but also of law and culture. They may be said indeed to represent two distinct and separate civilizations'. India Office Records, London, *Report of the Joint Select Committee on Indian Constitutional Reform, 1934*, Vol. 1, p. 1.

28 Quoted in M. H. Saiyid, *Mohammad Ali Jinnah: A Political Study*, Lahore: Ashraf, 1953, p. 67.

29 India Office Library, L/PO/78 (I), The Prime Minister's statement for release in the afternoon of Tuesday, 16 August, in time for publication in the morning newspapers in India and UK of Wednesday, 17 August 1932.

30 India Office Library, L/PO/49 (ii), John Lothian (The Chairman of the Franchise Committee, 1932), to the Viceroy, Government of India, 8 August 1932.

31 India Office Library, CMD 2360, Volume XVI, memorandum by A. K. Ghuznavi, p. 188.

32 India Office Library, L/PO/48 (ii). Muslim demands including the Fourteen Points Programme of Jinnah were placed at the open meeting of the All India Muslim League in Delhi in March 1929.

33 The Lucknow pact, 1916 is the first political arrangement at the all-India level dividing the two principal communities, Hindus and Muslims. In his study of the Lucknow Pact, Hugh Owen has shown that even the two bodies who made the Pact, the Congress and Muslim League, 'were quite fundamentally arrayed against each other in their notions of their own identity. The Congress claimed to speak for all Indians, including Muslims, whereas the Muslim League claimed to speak for the Indian Muslims, and had in fact spoken with some success for them in the years preceding the Pact. In terms of the objects of these two organizations, Congress under the moderate leadership had worked for a secular India and had repeatedly deplored recognition of communal or religious distinctions in political matters, whereas the Muslims League asserted that Indian Muslims must work as members of the Muslim community for

representation and safeguards for that community as such.' Hugh Owen, 'Negotiating the Lucknow Pact', *Journal of Asian Studies*, 31 (3), 1972, p. 561.

34 Ujjwalkanti Das, 'The Bengal Hindu–Muslim Pact', *Bengal Past and Present*, 99 (188), 1980. The idea of composite culture that informed the Bengal pact was not novel, for Bipin Chandra Pal had visualized a federal India in which units were to be the religious communities – Hindu, Muslim, Christian and aboriginal. Rabindranath Tagore had wanted a *swadeshi samaj* under the joint control of a Hindu and a Muslim. The *Bangabasi* suggested in 1908 that the adherents of different religions should each form a party of their own and then cooperate among themselves. Sumit Sarkar, *The Swadeshi Movement in Bengal, 1903–1908*, New Delhi: People's Publishing House, 1973, pp. 422–4.

35 Mahatma Gandhi, for instance, insisted that the scheduled castes were a part of Hindu society and separating the two would be detrimental to the interests of the nation. Hence he opposed the plea of for separate electorates for scheduled castes. He however accepted the idea of reservations through a system of joint electorates. One of the best literary works on both the socio-political background and the consequences thereof is Mulk Raj Anand's *Untouchable* – a novel that defended Gandhi as against Ambedkar who, according to the novelist, sought to undermine the manifesto of political freedom on which the Indian nationalist movement was based. See *Untouchable* (preface by E. M. Foster), London: Penguin Books, 1940 (reprint). In her *Children of God*, Shanta Rameshwar Rao dealt with the Gandhi–Ambedkar controversy on the issues raised in the Poona Pact. See *Children of God*, Calcutta: Orient Longman, 1992 (reprint). The occlusion of Ambedkar in both these novels is consistent with a certain tradition of writing about 'untouchability' that has its root in the antagonistic rhetoric of the Indian National Congress, which responded to Ambedkar's threat of splitting the leadership with disdain and fear. Apart from literary works, the Poona Pact appears to be an under-researched subject. However, the following two articles are indicative of the mindset that appeared to have significantly influenced the Pact and its critic: Ravinder Kumar, 'Ambedkar, Gandhi and the Poona Pact', Occasional Paper on Society and History No. 20, New Delhi: Nehru Memorial Museum and Library, 1985; Valerian Rodrigues, 'Between tradition and modernity: the Gandhi–Ambedkar debate', in A. K. Narain and D. C. Ahir (eds), *Dr. Ambedkar, Buddhism and Social Change*, Delhi: B. R. Publishing, 1994.

36 Gauri Viswanathan, *Outside the Fold: Conversion, Modernity and Belief*, Delhi: Oxford University Press, 1998, p. 213.

37 For an elaboration of this argument, see Viswanathan, *Outside the Fold*, ch. 7 (pp. 211–39).

38 In his 1940 Ramgarh presidential address, Abul Kalam Azad argues that, '[f]or a hundred and fifty years, British imperialism has pursued the policy of divide and rule, and, by emphasizing internal differences, sought to use various groups for the consolidation of its own power. That was the inevitable result of India's political subjection, and it is folly for us to complain and grow bitter. A foreign government can never encourage internal unity in the subject country, for disunity is the surest guarantee for the continuance of its own domination.' Azad's presidential address at Ramgarh, 1940, in A. M. Zaidi and S. G. Zaidi (eds), *The Encyclopedia of the Indian National Congress*, Vol. 12, New Delhi: Chand, 1981, pp. 355–6.

39 Reiterating the famous 1940 Lahore resolution of the All India Muslim League demanding an independent state for the Muslims since they constituted a separate nation, Jinnah always insisted that 'there are two major nations [in India]. This is the root cause and essence of our troubles. When there are two major nations how can you talk of democracy which means that one nation majority will decide everything for the other nation although it may be unanimous in its opposition. . . . these two nations cannot be judged by western democracy. But they should each be treated equals and attempts should be made to solve the difficulties by acknowledging the fact.' Jinnah's press statement on 31 July 1946, *The Dawn*, 1 August 1946. It is however debatable

whether the highly publicized conflicting ideas and conceptions lay at the root of Hindu–Muslim chasm at the grassroots since it has been amply demonstrated that 'explicit rivalries between the [principal] communities tended to exist [during the period preceding partition] at . . . the level of organized politics at the top where Hindu and Muslim elites were rivals for influence with government and eventually for the control of government itself'. Ayesha Jalal and Anil Seal, 'Alternative to partition: Muslim politics between the wars', *Modern Asian Studies*, 15 (3), 1984, p. 415.

40 Sushil Srivastava, 'Constructing the Hindu identity: European moral and intellectual adventurism in 18th century India', *Economic and Political Weekly*, 16–22 September, 1998, p. 1186. According to Srivastava, 'English writing on India that appeared after 1780 was preoccupied with the obligation [*sic*] to expound and glorify the literary and other achievements of the ancient past of the Hindoos. In this process, the Brahminical system and practices were naturally glorified and the newly discovered Sanskrit language was said to be the only source that could open the unknown mystifying world of brahmans. Sanskrit literature was alone distinguished as the sole source of knowledge that could unravel the mysteries of the glory that was India.'

41 *The Tribune*, Lahore, 24 August 1906, quoted in John Zavos, 'Searching for Hindu nationalism in modern Indian history: analysis of some early ideological developments', *Economic and Political Weekly*, 7 August, 1999, p. 2272. According to Zavos, '[t]he representation of the community of Hindus, an idea which underpinned the Sabha movement at the outset, was related to struggles within the Congress over how precisely the Indian nation was to be represented. It is this notion of representation, indeed, which dominated the politics of [the first ten years of the twentieth century] and in a sense, provided the space for the articulation of the community of Hindus.'

42 V. D. Savarkar, *Who is a Hindu? Hindutva*, Poona: S. P. Gokhale, 1949. According to Ashis Nandy, Savarkar appeared to have borrowed this formaulation from those thinkers in nineteenth-century Bengal who put forward more or less this definition. Ashis Nandy, Shikha Trivedy, Shail Mayaram and Achyut Yagnik, *Creating a Nationality: The Ramjanmabhumi Movement and Fear of the Self*, Delhi: Oxford University Press, 1995, p. 67.

43 Ashutosh Varshney, 'Contested Meanings: Hindu Nationalism, India's National Identity, and the Politics of Anxiety', *Daedalus*, 122 (3), 1993, pp. 227–61.

44 D. H. Dhanagare, 'Three constraints of Hinduism', *Seminar*, 411, November 1993, p. 25.

45 Stuart Corbridge and John Harriss, *Reinventing India: Liberalization, Hindu Nationalsim and Popular Democracy*, New Delhi: Oxford University Press, 2000, p. 182.

46 M. S. Golwalkar, *Bunch of Thoughts*, Bangalore: Jagarana Prakashan, 1980 (reprint), pp. 123–4. For a detailed analysis of the evolution of the concept of Hindu community, see Tapan Basu, Pradip Datta, Sumit Sarkar, Tanika Sarcar and Sambuddha Sen, *Khaki Shorts and Saffron Flags: A Critique of the Hindu Right*, Delhi: Orient Longman, 1993, pp. 12–55, and Pralaya Ranjan Kanungo, *Politics and Ideology of the Rashtriya Swyam Sevak Sangh, 1973–1990*, unpublished PhD dissertation, University of Delhi, 1997, pp. 98–153.

47 Golwalkar, *Bunch of Thoughts*, p. 52.

48 Not only did they seek to organize Hindu men, a concerted effort was also made to bring the Hindu women under a platform to champion the cause of the Hindus. Tanika Sarkar has shown that in 1936, eleven years after the formation of the RSS, a women's organization, the Rashtrasevika Samiti, was founded with daily shakhas that provided training in physical, martial arts as well as ideology or 'boudhik'. Tanika Sarkar, 'Pragmatics of the Hindu right: politics of women's organizations', *Economic and Political Weekly*, 31 July 1999, pp. 2159–67.

49 Golwalkar, *Bunch of Thoughts*, p. 128, emphasis added.

50 What is most critical in Golwalkar's conceptualization of Hindutva is 'the arrogance and insolence of Muslims' – a theme to which he returned to with metronomic regularity, as Jyotirmaya Sharma argues. For Golwalkar, according to Sharma, 'the

Muslims posed a greater danger than anyone else. The European colonial masters had left, but the Muslims remained in the country. The first round of aliens came to this land, observes Golwalkar, taking advantage of Hindu disunity. The Muslims who remained in India, he felt, still thought of themselves as victors and rulers. They still harboured dreams of an empire and were bound to make good use of any semblance of disunity among the Hindus. Politicians greedy for their votes were bound to support their cause, and the Muslims, in turn, would make themselves indispensable to any political formation'. Jyotirmaya Sharma, *Terrifying Vision: MS Golwalkar, the RSS and India*, Delhi: Penguin, 2007, p. 73.

51 For details of the trajectory of the evolution of Hindu nationalism, see John Zavos, 'The shapes of Hindu nationalism', in Katherine Adney and Lawrence Saez (eds), *Coalition Politics and Hindu Nationalism*, London: Routledge, 2005, pp. 36–54; Corbridge and Harris, *Reinventing India*, pp. 181–3.

52 Penderel Moon, *Divide and Quit: An Eyewitness Account of the Partition of India*, Delhi: Oxford University Press, 1998 (reprint), ch. 1 (pp. 11–28).

53 In the Constituent Assembly, the speeches of representatives belonging to most religious communities reflected concerns regarding the submerging of a distinct cultural identity in independent India. Considerations of cultural autonomy were sought to be rendered compatible with the nationalist elite's concerns regarding national unity. It was emphasized that only through the retention of their own distinct culture could members of these communities contribute effectively to the nation. Their arguments drew on early nationalist conceptions that regarded communities, defined in religious, caste and linguistic terms, rather than individual citizens as the building blocks of the nation. The anxiety for a strongly centralized identity is comprehensible in a newly fledged nation that absorbed the trauma of partition. For a critical analysis of the debates on the minorities in the Constituent Assembly, see Rochana Bajpai, 'Constituent Assembly debates and minority rights', *Economic and Political Weekly*, 27 May 2000, pp. 1837–45.

54 The dominant opinion during this period regarded 'socio-economic backwardness' as constituting a legitimate basis for claims for special provision and this criterion was applicable only to the lower castes and tribal groups and not to the religious minorities. Opposing an amendment initiated by Sikh representatives for consideration for all minorities in the matter of appointments to the public service, Vallabhbhai Patel argued, '[a]fter all, what is the Sikh community backward in? Is it backward in industry, or commerce or anything?' *CAD*, Vol. 10, 1949, pp. 247–9.

55 The Motilal Nehru Committee Report reproduced in B. Shiva Rao (ed.), *The Framing of India's Constitution: Select Documents*, Vol. 1, New Delhi: Universal Law Publishing Co., 2004 (reprint), p. 74.

56 Rochana Bajpai, 'Constituent Assembly debates and minority rights', *Economic and Political Weekly*, 27 May 2000, p. 1837.

57 Ralph H. Retzlaff, 'The problem of communal minorities in the drafting of the Indian Constitution', in R. N. Spann (ed.), *Constitutionalism in Asia*, Bombay: Asia Publishing House, 1963, p. 59.

58 James Chiriyankandath, 'Creating a secular state in a religious country: the debate in the Indian Constituent Assembly', *Journal of Commonwealth and Comparative Politics*, 38 (2), 2000, p. 12.

59 Rao, *The Framing of India's Constitution: Select Documents*, Vol. II, p. 113.

60 Rao, *The Framing of India's Constitution: Select Documents*, Vol. II, p. 412.

61 Jawaharlal Nehru's statement quoted in K. M. Munshi, *Indian Constitutional Documents*, Vol. I, Delhi: Bharatiya Vidya Bhavan, 1967, p. 209.

62 The majority section of the Muslim League did not join the Constituent Assembly since the idea of a drafting Assembly was suggested by the Cabinet Mission, which never agreed to the idea of partition of British India. Hence, when the debates on the issue of safeguard took place, the Muslims were no longer able to speak with

authority. In the same month, the Akali Dal decided to disband the Sikh Panthic Party, both in the East Punjab Assembly and in the Constituent Assembly. Members of the Panthic Party were advised to sign the Congress pledge and to unconditionally join the Congress Party in the central and provincial legislatures. As a result, the Sikhs also split into several groups, one of which, led by Master Tara Singh, strongly maintained the separate identity of the Sikh community for political purposes. Ralph H. Retzlaff, 'The problem of communal minorities in the drafting of the Indian Constitution', in R. N. Spann (ed.), *Constitutionalism in Asia*, Bombay: Asia Publishing House, 1963, p. 67.

63 In elaborating the arguments raised in the Constituent Assembly debates on the minority question, I have drawn on Bajpai, 'Constituent Assembly debates and minority rights', p. 1840.

64 Chiriyankandath, 'Creating a secular state in a religious country', p. 13.

65 Patel's statement defending abdication of separate electorates in the Assembly, *CAD*, Vol. VIII, p. 354.

66 The Conference resolved, 'if a province has to educate itself and do its daily work through the medium of its own language, it must necessarily be a linguistic area. . . . Hence it becomes most desirable for provinces to be regrouped on a linguistic basis.' *The Report of the All Parties Conference*, Allahabad: All India Congress Committee, 1928, p. 62.

67 For a critical analysis of the arguments and counter-arguments made by Jawaharlal Nehru and his colleagues in the Congress Party on the linguistic regrouping of the provinces, see Robert D. King, *Nehru and the Language Politics of India*, Delhi: Oxford University Press, 1997.

68 *The Report of the State Reorganization Commission, 1955* is instructive and even-handed both in its exposition of the history of the movement towards linguistic provinces and in explaining its recommendations on where to draw the state boundaries whether one agrees with either the logic or reasoning of the Commission or its recommendations. One of the first and also finest studies of the linguistic identities that surfaced before and after independence is Jyotirindra Dasgupta, *Language Conflict and National Development*, Berkeley: University of California Press, 1970; see also Prakash Karat, *Language and Nationality Politics in India*, New Delhi: Orient Longman, 1973; Paul Brass, *Language, Religion and Politics*, Berkeley: University of California Press, 1974; Robert D. King, *Nehru and the Language Politics of India*, Delhi: Oxford University Press, 1997, especially ch. 3 (pp. 52–96).

69 Dipankar Gupta, *Nativism in a Metropolis: The Shiv Sena in Bombay*, Delhi: Manohar, 1982; Myron Weiner, *Sons of the Soil, the Assam Movement*, Princeton, NJ: Princeton University Press, 1978; and also Sanjib Baruah, *India against Itself: Assam and the Politics of Nationality*, Philadelphia, PA: University of Pennsylvania Press, 1999.

70 The search for a separate regional identity and its articulation in the form of movements led to the rise of the Akali Dal, the DMK and the Telugu Desam – which succeeded in infusing the identity aspirations of the concerned communities with a political content in Punjab, Tamil Nadu and Andhra Pradesh respectively. Reasons attributed to the search for regional identity are generally (a) influx of migrants, (b) cultural differences between the migrants and local people, (c) restricted job opportunities for the indigenous middle class, (d) immobility of local population, (e) rapid growth of education among the lower middle classes, (f) a competitive labour market, (g) language domination or a sense of insecurity of language-culture-religion and so on. Robert Hardgrave's analysis of the Dravidian movement that led to the emergence of the DMK in Tamil Nadu is an evenly balanced study of the factors contributing to the consolidation of regional identity in the post-1947 era. Robert L. Hardgrave, *The Dravidian Movement*, Bombay: Popular Prakashan, 1965; Sajal Basu, *Regional Movements: Politics of Language, Ethnicity-Identity*, New Delhi: Manohar, 1992, ch. 3 (pp. 46–70); Baldev Raj Nayer, *Minority Politics in the Punjab*, Princeton, NJ:

Princeton University Press, 1966, ch. 2 (the chapter seeks to identify those factors shaping the nature of regional aspiration, as witnessed in Punjab in the early 1960s).

71 Paul Brass, *Ethnicity and Nationalism: Theory and Comparison*, New Delhi: Sage, 1991, p. 21.

72 S. J. Tambiah, *Levelling Crowds: Ethnonationalist Conflict and Collective Violence in South Asia*, Berkeley, CA: University of California Press, 1996, p. 217.

73 Dipankar Gupta, *The Politics of Ethnicity: Sikh Identity in a Comparative Perspective*, Delhi: Oxford University Press, 1996, pp. 102–15.

74 There are a good number of studies focusing exclusively on caste as a factor in ascriptive identity. Andre Beteille's work on Tamil Nadu, however, stands apart for having lucidly dealt with the question in the context of a rather conservative society, which had experienced several violent movements that successfully challenged the upper-caste hegemony. Andre Beteille, *Society and Politics in India: Essays in a Comparative Perspective*, Delhi: Oxford University Press, 1991, pp. 89–121.

75 The Mandal Commission Report draws on and adds to the 1955 Kelkar Commission Report, which identified 2399 castes as OBCs. The report of the Mandal Commission is an in-depth analysis of the caste configuration in India that goes beyond the stereotyped division of the ascriptive identity in terms of four major castes.

76 Susana B. C. Devalle dwells on the tribal perception in the Jharkhand areas in her ch. 6, 'The culture of protest' (pp. 210–27), in *Discourses of Ethnicity: Culture and Protest in Jharkhand*, New Delhi: Sage, 1992. S. K. Chaube deals with the complexity of identity formation in the context of north-east India, which had a completely different kind of ramifications. See his 'Tribal societies and nation building in north east India', in B. Pakem (ed.), *Nationality, Ethnicity and Cultural Identity in North East India*, Gwahati: Omsons, 1990, pp. 15–26.

77 Sunil Khilnani, *The Idea of India*, London: Hamish Hamilton, 1997, p. 12.

78 Sudipta Kaviraj, 'Modernity and politics in India', *Daedalus*, 129 (1), 2000, p. 153.

79 With remarkable clarity of vision, Rabindranath Tagore succinctly wrote about his views on nation in a rather small piece, entitled *Nation Ki* (What is a Nation) in Bengali. During his lecture tour in America, 1916–17, he elaborated some of these points, including his views on nationalism in India. See *Nationalism*, Delhi: Rupa, 1994 (reprint of the collection, originally published in 1917), pp. 77–99.

80 Tagore, *Nationalism*, p. 89.

81 Rabindranath Tagore to Amiya Chakrabarty, no date, in Sabyasachi Bhattacharya (ed.), *The Mahatma and the Poet: Letters and Debates between Gandhi and Tagore, 1915–1941*, New Delhi: National Book Trust, 1997, p. 172.

82 Ashis Nandy, *The Illegitimacy of Nationalism*, New Delhi: Oxford University Press, 1994, p. 89.

83 Tagore, *Nationalism*, p. 90.

84 Ashis Nandy aptly comments that Jana Gana Mana 'could only be the anthem of a state rooted in the Indian civilization [and] not of the Indian nation-state trying to be the heir to the British-Indian empire'. *The Illegitimacy of Nationalism*, p. 88.

85 Linda Martin Alcoff, *Visible Identities: Race, Gender and Self*, New York: Oxford University Press, 2006, p. 5.

86 Susan Bayly's thorough study of caste, society and politics in India since the eighteenth century confirms that 'India is not and never has been a "monolithic" caste society'. Susan Bayly, *Caste, Society and Politics: From the Eighteenth Century to the Modern Age*, Cambridge: Cambridge University Press, 1999, p. 382.

87 Amartya Sen 'India's pluralism', *India International Quarterly*, 20 (3), 1993, p. 37.

88 Indian identity cannot be 'totalized', because, as Yogesh Atal argues, the distinctiveness of India as a socio-cultural conglomeration lies 'in plurality of people and multiplicity of identities [that] characterize the conglomerate Indian culture'. India's emergent composite culture, he further asserts, 'allowed for the survival of diversities – insiders of the composite culture of Indian simultaneously enjoy outsider and insider statuses

through their membership of various subcultures and groups within the broader society'. Yogesh Atal, 'Subcultures and groups', *Economic and Political Weekly*, 8 September 2001, p. 3460.

89 Amartya Sen, *The Argumentative Indian: Writings on Indian History, Culture and Identity*, London: Allen Lane, 2005, p. 354

90 Sen, *The Argumentative Indian*, p. 356.

91 John Zavos pursues this argument at length in his 'The shapes of nationalism', in Katherine Adney and Lawrence Saez (eds), *Coalition Politics and Hindu Nationalism*, London: Routledge, 2005, pp. 41–5.

92 Jawaharlal Nehru's statement in the Constituent Assembly, *CAD*, Vol. VII, 1948, pp. 991–2.

93 Malini Parthasarathi, 'A souvenir, not an emblem', *The Hindu*, 6 June 2006.

94 Shankar Gopalakrishnan pursues this argument at length in his 'Defining, constructing and policing a new India: relationship between neoliberalism and Hindutva', *Economic and Political Weekly*, 30 June 2006, pp. 2803–13.

3 Indian democracy

1 Pratap Bhanu Mehta, *The Burden of Democracy*, New Delhi: Penguin, 2003, p. 2. According to Mehta, 'no body of European social thinking on the prospects of democracy would have counseled such a course; there was no instance from the past that could be the basis for confidence that this experiment would work. No political formation that could provide an instructive example of how to make in such seemingly unpropitious circumstances: unbound poverty, illiteracy, the absence of a middle class, immense and deeply entrenched social cleavages.' pp. 1–2.

2 Achin Vanaik, *The Painful Transition: Bourgeois Democracy in India*, London: Verso, 1990, p. 93

3 L. I. and S. H. Rudolph, *In Pursuit of Lakshmi: The Political Economy of the Indian State*, New Delhi: Orient Longman, 1987, ch. 4.

4 Vanaik, *The Painful Transition*, pp. 93–7.

5 John Mcguire and Peter Reeves, 'What are the politics of economic liberalization in India? The case of West Bengal', *Asian Studies Review*, 1 (3), 1996, pp. 30–7.

6 D. K. Guha recollects his experience as a chief electoral officer in the 1952 election in his 'Ballot vs. bullet', *The Statesman*, 13 May 1991.

7 This discussion will be pursued later in the section on the Mandal Commission and after. I owe a great deal to Nawal Kishore Yadav who in his piece 'Criminalization of politics' puts forward this point sharply. See Nawal Kishore Yadav, 'Elections test bullet and brawn in north India', in *The Times of India*, Lucknow, 5 November 1989.

8 S. Nihar Singh, 'Will the country now take stock of its failings?', *The Telegraph*, 24 May 1991.

9 For details, see Vijay Dutt's 'Will the past haunt?', *The Hindustan Times*, New Delhi, 17 March 1991.

10 Rajni Kothari, 'The Congress system in India', *Asian Survey*, March 1964, p. 1170, and also 'Integration and exclusion in Indian politics', in *Economic and Political Weekly*, 12–18 September 1988, p. 2224; W. H. Morris-Jones, 'Stability and change in Indian politics', in Saul Rose (ed.), *Politics in Southern Asia*, London: Macmillan, 1963, pp. 9–32.

11 James Manor, 'Party decay and political crisis in India', *The Washington Quarterly*, Summer, 1981, p. 26.

12 Rakhahari Chatterjee, 'Democracy and opposition in India', *Economic and Political Weekly*, 7–13 June 1988, p. 847.

13 Rajni Kothari, *State against Democracy: In Search of Humane Governance*, Delhi: Ajanta, 1988, p. 30.

14 Rajni Kothari, 'Integration and exclusion', *Economic and Political Weekly*, 12–18 September 1988, p. 2225.

15 Ibid.

16 Rudolph and Rudolph, *In Pursuit of Lakshmi*, p. 99.

17 Rudolph and Rudolph, *In Pursuit of Lakshmi*, p. 134.

18 Kothari, 'Integration and exclusion', p. 2226.

19 'Legitimacy can only have meaning in a historical content – it cannot be considered in an historical asocial fashion. Broader structural factors (class relations) and social processes (levels of class struggle) shape the meaning of legitimacy . . . . While legitimacy is derivative of larger societal processes, it plays an important role in reinforcing outcomes.' See James Petras, 'Class politics, state power and legitimacy', in *Economic and Political Weekly*, 2–8 August 1989, p. 1957.

20 Kothari, 'Integration and exclusion', p. 2226.

21 Partha Chatterjee explains this as illustrative of the politics of 'appropriation' and 'opposition'. For details see his 'The follies of appropriation and opposition', *Frontier*, 8–10 (11–25), 1986, pp. 30–6.

22 Vanaik, *The Painful Transition*, p. 99.

23 Vanaik, *The Painful Transition*, p. 103.

24 Achin Vanaik, 'Flexibility of Indian centrism', *The Sunday Observer*, New Delhi, 28 April 1991.

25 Ibid.

26 Ibid.

27 For details see Paul Brass, *The Politics of India since Independence*, Delhi: Orient Longman (reprint), 1990; Rudolph and Rudolph, *In Pursuit of Lakshmi*.

28 Rudolph and Rudolph, *In Pursuit of Lakshmi*, p. 137.

29 M. J. Akbar, 'Wolves at the dynasty's door', *The Telegraph*, 2 June 1991.

30 Khushwant Singh described the people surrounding the Congress (I) leader in a more pejorative way: 'Whatever political importance they got in the past was as chamchas [parasites] hanging round our recently assassinated former Prime Minister and his family'; see Khushwant Singh's column in the *The Telegraph*, Calcutta, 3 June 1991.

31 Madhav Godbole, *Unfinished Innings : Recollections and Reflections of a Civil Servant*, New Delhi: Orient Longman, 1996. Godbole was the Home Secretary in the Union government when the controversial mosque was brought down.

32 One of the reasons which prevented the successive Union governments from formally adopting the reservation scheme for the OBCs was connected with the 1985 Gujarat riot, which demonstrated the impossibility of ignoring the opposition and resentments of the upper and middle castes, who remain powerful and numerous, in implementing an expanded reservations policy. Brass, *The Politics of India since Independence*, pp. 215–22.

33 For a descriptive account of the nature and recommendation of the Mandal Commission, see Dharma Kumar, 'The affirmative action debate in India', *Asian Survey*, 32 (3), 1992, pp. 290–302.

34 Nitya Rao, 'Social justice and empowerment of the weaker sections and gender rights', in Katharine Adeney and Lawrence Saez (eds), *Coalition Politics and Hindu Nationalism*, London: Routledge, 2005, p. 119.

35 Niraja Jayal Gopal, *Representing India: Ethnic Diversity and the Governance of Public Institutions*, London: Palgrave, 2006, p. 191.

36 Susie Tharu, M. Madhava Prasad, Rekha Pappu and K. Satyanarayana, 'Reservation and return to politics', *Economic and Political Weekly*, 8 December 2007, pp. 40–1.

37 Sunanda K. Dutta Ray, 'Darkness at noon: implications of student riots', *The Statesman*, Calcutta, 30 September 1990.

38 Rosalind O'Hanlon, *Caste, Conflict and Ideology: Mahatma Jotirao Phule and Low Caste Protest in Nineteenth Century Western India*, Cambridge: Cambridge University Press, 1985.

39 Andre Beteille, 'Caste and politics: subversion of public institutions', *The Times of India*, Lucknow, 12 September 1990.

40 The Karpoori Thakur formula is as follows: statutory reservation to the Scheduled Caste and Scheduled Tribe (Notification Nos 755, 756, 757 of 10 November 1979, Government of Bihar) 12 per cent reservation for the extremely backward class, 8 per cent reservation for the backward, 3 per cent reservation for women of all castes, 3 per cent reservation for the extremely backward upper castes.

41 V. N. Srinivas, 'The Mandal formula: backwardness – caste vs. individuals', *The Times of India*, Lucknow, 18 September 1990.

42 Mihir Desai, 'The need for reservation: a reply to Shourie and others', *Lokayan Bulletin*, 8 (4), 1990, p. 54.

43 Chandan Mitra, 'Moulded in caste: electoral patterns in north India since Nehru', in Bidyut Chakrabarty (ed.), *Whither India's Democracy*, Calcutta: KP Bagchi & Co, 1993.

44 Francine R. Frankel, *India's Political Economy, 1947–77: The Gradual Revolution*, Princeton, NJ: Princeton University Press, 1978; Pranab Bardhan, *The Political Economy of Development in India*, Oxford: Oxford University Press, 1984; Atul Kohli, *The State and Poverty in India: Decline of a Social Order*, Vols I and II, Delhi: Oxford University Press, 1990.

45 Ashok Guha, 'Reservation in myth and reality', *Economic and Political Weekly*, 15 December 1990, p. 2716.

46 M. N. Srinivas, 'End of an egalitarian dream', *The Sunday Observer*, New Delhi, 12 August 1990.

47 Chandra Bhan Prasad, 'Mandal's true inheritors: reservations should go to MBCs (most backward castes), not OBCs (other backward castes)', *The Times of India*, 12 April 2006. Prasad defends his argument with reference to L. R. Naik's note of dissent on the main recommendations of the Mandal Commission. According to Naik, as Prasad argues, OBCs were made of two large social blocks – landowning OBCs whom he described as intermediate backward classes and artisan OBCs whom he described as depressed backward classes. Intermediate backward classes or upper OBCs (Yadavs, Kurmis, Jats among others) who have now turned into landowning castes are relatively powerful while the depressed backward classes or most backward classes (MBCs) remain economically marginalized. Naik thus suggested preferential treatment for the MBCs within the OBCs in order to safeguard interests of the MBCs, otherwise the upper OBCs would monopolize Mandal jobs.

48 C. P. Bhambri, 'The politics of caste alliance: alignments on a caste basis have sharpened and legitimized the rich-poor divide', *The Telegraph*, 23 May 1991.

49 Manoranjan Mohanty, 'The relevance of reservation', *Lokayan Bulletin*, 8 (4/5), p. 143; Upendra Baxi, 'Justice: journey of the backward classes', *Lokayan Bulletin*, 8 (4/5), pp. 117–26.

50 Ramchandra Guha, *India after Gandhi: The History of the World's Largest Democracy*, London: Picador, 2007, p. 611.

51 Drawn from *The Times of India*, 10 April 2006.

52 Yogendra Yadav and Satish Deshpande, 'Wrong route, right direction: reservation policy needs to be fine-tuned', *The Times of India*, 31 May 2006.

53 V. P. Singh's press interview, *The Hindu*, 14 June 2006.

54 Christophe Jaffrelot, *India's Silent Revolution: The Rise of the Low Castes in North Indian Politics*, New Delhi: Permanent Black, 2006, p. 493.

55 Bhagwan Das, 'Moments in a history of reservations', *Economic and Political Weekly*, 28 October 2000, pp. 3834–8. Especially in view of the Supreme Court judgment in the Indira Sawhney case, the government is under pressure 'to enact a law so that the judiciary may not decide against the disadvantaged sections of society'.

56 Neera Chandhoke, 'Three myths about reservations', *Economic and Political Weekly*, 10 June 2006, p. 2289.

57 Sukhadeo Thorat and Paul Attewell, 'The legacy of social exclusion: a correspondence study of job discrimination in India', *Economic and Political Weekly*, 13 October 2007, pp. 4141–5.
58 Zoya Hasan, 'Countering social discrimination', *The Hindu*, 2 June 2006.
59 Tharu *et al.*, 'Reservation and return to politics', p. 45.
60 Jaffrelot, *India's Silent Revolution*, p. 494.
61 While identifying the aims of the Oversight Committee, M. Veerappa Moily, the chairman, underlines that 'the idea is to have expansion, inclusion and excellence. And, to utilize this opportunity to build a knowledge society. We are trying to build an inclusive society; the idea is not to exclude anybody but include everybody.' M. Veerappa Moily's press interview, *The Hindu*, 18 June 2006.
62 Harish Khare, 'Lessons from the new intolerance', *The Hindu,* 12 April 2006.
63 Javeed Alam pursues this argument at a greater length in his *Who Wants Democracy?*, New Delhi: Orient Longman, 2006, pp. 9–11.
64 Rochana Bajpai, 'Redefining equality: social justice in the Mandal debate, 1990', in V. R. Mehta and Thomas Pantham (eds), *Political Ideas in Modern India*, New Delhi: Sage, 2006, p. 335.
65 Chandhoke, 'Three myths about reservations', p. 2290.
66 Bhikhu Parekh, 'Limits of the Indian political imagination', in V. R. Mehta and Thomas Pantham (eds), *Political Ideas in Modern India*, New Delhi: Sage, 2006, p. 443.
67 Vir Sanghvi, 'The debate over reservation', *Hindustan Times*, 30 April 2006.
68 Parekh, 'Limits of the Indian political imagination', p. 442. Bhikhu Parekh elaborates the argument further by saying that 'the middle classes support it because of residual sense of historical guilt and because it spares them the likely disorder and the heavier taxation entailed by redistributive programme. The reservation policy helps the better off among the scheduled castes, the scheduled tribes and the OBCs, who have an obvious interest in defending it. And as for the rest of the members of these communities, they support it because of its trickle down effect, because it is the only thing they think they are ever likely to get, and because it reassures them that they matter to the otherwise indifferent Indian state. Although resented in some circles, the reservations policy therefore continues to enjoy a broad-based support.'
69 Pratap Bhanu Mehta, *The Burden of Democracy*, New Delhi: Penguin, 2003, p. 163.
70 W. H. Morris-Jones, *The Government and Politics of India*, New Delhi: BI Publications, 1974, pp. 215–17.
71 Sunil Khilnani pursues this argument in his *The Idea of India*, London: Hamish Hamilton, 1997, pp. 56–61.
72 Paul R. Brass, *The Politics of India since Independence*, Cambridge: Cambridge University Press, 1990, p. 64.
73 L. I. and S. H. Rudolph, *The Modernity of Tradition: Political Development in India*, Chicago: University of Chicago Press, 1967, p. 27.
74 For details on the rise and failure of the Bharatiya Jana Sangh, see Bruce D. Graham, *Hindu Nationalism and Indian Politics: The Origins and Development of the Bharatiya Jana Sangh*, Cambridge: Cambridge University Press, 1990; Craig Baxter, *The Jana Sangh: A Biography of an Indian Political Party*, Delhi: Oxford University Press, 1971.
75 Kanchan Chandra, *Why Ethnic Parties Succeed: Patronage, Ethnic Headcounts in India*, Cambridge: Cambridge University Press, 2004.
76 I borrow this expression from Kanchan Chandra. See her 'Post-Congress politics in Uttar Pradesh: the ethnification of the party system and its consequences', in Paul Wallace and Ramshray Roy, *Indian Politics and the 1998 Election: Regionalism, Hindutva and State Politics*, New Delhi: Sage, 1999, pp. 55–104.
77 Ashutosh Kuman, 'Dissonance between economic reforms and democracy', *Economic and Political Weekly*, 5 January 2007, p. 54.

78 For details of caste politics in the 1960s, see Rudolph and Rudolph, *The Modernity of Tradition*, pp. 79–82.
79 Author's personal interview in Allahabad, 18 April, 2007.
80 Dipankar Gupta and Yogesh Kumar, 'When the caste calculus fails: analyzing BSP's victory in UP', *Economic and Political Weekly*, 18 August 2007, pp. 3388–96.
81 Christophe Jaffrelot, *Dr. Ambedkar and Untouchability*, London: Hurst & Co., 2000, p. 157.
82 Yogendra Yadav, 'Reconfiguration in Indian politics', *Economic and Political Weekly*, 13 and 20 January, 1996, pp. 95–104.
83 Chandra, *Why Ethnic Parties Succeed*, p. 142.
84 Chandra, *Why Ethnic Parties Succeed*, p. 292.
85 According to Kanchan Chandra, the growing ethnification of political parties in India is inevitable. As she elaborates, 'ethnic parties are most likely to succeed in patronage-democracies when they have competitive rules for intra-party advancement. The adoption of centralized rule for intra-party advancement and/or a negative difference between the size of the target ethnic constituency and the threshold of winning or influence, increase the likelihood of failure.' *Why Ethnic Parties Succeed*, p. 15.
86 The *mandir* slogan paid massive electoral dividends to the BJP. In the aftermath of the controversial Rath Yatra in 1990, the BJP, for instance, almost doubled its popular vote from 11 per cent in 1989 to 21 per cent in 1991, winning 119 Lok Sabha seats. That was perhaps the upper limit of what a typical Hindutva slogan could achieve in terms of seats in parliament. Its increased tally of 182 seats in 1999 national poll was linked to a large extent with the failure of other parties to emerge as effective alternatives to the BJP.
87 Bhikhu Parekh, 'Limits of the Indian political imagination', in V. R. Mehta and Thomas Pantham (eds), *Political Ideas in Modern India*, New Delhi: Sage, 2006, p. 452.
88 Satish Deshpande, *Contemporary India*, New Delhi: Penguin, 2004, pp. 84–97.
89 Bhikhu Parekh, 'Limits of the Indian political imagination', p. 452.
90 Sumit Ganguly, 'The crisis of Indian secularism', *Journal of Democracy*, 14 (4), 2003, p. 23.
91 John Zavos, 'The shapes of Hindu nationalism', in Katherine Adney and Lawrence Saez (eds), *Coalition Politics and Hindu Nationalism*, London: Routledge, 2005, p. 53.
92 Christophe Jaffrelot characterizes this process as 'a silent revolution' in his *India's Silent Revolution: The Rise of the Low Castes in North Indian Politics*, New Delhi: Permanent Black, 2005.
93 Oliver Heath, 'Anatomy of BJP's rise to power: social, regional and political expansion in 1990s', *Economic and Political Weekly*, 21 August 1999, pp. 2516–17.
94 Thomas Blom Hansen and Christophe Jaffrelot (eds), *The BJP and the Compulsions of Politics in India*, Delhi: Oxford University Press, 1998, p. 10. This confluence, argue Hansen and Jaffrelot, resulted in the eclipse of the Congress in Tamil Nadu in the 1960s, Andhra Pradesh and Karnataka in the 1980s and most of north India especially from the late 1980s onwards. The interesting feature of especially northern and western India is, they further state, 'that the protracted demise of the Congress here has been executed interchangeably by the Janata Party, Samarwadi Party and other parties appealing to the upward-mobile OBCs and peasant communities'.
95 Heath, 'Anatomy of BJP's rise to power', p. 2517.
96 Suhas Palshikar, 'The regional parties and democracy: romantic rendezvous or localized legitimation?', in Ajay K. Mehra, D. D. Khanna and Gert Kueck (eds), *Political Parties and Party Systems*, New Delhi: Sage, 2003, p. 329.
97 While pondering over 'the politics of coalition' in the context of the 2004 Lok Sabha poll, representatives from the Congress, CPI(M) and Rashtriya Janata Dal were unanimous on the 'inevitability' of coalition government at the centre. But there were

sharp differences on whether it was an outcome of political expediency, simply a question of political accommodation or one that should only be determined by a common minimum programme. For the BJP spokesperson, coalition politics 'has ceased to be a question of preferences, it has become inevitable', whereas Laloo Prasad Yadav, the Rashtriya Janata leader, attributed the success of a coalition to a common minimum programme of 'ousting the BJP and its frontal organizations and save the country from disaster'. Concurring that coalition politics has emerged as 'a viable option', the CPI(M) chief minister of West Bengal referred to the left front experiment in West Bengal as an example of a coalition demonstrating that coming together of parties is possible 'without stooping to political opportunism'. Critical of the fragile basis of the NDA that drew on inherent contradictions of Hindutva, and by underscoring the necessity of 'political morality', he further argued that 'without ideological coalition no coalition can survive'. *The Hindu*, 2 March 2004.

98 Yogendra Yadav, 'Reconfiguration in Indian politics: state assembly elections, 1993–1995', *Economic and Political Weekly*, 13–20 January 1996, pp. 96–100.
99 Gurcharan Das, 'The hope of a new politics', *The Times of India*, 22 February 2004.
100 Paranjoy Guha Thakurta and Shankar Raghuraman, *A Time of Coalitions: Divided We Stand*, New Delhi: Sage, 2004, pp. 310–12.
101 This is the main argument in a recent publication: Katherine Adeney and Lawrence Saez, *Coalition Politics and Hindu Nationalism*, London: Routledge, 2005.
102 Adeney and Saez, *Coalition Politics and Hindu Nationalism*, p. 93.
103 Adeney and Saez, *Coalition Politics and Hindu Nationalism*, pp. 97–115.
104 Adeney and Saez, *Coalition Politics and Hindu Nationalism*, pp. 193–211.
105 Adeney and Saez, *Coalition Politics and Hindu Nationalism*, pp. 153–70.
106 Adeney and Saez, *Coalition Politics and Hindu Nationalism*, p. 168.
107 Adeney and Saez, *Coalition Politics and Hindu Nationalism*, p. 191.
108 Adeney and Saez, *Coalition Politics and Hindu Nationalism*, pp. 258–60.
109 The Indian experience is a creative response to democratic theory. Its paradox is a paradox only, argues Javeed Alam, 'in relation to received theory'. Javeed Alam, *Who Wants Democracy?*, New Delhi: Orient Longman, 2004, p. 131.
110 Rajni Kothari, *Rethinking Democracy*, New Delhi: Orient Longman, 2005, p. 123. Critical of the age-old government-centric conceptualization, Kothari defines democracy as an ideology that encompasses 'the many facets and diversities of a complex social reality, without falling prey to the homogenizing and oppressive thrust of the modern state, economy and technology'.
111 Amit Bhaduri, *Development with Dignity: A Case for Full Employment*, New Delhi: National Book Trust, 2006, p. 3.
112 *CAD*, Vol. X, p. 979.
113 Sunil Khilnani, *The Idea of India*, London: Hamish Hamilton, 1997, p. 13.
114 Alam, *Who Wants Democracy?*, p. 25.
115 The literature on deliberative democracy is rich and includes: John Dryzek, *Deliberative Democracy and Beyond: Liberals, Critics and Contestations*, Oxford: Oxford University Press, 2000; John Dryzek, 'Legitimacy and economy in deliberative democracy', *Political Theory*, 29 (5), 2001, pp. 651–69; Jurgen Habermas, *Between Facts and Norms: Contributions to a Discourse Theory of Law and Democracy*, Cambridge, MA: MIT Press, 1996; Ian Shapiro, *Democratic Justice*, New Haven, CT: Yale University Press, 1999; Marion Iris Young, *Inclusion and Democracy*, Oxford: Oxford University Press, 2000.

4 Parliamentary federalism

1 Katy Le Roy and Cheryl Saunders (eds), *Legislative, Executive and Judicial Governance in Federal Countries: A Global Dialogue on Federalism*, Kingston, Ont.: Queen's University Press, 2006, pp. 37–70, 101–34.

2 Ronald L. Watts, *Comparing Federal Systems*, Kingston, Ont.: Queen's University Press, 1999, pp. 23–5.

3 Canada is another hybrid system that combines the British tradition with American principles. Based on 'parliamentary federation', Canada is a political system with a strong central government that occasionally ignores the constituent provinces in the interest of the nation. For details of the development in Canada, see Douglas V. Varney, 'From executive to legislative federalism? The transformation of the political system in Canada and India', *The Review of Politics*, 3, 1989, pp. 241–63; D. V. Smiley, *Canada in Question: Federalism in the Eighties*, Toronto: McGraw Hill, 1980; Ronald L. Watts, 'Parliamentary federations: Canada and India', in Balveer Arora and Douglas V. Varney, *Multiple Identities in Single State*, Delhi: Konark, 1995, pp. 60–70.

4 Sudipta Kaviraj, 'Modernity and politics in India', *Daedalus*, 129, 2000, p. 155.

5 A. V. Dicey, *An Introduction to the Study of the Law of the Constitution*, Delhi: Universal Book Traders (Indian reprint), 1994, pp. 39–40.

6 Dicey, *An Introduction to the Law of the Constitution*, p. 414.

7 Dicey, *An introduction to the Law of the Constitution*, p. 143.

8 Dicey, *An Introduction to the Law of the Constitution*, p. 144.

9 Arend Lijphart, *Democracy in Plural Societies: A Comparative Exploration*, Bombay: Popular (Indian edition), 1989, p. 42.

10 For details, see Arend Lijphart, *Democracies: Patterns of Majoritarian and Consensus Government in Twenty-one Countries*, New Haven, CT: Yale University Press, 1984, pp. 23–30.

11 Lijphart, *Democracies*, pp. 208, 210.

12 Paul Brass pursues this argument in his 'The strong state and the fear of disorder', in Francine Frankel, Zoya Hasan, Rajeev Bhargava and Balveer Arora (eds), *Transforming India: Social and Political Dynamics of Democracy*, Delhi: Oxford University Press, 2000.

13 *CAD*, Vol. VII, p. 43.

14 Stuart Corbridge and John Harriss, *Reinventing India: Liberalization, Hindu Nationalism and Popular Democracy*, Delhi: Oxford University Press, 2000, p. 29.

15 As early as December 1946, G. B. Pant declared that 'the Constituent Assembly is resolved to set up a suitable republic for independent India. The recognition of the unity of India forms the cornerstone of this scheme. We do not know what will exactly be the subjects reserved for the Centre, but we know that the integrity and unity of India shall be preserved. The sentiment of unity will not be impaired in any way. That is first fundamental condition, as without it no constitution can be formulated and none can last for a day.' G. B. Pant's convocation address at Allahabad University on 21 December 1946. See *Selected Works of Govind Ballabh Pant*, Vol. 11, New Delhi: Oxford University Press, 1998, p. 425.

16 Quoted from M. Govinda Rao and Nirvikar Singh, *Political Economy of Federalism in India*, Delhi: Oxford University Press, 2005, p. 47.

17 *CAD*, Vol. VII, p. 892.

18 For a detailed discussion of the historical background, see W. H. Morris-Jones, *Parliament in India*, London: Longmans, 1957, pp. 73–81; W. H. Morris-Jones, *The Government and Politics of India*, Bombay: B. I. Publications, 1974 (Indian reprint), pp. 40–2, 79–80, 230–9.

19 *The Report of the All-Parties Conference*, part I (report of the committee appointed by the conference to determine the principles of the Constitution of India), Allahabad: All India Congress Committee, 1928, pp. 6–7.

20 For an incisive and detailed study on the formation of the Constituent Assembly in India, see Shibanikinkar Chaube, *Constituent Assembly of India: Springboard of Revolution*, 2nd edn, New Delhi: Manohar, 2000; Granville Austin, *The Indian Constitution: Cornerstone of a Nation*, New Delhi: Oxford University Press, 1996 (Indian reprint).

21 *CAD*, Vol. I, pp. 3–4.
22 *CAD*, Vol. I, pp. 57, 60.
23 *CAD*, Vol. IV, pp. 579–80.
24 *CAD*, Vol. IV, pp. 640, 637.
25 *CAD*, Vol. IV, p. 916.
26 Opposed to the parliamentary form of government, the Muslim League members (Aziz Ahmed Khan, Begum Aizaz Rasul, Chaudhuri Khaliquzzaman, to name a few prominent League members) recorded their views. For details, see *CAD*, Vol. IV, pp. 633–58. Once Pakistan was conceded, the League boycott ceased and its members from constituencies in independent India participated in the Assembly's deliberations.
27 *CAD*, Vol. VII, p. 33.
28 Morris-Jones, *Parliament in India*, p. 87.
29 *CAD*, Vol. VII, p. 984–5.
30 Chapter II of Part V to *The Constitution of India* incorporates the provision for Parliament in India.
31 Speech of Lokanath Mishra, *CAD*, Vol. VII, p. 242.
32 Speech of Lakshminarayan Sahu, *CAD*, Vol. XI, p. 613. Granville Austin, however, does not agree with the view that Gandhians, in order to reiterate their faith in the village panchayats, rejected the parliamentary form of government in its entirety. In his words, 'the debate in the Constituent Assembly in November, 1948 on the Draft Constitution confirmed the popularity of panchayats whilst emphasizing that support for them was not a rejection of either parliamentary government or Indian federalism.' Granville Austin, *The Indian Constitution*, p. 36.
33 *CAD*, Vol. 7, p. 241.
34 Speech of K. Hanumanthaiya, *CAD*, Vol. XI, p. 616.
35 Speech of Ramnarayan Singh, *CAD*, Vol. XI, pp. 639–42.
36 W. H. Morris-Jones, *The Government and Politics of India*, pp. 237–8.
37 In the first bicameral legislature established by the 1919 Government of India Act, the upper house was never to have a 'federal' role of providing for the equal representation of the various regions in the country. Four reasons were put forward in its defence: tradition, the desire of the propertied few to protect their interests, the desire to provide a second forum to reconsider some hasty decisions passed by the lower house and finally the desire to provide representation for interests difficult to accommodate in the lower house. For details, see Nalini Rajan, *Democracy and the Limits of Minority Rights*, New Delhi: Sage Publications, 2002, pp. 206–11.
38 This is how the role of the Rajya Sabha was articulated by *The Sarkaria Commission*, New Delhi: Publication Division, Government of India, 1988, p. 68. For a critical assessment of the report of the Sarkaria Commission on centre–state relations, see Lawrence Saez, *Federalism without a Centre: The Impact of Political and Economic Reform on India's Federal System*, New Delhi: Sage, 2002, pp. 71–100, 110–114.
39 *CAD*, Vol. IV, p. 876.
40 Morris-Jones, *The Government and Politics of India*, p. 232.
41 This is how Gopalaswamy Ayyangar defined the role of Rajya Sabha in the Constituent Assembly; *CAD*, Vol. IV, p. 876.
42 *CAD*, Vol. VII, pp. 1208–9.
43 Report of the Sarkaria Commission, p. 69.
44 For a lucid account of the political development in India in the aftermath of independence, see Partha Chatterjee (ed.), *State and Politics in India*, New Delhi: Oxford University Press, 1997, pp. 1–39.
45 Era Sezhiyan, 'Council of States or Council of Nominees?', *The Hindu*, 3 February 2006.
46 The recent examples are Spain and Belgium. In the former, the centre agreed to devolve power to hold the constituent provinces together after the collapse of the

Franco regime in 1975; the latter, in order to hold the Flemish and Walloon communities together, adopted a federal constitution in 1993. For details, see Alfred Stepan, 'Toward a new comparative politics of federalism, multi-nationalism and democracy: beyond Rikerian federalism', in *Arguing Comparative Politics*, Oxford: Oxford University Press, 2001, pp. 315–61.

47 *CAD*, Vol. XII, p. 976.

48 *CAD*, Vol. VII, pp. 34–5.

49 This discussion draws on B. R. Ambedkar's address to the Constituent Assembly on 4 November 1948. *CAD*, Vol. VII, pp. 36–7.

50 Quoted in M. Govinda Rao and Nirvikar Singh, *Political Economy of Federalism in India*, Delhi: Oxford University Press, 2005, p. 44.

51 *All Parties Conference, 1928* (report of the committee appointed by the conference to determine the principles of the Constitution of India), Allahabad: All India Congress Committee, 1928, pp. 62–3, emphasis added.

52 *CAD*, Vol. XI, p. 976.

53 India's federal system presents some peculiarities and adaptations of a well-known form of government. Although politics in India are more regionalized than in any other federal polity, reflecting the unrivalled cultural diversity of the country, the system has more unitary features than most federal systems, including the US, Canada and Australia. For details, see Paul Brass, *The Politics of India since Independence*, Cambridge: Cambridge University Press, 1990, pp. 59–63.

54 Mahendra Ved, 'Honouring Sardar Patel: Bismarck of India', *The Times of India*, 22 August 1998.

55 Ravinder Kumar elaborated this point in his 'Securing Stability: No Cause for Constitutional Reforms', *The Times of India*, 15 September 1998.

56 Paul Brass, *The Politics of India since Independence*, p. 63. Underlining the various countervailing tendencies within what eventually emerged as India's federal system, this argument is a pointer to the future direction of Indian polity following the disintegration of the Congress Party as an umbrella organization.

57 This discussion is drawn from Rekha Saxena and M. P. Singh, *Indian Politics: Shifts without a Paradigm*, New Delhi: Prentice Hall (forthcoming).

58 T. T. Krishmachari's address to the Constituent Assembly, 25 November 1949, *CAD*, Vol. XII, p. 950.

59 Rajni Kothari, 'The Congress System in India', *Asian Survey*, December 1964. When reviewing his model in 1974, Kothari reiterated his faith in the Congress system as the most effective means of countering 'the challenges that the country faces'. Hence, his suggestion included, 'rebuild the Congress Party and its regional infrastructure that has become so weak of late, reinvest the electoral process with legitimacy, restore to the opposition parties their due role in parliamentary politics and at regional levels, and restructure the communication linkage between government, party units and the people, so that the system becomes more responsive and has to rely less on coercion'. See Rajni Kothari, 'The Congress System Revisited: A Decennial Review', *Asian Survey*, December 1974, pp. 1052–3. Over a period of time, however, the situation has changed radically and the Congress system has largely lost its grip over the Indian reality. In the words of Kothari, '[b]uilt as it was around a system of one party dominance the Congress system while allowing a great deal of internal flexibility and a long period of stable democratic functioning, nonetheless produced a centralized, bureaucratic apparatus that was lacking in effective distributive policies and any sound philosophy of justice, it eventually ended up in a neo-liberal, marketized doctrine (popularly described as liberalization and globalization) that led to consequences which produced a sharp reaction from the people at large. An electoral democracy . . . [that had] broadened its social base and shown special regard for diverse types of minorities and hence gained so much legitimacy got eroded over time and forced the political managers to compromise with and ultimately become party to monied

and "mafia" interests, in the process undermining the autonomy of the state and the political system.' See Rajni Kothari, 'The democratic experience', in Partha Chatterjee (ed.), *Wages of Freedom*, Delhi: Oxford University Press, 1998, pp. 27–8.

60   I borrow this explanation from Kanchan Chandra, 'Elite incorporation in multi-ethnic societies', *Asian Survey*, September/October 2000, pp. 22–3.

61   Ravinder Kumar, 'Winds of change across India and the shaping of a new polity', *South Asia*, 19 (1), 2006, p. 164.

62   Rajni Kothari, *State against Democracy: In Search of Humane Governance*, Delhi: Ajanta, 1988, p. 157.

63   Amal Ray, 'Coordinating pluralism: the federal experience in India', in Rasheeduddin Khan (ed.), *Rethinking Indian Federalism*, Shimla: Indian Institute of Advanced Studies, 1997, pp. 98–102.

64   Francine Frankel, 'Decline of a social order', in Francine Frankel and M. S. A. Rao (eds), *Dominance and State Power in Modern India: Decline of a Social Order*, Vol. II, Delhi: Oxford University Press, 1990, p. 502.

65   Sudipta Kaviraj, 'On state, society and discourse in India', in James Manor (ed.) *Rethinking Third World Politics*, London: Longman, 1991, pp. 87–8.

66   Rakhahari Chatterjee, 'Democracy and opposition in India', *Economic and Political Weekly*, 23 April 1988, p. 847.

67   Ramshray Roy, *Democracy in India: Form and Substance*, New Delhi: Shipra, 2005, p. 215.

68   Sunil Khilnani, *The Idea of India*, London: Hamish Hamilton, 1997, p. 182.

69   Kothari, *State against Democracy*, p. 30.

70   L. I. Rudolph and S. H. Rudolph, *In Pursuit of Lakshmi: The Political Economy of the Indian State*, Hyderabad: Orient Longman (reprint), 1987, p. 99. Making the same point more sharply, Kaviraj writes, 'initially the federal structure worked through the federalism inside the Congress party rather than constitutional channels'. See his 'On state, society and discourse in India', p. 88.

71   Rudolph and Rudolph, *In Pursuit of Lakshmi*, p. 138.

72   Rajni Kothari, 'Integration and exclusion', *Economic and Political Weekly*, October 1988, p. 2226.

73   T. V. Sathyamurthy, 'Impact of centre–state relations on Indian politics: an interpretative reckoning, 1947–1987', in Partha Chatterjee (ed.), *State and Politics India*, Delhi: Oxford University Press, 1997, p. 250.

74   In his analysis of the decay of political institutions, Kaviraj argues that, as power has accumulated in the centre, institutions designed to safeguard democratic functioning of the state have weakened. See his 'On the crisis of political institutions in India', *Contributions to Indian Sociology* (New Series), 18 (2), 1984, pp. 223–43.

75   Subrata Kumar Mitra, 'Democracy and political change in India', *Journal of Commonwealth & Comparative Politics*, 30 (1), 1992, p. 27.

76   Kothari, *State against Democracy*, p. 175.

77   For an interesting exposition of this phenomenon, see Rajni Kothari, 'Rise of the dalits and the renewed debate on caste', *Economic and Political Weekly*, 25 June 1994.

78   Amartya Sen, 'India in the world', *The Hindu*, 15 August 2007, p. 2.

79   For details of the 1973 Kesavananda Bharati case, see Granville Austin, *Working a Democratic Constitution: A History of the Indian Experience*, New Delhi: Oxford University Press, 1999, pp. 258–77.

80   Arun Shourie, *The Parliamentary System: What We have Made of It, What We can Make of It*, New Delhi: Rupa, 2007, p. 194.

81   Somnath Chatterjee's foreword in Pran Chopra (ed.), *The Supreme Court Versus the Constitution: A Challenge to Federalism*, New Delhi: Sage, 2006, p. 13.

82   This discussion draws on Ramaswamy R. Iyer, 'Some constitutional dilemmas', *Economic and Political Weekly*, 27 June 2006, pp. 2066–8.

83 Granville Austin, *Working a Democratic Constitution*, p. 652.
84 Pratap Bhanu Mehta, 'The inner conflict of constitutionalism: judicial review and the "Basic Structure" ', in Zoya Hasan, E. Sridharan and R. Sudarshan (eds), *India's Living Constitution: Ideas, Practices and Controversies*, New Delhi: Permanent Black, 2002, p. 180.
85 Rajeev Dhavan and Rekha Saxena, 'Republic of India', in Katy Le Roy and Cheryl Saunders (ed.), *Legislative, Executive and Judicial Governance in Federal Countries*, London: McGill–Queen's University Press, 2006, p. 179.
86 Rudolph and Rudolph, *In Pursuit of Lakshmi*, p. 105.
87 Under economic liberalization policies, there have been no fundamental changes in the state or central power. The impact on the states of the centre's treaty-making power has always been there. Only in the US and Canadian constitutions is there a constitutional bar on the role of the state vis-à-vis treaty-making; in the Australian constitution, no such embargo is evident.
88 Rajeev Dhawan and Geetanjali Goel, 'Indian federalism and its discontents', in Gert Kueck and others (ed.), *Federalism and Decentralization: Centre–State Relations in India and Germany*, New Delhi: Mudrit, 1998, p. 54.
89 L. I. and S. H. Rudolph, 'The iconization of Chandrababu: sharing of sovereignty in India's federal market economy', *Economic and Political Weekly*, 5 May 2001, p. 1546.
90 The World Bank report entitled 'Bolstering state reform programs for faster growth and poverty reduction in India', quoted in Aseema Sinha, 'The changing political economy of federalism in India: a historical institutional approach', *India Review*, 3 (1), 2004, p. 50.
91 The Bommai judgment is quoted from Era Sezhiyan, 'Council of States or council of nominees?', *The Hindu*, 3 February 2006.
92 Sinha, 'The changing political economy of federalism in India', p. 32.
93 Rajni Kothari suggests a Pradesh Sabha to make the second chamber more effective in governance. According to him, 'the central Parliament should consist of a directly elected Lok Sabha and an indirectly elected Pradesh Sabha, to which each state electoral college consisting of elected representatives of the district councils and the state legislature elect an equal number of representatives. Unlike the Rajya Sabha which has become a tame replica of the Lok Sabha, the function of the Pradesh Sabha should be to represent the interests of the lower rungs of the political structure in national deliberation and, at the same time, act as a channel and a training ground for regional cadres in national affairs. A convention should be established that only those who have had experience in district or state bodies should contest the election to the Pradesh Sabha. They would thus bring a fund of experience to bear upon parliamentary deliberations.' Rajni Kothari, *Democratic Polity and Social Change in India: Crisis and Opportunities*, Bombay: Allied Publishers, 1976, p. 83.
94 The forums and agencies that constitute the lifeline of the process of federalization in India are: (a) inter-governmental agencies, *viz.* National Development Council, Inter-State Council and ministerial and secretarial-level meetings; (b) federal agencies having implications for states as well – for instance, the Finance Commission, the Planning Commission, a number of independent regulatory authorities in sectors such as electricity, telecommunications, Central Vigilance Commission, Central Bureau of Investigation, Central Reserve Police Force – and (c) inter-state conferences of Chief Ministers, either all of them or those from one particular political persuasion. Apart from these agencies, there is also the National Integration Council, created by Jawaharlal Nehru in the wake of the 1962 war with China, another inter-governmental device involving also important personalities from all walks of life besides those associated with the functioning of the government machinery both at the central and state levels. For a detailed description of these agencies, see Rekha Saxena, 'Role of inter-governmental agencies', *The Hindu,* 29 January 2002.

95 Lawrence Saez, *Federalism without a Centre: The Impact of Political and Economic Reform on India's Federal System*, New Delhi: Sage, 2002, p. 158.
96 Granville Austin, 'The expected and the unintended in working a democratic constitution', in Hasan *et al.* (eds), *India's Living Constitution*, p. 342.
97 The rise of the regional parties in several states has radically altered the composition of the Rajya Sabha. In other words, parties other than the ruling party at the centre are able to send more representatives to the Rajya Sabha. As a result, ruling parties have invariably fewer members in the upper house than before. There have been occasions when the ruling party has failed to muster the required two-thirds majority in the Rajya Sabha to pass constitutional amendments, as was the case with the Forty-Third and Forty-Fourth constitutional amendments.
98 The fate of federalism in India is quite mixed. Federalism was eroded in the 1970s and 1980s and the imperatives of party politics seem to have strengthened it during the 1990s. Even during the heyday of the Congress rule during the single-party dominance phase (1947–66), no state has ever been held responsible for 'fiscal' indiscipline. Indeed the constitutional provision for declaring financial emergencies in states has never been used since independence despite appalling financial conditions in some states. What it means is that even during the heyday of 'centralization' the centre was not able to exercise leverage over the states as much as we seem to think, though the centre intervened to change Chief Ministers and dismiss governments, which is certainly a significant dimension of centralization.

5 The chaotic 1960s

1 The 1967 assembly elections led to the formation of non-Congress (typically coalitional) governments in nine states across India: Punjab, Haryana, Uttar Pradesh, Madhya Pradesh, Bihar, West Bengal, Orissa, Tamil Nadu and Kerala.
2 This trend is best exemplified during the period when Indira Gandhi held power. By her capacity to directly communicate with the electorate, Mrs Gandhi could afford to ignore the party organization, which gradually became dependent on her charisma for its viability. Sudipta Kaviraj has graphically illustrated the process that ultimately contributed to the decline of the Congress as an institutionalized party with its organizational tentacles spread all over India for historical reasons. Sudipta Kaviraj, 'A critique of passive revolution', *Economic and Political Weekly*, 23 (45–7), pp. 2429–44.
3 Paul Brass, *The Politics of India since Independence*, Cambridge: Cambridge University Press, 1990, p. 63.
4 N. C. B. Ray Chaudhury, 'The politics of India's coalitions', *The Political Quarterly*, 40 (3), 1969, pp. 296–7.
5 Chaudhury, 'The politics of India's coalitions', p. 297.
6 Communist Party of India (Marxist), Central Committee Political Report, 10–16 April 1967, *New Situation and Party's Tasks*, p. 70.
7 CPI(M), *New Situation and Party's Tasks*, p. 32
8 Ross Mallick, *Indian Communism: Opposition, Collaboration and Institutionalization*, Delhi: Oxford University Press, 1994, p. 102.
9 CPI(M), *New Situation and Party's Tasks*, p. 84.
10 For a very critical analysis of the 1967 poll results, see Atul Kohli, *Democracy and Discontent: India's Growing Crisis of Governability*, Cambridge: Cambridge University Press, 1991, pp. 274–6.
11 Sankar Ghosh, *The Disinherited State: A Study of West Bengal, 1967–70*, Calcutta: Orient Longman, 1971, p. 156.
12 By the late 1960s, there emerged, Zoya Hasan reports, 'a coalition of groups representing the interests of rich and middle peasantry that showed the potential to displace the ruling party. This section made political demands that could not be incorporated

within the Congress system. instead they were courted by the Bharatiya Kranti Dal (BKD) which [rose] as an alternative formation under Charan Singh.' In forging anti-Congress oppositional alliances, Singh was supported by the Jana Sangh and socialists. Zoya Hasan, *Quest for Power: Oppositional Movements and Post-Congress Politics in Uttar Pradesh*, Delhi: Oxford University Press, 1998, p. 28.

13 *Hindustan Times*, 9 April 1967.

14 Charan Singh formed the Bharatiya Kranti Dal on 5 May 1967, and on 27 November 1967 the Jana Congress merged with it. Sudha Pai, *Uttar Pradesh: Agrarian Change and Electoral Politics*, New Delhi: Shipra, 1993, p. 77.

15 *National Herald*, 7 April 1967.

16 *National Herald*, 26 June 1967.

17 *National Herald*, 2 July 1967. In its editorial, the *National Herald* even characterized the SVD government as nothing but endorsing 'the Jana Sangh rule'.

18 *The Times of India*, 17 August 1967.

19 Article 356 of India's Constitution empowers the president of India to declare a state of emergency 'if the President, on receipt of a report from the Governor of a State or otherwise, is satisfied that a situation has arisen in which the government of the State cannot be carried on in accordance with the provisions of this Constitution'. The media was full of reports of blame and counter-blame by the constituents of the SVD once the Charan Singh ministry collapsed. *Hindustan Times*, 18 February 1968; *The Times of India*, 18 February 1968; *National Herald*, 18 February 1968.

20 The 1969 elections reestablished the Congress hegemony in the state. Not only did it capture 211 seats in the legislative assembly, it had won 33.7 per cent of votes, which was was nearly 1.5 per cent more than its share in 1967. For details, see V. K. Pai, 'In search of a new balance: caste, region and community in Uttar Pradesh', *Economic and Political Weekly*, 21 August 1999.

21 Chaudhury, 'The politics of India's coalitions', p. 299.

22 *The Times of India*, 8 August 1967; *Hindustan Times*, 9 August 1967.

23 *The Times of India*, 22 November 1967.

24 For a detailed exposition of this experiment, see H. Austin, *Anatomy of the Kerala Coup*, New Delhi: People's Publishing House, 1959; Victor M. Fic, *Painful Transition to Communism in India: Strategy of the Communist Party*, Bombay: Nachiketa Publications, 1969; Victor M. Fic, *Yenan of India*, Bombay: Nachiketa Publications, 1970; George K. Lieten, *The First Communist Ministry in Kerala*, Calcutta: KP Bagchi & Co., 1982.

25 For details, see M. K. Das and N. P. Che Kutty, 'Coalition government – Kerala experiment', in Lakshmi Krishnamurti and Gert W. Kueck (eds), *Making a Success of Coalitions*, Chennai: East West Books, 2000, pp. 134–5.

26 S. N. Sadsivan, *Administration and Social Development in Kerala: A Study in Administrative Sociology*, New Delhi: IIPA, 1988, p. 16.

27 These demographic figures are taken from T. J. Nossiter, *Marxist Governments in India: Politics, Economic and Society*, London: Pinter Publishers, 1988, p. 61.

28 B. T. Randive, *Lessons of the Break-up of Kerala United Front*, Calcutta: Communist Party of India (Marxist), 1970, p. 18.

29 For details see P. John John, *Coalition Government in Kerala*, Trivandrum: Institute of Public Policy and Management, 1983, pp. 129, 134–42.

30 John, *Coalition Government in Kerala*, p. 142.

31 E. M. S. Namboodripad, *Anti-Communist Gang-up in Kerala Betrayers of UF Set-up Anti-people Government*, Calcutta: Communist Party of India (Marxist), 1970, p. 28.

32 'The trouble in Kerala', *Economic and Political Weekly*, 18 November 1967, p. 1973; E. J. Thomas, *Coalition Game Politics in Kerala after Independence*, New Delhi: Intellectual Publishing, 1985, pp. 134–6.

33 For details, see T. J. Nossiter, *Communism in Kerala: A Study in Political Adaptation*, New Delhi: Oxford University Press, 1982, ch. 3 and 4.

34 T. J. Nossiter, *Marxist Governments in India*, p. 101.
35 Nossiter, *Marxist Governments in India*, p. 107.
36 Balraj Madhok, 'The future of the parties', *The Pioneer*, 14 January 1964.
37 Central General Council, Delhi, Bharatiya Jana Sangh documents, Vol. IV, p. 196, 21 April 1967.
38 Bruce Graham, *Hindu Nationalism and Indian Politics: The Origins and Development of Bahratiya Jana Sangh*, Cambridge: Cambridge University Press, 1990, p. 219.
39 In articulating this approach, Atal Bihari Vajpayee referred to the events that brought the Jana Sangh to the centre stage of UP politics in the aftermath of the 1967 elections. In his words, 'even though the Jana Sangh was the largest single group in the opposition in UP, it had suggested Shri Charan Singh that he might form his Government without the Jana Sangh. The Jan Sangh had assured him full support from outside. Shri Charan Singh point-blank refused to accept the suggestion and said that he could not contemplate a non-Congress Government in UP without the Jana Sangh.' Atal Bihari Vajpayee's statement in *The Times of India*, 23 April 1967; *Hindustan Times*, 23 April 1967.
40 N. C. B. Ray Chaudhury, 'The politics of India's coalitions', *The Political Quarterly*, Vol. 40 (3), 1969, p. 303.
41 In Haryana, where defection was first initiated, the phenomenon was described in such a way.
42 W. H. Morris-Jones, 'From monopoly to competition', in *Politics Mainly India*, Madras: Orient Longman, 1978, p. 155.
43 James Manor, 'Parties and the party system', in Zoya Hasan (ed.), *Parties and Party Politics in India*, New Delhi: Oxford University Press, 2002, p. 438.
44 Bipan Chandra, Mridula Mukherjee and Aditya Mukherjee, *India after Independence, 1947–2000*, New Delhi: Penguin, 2000, p. 228.
45 Rajni Kothari, *Politics in India*, New Delhi: Orient Longman, 1986 (reprint), p. 183.

6 The Left Front and the 2006 assembly elections in West Bengal

1 Atul Kohli, *Democracy and Discontent: India's Growing Crisis of Governability*, Cambridge: Cambridge University Press, 1991, p. 267.
2 Dwaipayan Bhattacharya pursues this argument in his 'Road to revolution: land reform to industrialization', *Hindustan Times*, 21 June 2007.
3 Sumanta Banerjee, 'Assembly Polls, 2006: elections, *jatra* style, in West Bengal', *Economic and Political Weekly*, 26 May 2006, p. 864.
4 AM, 'Suffrage in West Bengal', *Economic and Political Weekly*, 26 May 2006, p. 2048.
5 Author's personal interaction with voters in the districts of Birbhum and Calcutta. This assertion is also corroborated by findings from other districts of West Bengal.
6 Ashok Mitra, 'Take it as red', *The Telegraph*, 13 May 2006.
7 That the names of genuine voters were deleted became a bone of contention and the Election Commission was inundated with complaints from West Bengal voters. In a large number of booths in Calcutta and some of its adjoining districts which are CPI(M)'s strongholds, several genuine voters were denied entry simply because in the revised list their names did not figure.
8 The major Bengali newspapers, such as *Anadabazar Patrika* and *Bartaman*, devoted a lot of space on the activities of these 'central' observers and hailed their role 'in restoring democracy' in West Bengal by ensuring a free and fair poll.
9 D. Bandyopadhyay, 'Elections and bureaucracy in West Bengal', *Economic and Political Weekly*, 21 April 2006, p. 1417.
10 Yogendra Yadav, 'The opportunities and the challenges', *The Hindu*, 16 May 2006.
11 Marcus Dam, 'Left Front's support base widens', *The Hindu*, 13 May 2006.
12 The expression 'Brand Buddha' refers to a specific style of electoral campaign that the

incumbent chief minister, Buddhadeb Bhattacharjee, undertook in the 2006 election. Designed to win over urban voters disenchanted with the Left Front, the campaign drew on well-defined plans and programmes for regeneration of hope and addressed the grievances of urban dwellers by proposing rapid industrialization, even by inviting private industrialists and also FDI (foreign direct investment) in West Bengal. This does not appear to sit well with the Left Front leadership, which explains the historic victory in terms of 'organization' and pro-people policies of the government over a lengthy period. The Left Front Chairman, Biman Bose, made this point in his press statement on 15 May 2006. *Anandabazar Patrika*, 16 May 2006.

13 Atul Kohli, *Democracy and Discontent: India's Growing Crisis of Governability*, Cambridge: Cambridge University Press, 1991, pp. 267–96.

14 Articulating the views of those who are critical of the West Bengal panchayats, Poromesh Acharya argues that '[n]o doubt, there emerged a new generation of leadership in rural West Bengal but the class and caste background of the new leadership' remain more or less unchanged. 'There developed a new institutional structure, decentralized in form but still dominated by the middle and rich peasants. The agricultural labourers and poor peasants, though not in proportion, have their representatives in the new structure but their participation in the decision making process is still a far cry.' See Poromesh Acharya, 'Panchayats and left politics in West Bengal', *Economic and Political Weekly*, 29 May 1993, p. 1080.

15 D. Bandyopadhyay, 'Caucus and masses: West Bengal Panchayats', *Economic and Political Weekly*, 21 November 2003, p. 4826.

16 Dwaipayan Bhattacharya, 'Limits to legal radicalism: land reform and the Left Front in West Bengal', *Calcutta Historical Journal*, 16 (1), 1994, p. 86.

17 The West Bengal CPI(M) State Committee directives on Panchayats, CPI(M) State Committee, 31 January 1994 (unpublished), courtesy of the late B. T. Ranadeve.

18 Ibid.

19 Maitreesh Ghatak and Maitreya Ghatak, 'Recent reforms in the panchayat system in West Bengal: toward greater participatory governance?', *Economic and Political Weekly*, 11 January 2002, p. 56.

20 A press statement by Maheshwar Murmu, the minister for tribal affairs, on 29 July 2005. *Dainik Statesman*, 30 July 2005.

21 Yogendra Yadav and Sanjay Kumar, 'Why the left will win once again', *The Hindu*, 16 April 2006.

22 Suhrid Sankar Chattopadhyay, 'Left landslide', *Frontline,* 2 June 2006, p. 10.

23 Buddhadeb Bhattacharjee, statement to press conference, 12 May 2006. *Anandabazar Patrika*, 13 May 2006.

24 This summary of the press conference addressed by Bhattacharjee is drawn from Suhrid Sankar Chattopadhyay, 'Left landslide', *Frontline,* 2 June 2006, p. 10.

25 Buddhadeb Bhattacharjee, statement to press conference, 12 May 2006. *Anandabazar Patrika*, 13 May 2006.

26 Buddhadeb Bhattacharjee's press release in *The Statesman*, 12 May 2006.

27 This is drawn from Buddhadeb Bhattacharjee's press conference held on 15 May 2006. *Anandabazar Patrika* reproduced the views in its edition of 16 May 2006.

28 The figures are drawn from Yogendra Yadav, 'The opportunities and the challenges', *The Hindu*, 16 May 2006.

29 Thus it was not surprising that the strike over the hike in petrol prices on 13 June 2006 was observed by resorting to only 'five minute *chakka* jam' (blockading of traffic) and street-corner meetings. This was inconceivable in the immediate past when the CPI(M) cadres were instructed to paralyse the civic life. The CPI(M) leadership announced that it would restrict the strike to 'token protest' because, as the Chief Minister stated, 'it would give wrong signals to the investors'. In order to highlight the changed perception of the Left Front, a newspaper reports, 'while Left MPs in Delhi were busy courting arrest, Buddhadeb Bhattacharjee's cabinet colleagues and senior

bureaucrats were working on details of the land acquisition plan for the state's FDI projects of Indonesia's Salem Group'. *Indian Express*, 14 June 2006.

30 Paranjoy Guha Thakurta dwells on this question in his 'When left is right', *The Times of India*, 17 May 2006.

31 In terms of organizational network, the closest parallel is the Bahujan Samaj Party (BSP), which supports its electoral campaign with a well-entrenched election machinery. The BSP begins its electoral drill well in advance by choosing the candidates for most of the constituencies for better and intimate interaction between them and the voters. Divided into twenty-five sectors (with ten polling booths in one sector), each constituency is being looked after by the High Command. Each booth, with roughly 1000 voters, is the responsibility of a nine-member committee comprising at least one woman to motivate and mobilize women voters.

32 Banerjee, 'Assembly Polls, 2006', p. 865.

33 Yogendra Yadav, 'How West Bengal voted', *The Hindu*, 16 May 2006.

34 Bhaskar Ghose, 'A necessary ritual', *The Telegraph*, 9 June 2004.

35 Mitra, 'Take it as red'.

36 The height of the Congress factional fight was witnessed in Murshidabad where the district president, who is an MP, set up candidates in two constituencies in his district to contest against the party's official nominees. Such is the state of affairs in the party that he cannot be disciplined. He, in fact, shared the dais with the all-Indian party president, Sonia Gandhi, during the campaign, and nobody dared to even mildly reprimand him. *The Telegraph*, 12 May 2006.

37 Banerjee, 'Assembly Polls, 2006', p. 866.

38 Mitra, 'Take it as red'.

39 Ravinder Kumar, 'Winds of change across India and the shaping of a new polity', *South Asia*, 29 (1), 2006, p. 164.

40 Rajni Kothari, 'The Congress system in India', *Asian Survey*, December 1964.

41 Amal Ray, 'Coordinating pluralism: the federal experience in India', in Rasheeduddin Khan (ed.), *Rethinking Indian Federalism*, Shimla: Indian Institute of Advanced Studies, 1997, pp. 98–102.

42 Dwaipayan Bhattacharya pursues this argument in his 'Road to revolution: land reform to industrialization', *Hindustan Times*, Delhi, 21 June 2007.

43 Partha Pratim Basu, 'Brand Buddha in India's West Bengal', *Asian Survey*, 47 (2), 2007, p. 305.

44 Seeking to create an environment conducive for private business, the Left Front government adopted the SEZ Act in 2003, two years before it was adopted by the union government. SEZs are generally defined as specially demarcated zones that are exempt from various duties and tariffs by virtue of their treatment as a foreign territory for the purposes of trade operations. The scheme offers a vast range of economic activities including manufacturing, services, trading, reconditioning, labelling, repacking and warehousing.

45 Author's interview with Harihar Mondal, a Nandigram farmer, 29 March 2007.

46 Press statement of Prakash Karat, CPI(M) general secretary, *The Times of India*, 24 March 2007.

47 Press statement of A. B. Bardhan, CPI general secretary, *The Times of India*, 23 March 2007.

48 *Anandabazar Patrika*, 13 November 2007.

49 Dipanjan Rai Chaudhuri and Satya Sivaraman, 'Nandigram: six months later', *Economic and Political Weekly*, 13 October 2007, p. 4103.

50 The chief minister was forced to scrap the SEZ in Nandigram as a result of popular resentment against his government's heavy-handed attempt to steamroller the SEZ, which left the Left allies fuming and even the party leadership deeply unhappy. The chief minister's press statement on 18 December 2007, *Anandabazar Patrika*, 19 December 2007.

51 Bolan Bandyopadhyay, 'The Left Front does not require the poor peasants' (Bengali), *Anandabazar Patrika*, 7 September, 2006

7 Coalition politics in India

1 Of the successful experiments, the Olive Tree coalition in Italy on the basis of a compromise between the Catholic Church and the Communists was possible once the contentious issues were swept under the carpet. In Germany, the Christian Democratic Party and Social Democratic Party continue to remain important ingredients in the coalition government. Switzerland is another successful experiment in coalition government seeking to merge the interests of the three major language groups (French, German and Italian). Outside Europe, Israel is perhaps the best example of power-sharing and a Prime Minister by rotation. Israel had a coalition government of the Likud Party and Labour Party from 1984 to 1988. For the first two years, Shimon Peres was the premier and Yitzhak Shamir the Foreign Minister, followed by a reversal of roles in the next two years. The Israel example was suggested when the National Front came to power in India in 1989.

2 *Swadeshi* is an Indian expression, popularized and loaded with meaning in the course of the freedom struggle. It means (a) collective pride, (b) ancestral loyalty and (c) communal integrity or amity.

3 Bhikhu Parekh, 'Ethnocentricity of the nationalist discourse', *Nations and Nationalism*, 1 (1), 1995, p. 39.

4 Gandhi defined Swaraj as separate from 'freedom' and 'independence', which he claimed 'were English words lacking such connotations and which could be taken to mean a license to do whatever one wishes'. His Swaraj 'allowed no such irresponsible freedom and demanded rather a rigorous moulding of the self and a heavy sense of responsibility'. David Hardiman, *Gandhi in His Time and Ours*, New Delhi: Permanent Black, 2003, p. 26.

5 Granville Austin, *The Indian Constitution: Cornerstone of a Nation*, New Delhi: Oxford University Press, 1999, pp. 309–10.

6 Vir Sanghvi, 'Neither fair nor stable', *Hindustan Times*, 25 March 2007.

7 Jayaprakash Narayan, 'The crisis of governance', in Rajesh Tandon and Ranjita Mohanty (eds), *Does Civil Society Matter: Governance in Contemporary India*, New Delhi: Sage, 2005 (reprint), p. 101.

8 Austin, *The Indian Constitution*, p. 318.

9 Built as it was around a system of one-party dominance, the Congress system allowed a great deal of internal flexibility and a long period of stable democratic functioning defused tension within the organization, which accounted for its survival for more than four decades after independence. For details, see Rajni Kothari, 'The Congress System in India', *Asian Survey*, December 1964.

10 Rajni Kothari, 'Continuity and change in the Indian party system', *Asian Survey*, November 1970, p. 939.

11 Sunil Khilnani, *The Idea of India*, p. 184.

12 Khilnani, *The Idea of India*, p. 57.

13 For details of this argument, see Lawrence Saez, *Federalism without a Centre: The Impact of Political and Economic Reform on India's Federal System*, New Delhi: Sage, 2002.

14 Christophe Jaffrelot, *India's Silent Revolution: The Rise of Low Castes in North Indian Politics*, New Delhi: Permanent Black, 2003.

15 Rammanohar Lohia's political vision was articulated in *saptakranti* (revolutions for seven goals), which consists of revolutions (1) for man–woman equality, (2) against inequality based on colour, (3) against social inequality and caste and for special opportunities, (4) against colonialism and foreign rule, (5) for maximum achievable economic equality, (6) for privacy and democratic rights and (7) against weapons

of mass destruction. Rammonohar Lohia, *Election Manifesto of the Socialist Party*, 1962, p. 3 – quoted in Madhu Limaye, *Janata Party Experiment: An Insider's Account of Opposition Politics, 1977–80*, Vol. 2, New Delhi: DK Publishers, 1994, p. 543.

16 Rammanohar Lohia, *Note and Comments, the Elections, 1967 and After*, Vol. 2, pp. 247–52, quoted in Madhu Limaye, *Janata Party Experiment*, Vol. 2, p. 542.

17 Emma Tarlo, *Unsettling Memories: Narratives of India's Emergency*, New Delhi: Permanent Black, 2003.

18 The Left Front parties, for instance, oppose the Congress in states such as Kerala, West Bengal and Tripura where they are the governing coalitions though they are a critical part of the Congress-led United Progressive Alliance at the centre.

19 For a definite account of the changing nature of parliament, see Bimal Jalan, *India's Politics: A View from the Backbench*, New Delhi: Penguin, 2007, p. 27.

20 The Second Backward Classes Commission, known as the Mandal Commission, appointed in 1978, revived interest in formulating a national policy for OBCs. The Commission suggested that OBCs, who form 54.5 per cent of the country's population, require special concession to correct the social imbalance. As is evident, the Mandal formula rests on two premises: (a) the OBCs comprise a very large segment of India's population and (b) their representation (only 5 per cent) in the public sector is abysmally poor. Hence the recommendations ensuring 27 per cent reservations in central jobs and education for the OBCs appear revolutionary.

21 Padmanand Jha, 'An election without an issue', *Outlook*, 1 May 1996, p. 4.

22 Khilnani, *The Idea of India*, p. 57.

23 Stuart Corbridge and John Harris, *Reinventing India: Liberalization, Hindu Nationalism and Popular Democracy*, New Delhi: Oxford University Press, 2001, p. 133.

24 Yogendra Yadav, 'Politics', in Marshall Bouton and Phillip Oldenburg (eds), *Indian Briefing: A Transformative Fifty Years*, Delhi: Mudrit, 2001, p. 38.

25 Yogendra Yadav, 'Electoral politics in the time of change: India's third electoral system, 1989–1999', *Economic and Political Weekly*, 21–28 August/3 September 1999, p. 2397.

26 Alfred Stepan, 'Federalism, multi-national states and democracy: a theoretical framework, the Indian model and a Tamil case study', in K. Shankar Bajpai (ed.), *Democracy and Diversity: India and the American Experience*, New Delhi: Oxford University Press, 2007, pp. 240–4.

27 Balveer Arora, 'Negotiating differences: federal coalitions and national cohesion', in Francine R. Frankel, Zoya Hasan, Rajeev Bhargava and Balveer Arora (eds), *Transforming India: Social and Political Dynamics of Democracy*, New Delhi: Oxford University Press, 2000, p. 191.

28 'Unity in unhappiness', editorial, *The Economic Times*, 13 August 1996.

29 Suresh D. Tendulkar and T. A. Bhavani, *Understanding Reforms: post 1991 India*, Oxford University Press, New Delhi, 2007, p. 91.

Conclusion

1 Ramchandra Guha pursues this argument in his *India after Gandhi: The History of the World's Largest Democracy*, London: Picador, 2007, pp. 767–71.

2 Quoted in Guha, *India after Gandhi*, p. xvi.

3 I borrow this expression from Katharine Adeney and Andrew Wyatt, 'Democracy in South Asia: getting beyond the structure–agency dichotomy', *Political Studies*, 50 (1), 2004, p. 2.

4 I borrow the expression 'the banyan tree democracy' from John Keane, 'Banyan democracy of India', *Indian Express*, 15 August 2007.

5 V. S. Naipaul, *A Million Mutinies*, London: Heinemann, 1991, p. 106. According to Naipaul, every protest movement strengthens the state 'defining it as the source of law and civility and reasonableness'. The institutionalization of power in the form of

democratic state gives 'people a second chance, calling them back from the excesses with which, in another century, or in other circumstances (as neighbouring countries showed), they might have had to live: the destructive chauvinism of the *Shiv Sena*, the tyranny of many kinds of religious fundamentalism . . . the film-star corruption and the racial politics of the South, the pious Marxist idleness and nullity of Bengal'.

6　Subrata Mitra pursues this argument in his 'Crisis and resilience in Indian democracy', *International Social Science Journal*, 129, 1991, pp. 567–8.

7　Sudipta Kaviraj, 'Modernity and politics in India', *Daedalus*, 129 (1), 2000, pp. 156–7.

8　Adeney and Wyatt, 'Democracy in South Asia', p. 1.

9　Javeed Alam, *Who Wants Democracy?*, New Delhi: Orient Longman, 2004, p. 22. According to Alam, 'democracy in India is an assertion of the urge for more self-respect and the ability to better oneself'.

10　Christophe Jaffrelot, *India's Silent Revolution: The Rise of the Low Castes in North Indian Politics*, New Delhi: Permanent Black, 2005.

11　Rajni Kothari, *Memoirs*, New Delhi: Rupa, 2002, p. 200.

12　Literature on Indian secularism is plentiful. Rajeev Bhargava's *Secularism and its Critics* (New Delhi: Oxford University Press, 1998) is an exhaustive survey of the literature. The other noteworthy works include Neera Chandhoke, *Beyond Secularism: The Rights of Religious Minorities*, New Delhi: Oxford University Press, 1999; Partha Chatterjee, 'Secularism and toleration', in his *A Possible India: Essays in Political Criticism*, Delhi: Oxford University Press, 1997, pp. 228–62; Akeel Bilgrami, 'Two concepts of secularism, reason, modernity and Archemedial ideal', *Economic and Political Weekly*, 9 July 1994; T. N. Madan *Modern Myths, Locked Myths*, Delhi: Oxford University Press, 1996; Ashis Nandy, 'The politics of secularism and the recovery of religious tolerance', in Veena Das (ed.), *Mirrors and Violence: Communities, Riots and Survivors in South Asia*, Delhi: Oxford University Press, 1990.

13　For a thorough study of the issues raised in the Constituent Assembly during the debate, see Shefali Jha, 'Secularism in the Constituent Assembly Debates, 1946–1950', *Economic and Political Weekly*, 27 July 2002. The Indian version of secularism was articulated, as Jha has shown, out of dialogue, debate and contestation among the Assembly members endorsing (a) separation between religion and state and (b) equal respect for all religions.

14　Jawaharlal Nehru's statement in the Constituent Assembly, *CAD*, Vol. 9, p. 401.

15　Paul Brass, 'The strong state and the fear of disorder', in Francine Frankel, Zoya Hasan, Rajeev Bhargava and Balveer Arora (eds), *Transforming India: Social and Political Dynamics of Democracy*, Delhi: Oxford University Press, 2000, p. 79.

16　Subrata Mitra, 'Desecularising the state: religion and politics in India after independence', *Comparative Studies in Society and History*, 33 (4), 1991, p. 775.

17　Jawaharlal Nehru's intervention in the Lok Sabha debate on the Hindu Marriage Bill, *The Lok Sabha Debates*, 5 May 1955, p. 7963; quoted in Subrata Mitra, 'Desecularising the state', p. 770.

18　Quoted in Bimal Prasad, *Gandhi, Nehru and JP: Studies in Leadership*, Delhi: Chanakya, 1985, p. 136.

19　Sunil Khilnani, *The Idea of India*, London: Hamish Hamilton, 1997, p. 41. Khilnani further argues, 'the state was enlarged, its ambitions inflated and it was transformed from a distant, alien object into one that aspired to infiltrate the everyday lives of Indians, proclaiming itself responsible for everything they could desire: jobs, ration cards, educational places, security, cultural recognition'.

20　Sanghamitra Padhy, 'Secularism and justice: a review of Indian Supreme Court judgments', *Economic and Political Weekly*, 20 November 2004.

21　B. Shiva Rao, *The Framing of India's Constitutions: Select Documents*, Vol. 2, p. 89.

22　Sanghamitra Padhy provides a detailed historical account of how the Supreme Court arrived at the judgment and its repercussions in Indian politics in 'Secularism and justice'.

23 This section draws on Samita Sen, 'Towards a feminist politics? The Indian women's movement in historical perspective', unpublished policy research report on gender and development, Working Paper Series No. 9, The World Bank, April 2000, pp. 28–42. Also, Madhu Kishwar, 'Pro-women or anti-Muslim? The Shaho Bano controversy', *Manushi*, 6 (2), 1986; Iqbal A. Ansari, 'Muslim womens' rights, goals and strategy of reform', *Economic and Political Weekly*, 27 April 1991; Avneshi, 'Is gender justice only a legal issue? Political stakes in the UCC (uniform civil code) debate', *Economic and Political Weekly*, 1 March 1997.

24 This section draws on Sen, 'Towards a feminist politics?', pp. 43–56.

25 Sumanta Banerjee, 'Salvaging an endangered institution', *Economic and Political Weekly*, 9 September 2006, p. 3838. According to Banerjee, there were 'two major watersheds' in the history of Lok Sabha: the first was in 1967 when the fifteen-year-old two-thirds majority of Congress came to an end, and the vacuum was filled by a new breed of elected representatives, well-versed with the issues, which they raised in parliament in a dignified way. The second watershed was in 1980, which inaugurated a process of devaluation of old conventional parliamentary norms. Consequently, well-argued debates and patient discussions gradually receded into the background to give way to 'slanging matches', often leading to physical confrontation in the well of the House – which has now become a common practice in the Lok Sabha.

26 L. I. Rudolph and S. H. Rudolph, 'Redoing the constitutional design: from an interventionist to a regulatory state', in Atul Kohli (ed.), *The Success of India's Democracy*, Cambridge: Cambridge University Press, 2002, p. 141.

27 For details of the UP case, see A. G. Noorani, *Constitutional Questions in India*, New Delhi: Oxford University Press, pp. 328–39.

28 James Manor, 'The Presidency', in Devesh Kapur and Pratap Bhanu Mehta (ed.), *Public Institutions in India: Performance and Design*, New Delhi: Oxford University Press, p. 116.

29 Rudolph and Rudolph, 'Redoing the constitutional design', p. 150.

30 In elaborating the office of profit controversy, I have drawn on an unpublished article by J. S. Verma, the former chief justice of India. I am thankful to Justice Verma for having shared this unpublished article, a part of which was printed in *The Times of India*, 4 September 2006.

31 *S. R. Bommai vs. Union of India*, *AIR*, The Supreme Court of India, December 1994.

32 For a descriptive account of the Election Commission, see Ujjwal K. Singh, *Institutions and Democratic Governance: A Study of the Election Commission and Electoral Governance in India*, New Delhi: Nehru Memorial Museum and Library, 2004; Manjari Katju, 'Election Commission and functioning of democracy', *Economic and Political Weekly*, 29 April 2006.

33 The figure is taken from Sumanta Banerjee, 'Assembly Polls, 2006: elections, *jatra* style, in West Bengal', *Economic and Political Weekly*, 26 May 2006, p. 864.

34 I have dwelt on the role of the Election Commission in the 2006 West Bengal assembly election at some length in my 'Left Front's 2006 victory in West Bengal: continuity or a trendsetter', *Economic and Political Weekly*, 12 August 2006.

35 An expression used by Christophe Jaffrelot in his *India's Silent Revolution: The Rise of the Low Castes in North Indian Politics*, New Delhi: Permanent Black, 2006, p. 492.

36 Guha, *India after Gandhi*, p. 667.

37 Dipesh Chakrabarty raises certain fundamental difficulties in conceptualizing modernity by saying that 'modernity is easy to habitate, but difficult to define. If modernity is to be a definable, delimited concept, we must identify some people or practices or concepts as pre-modern. . . . Following the tenets of the European Enlightenment, many Western intellectuals thought of modernity as the rule of institutions that delivered us from the thrall of all that was unreasonable and irrational. Those who felt

outside its ambit could be described as pre-modern. Western powers in their imperial mode saw modernity as coeval with the idea of progress. Nationalists saw in it the promise of development.' Dipesh Chakrabarty, *Habitations of Modernity: Essays in the Wake of Subaltern Studies*, Chicago, IL: University of Chicago Press, 2002, p. xix.

Annotated bibliography

1 I thankfully acknowledge the contribution of my graduate students, Dr Rajender Pandey and Dr Prakash Chand in preparing this annotated bibliography.

Index

administration: debureaucratization 32; hierarchical Weberian 29, 32; in India 26–9; as legacy of the British Raj 2; in a network society 32–3; openness in 31; over-regulation of 32

administrators/bureaucrats: as facilitators and not regulators 33; generalist 26; as 'rent-seekers' 33

adult suffrage 4

adulthood, of Indian states 179–81

Advisory Committee on Minorities 49

AGP 180

agriculture: shifting of resources to 11; suicide of indebted farmers 106

AIADMK 12, 73, 160

AJGAR 66

Akali Dal, in Punjab 73

All Bengal Teachers' Association 143

All Parties Conference (1928) 49

Ambedkar, B. R. 6, 48, 76, 83, 172, 178; and federalism 95–6

American federal legacy 108, 109

Amlasole 141

Andhra Pradesh 106

'atomized' individuals, absence of 171

Annadurai , C. 111

anti-Congress movement 130

anti-poverty programmes 23

Article 311 27

Article 324 179

Article 356 125, 178

Article 371 98

asymmetrical federalism 98

atheistic communism 170

autonomy and separation, in Kashmir and Punjab 157

Avadi session of the Congress (1955) 20

aya ram gaya ram 129

Babri Masjid 173

backward castes, rise of 56; *see also* Other Backward Castes (OBC)

Bahujan Samaj Party 74

Banaras resolution (1934) 21

Bengal Pact (1923) 43

Bharatiya Jana Sangh 46

Bharatiya Janata Party (BJP) 11; rise of, factors in 80–1; sentiments against, and UPA coalition 169

Bharatiya Lok Dal 10

Bhumi Ucched Pratirodh Committee 151

bicameralism 108

Bihar formula and election 136

binodal party system 168

BKD, in Uttar Pradesh 119

Bombay Provincial Conference, 1916 42

Bommai judgment (1994) 106, 173

Bose, Subhas 22

Brand Buddha: in rural Bengal 138–41; in urban Bengal 141–3

brhamon jodo 74

British Conservative Party 133

British North America Act (1867) 3

BSP, in Uttar Pradesh 13, 74–8

bureaucracy (see administration)

bureacrats (see administrators/bureaucrats)

Cabinet Mission (1946) 6, 89

Canning Lane Group 7

caste(s): backward, rise of 56; conflicts based on, and reservation 71; economically prosperous 56, 65; identity drawn on 171; Other Backward (OBC) 50, 64, 175; in public-political domain 164; as representational 181; upper 56, 65; *see also* reservation

centralization: as 'an instrument of